Bottom Line's

ENCYCLOPEDIA OF
Alternative Healing

24 Volumes of Our Best-Ever All Natural Remedies and Cures

Bottom Line Books

www.BottomLineSecrets.com

Contents

■ Contents ■

■ *Contents* ■

Volume 1
Cancer Fighters

Wheat Germ Extract: A Promising New Cancer Fighter

Wheat germ was one of the original health foods. The "germ" is the most nutritious part of the wheat seed. Today *fermented wheat germ extract* (FWGE) is showing promise as a potential breakthrough for treating cancer patients.

The evidence: A number of cell, animal and human studies support the use and benefits of FWGE as an adjunct therapy, meaning one that is used as part of a broader treatment program.

• **Colorectal cancer.** A study of 170 patients who had received conventional treatments for colorectal cancer found that those who also took 9 grams (g) of FWGE daily for six months had less risk of developing new cancers. The cancer spread among only 8% of the patients receiving FWGE, compared with 23% of those getting only conventional treatment.

• **Oral cancer.** Researchers compared 22 patients with oral cancer who took FWGE with 21 patients not receiving the supplement. FWGE reduced the risk for cancer progression by 85%.

• **Melanoma.** For one year, FWGE was given to 22 patients with advanced (stage 3) melanoma, and their progress was compared with 24 similar patients not receiving FWGE. Patients taking FWGE were half as likely to die from melanoma during this time.

• **Chemotherapy-induced infections.** Researchers studied 22 children and teenagers with different types of cancer. The 11 children

Mark A. Stengler, NMD, licensed naturopathic medical doctor in private practice, La Jolla, California…adjunct associate clinical professor at the National College of Natural Medicine, Portland, Oregon…author of many books, including *The Natural Physician's Healing Therapies* and coauthor of *Prescription for Natural Cures* (both from Bottom Line Books)…and author of the *Bottom Line/Natural Healing* newsletter.

1

who received FWGE had significantly fewer infections and fevers while receiving chemotherapy.

• **Animal studies.** Numerous studies suggest benefits from FWGE for leukemia as well as breast, ovarian, gastric and thyroid cancers. In one study, laboratory rats received both FWGE and vitamin C in the treatment of lung, skin and colon cancers. The combination prevented the cancer from spreading, but vitamin C alone did not. In another study, FWGE worked better alone than it did with vitamin C to treat kidney cancer.

HOW IT WORKS

FWGE appears to work by starving cancer cells of glucose, prompting their death...and by enhancing immune cell activity. Wheat germ contains chemicals that seem to have anticancer properties, and fermentation increases their concentration.

Note: FWGE is very different from the regular wheat germ you can buy at health-food stores. It comes in a powder and is sold in health-food stores and online.

Good brands: Avemar (*www.avemar-alternativetherapy.com*) and OncoMar (800-647-6100, *www.xymogen.com*).

MY ADVICE

If you would like to begin taking FWGE, check with your physician about incorporating it into your treatment program. I recommend one packet a day, which equals 9 g. You can mix it into a glass of cold water and then drink it—or substitute a non-citrus juice, such as apple or cranberry (citrus can deactivate FWGE's active ingredient).

FWGE is not cheap—it costs about $160/month—but I think the expense is worth it, given the early indications that it may improve cancer survival rates.

Good news: FWGE is generally safe, and any side effects, such as diarrhea and flatulence, occur only occasionally.

Apple Skins Fight Alzheimer's Disease And Cancer

They contain high levels of *quercetin*, an antioxidant that may fight cell damage linked with these diseases.

Best: Eat at least one red apple a day. Quercetin also can be found in onions, raspberries, cherries, red wine, red grapes, citrus fruits, broccoli, leafy greens and green and black tea.

Chang Y. Lee, PhD, professor and department chairman, department of food science and technology, Cornell University, Geneva, New York.

Magical Food Combos That Fight Cancer

Karen Collins, MSRD, registered dietitian and nutrition adviser to the American Institute for Cancer Research (*www.aicr.org*). A syndicated newspaper columnist and public speaker, she maintains a private nutrition counseling practice in Washington, DC.

Researchers know that some foods can help prevent cancer. Now there is growing evidence that certain food combinations may offer more protection against cancer than any one specific food.

The following combinations of foods are especially beneficial. *Eat them regularly—either at the same meal or separately throughout the week...*

TOMATOES AND BROCCOLI

Results of an animal study presented at the American Institute for Cancer Research International Research Conference showed that rats with tumors that were given a diet of tomatoes and broccoli had significantly smaller tumors than animals fed one of these foods.

The *lycopene* in tomatoes is an antioxidant. Antioxidants are crucial for preventing cancer because they help prevent unstable molecules, called free radicals, from damaging cell structures and DNA. Broccoli contains chemical compounds known as *glucosinolates*, which may be effective in flushing carcinogens from the body.

Also helpful: Combine broccoli or other cruciferous vegetables, such as brussels sprouts and cabbage, with foods that are high in selenium, such as shellfish and Brazil nuts. A study published by the UK's Institute of Food Research found that the combination of broccoli's glucosinolates and selenium has more powerful anticancer effects than either food eaten alone.

BRUSSELS SPROUTS AND BROCCOLI

These potent cancer-fighting vegetables also are rich in vitamin C and folate, as well as phytonutrients that deactivate carcinogens. When eaten in combination, brussels sprouts and broccoli may provide more protection than either one eaten alone.

Brussels sprouts have the phytonutrient *crambene*, which stimulates phase-2 enzymes, substances that help prevent carcinogens from damaging DNA. Broccoli is high in *indole-3-carbinol*, a phytonutrient that also stimulates phase-2 enzymes—but in a different way.

ORANGES, APPLES, GRAPES AND BLUEBERRIES

Each of these foods is very high in antioxidants. In a recent laboratory analysis, researchers measured the amount of antioxidants in each of these fruits individually. Then they combined them and still took additional measurements.

Result: The mixture of fruits was more powerful against free radicals than any one fruit alone.

CURCUMIN AND QUERCETIN

Curcumin is a phytonutrient found in the spice turmeric. *Quercetin* is a phytonutrient that is abundant in yellow onions, especially in the outermost rings. According to a small study in *Clinical Gastroenterology and Hepatology*, people who consumed large amounts of these two phytonutrients had a reduction in

the number of colon polyps, growths that may turn into cancer.

The study looked at a small number of people with *familial adenomatous polyposis*, a hereditary condition that increases the likelihood of developing polyps. The phytochemical combination reduced the number of polyps by 60%. It also caused some polyps to shrink.

The researchers used concentrated forms of curcumin and quercetin. You would have to eat two-and-a-half tablespoons of turmeric daily to get a comparable amount. To get the necessary amount of quercetin, you would need to have about two-thirds cup of chopped onions daily.

Recommended: Eat a variety of herbs and spices to get the most phytonutrient protection. Even small amounts used frequently will impact your health over time. Among herbs, rosemary and oregano rank among the best phytonutrient sources. Ginger is another powerful spice.

TOMATOES AND FAT

The lycopene in tomatoes is particularly effective against prostate cancer—but only when it's consumed with a small amount of fat. Lycopene, like other members of the carotenoid chemical family, is a fat-soluble substance. The body can't absorb it efficiently in the absence of fat.

It takes only three to five grams of fat (about one teaspoon of oil) to improve the absorption of lycopene from tomatoes. For example, you could have a salad with an oil-based dressing. The type of fat doesn't matter for absorption of lycopene and other carotenoids, but you might as well choose a fat that promotes health. Olive oil and canola oil are good choices.

MORE VARIETY, LESS CANCER

In a recent study published in *The Journal of Nutrition*, researchers divided 106 women into two groups. All of the women were asked to eat eight to 10 servings of fruits and vegetables daily for two weeks. However, one of the groups (the high-diversity group) was told to include foods from 18 different botanical groups, including onions and garlic from the allium family, legumes, cruciferous vegetables, etc. The other group (the low-diversity one) was asked to concentrate all its choices among only five major groups.

Results: Women in both groups showed a decrease in *lipid peroxidation*—important for reducing the risk of cancer and heart disease. However, only the women in the high-diversity group showed a decrease in DNA oxidation, which is one of the steps that initiates cancer development.

The ways that chemicals work in the body, known as metabolic pathways, have a rate-limiting effect. This means that beyond a certain point, eating more of a specific food won't provide additional protection. Eating a wide variety of foods brings more metabolic pathways into play, thus bypassing this limiting effect.

REPORT #4
A Medicinal Mushroom For Cancer?

Mark A. Stengler, NMD, licensed naturopathic medical doctor in private practice, La Jolla, California…adjunct associate clinical professor at the National College of Natural Medicine, Portland, Oregon…author of many books, including *The Natural Physician's Healing Therapies* and coauthor of *Prescription for Natural Cures* (both from Bottom Line Books)…and author of the *Bottom Line/Natural Healing* newsletter.

Researchers have been studying the health benefits of *Agaricus blazei* (A. blazei), an edible mushroom native to Brazil.

A. blazei appears to act as an antioxidant, to balance glucose within the body, prevent abnormal cell growth, bolster the immune system and attack existing tumor cells. Is it worth taking in supplement form?

HEALTH BENEFITS

Studies show the benefits of A. blazei for the following conditions…

•**Cancer.** In one study, patients with cervical, ovarian or endometrial cancer were treated with chemotherapy, plus either an oral A. blazei extract or a placebo. The activity of tumor-fighting cells was significantly higher in those taking A. blazei compared with those who took the placebo. Most striking: Patients taking A. blazei also suffered fewer side effects of chemotherapy, including hair loss, weakness and decreased appetite.

•**Hepatitis C.** A study in *Japanese Pharmacology & Therapeutics* suggests that A. blazei extract may be effective in treating hepatitis C. In 80% of study participants, A. blazei extract appeared to reduce levels of the liver enzyme *gamma-glutamyl transpeptidase* (GGT), an indicator of liver damage.

MY ADVICE

For those with any type of cancer (particularly those noted above) or hepatitis C, I recommend 1,500 milligrams (mg) to 3,000 mg daily of A. blazei. Have your doctor determine the dose and monitor your response, including blood glucose levels. (A. blazei can improve insulin resistance, a condition in which the body doesn't use insulin properly.)

Caution: A. blazei should not be taken by anyone on immune-suppressing transplant medications—these patients do not want their immune system to reject the new organ. Avoid A. blazei if you have an autoimmune disease (such as rheumatoid arthritis) in which the immune system already is overactive. Good choice: Nutraceutics Rx AgariPure Agaricus Blazei Murrill extract by American Nutrition (800-454-3724, *www.americannutrition.com*, $29.95 for 120 500-mg capsules).

REPORT #5
Another Reason to Love Olive Oil

Henrik E. Poulsen, MD, professor of clinical pharmacology and the head of the department of clinical pharmacology at Rigshospitalet, University Hospital, Copenhagen, Denmark.

It's no news that omega-3 fatty acid and phenolic-rich olive oil is good for your heart. However, the virtues of olive oil seem now to extend into the rest of the body as well, according to new research. Noting that the incidence of breast, large bowel, ovary and prostate cancer is lower in Mediterranean countries than in Northern Europe —and that the association between olive oil and cancer reduction has been established— researchers wondered whether olive oil with higher amounts of phenolic compounds may be even more protective.

WHAT'S HEALTHY ABOUT OLIVE OIL?

Researchers believed it was probably the phenolic compounds—healthful plant compounds, abundant in olive oil—that were delivering the cancer-fighting benefits, so they tested three different olive oils with three different phenolic concentrations—high, medium and low. For the study, they divided 182 healthy European men between 20 and 60 years old, from five different countries (Denmark, Finland, Germany, Italy and Spain) into three groups. Each group consumed 25 milliliters (0.84 oz.) of one kind of the olive oils at a time. After three weeks on each of the three olive oils, with a two-week washout period in between, their urine was tested for presence of a substance (8oxodG) considered a reliable measure of oxidative damage.

It turned out to not even matter which kind of olive oil the men had been consuming, since all had noticeably reduced measures of 8oxodG. It seems to have been the olive oil itself that had made the difference, regardless of phenol content. "It is likely the monounsaturated fat in the olive oil is the protective element," one of the study's co-authors, Henrik Poulsen, MD, professor of clinical pharmacology, Rigshospitalet, University Hospital, Copenhagen, Denmark, told me, since it is known to have anti-inflammatory properties. Dr. Poulsen speculates that other oils high in monounsaturated fat, such as macadamia nut oil and almond oil, may be cancer-protective as well, though this study only examined olive oil.

EXTRA VIRGIN WORTH EXTRA INVESTMENT

Phenolic compounds are always touted as one of the virtues of extra-virgin olive oil, since they are better preserved than in the other, less expensive olive oils. I asked Dr. Poulsen if there was any benefit to paying the higher price for these. Yes, he said, the extra virgin olive oil is worth the extra investment. Not only is it subject to the least processing and heat exposure, but it also works harder for your health than regular or light olive oils. "Our other research shows that the high phenolic content of extra virgin olive oil is what's protective against arteriosclerosis," he told me. "Extra virgin olive oil gives you the best of both worlds."

REPORT #6
Exercise and Coffee May Fight Skin Cancer

Skin cancer develops in cells whose DNA has been damaged by UV radiation—but damaged cells often die before becoming malignant. The death rate of precancerous skin cells in mice that received exercise and oral caffeine was nearly 400% greater than in mice that had neither exercise nor caffeine.

Allan Conney, PhD, Professor of Pharmacology and director of the Susan Lehman Cullman Laboratory for Cancer Research, Rutgers State University of New Jersey, Piscataway, and coauthor of a study published in *Proceedings of the National Academy of Sciences.*

REPORT #7
Lentils May Prevent Breast Cancer

Women who ate one-half cup of lentils at least twice a week were 24% less likely to develop breast cancer, compared with women who ate the same amount of lentils less than once a month or not at all.

Theory: Lentils' protective effects may be due to particular types of phytochemicals. One-half cup of lentils has 9 grams (g) of protein, 8 g of fiber, 3 milligrams of iron and only 115 calories. And they are inexpensive. Add lentils while cooking soups and whole grains, and use cooked lentils in salads.

Clement A. Adebamowo, MD, ScD, associate professor of epidemiology, department of epidemiology and preventive medicine, Institute of Human Virology, member of the Greenebaum Cancer Center, School of Medicine, University of Maryland, Baltimore, and co-author of a study of 90,630 women, published in *International Journal of Cancer*.

REPORT #8
Cancer-Prevention Pill

Mark A. Stengler, NMD, licensed naturopathic medical doctor in private practice, La Jolla, California…adjunct associate clinical professor at the National College of Natural Medicine, Portland, Oregon…author of many books, including *The Natural Physician's Healing Therapies* and coauthor of *Prescription for Natural Cures* (both from Bottom Line Books)…and author of the *Bottom Line/Natural Healing* newsletter.

S ome people don't have the time—or taste buds—for a full day's worth of fruits and vegetables. That's when the capsule form of the cancer-fighting compound *sulphoraphane glucosinolate* (SGS) comes in handy. I recommend it for people with a family history of cancer…as a complement to ongoing cancer treatments (with your doctor's approval)…for those who have been exposed to toxins…and for all who want to reduce their risk of cancer.

The supplement company Xymogen (*www.xymogen.com*) markets OncoPlex SGS, which contains 30 mg of SGS per capsule. Though it does not require a prescription, it is not sold in health-food stores and usually is purchased through holistic doctors.

In general, I advise taking one capsule daily. If you have had cancer or are undergoing cancer treatment, increase to two to four capsules daily, under the supervision of your doctor.

REPORT #9
Red Wine—It's Like the New Green Vegetable

Jeffrey B. Schwimmer, MD, director, Fatty Liver Clinic, associate professor of pediatrics and director, quality improvement, Division of Gastroenterology, Hepatology, and Nutrition, Department of Pediatrics, University of California, San Diego, California.

R ed wine seems to be the new "green vegetable"…good for practically everything. New research points to a surprising and counterintuitive connection between moderate wine consumption and the lower risk of a certain kind of liver disease… plus, I recently saw another study that suggests serving red wine with steaks can help diminish the harmful effects associated with eating red meat. Once again it appears that modern science is confirming age-old wisdom, in this case those who revered the "nectar of the Gods."

SHALL WE DRINK TO THAT?

Of course, experts are quick to point out that wine is beneficial to your health in moderation only. *That said, following are a sample of the many benefits that moderate wine consumption may confer upon your health…*

• **Lowers risk of liver disease.** Considered by some to be an emerging epidemic, *nonalcoholic fatty liver disease* (NAFLD) has become the most common chronic liver disease in the United States today, due in large part to our Western lifestyle and obesity, notes study author Jeffrey B. Schwimmer, MD, at the University of California, San Diego. He and his colleagues found that moderate wine drinkers are significantly less likely to develop NAFLD than nondrinkers, even after controlling for other possible contributing factors.

• **Healthier heart.** Wine in particular possesses potent heart-healthy benefits, according to a large-scale study, published in 2000, which included Copenhagen City Heart Study data. Researchers found the risk of death significantly lower than for people who did not drink wine and believe it's due to ethanol and the substances in wine. Other research shows that the high polyphenol content in red wine protects the linings of cardiovascular blood vessels and may inhibit plaque formation.

• **Prostate cancer protection.** Men who drink four to seven glasses of red wine weekly are half as likely to be diagnosed with prostate cancer as men who do not drink red wine, according to research from the Fred Hutchinson Cancer Research Center in Seattle. Doctors speculate that healthful antioxidant compounds such as flavonoids and resveratrol are responsible for this effect. White wine was helpful too, but not as much as red wine, which is a richer source of these health-promoting compounds.

• **Kidney care.** Drinking at least two glasses of red wine a week may lower the risk of kidney cancer, say doctors at the Karolinska Institutet in Sweden. Beneficial effects were also found with white wine and strong beer, but not liquor. Other research, conducted in part at Harvard Medical School, suggests that men who consume seven or more drinks weekly have a 29% lower risk of developing kidney problems.

• **Longer life.** One day resveratrol may prove to be the key to unlocking the secret of lasting youth. Laboratory tests demonstrate that this antioxidant compound in red wine prevents early death in mice that were fed high-fat diets. Yet so far no human research has taken place, so further study is needed.

TO YOUR HEALTH

So it seems there's some merit to such toasts as "salud" (health) and "l'chaim" (to life). Enjoying a glass of red wine with your evening meal may indeed improve your health and extend your life -- but do so with restraint, and drink at mealtime, since food slows alcohol absorption. Most experts suggest that an intake of one to two glasses of wine a day for men and one for women is optimal for health benefits. More, however, may increase the risk of some of the consequences of excessive alcohol consumption. Red wines have more polyphenols than white (which, as noted above, can also be beneficial) but not all red wines offer equal potency of this health-promoting compound. A study in the scientific journal *Nature* reported that the most powerful heart-healthy polyphenols are procyanidins, which is the main source of the vascular health benefits in red wine. Wines from Southern France and Sardinia were found to have higher concentrations, due to production methods. Other research shows that the darker the wine, in general, the healthier.

However none of this is meant to suggest you ought to cultivate a wine habit if you don't want to or don't particularly enjoy it. Immoderate alcohol consumption has a greater negative effect than the positive beneficial effects. Dr. Schwimmer takes cautionary advice a step further, warning that people at risk for alcohol abuse or alcoholism (for example, those with a personal or family history) should not consume wine or other alcoholic beverages. Fortunately for teetotalers, there's an excellent alternative—red grape juice and grapes themselves are rich sources of many of the same beneficial compounds as red wine. Other antioxidant-packed options include blueberries, cranberries, elderberries and pomegranates. If you're worried about the consequences of imbibing too much nectar of the Gods, just reach for a bunch of grapes.

REPORT #10
The Power of Yogurt

Yogurt reduces risk for bladder cancer. A recent study found that consuming two or more servings of yogurt a day was associated with a 45% reduction in bladder cancer for women and a 36% reduction in men, compared with people who didn't consume yogurt.

Why: The researchers believe that lactic acid bacteria in yogurt may destroy harmful carcinogens that otherwise may form in the bladder.

Susanna C. Larsson, PhD, division of nutritional epidemiology, National Institute of Environmental Medicine, Karolinska Institutet, Stockholm, Sweden.

REPORT #11
Onions and Garlic Curb Cancer Risk

In a 13-year study of the diets of about 25,000 people, participants who ate the most onions and/or garlic were 10% to 88% less likely to develop several types of cancer—including colorectal, esophageal, oral and ovarian—than those who ate the least. *Theory:* Onions and garlic contain antioxidants, including allicin and quercetin, that prevent cell damage that can lead to cancer. *Self-defense:* Aim to eat one-half cup of onions (any type) and/or one to two cloves of garlic (chopped or crushed) several times weekly.

Carlotta Galeone, PhD, researcher, Mario Negri Institute of Pharmacological Research, Milan, Italy.

REPORT #12
Ultimate Cancer-Fighting Food…Now in Capsule Form, Too

Mark A. Stengler, NMD, licensed naturopathic medical doctor in private practice, La Jolla, California…adjunct associate clinical professor at the National College of Natural Medicine, Portland, Oregon…author of many books, including *The Natural Physician's Healing Therapies* and coauthor of *Prescription for Natural Cures* (both from Bottom Line Books)…and author of the *Bottom Line/Natural Healing* newsletter.

I do not like broccoli. I haven't liked it since I was a little kid and my mother made me eat it. I'm president of the United States, and I'm not going to eat any more broccoli!" George H.W. Bush spoke these words early in his tenure at the White House. Unfortunately, he is missing out on a potent cancer-fighting food.

If you share the former president's aversion to broccoli, you'll be happy to learn of new alternatives that offer even more health benefits. *First, some background information…*

DEFICIENT DIETS

Researchers have published eye-opening studies on the compound *sulforaphane*, found in broccoli and similar vegetables. Sulforaphane helps prevent cancers of the breast, ovary, prostate, bone, brain, bladder, liver, lung and stomach, and combats other conditions associated with aging and cell death.

It is no secret that the average American fails to consume the seven to nine daily servings of fruits and vegetables recommended to provide dietary protection against cancer and other diseases. And for many people, the produce they do eat seldom includes the recommended one to two daily servings of cruciferous vegetables (so called because the plants' flowers have four petals arranged like a crucifix), such as cauliflower, kale, bok choy, rutabagas, radishes, turnips, brussels sprouts and, of course, broccoli. An analysis published in *The Journal of Nutrition*, which looked at dietary data on 4,806 men and women ages 25 to 75, revealed that just 3% of the group consumed broccoli during either of two typical days. Consumption of dark green vegetables averaged just one-fifth of a serving per day.

Cruciferous vegetables are a rich source of healthful plant chemicals called phytochemicals or phytonutrients. These include cancer-fighting *thiols* (such as the sulfur-containing glucosinolates) and *indoles* (which bind chemical carcinogens and activate detoxifying enzymes). Yet even veggie lovers may find it difficult to ingest therapeutic amounts of cruciferous vegetables on a regular basis. This problem is compounded by the fact that cooking can destroy phytonutrients, so health benefits are diminished unless the vegetables are consumed raw or lightly steamed.

SGS DISCOVERED

Scientists at the Johns Hopkins University School of Medicine identified the compound *sulforaphane glucosinolate* (SGS)—a naturally occurring precursor to sulforaphane—in 1992 and began to research its cancer-fighting potential. Leading this effort was Paul Talalay, MD, a professor of pharmacology and director of the university's Laboratory for Molecular Sciences.

His strategy: To support the body's natural detoxification capacity to fight cancer-causing chemicals and cell-damaging free radicals. It is well accepted that cell DNA controls replication of cells and that damage to cell DNA is an important factor in the development of cancer.

In 1994, Dr. Talalay looked at the impact of SGS on mammary (breast) tumors in rats exposed to a potent carcinogen. Results were astounding. The number of rats that developed tumors was reduced by as much as 60%...the number of tumors in each animal was reduced by 80%...and the size of the tumors that did develop was reduced by 75%. Subsequently, hundreds of other test tube and animal studies have confirmed the anticancer properties of sulforaphane.

Toxins (natural and man-made) go through phases of breakdown in the cells of the body, particularly the liver. *Sulforaphane promotes detoxification by...*

• **Supporting enzymes that destroy carcinogens.**

• **Stimulating longer-lasting protective antioxidant effects than other nutrients do.**

• **Replenishing the cells' levels of the amino acid glutathione, strengthening the immune system.**

• **Inhibiting COX-2, an inflammatory enzyme that contributes to cancerous changes in cells.**

• **Limiting DNA damage and abnormal cell growth.**

SUPER SPROUTS

Dr. Talalay discovered that various types of fresh and frozen broccoli differed significantly in the amounts of SGS they contained—and that the older the broccoli was, the lower its SGS. Painstaking research uncovered certain varieties of three-day-old broccoli sprouts—which look like a cross between alfalfa sprouts and bean sprouts—that contained up to 50 times more SGS than mature, cooked broccoli. One ounce of these sprouts could provide as much SGS as three pounds of cooked broccoli.

This set the stage for a fascinating study, published in *Cancer Epidemiology Biomarkers & Prevention.* The study was conducted in a rural area near Shanghai where liver cancer is common because local grain is contaminated with *aflatoxin*, a carcinogen produced by mold.

In the study, broccoli sprouts with known levels of SGS were grown at the site in China. Three days after the shoots emerged from the soil, the sprouts were picked and used to prepare a liquid extract to ensure standard dosages. One hundred local residents drank five ounces of diluted extract in tea form (equal to eating two ounces of sprouts) daily for two weeks. A control group drank a tea indistinguishable in taste and appearance but containing no SGS.

Great results: Analysis of the participants' urine showed that in people who drank the SGS extract, carcinogens were being removed from the body—providing the first direct evidence that broccoli sprouts can enhance the human body's detoxifying system, reducing the risk of cancer.

NEW WAYS TO GET GREENS

Broccoli sprouts and SGS are safe for everyone. (If you have thyroid problems, check with your doctor—there is a slight risk that broccoli sprouts may suppress thyroid function. There is no concern with the SGS supplement.) Because the SGS content of broccoli sprouts can vary greatly depending on seed type and growing methods, I recommend the sprouts developed by the Johns Hopkins team. These are now available under the brand name BroccoSprouts, from Brassica Protection Products LLC (877-747-1277, *www.brassica.com*). Sold in health-food and grocery stores nationwide, these broccoli sprouts contain standardized and therapeutic amounts of sulforaphane.

Alternatively, you can grow your own sprouts using BroccoSprout seeds. Order the kit from Caudill Seed Company (800-626-5357).

For optimal health, eat one-half cup (one ounce) of BroccoSprouts every other day. Each serving contains 73 mg of SGS. They are most beneficial when eaten raw, so sprinkle them on salads and sandwiches. The taste is similar to that of a radish, with a spicy flavor that results from the release of sulforaphane as you chew. Even people who hate broccoli usually enjoy the tangy taste of broccoli sprouts.

REPORT #13
Miracles Do Happen— True Stories of Spontaneous Healing

Joan Borysenko, PhD, cofounder and former director of the mind-body clinical programs at two Harvard Medical School hospitals, now merged as Boston's Beth Israel Deaconess Medical Center. Based in Boulder, Colorado, she runs workshops and conducts lectures on mind-body healing. *Minding the Body, Mending the Mind* (Da Capo). *joanborysenko.com*. She is also founding partner of Mind/Body Health Sciences, LLC in Boulder.

On occasion, a health problem that was expected to be permanent or fatal instead disappears without medical intervention. The limited research that has been done suggests that the reason why one person recovers when most others do not might have as much to do with the mind as the body.

We interviewed Joan Borysenko, PhD, a former Harvard medical scientist who is a renowned expert in the field of mind/body healing. *She relayed these true stories of spontaneous healing…*

MIND/BODY CURE

In 1985, Alice Epstein, a sociology doctoral student at the University of Massachusetts, was diagnosed with kidney cancer. One of her kidneys was removed, but it was no use—the cancer had spread to her lungs, and treatment was impossible. Epstein was told she had only a few more months to live.

With no way to treat the physical problem, Epstein and her psychology-professor husband decided to treat her mind. Epstein used meditation to reduce her stress, and psychotherapy to deal with the angry, unhappy component of her personality. Within six weeks,

tests showed that her cancer was going into remission. Her progress slowed when she took time off from the intensive psychotherapy but resumed once the psychotherapy resumed. The cancer eventually disappeared. Epstein earned her PhD and is still alive today, more than 20 years later.

What may have happened. Eliminating stress and anger will not cure every disease, but it can trigger a host of biochemical changes in the body—including providing a boost to the immune system. It is possible that Epstein's aggressive mental treatments played a role in her return to physical health.

A VISION IN LOURDES

Nearly 150 years ago, a teenage girl in Lourdes, France, reported seeing a vision of the Virgin Mary. Ever since, the waters in that area have been credited with healing powers. Most of these incidents involve cancer, multiple sclerosis and other diseases that occasionally go into remission, even without a visit to Lourdes.

The 1908 case of Marie Bire is more interesting. The 41-year-old French woman was blind as a result of optic atrophy—the degeneration of her optic nerve. According to medical science, it should not have been possible for optic nerves to recover from such a condition.

At Lourdes, the blind Bire attended Mass and received Holy Communion. Then, as the Blessed Sacrament in procession was passing the place where she sat, she suddenly regained her sight. Ten doctors examined Bire. They all found that her optic nerves were still withered but that she could see.

What may have happened. We do not have to believe in divine miracles to believe that Bire's faith might have played a role in her recovery. Studies have found that depending upon the medical condition, between 30% and 50% of people respond to placebos. If you tell these people that you have given them painkillers, their brain activity will show that they actually feel less pain.

CONFIDENCE DESPITE THE ODDS

In 1975, Ian Gawler, a 24-year-old Australian veterinarian and decathlete, learned that he had bone cancer in his right leg. The leg was amputated, but the cancer reappeared later that year and spread throughout his body. In 1976, Gawler was given two weeks to live. No one had ever been known to recover from such an advanced case of this form of cancer. As a doctor, Gawler knew that the reasonable response was to prepare for death. Instead, he remained certain that he would recover. He focused on meditation, positive thinking and a natural diet.

Gawler did recover. He now runs The Gawler Foundation (*www.gawler.org*), which provides support for others suffering from serious illnesses. The foundation stresses healthy food, meditation and belief in recovery.

What may have happened. We cannot simply imagine cancer away, but there is reason to think that believing in the desired health outcome might improve the odds that it will occur.

SURROUNDED BY LOVE

Fifty years ago, the outlook was bleak for those suffering psychotic hallucinations. Today's pharmaceuticals and cognitive behavior therapy were not yet available. Recovery was very rare.

That was bad news for one previously healthy 10-year-old girl growing up in the 1950s. Her nightmares had entered her waking life—she saw snakes, scorpions and head-hunters. The girl believed that these tormentors were going to kill her family and that the only way she could stop them was to repeat obsessive-compulsive behaviors, such as scraping the inside of her mouth with her fingernails, reading books only upside down and backward, rereading each sentence three times and erasing everything she wrote three times before continuing. The girl eventually was pulled from school and lived each day in a landscape of terror.

For months, she prayed intensely for a cure. One day during these prayers, she suddenly felt surrounded by love and wisdom, as though she were being held in the arms of God. Her fear instantly disappeared, and she stopped her obsessive-compulsive behavior cold turkey. Within days, all of her symptoms were gone, never to return.

I was that little girl. The experience sparked my lifelong interest in psychology and spirituality.

What may have happened. Most people with mental disorders cannot just pray their way to recovery. Still, it is worth noting that many people who experience spontaneous healing also experience a transformative spiritual episode similar to mine—a single moment when they feel aided by a loving, powerful outside force.

HOW TO USE
YOUR MIND TO HEAL

Some things we can do when we are seriously ill that will benefit our overall health…

Do not let your mind be pulled into worry or into the past or the future. Spend time each day doing something that makes you feel good and keeps you in the present, whether it is gardening, meditating or walking in nature.

Forgive any wrongs that have been done to you. Letting go of anger and regrets can reduce stress and boost your immune system.

Have gratitude. Before going to bed, be truly grateful for something that happened that day. Wasn't it wonderful when someone smiled at you? Soak up these positive feelings.

Imagine the health outcome that you desire. Picture the disease disappearing from your body. If you have trouble visualizing a positive health outcome, begin by picturing other things that make you happy.

REPORT #14
Sweet Cancer Prevention

The sweet-tasting compound in licorice, *glycyrrhizic acid*, has been shown in animal studies to help stop the progression of colon cancer. The finding may lead to new approaches to preventing malignancies of the colon.

Vanderbilt University Medical Center.

REPORT #15
Heat Is Good

Heat may kill some cancer cells directly and render others more responsive to radiation treatment.

Recent finding: Treating superficial (or "contained") tumors in tissue of the breast, cervix, head, neck and skin with hyperthermia—gradually increasing the temperature of the cancerous tissue to between 105°F and 113°F—reduced the risk of recurrence by 68%.

Ellen Jones, MD, PhD, associate professor, department of radiation oncology, Duke University School of Medicine, Durham, North Carolina, and leader of a study of 109 patients with recurrent, superficial cancers, published in *Journal of Clinical Oncology*.

REPORT #16
Breast Cancers That Disappear Without Treatment

Susan Love, MD, clinical professor of surgery, David Geffen School of Medicine, UCLA, Los Angeles, California. Dr. Love is founder, president and medical director of the Dr. Susan Love Research Foundation (*www.dslrf.org*) and author of *Dr. Susan Love's Breast Book* (Da Capo).

Mammograms save many lives, but screening for breast cancer also produces many false positive results—leading to unnecessary, invasive testing, not to mention untold anxiety for women and their loved ones. A recent study has identified yet another concern. In Norway, investigators found that women who underwent screening mammography were significantly more likely to be diagnosed with breast cancer than those who did not get screened, leading to the possibility that some breast cancers disappear spontaneously on their own without treatment. It's an intriguing finding, given how much time, cost and anxiety is associated

with diagnosing breast cancer—even more so when you consider how many women might not require aggressive treatment, including potent drugs, powerful radiation and painful, disfiguring surgery, for cancers that might disappear on their own.

We spoke with one of the country's leading breast cancer authorities, Susan Love, MD, a clinical professor of surgery at UCLA's David Geffen School of Medicine, founder of the Dr. Susan Love Research Foundation (*www.dslrf. org*) and author of *Dr. Susan Love's Breast Book*. She called the study "extremely encouraging," noting it might someday enable researchers to identify which types of breast cancers require treatment and which can simply be monitored…but she cautions that we're not there yet. At present, women should continue to get their regularly scheduled mammograms.

MORE SCREENING = MORE POSITIVE DIAGNOSES

In the study, investigators compared the number of breast cancers detected in two groups of Norwegian women, ages 50 to 64 (over 100,000 participants), who underwent mammography screening. One group received three mammograms between 1996 and 2001 as part of a new national screening program. The other group had just a single screening in 1997.

Theoretically, these comparable groups should have the same number of cancers, says Dr. Love. Yet that did not prove to be the case. Researchers found 22% more breast cancers in the women who underwent more frequent mammograms. This raises the possibility that left untreated, these tumors might have spontaneously regressed. It's not such a far-fetched theory, given that scientists already know of at least one other cancer—a rare childhood cancer called a *neuroblastoma*—that is known to regress without treatment in as many as 7% of cases that are detected through screening.

These results were published in the *Archives of Internal Medicine*. Though the study results raised a hubbub, Dr. Love didn't find them surprising and said she suspects the type that disappears on its own might be one called "almost normal" breast cancer because it is so non-aggressive. "It's just a hunch though," she notes—agreeing with the researchers that further study is required.

"WATCH AND WAIT" A POSSIBLE NEW APPROACH?

Just as "watch and wait" is a treatment strategy for some prostate cancers, perhaps research will identify certain types of breast cancers that can safely be approached in the same way, says Dr. Love. Looking ahead, she notes that this and similar studies may even lead to changes in what's considered "cancer." It may be that in some people, some groups of abnormal cells may appear that will never develop into a life-threatening tumor and should not be referred to—or more importantly treated as—cancer.

As things now stand, though, it's impossible to predict whether a tumor will spontaneously regress, nor will that likely be possible anytime soon. For now, the American Cancer Society (*www.cancer.org*) recommends that women get an annual mammogram beginning at age 40. Women at high risk—those with a family history of breast cancer or who test positive for a genetic mutation in BRCA 1 or BRCA 2 genes—should also get an MRI. If you are uncertain, consult your physician to determine your risk level.

REPORT #17
Raspberries May Prevent Oral Cancer

The pulp of black raspberries contains antioxidants and anti-inflammatory acids that may slow the growth of—or even eliminate—cancerous lesions in the mouth. Researchers now are testing a raspberry-based gel for treatment of lesions. Oral cancer, generally associated with alcohol and tobacco use, causes 8,000 deaths in the US each year.

Russell J. Mumper, PhD, vice chair and associate professor of pharmaceutical sciences, University of Kentucky, Lexington.

REPORT #18
Vitamin C...A Natural Form of Chemotherapy

Mark A. Stengler, NMD, licensed naturopathic medical doctor in private practice, La Jolla, California...adjunct associate clinical professor at the National College of Natural Medicine, Portland, Oregon...author of many books, including *The Natural Physician's Healing Therapies* and coauthor of *Prescription for Natural Cures* (both from Bottom Line Books)...and author of the *Bottom Line/Natural Healing* newsletter.

Most people have never heard of intravenous (IV) vitamin C, and yet it is one of the best alternative therapies to fight cancer. As most people know, vitamin C is an antioxidant with an immune-boosting effect. But when I—and a host of other natural physicians—administer it at very high doses, it plays an altogether different role, acting like a type of natural chemotherapy and killing cancer cells. When used in conjunction with regular chemotherapy, IV vitamin C works right alongside it, helping to kill cancer cells while also boosting the immune system and helping the body to rid itself of unwanted waste products.

At my clinic, I use IV vitamin C treatment for patients at all stages of cancer. All of these patients are also under the care of an oncologist. I give IV vitamin C to cancer patients at the outset of their treatment, to those who have tried conventional treatments to no avail and to those in remission who want an immune system boost. For patients with terminal disease, it helps to improve quality of life by increasing their energy and reducing nausea.

The use of vitamins in the treatment of cancer is controversial, extending back 40 years to when Nobel Laureate Linus Pauling, PhD, first proposed the use of high-dose vitamin C in the treatment of cancer. Many oncologists today remain skeptical about using any type of vitamin therapy in the treatment of cancer. Cancer specialists maintain that some types of chemotherapy and radiation kill cancer cells by generating large numbers of destructive free radicals. Because vitamin C is an antioxidant, they believe that it will neutralize these free radicals and reduce the effectiveness of chemotherapy and radiation.

I think this view is simplistic. At low doses (under 25 grams, or 25,000 milligrams), vitamin C's antioxidant properties do help to neutralize disease-causing free radicals. But at doses higher than 25 grams, vitamin C has a pro-oxidant effect that exploits a weakness in the biochemistry of cancer cells and increases production of hydrogen peroxide, an acid that has been shown to kill cancer cells without harming healthy cells.

It's impossible to achieve the required high concentrations of vitamin C through oral supplements alone. The body regulates the amount of vitamin C that can be absorbed through the gut, and very large amounts of the vitamin will cause diarrhea. Intravenous vitamin C bypasses this problem because it goes directly into the bloodstream. I provide my patients with IV vitamin C in the office. They lie comfortably in a reclining chair during a one- to two-hour treatment session, at which time they receive doses of 30 grams to 75 grams of vitamin C.

PROMISING RESEARCH

The benefits of IV vitamin C for cancer patients has been demonstrated in studies, including those by researchers at the National Institutes of Health. Laboratory studies have shown that IV vitamin C kills cancer cells but not normal cells. Studies by physicians at University of Kansas Medical Center in Kansas City, for example, described two cases in which patients suffering from advanced ovarian cancer underwent surgery and then received chemotherapy and IV vitamin C. Three years after treatment, both women had no sign of disease, which is quite unusual, because the prognosis for ovarian cancer typically is quite poor. Other research has shown the benefit of this treatment for terminally ill patients. A Korean study found that a combination of IV and oral vitamin C improved quality of life, reducing nausea and increasing energy in terminally ill patients.

Most researchers agree that data from large clinical trials is needed. Several clinical trials currently are under way to assess the effect of IV vitamin C and other antioxidants on different types of cancers.

WHAT TO DO

Many oncologists will not advocate vitamin therapy in any form.

My advice: While you're undergoing conventional therapy, look for a medical doctor or naturopathic physician experienced in IV therapies to work with your oncologist. You and your doctors can decide whether to administer IV vitamins during or immediately after receiving conventional therapies. Your doctor will determine the number of treatments you need. Some patients get one or two IV vitamin C infusions weekly for the first year after diagnosis and initial treatment for cancer, and then every other week for a few years to help prevent cancer cells from returning and to boost the immune system.

Large amounts of vitamin C are nontoxic and generally safe for everyone except those with kidney failure, who can't tolerate large amounts. In addition, a small percentage of people are deficient in the enzyme *glucose-6-phosphate dehydrogenase* (G6PD), which is needed to maintain normal red blood cells. Without this enzyme, large amounts of vitamin C can cause *hemolytic anemia*, a type of anemia that involves the abnormal breakdown of red blood cells. Before receiving IV vitamin C, ask your doctor to test you for this deficiency. If you have it, you should not have IV vitamin C.

Note that patients' response to cancer treatment of any kind varies, and no physician can ever know for certain how a tumor will respond to a specific treatment.

REPORT #19
Red Chili Pepper Fights Cancer

It contains *capsaicin*, an anti-inflammatory that is effective against cancer cells. In tests, capsaicin caused cancer cells to die without damaging normal ones. Though clinical trials are needed before a recommendation to eat chili pepper can be made, it can be enjoyed as part of your regular diet.

Sanjay K. Srivastava, PhD, associate professor of biomedical sciences Texas Tech University Health Sciences Center School of Pharmacy, Amarillo, Texas.

REPORT #20
Healing Outside the Box of Mainstream Medicine

Mark A. Stengler, NMD, licensed naturopathic medical doctor in private practice, La Jolla, California...adjunct associate clinical professor at the National College of Natural Medicine, Portland, Oregon...author of many books, including *The Natural Physician's Healing Therapies* and coauthor of *Prescription for Natural Cures* (both from Bottom Line Books)...and author of the *Bottom Line/Natural Healing* newsletter.

Almost invariably, new patients tell me, "Conventional medicine is not helping me. I'm here to try something different." Americans are waking up to the fact that most diseases can be helped or healed through natural medicine. Yet success requires that patients and their doctors "think outside the box" of mainstream medicine.

Healing sometimes takes more than an open mind, however. I'm often impressed by my patients who demonstrate dedication to a new lifestyle...perseverance despite setbacks...and courage to combat a discouraging prognosis. Here are the stories of four patients from whom I've learned invaluable lessons. I hope you find them inspiring, too.

LISTEN TO YOUR BODY

"I've lost track of how many different doctors I've seen in the past three years," said Nancy, 39, a real estate agent and mother of four. "They never agree on what's wrong, other than to imply that my problems are in my head. But I believe in listening to my body—and it's telling me that something isn't right."

Nancy had a daunting list of two dozen symptoms, including relentless fatigue, widespread muscle pain, dry skin, hair loss, weight gain, hypoglycemia (low blood sugar), recurring respiratory infections, dizzy spells, panic attacks and heart palpitations. Her various medical doctors had run numerous blood tests and other laboratory analyses over the years, but the results had always been "normal." Several times Nancy was offered antidepressants, which she refused. "I'm not sick because I'm depressed—I'm depressed because I'm sick," she told me.

Instead of trying to treat Nancy's symptoms one by one, I looked for a connection among her seemingly disparate problems—and recognized that many of them suggested low thyroid function. I ordered a blood test for free T3, the most specific marker of thyroid function available. (T3 is one of the thyroid hormones, and the "free" level is the amount not bound to protein and therefore available for use by the body's cells.) This test is not routinely ordered by most doctors, though I think it should be used more often.

The test confirmed that Nancy's free T3 level was low. I prescribed Armour Thyroid, a brand of natural thyroid hormone in tablet form that contains T3 and a blend of other thyroid hormones found in the human body. Most thyroid prescriptions do not contain T3, but instead contain only T4, a less potent and less effective thyroid hormone.

The results were fantastic. Within one week, Nancy's fatigue had eased and her mood had improved. Over the next three months, her energy level returned to normal...muscle pain disappeared...respiratory infections cleared up...weight and blood sugar stabilized...skin and hair condition improved...and mood lifted. Nancy said, "I can hardly believe how well I feel from just one simple type of treatment."

Self-help strategy: Before seeing a dozen different specialists for a dozen different symptoms, consult a holistic doctor. He/she will evaluate you as a whole person, rather than as a collection of problematic body parts—and may identify a single root cause behind all your symptoms. A good holistic doctor also will acknowledge that you know your own body best and will take all your concerns seriously.

HELP CELLS TO HELP THEMSELVES

A dedicated farmer and proud new grandparent, David was devastated when his oncologist reported that his prostate cancer had spread to his breastbone and that chemotherapy could not help. In an attempt to keep the cancer from spreading further, David underwent radiation treatments. He also received injections of drugs to reduce his body's production of testosterone and estrogen, since these hormones are associated with prostate cancer. Despite these measures, his prognosis was bleak. "Get your affairs in order," his doctor advised. "You've got about 12 months." David was 55 years old.

Though he had never given credence to alternative medicine, David decided that he had nothing to lose. At his son-in-law's urging, he came to see me.

I emphasized the need for David to help his cells detoxify—to release toxins that could be causing the cancer and to minimize the harmful side effects of the radiation treatments. I also recommended that we stimulate his immune system so that it could more effectively combat the disease.

First line of defense: A detoxifying diet.

Although he had been a lifelong beef lover, frequent beer drinker and occasional cake baker, David immediately gave up red meat, alcohol and sugary foods, and greatly increased his intake of nutritious vegetables and fish. He also began taking daily supplements of cancer-fighting vitamin C and selenium... the herbal detoxifiers dandelion root, burdock root and milk thistle...and various natural immune boosters, including echinacea and Oregon grape root.

The nutrients did their job better than David had dared to hope. He is now cancer-free—10 years after his doctor had predicted his imminent demise. David remains conscientious about his detoxifying diet-and-supplement regimen. "It's the reason I'm here today," he says, "watching my grandson grow up."

Self-help strategy: By detoxifying the body, it's often possible to fight serious diseases at the most basic cellular level. By being open-minded about alternative therapies, you expand your treatment options and optimize healing.

SAY NO TO DRUGS...AND YES TO NUTRITION

Victor, 12, was in trouble at school. For years, the boy's behavior had caused problems in the classroom, and recently his restlessness and outbursts had worsened. His grades, never good, had dropped perilously close to failing. After Victor's pediatrician diagnosed *attention-deficit/hyperactivity disorder* (ADHD), the school psychologist and principal pressured the boy's parents, warning, "If Victor does not go on ADHD medication, he will be asked to leave the school."

But Victor's mother stood firm—"Those drugs can have serious side effects. We need to explore all other options first." That's when the family contacted me.

I shared the family's concerns about ADHD drugs, such as *methylphenidate* (Ritalin) and *amphetamine/dextroamphetamine* (Adderall XR), which can cause nausea, loss of appetite and stunted growth...headaches, dizziness and tics...insomnia and fatigue...irritability and mood swings...and heart palpitations, blood pressure changes and an increased risk of heart attack. We agreed to try nutritional therapies first and to use drugs only as a last resort.

Fortunately, we had summer vacation to address Victor's problems. The boy's diet was already good—but nonetheless, I suspected a deficiency of essential fatty acids (EFAs), which are vital structural components of cell membranes that affect the health of the brain, nervous system and cardiovascular system. The clue: Victor's skin was extremely dry. EFA deficiency is a common cause of dry skin, and studies show that EFA supplementation improves mood and focus in some children with ADHD.

To boost Victor's intake of EFAs, I started him on daily supplements of fish oil (Nordic Naturals Pro DHA, 800-662-2544, *www.nordicnaturals.com*) and evening primrose oil. In addition, I prescribed the homeopathic remedy *Lycopodium clavatum*, made from club moss, to improve mood and concentration. I also had Victor take daily supplements of *phospha-*

tidylserine—a nutrient essential for the normal functioning of brain cell membranes and naturally found in soy, rice, fish and leafy green vegetables.

Victor was tested by a child psychologist before starting his treatment with me and again after 10 weeks. To the psychologist's amazement, Victor improved so markedly that he was no longer considered to have ADHD. During the ensuing school year, his teachers reported that Victor's behavior was exemplary. When I asked the boy during a follow-up visit, "How are your grades?" he grinned from ear to ear as he answered, "I made the honor roll!"

Self-help strategy: Many behavioral problems result from biochemical imbalances. Before resorting to drugs, investigate potential side effects—and explore natural alternatives that can safely restore the body to its proper balance.

PERSEVERANCE PAYS OFF

Turning 40, Joanne laughed at the idea of a midlife crisis. She was happily married and had a busy, successful medical practice as a doctor of chiropractic. Life was good, and the future looked bright.

But then Joanne began to experience recurring pain in her bladder and the surrounding pelvic area, plus a frequent and urgent need to urinate. Her doctor diagnosed *interstitial cystitis* (IC), a condition that affects more than 700,000 people in the US (primarily women), yet is still not well understood. Joanne tried every treatment her doctors could suggest—including the prescription drug *pentosan polysulfate* (Elmiron), which is intended to repair the bladder lining, and a surgical procedure called bladder distension, which stretches the bladder by filling it with gas or water to increase its capacity—but nothing brought relief.

After five years, Joanne was in such severe and incessant pain that she could no longer see patients, take care of her two-year-old or find any pleasure in sex. Compounding her problems, she also experienced an early menopause, with symptoms that included dozens of hot flashes a day, frequent insomnia and severe fatigue, heart palpitations, anxiety, mood swings and trouble concentrating.

As I took her medical history, I noticed that her IC symptoms had eased during her pregnancy. This suggested that her IC was connected to her hormone balance and that menopause was aggravating the condition. Blood and saliva tests confirmed that she had a deficiency of estrogen, progesterone and thyroid hormones.

Finding the root of Joanne's problem was easier than treating it. For seven months, we used a trial-and-error approach, looking for a precise mix of hormone replacement therapies to alleviate her IC and menopausal symptoms. Finally, we hit upon the solution—a mix of an *estriol* (estrogen) vaginal cream...an estrogen/progesterone combination transdermal (skin) cream...and oral thyroid hormone tablets. Two months later, Joanne's pelvic pain and urinary urgency were gone, her menopausal symptoms had abated, and her sex life was back on track. "I'm enjoying being a mom," she reported, "and I may reopen my chiropractic practice. I've got my life back!"

Self-help strategy: Joanne deserves credit for her patience as we worked to figure out the best treatment for her individual needs. Too many people give up if they don't find a quick fix. For health problems—as with most of life's challenges—perseverance is the key to finding a solution.

WHEN YOU NEED SUPPORT

Facing a medical problem? Reach out for help. These organizations can provide physician referrals...information on conditions, treatments and research...and/or emotional support.

Complementary and Alternative Medicine

●**American Association of Naturopathic Physicians,** 866-538-2267, *www.naturopathic. org.*

●**American Association of Acupuncture and Oriental Medicine,** 866-455-7999, *www. aaaom.org.*

●**American College for Advancement in Medicine,** 888-439-6891, *www.acamnet.org.*

●**National Center for Homeopathy,** 703-548-7790, *www.nationalcenterforhomeopathy. org.*

Mainstream Medicine

- **American Autoimmune Related Diseases Association,** 202-466-8511, *www.aarda.org.*

- **American Cancer Society,** 800-227-2345, *www.cancer.org.*

- **American Diabetes Association,** 800-342-2383, *www.diabetes.org.*

- **American Heart Association,** 800-242-8721, *www.heart.org.*

- **American Lung Association,** 800-586-4872, *www.lungusa.org.*

- **National Alliance on Mental Illness,** 800-950-6264, *www.nami.org.*

REPORT #21
Marijuana Compound May Stop Metastatic Breast Cancer

Sean D. McAllister, PhD, Basic Science Researcher, California Pacific Medical Center Research Institute, San Francisco.

Pierre-Yves Desprez, PhD, Basic Science Researcher, California Pacific Medical Center Research Institute, San Francisco.

Manuel Guzman, PhD, professor, biochemistry and molecular biology, Complutense University, Madrid, Spain.

Molecular Cancer Therapeutics.

A nontoxic, nonpsychoactive compound in marijuana may block the progress of metastatic breast cancer, according to a new study by researchers in California.

"This is a new way to treat a patient that is not toxic like chemotherapy or radiotherapy. It is a new approach for metastatic cancer," said lead researcher Sean D. McAllister, PhD, an associate scientist at the California Pacific Medical Center Research Institute in San Francisco.

HOW IT WORKS

The compound found in cannabis, called *cannabidiol* (CBD), inhibits a gene, Id-1, that researchers believe is responsible for the metastatic process that spreads cells from the original tumor throughout the body.

Opting for a musical metaphor, senior researcher Pierre-Yves Desprez, PhD, likened Id-1 to "an (orchestra) conductor. In this case, you shoot the conductor, and the whole orchestra is going to stop. If you shoot the violinist, the orchestra just continues to play."

In humans, the Id-1 gene is found only in metastatic cancer cells, said Dr. Desprez, a staff scientist at the institute. Before birth, they are present and involved in the development of human embryos, but after birth, they go silent—and should stay that way, he said.

But in metastatic cancer "when (the genes) wake up, they are very bad," he said. "They push the cells to behave like embryonic cells and grow. They go crazy, they proliferate, they migrate." Dr. Desprez said, "We need to be able to turn them off."

NEW FINDINGS

According to the new study, CBD does exactly that.

"We are focusing on the latest stages of cancer," Dr. Desprez added. The cancer cell itself is not the problem, because a tumor can be "removed easily by surgery," he said. The problem is the development of metastatic cells, which is "conducted" by Id-1.

Drs. McAllister and Desprez said they are not suggesting that patients with hormone-independent metastatic breast cancer smoke marijuana. For one thing, a sufficient amount of CBD could never be obtained in that way, they said.

The research that has been done on marijuana and its compounds, however, is helpful, Dr. McAllister, said. CBD has been around for a long time, and researchers have found it is not psychoactive, and its "toxicity is very low," he added.

If Drs. McAllister and Desprez's work results in the development of a cancer treatment, someone with metastatic cancer might be placed on CBD for several years. That means low toxicity is important, Dr. McAllister explained.

Dr. McAllister also suggested that Id-1 is "so important in providing the [metastatic] mechanism in these cells in so many types of cancers" that they "provide us an opportunity potentially to target other types of cancers."

TREATMENT WITH CBD

Further study is needed before CBD can be conclusively identified as a treatment option, Drs. McAllister and Desprez said. "We need to involve a team of physicians, because we are bench (basic) scientists," Dr. McAllister noted.

One expert called the findings intriguing but preliminary.

"This is the first evidence that a cannabinoid can target the expression of an important breast cancer metastasis gene," noted Manuel Guzman, PhD, a Spanish expert on cannabinoids and cancer. He described the California study as giving "preliminary insight into the question of whether CBD could be used clinically to treat metastatic breast cancer."

However, "all the experiments in the paper have been conducted in cultured cells and none of them in any animal model of breast cancer, which would be one of the steps for further research," added Dr. Guzman, who is a professor of biochemistry and molecular biology at Complutense University in Madrid.

For more on breast cancer, go to the National Breast Cancer Foundation Web site at *www.nationalbreastcancer.org.*

Volume 2
Cholesterol and Heart Cures

The Food that Lowers Cholesterol 24%...In Just Five Weeks

If you're one of the millions of Americans with high cholesterol, chances are your doctor has told you what not to eat—high-fat meats and dairy, for example. But certain foods actually can lower your cholesterol and, in some cases, eliminate the need for cholesterol-lowering drugs. Regularly including these foods can have a particularly powerful effect on reducing LDL—the "bad" cholesterol that damages arteries and other blood vessels. High LDL levels are associated with an increased risk for heart attack and stroke.

OAT BRAN, BARLEY AND MORE

Soluble fiber is present in plant-based foods in the form of gums and pectins. The National Cholesterol Education Program Adult Treatment Panel states that five to 10 grams (g) of soluble fiber daily can help to lower LDL by as much as 5%.

A specific type of soluble fiber—*beta-glucan* (found in oat bran and barley)—has an even more potent cholesterol-lowering effect...

• **In a study, men eating 6g of soluble fiber from barley per day** lowered their LDL cholesterol by an average of 24% in five weeks.

• **In a study, men given 6g of beta-glucan in a fortified bread**—who also were following a low-fat diet and walking 60 minutes per day—experienced an average reduction in LDL cholesterol of 28%.

How it works: In the intestines, soluble fiber attaches itself to cholesterol and bile acids. Bile acids help with fat digestion. They are made from cholesterol, so when the body

Andrea Chernus, RD, is a registered dietitian, certified diabetes educator and exercise physiologist who maintains a private practice in New York City. She counsels patients on high cholesterol, diabetes, weight management and sports nutrition. She was formerly the clinical nutritionist for Columbia University, New York City. *www.nutritionhandouts.com.*

needs to make more bile acids, it pulls cholesterol from the bloodstream. The process of binding soluble fiber to bile acids forces the body to make more bile and use up cholesterol from the body's supply. Because fiber is not digested, it carries the cholesterol and bile acids out of the body, lowering the body's cholesterol.

Best sources of soluble fiber: Oat bran, oatmeal, barley, apples, citrus fruits, pears, kidney and lima beans, carrots, broccoli and brussels sprouts. Psyllium seed husks also are a good source and are found in some cereals, such as Kellogg's All-Bran Buds cereal.

Hot cereal made of 100% oat bran has about 3g of soluble fiber per serving...plain oatmeal has about 2g. Most cold oat-based cereals have one gram. Fruits and vegetables have 0.5g to 1g of soluble fiber per serving.

Beware: Commercially prepared muffins, pretzels and breads made with oat bran may not contain much soluble fiber. Also, some may be high in saturated or trans fats, sugars and sodium. As a rough guide, check the label to make sure oat bran is one of the first ingredients listed on the food label. (Soluble fiber does not have to be listed separately from total fiber.)

PLANT STEROLS AND STANOLS

Plant sterols (phytosterols) and plant stanols (phytostanols) are substances that block absorption of cholesterol. They are particularly high in vegetable oils and, to a lesser degree, in fruits, vegetables, nuts and seeds. More than 25 studies have proved their effectiveness in cholesterol reduction. *Examples...*

• **In a study, 155 adults with high cholesterol took in 1.5g per day of plant sterols from margarine.** After six months, they had an average reduction in LDL cholesterol of 11% (and 9% reduction in total cholesterol).

• **In another study, 72 adults with high cholesterol took in 2g per day of plant sterols from phytosterol-fortified orange juice.** After eight weeks, their average reduction in LDL cholesterol was 12% (7% reduction in total cholesterol).

How they work: Plant sterols and stanols help block the absorption of dietary cholesterol and the reabsorption of cholesterol back into our intestinal tract. They compete with cholesterol for incorporation into mixed micelles, which are composite molecules that contain both water- and fat-soluble substances. In the body, micelles are used to carry fats through the bloodstream. When cholesterol is blocked from being absorbed and incorporated into these molecules, it is excreted from the body.

Best sources: To get a cholesterol-lowering dose from ordinary food, you would have to eat hundreds of calories worth of oils per day or bushels of fruits and vegetables. But researchers have isolated plant sterols and stanols, and food companies have incorporated them into "functional foods."

Until recently, only certain margarines contained these cholesterol-lowering ingredients, but food companies now have put them into lower-fat foods, such as yogurts, juices, breads and more. A dose of 2g to 3g of plant sterols and stanols per day has the greatest impact on lowering LDL cholesterol, reducing it by 6% to 15%. Higher doses of sterols and stanols are not more effective.

Foods containing effective amounts of plant sterols and stanols include Promise, Benecol and Take Control margarines...Minute Maid Heartwise Orange Juice...Nature Valley Healthy Heart Granola Bars...Hain Celestial Rice Dream beverage...Lifetime low-fat cheese...Oroweat whole-grain bread...and VitaMuffins.

The FDA allows foods containing sterols and stanols that meet certain criteria to put a health claim on the label that they can help reduce the risk of coronary heart disease.

Beware: Margarines and juices are dense in calories. Check food labels to see how much you need to eat to obtain 2g to 3g of sterols and stanols.

If you're worried about calories, you can take sterol/stanol supplements. Generally, they are called beta-sitosterol or sitostanol. It is safe to use these supplements along with statin drugs for an additional cholesterol-lowering effect.

NUTS

People who are trying to lower cholesterol levels often eliminate nuts from their diets because nuts are high in fat and calories. But nuts contain mostly monounsaturated fats, which, when substituted for the saturated fats found in high-fat meats and dairy, not only can lower LDL levels but also boost HDL "good" cholesterol levels.

Studies have shown the greatest effect when nuts comprise 20% of one's total calories, which typically amounts to 1.5 to 3.5 ounces of nuts daily (about one-quarter to one-half cup).

On average, LDL cholesterol levels fall 8% to 12% when walnuts or almonds are substituted for saturated fats. HDL levels may increase by 9% to 20%. Other nuts, such as peanuts (technically a legume), pistachios and pecans, have been shown to lower cholesterol, but fewer studies are available on these varieties.

How they work: The exact mechanism of nuts' healthful effects hasn't been discovered yet, but nuts contain a combination of plant sterols, fiber and healthy fats.

Beware: Because nuts are high in calories, the trick is to substitute nuts for less healthful, high-fat foods, including cheese and meat.

REPORT #23
Pets May Prevent Heart Attacks

Adnan I. Qureshi, MD, executive director, Minnesota Stroke Initiative and professor of neurology, neurosurgery and radiology, University of Minnesota, Minneapolis.

Kathie Cole, RN, clinical nurse, UCLA Medical Center/School of Nursing, Los Angeles.

American Stroke Association International Stroke Conference, New Orleans.

Whether it's a frisky kitten or a tubby tabby, a cat at home could cut your heart attack risk by almost a third, according to recent research. The 10-year study of more than 4,300 Americans, suggests that the stress relief pets provide humans is heart-healthy.

Bonus: Dog lovers shouldn't feel left out. Although the study found no such benefit from "man's best friend," that's probably because there simply weren't enough dog own-

ers in the study to draw firm conclusions, the researchers said.

"For years we have known that psychological stress and anxiety are related to cardiovascular events, particularly heart attacks," noted study senior author Dr. Adnan Qureshi, executive director of the Stroke Center at the University of Minnesota in Minneapolis. According to Qureshi, the research shows that "essentially there is a benefit in relieving those inciting factors from pets."

The findings were presented during the American Stroke Association's International Stroke Conference in New Orleans.

The stress-cardiovascular disease link is very well-documented in scientific literature, and the affection and pleasure pets give humans is a known stress-buster. In fact, an earlier study presented at an American Heart Association meeting found that a single 12-minute visit with a dog improved the heart and lung function of people with heart failure.

In Qureshi's study, the team analyzed data on 4,435 Americans, aged 30 to 75, who took part in the federal government's second National Health and Nutrition Examination Study, which ran from 1976-1980. According to the data in the survey, 2,435 of the participants either owned a cat or had owned a cat in the past, while the remaining 2,000 had never done so.

Qureshi's team then tracked rates of death from all causes, including heart and stroke. Cat owners "appeared to have a lower rate of dying from heart attacks" over 10 years of follow-up compared to feline-free folk, Qureshi said.

The magnitude of the effect—a 30 percent reduction in heart attack risk—"was a little bit surprising," he added. "We certainly expected an effect, because we thought that there was a biologically plausible mechanism at work, but the magnitude of the effect was hard to predict."

Qureshi—proud owner of his own feline, Ninja—stressed that dogs probably would bring people the same kind of benefit, but the numbers of dog owners in the study wasn't big enough to count statistically.

Kathie Cole, a clinical nurse at the UCLA Medical Center and School of Nursing and the lead author of the dog-and-heart-failure study, said she wasn't surprised by the Minnesota findings.

"I would be inclined to think that any animal that is perceived as meaningful to a person in a positive way would have health benefits," Cole said. She pointed to multiple studies that have found that animal companions "have a calming effect in regard to mental stressors."

Both researchers believe pet ownership should be perceived as a low-cost, low-risk medical intervention that can potentially save or extend lives, especially for the elderly. "The problem right now is that so many apartment buildings or nursing homes aren't allowing animals in," Cole said. "That's the problem I see from a community standpoint."

Qureshi agreed that cats, dogs or other pets may bring tangible medical benefits to owners. "This opens a whole new avenue or intervention that we hadn't looked at before, one that can be made at the public level," he said. And unlike drugs or surgery, pet ownership "doesn't appear to have any risks to it," he added.

Helpful: If you are considering adopting a pet, contact the American Veterinary Medical Association (800-248-2862, *www.avma.org*) for information on responsible pet ownership.

REPORT #24
Tomatoes Are Good For You

When 21 healthy people ate a tomato-free diet for three weeks, followed by a three-week diet that included about two tablespoons of ketchup and nearly two cups of tomato juice daily, participants' LDL "bad" cholesterol levels decreased, on average, by 12.9%.

Theory: Antioxidants in tomatoes inhibit oxidation of fats.

For heart health: Add tomato products (such as low-sodium tomato juice) to your daily diet.

Sohvi Hörkkö, MD, PhD, researchers, Institute of Diagnostics, Department of Medical Microbiology, University of Oulu, Finland.

REPORT #25
You Don't Need Drugs to Control Your Cholesterol

Allan Magaziner, DO, a clinical instructor in the department of family practice at the Robert Wood Johnson University of Medicine and Dentistry in New Brunswick, New Jersey, and founder and medical director of the Magaziner Center for Wellness in Cherry Hill, New Jersey (*www.drmagaziner.com*). A past president of the American College for Advancement in Medicine, he is the author of *The All-Natural Cardio Cure* (Avery).

It's widely known that low cholesterol levels help prevent heart attack and stroke. But that's only part of the story. Levels of HDL "good" cholesterol must be high enough to carry harmful forms of cholesterol to the liver to be excreted.

Recent finding: Research has shown that decreasing LDL "bad" cholesterol by 40% and increasing HDL by 30% lowers the risk for heart attack or stroke by 70%—a much greater reduction of risk than occurs from lowering either total cholesterol or LDL levels.

The pharmaceutical industry has worked feverishly to develop a prescription medication that significantly increases HDL levels, to be used as a complement to cholesterol-lowering statins that focus primarily on lowering LDL levels.

Examples: The drug *torcetrapib* was pegged as a blockbuster that increases HDL levels by 60%—that is, until late-stage clinical trials showed that torcetrapib actually increased heart problems and death rates.

What you may not know: Therapeutic doses of niacin (vitamin B-3) effectively boost HDL levels—and lower LDL and total cholesterol.

THE "CHOLESTEROL VITAMIN"

Over fifty years ago, Canadian scientists discovered that high doses of *nicotinic acid*—a form of niacin—could lower total cholesterol. In a 1975 study of men with heart disease, niacin was shown to reduce the rate of second heart attacks. Later, niacin was found to boost heart-protective HDL levels.

Although niacin alone cannot help everyone with abnormal cholesterol levels—often it is best used in combination with a statin—the vitamin is one of the most effective nondrug therapies available.

Ask your doctor about taking niacin if after trying cholesterol-lowering medication you have suffered side effects or your cholesterol levels have not improved within three months of getting a cholesterol test. Or consider trying niacin with the nondrug therapies described below.

How to use: Start with 100 mg of niacin daily and build up over one week to 500 mg a day. Every week, increase the dose by 500 mg until you reach 2,000 mg a day, taken in three divided doses, with meals. Be certain to use nicotinic acid, not *niacinamide*, a form of B vitamin that does not improve cholesterol levels. Consult your doctor before taking niacin.

The most common side effect of niacin is flushing—a warm, itchy, rash-like reddening of the face, neck and chest, which lasts about 10 minutes. Flushing is caused by niacin's ability to trigger vasodilation (widening of blood vessels).

To lessen this side effect, choose a form of niacin known as *inositol hexanicotinate*. It helps prevent the flush without reducing niacin's effectiveness.

Caution: Niacin should be avoided by people with a history of liver disease or stomach ulcers and used with caution by patients with diabetes and/or gallbladder disease. In addition, high-dose niacin (2,000 mg or more) may interact with certain medications, including alpha-blockers, such as *doxazosin* (Cardura), and the diabetes drug *metformin* (Glucophage).

OTHER NONDRUG THERAPIES

A diet that keeps sugar and processed food to an absolute minimum and emphasizes fruits and vegetables...whole grains...beans...fish... lean meats...and nuts and seeds can help lower LDL cholesterol and raise HDL levels. So can regular exercise, such as brisk walking, and losing excess weight.

Other nondrug approaches can lower total and LDL cholesterol and boost HDL. *Combine the following nondrug therapies with niacin for maximum effectiveness...*

• **Red yeast rice.** This Chinese medicine—a yeast that is grown on white rice, then fermented—contains *monacolins*, substances that act as naturally occurring statins. Research in China shows that red yeast rice can lower total cholesterol by 11% to 30%. Typical use: Take 1,200 to 2,400 mg a day of red yeast rice, in two to four doses, with meals.

Not recommended: Policosanol—a supplement derived from cane sugar that also contains natural statins—has been widely promoted as effective for lowering cholesterol. However, several recent studies show that policosanol has no significant effect on cholesterol.

• **Fish oil and flaxseed.** Fish oil and flaxseed supply omega-3 fatty acids, which lower total cholesterol and LDL levels and raise HDL levels.

Typical dose: For fish oil, take supplements containing a total of 3 g daily of *eicosapentaenoic acid* (EPA) and *docosahexaenoic acid* (DHA). If you take a blood-thinning drug, such as aspirin or *warfarin* (Coumadin), check with your doctor before taking this dose of fish oil. Or use one to three teaspoons of ground flaxseed a day, sprinkled on food or mixed with water or juice. Flaxseed also can help relieve constipation and ease arthritis pain.

• **Soy.** Many studies show that soy can help lower total and LDL cholesterol.

Typical use: Try to get 20 g of soy protein a day—the equivalent of eight ounces of tofu... or one cup of edamame (soy) beans.

Important: Soy ice cream and other processed soy foods don't deliver enough soy to help reduce cholesterol.

Caution: If you have been diagnosed with a hormone-dependent cancer, such as some breast malignancies, or are at risk for such a condition, check with your doctor before adding soy to your diet.

• **Plant sterols.** These natural substances, which block the absorption of cholesterol in the intestines, are found in fruits, vegetables, beans, grains and other plants. Regular intake can reduce total cholesterol by 10% and LDL by 14%. Products with plant sterols (or a similar form, plant stanols) include spreads, salad dressings, snack bars and dietary supplements.

Typical use: Aim for 1 g to 2 g daily of plant sterols.

• **Walnuts.** A recent study published in the medical journal *Angiology* showed that people who ate a handful of walnuts daily for eight weeks had a 9% increase in HDL. Walnuts contain polyphenol antioxidants, which also inhibit oxidation of LDL cholesterol. Recommended intake: One ounce of raw walnuts three times daily.

REPORT #26
The Amazing Power of Aspirin

Randall S. Stafford, MD, PhD, medical director of Stanford Prevention Research Center, director of the Program on Prevention and Outcomes Practices at the Stanford Prevention Research Center and associate professor of medicine at Stanford University. Dr. Stafford is author or coauthor of more than 110 scientific papers in leading medical journals. He is on the advisory panel of experts of "Aspirin Talks," an educational campaign from the American College of Preventive Medicine.

It costs pennies a pill—but for heart disease and stroke, the number-one and number-three killers of Americans, aspirin can be just as powerfully preventive as more expensive medications, such as cholesterol-lowering statins.

Two-thirds of people at high risk for heart attack and stroke don't take aspirin daily—leading to an estimated yearly death toll of 45,000 people who might have lived if they had taken a low-dose aspirin every day. *And recent evidence shows that aspirin also plays a role in fighting colon cancer and possibly other diseases...*

PROTECTING DISEASED ARTERIES

If you've had a heart attack, taking aspirin daily reduces your risk for a second attack by 23%. If you have angina—chest pain that signals serious heart disease—daily aspirin reduces heart attack risk by 51%. Type 2 diabetes—which damages arteries, increasing risk for heart attack and stroke—is another reason for daily aspirin. Taking aspirin if you have diagnosed heart disease or type 2 diabetes is called secondary prevention—it's too late to prevent the problem, but you're controlling it.

What to do: If you have heart disease or type 2 diabetes, talk to your doctor about aspirin therapy. The recommended dosage for secondary prevention is 81 milligrams (mg) daily, or one "baby aspirin." There continues to be debate about whether 162 mg daily may be more protective for some people with heart disease or diabetes—ask your doctor.

PREVENTING HEART ATTACK

In March 2009, the US Preventive Services Task Force (USPSTF) recommended the daily use of aspirin for primary prevention—preventing heart attack and stroke in people who don't have diagnosed cardiovascular disease.

Because older age is a risk factor for heart attacks and strokes, the recommendation included all men between the ages of 45 and 79 and all women between the ages of 55 and 79.

Among these groups, the USPSTF said to use aspirin for primary prevention only in cases in which the benefits are likely to outweigh the risks. When aspirin blocks the production of blood-clotting *thromboxane*, it increases the risk for internal bleeding.

The benefits of taking aspirin are likely to be greater than the risks in those with an elevated risk for heart attack and stroke. These risk factors include high total cholesterol, lower than normal HDL (good) cholesterol, high blood pressure, smoking and older age.

Factors that may indicate aspirin is too risky for you include...

• **Recent bleeding from a stomach ulcer or hemorrhagic stroke,** caused by a ruptured blood vessel

- **History of gastrointestinal (GI) bleeding** caused by other nonsteroidal anti-inflammatory drugs (NSAIDs)

- **Taking an anti-inflammatory corticosteroid,** such as prednisone

- **Rheumatoid arthritis.**

AGE 80 OR OLDER

The USPSTF didn't include a recommendation for people age 80 or older, because there's not enough scientific evidence to know whether aspirin protects this age group. However, your risk for heart attack and stroke increases with age, so those over 80 are likely to benefit from aspirin, but they also are more likely to have GI or brain bleeding.

What to do: If you're 80 or older, ask your doctor about taking aspirin. You probably shouldn't take it if you have a history of GI bleeding or falls (a head injury is more likely to cause hemorrhagic stroke in someone taking aspirin).

COLON CANCER

A study by researchers at Harvard Medical School, published in *The Journal of the American Medical Association*, showed that people with colorectal cancer who began taking aspirin regularly after diagnosis had a 29% lower risk of dying from the disease than those who never used aspirin. Researchers also found that those who used aspirin regularly before their diagnosis had a 61% lower risk of dying from the disease. Aspirin reduces inflammation, which may play a role in the progress of colon cancer.

What to do: If you've been diagnosed with colorectal cancer, talk to your doctor about taking aspirin. There is not enough scientific evidence to justify taking aspirin to prevent colorectal cancer.

USING ASPIRIN WISELY

- **Don't worry about the formulation.** In most cases, aspirin doesn't cause GI bleeding because it irritates your GI tract—the bleeding is caused by a systemic effect on *cyclooxygenases* (COX). That means enteric-coated tablets don't decrease the risk for GI bleeding.

- **Be cautious of blood-thinning supplements.** Fish oil and the herb ginkgo biloba also affect platelets, increasing the risk for internal bleeding. If you're taking aspirin, talk to your doctor about whether it's safe to take those supplements.

- **Don't take aspirin and another NSAID at the same time.** Recent research shows that NSAIDs, such as *ibuprofen* and *naproxen* (Aleve, Naprosyn), interfere with aspirin's ability to affect COX. If you take another NSAID, take it four to six hours before or after taking aspirin.

- **Think twice about stopping aspirin before surgery.** Surgeons often ask patients to stop taking aspirin about two weeks before surgery. But if you take aspirin for secondary prevention, the risk for a heart attack may outweigh the risk for additional bleeding during surgery. Ask your physician.

- **If you think you're having a heart attack, call 911 immediately and take aspirin.** Chew an uncoated full-strength (325-mg) aspirin right away. Taking aspirin once a day for the next month can reduce the risk for death by 23% and may significantly reduce damage to the heart.

HOW ASPIRIN WORKS

Aspirin is *acetylsalicylic acid*—a compound that blocks the action of COX, enzymes that are found in every cell.

COX help manufacture prostaglandins, hormones that control pain, fever and inflammation. COX also help produce *thromboxane*, which allows cells in the bloodstream called platelets to stick together, forming blood clots.

By impeding prostaglandins, aspirin lowers fever, relieves acute pain such as headache, and eases the soreness that accompanies inflammation. By reducing thromboxane, aspirin helps stop the formation of blood clots, reducing the risk for a heart attack and stroke.

REPORT #27
The Truth About Aspirin—It May Not Protect Your Heart...But Natural Solutions Can

Mark A. Stengler, NMD, licensed naturopathic medical doctor in private practice, La Jolla, California...adjunct associate clinical professor at the National College of Natural Medicine, Portland, Oregon...author of many books, including *The Natural Physician's Healing Therapies* and coauthor of *Prescription for Natural Cures* (both from Bottom Line Books)...and author of the *Bottom Line/Natural Healing* newsletter.

Every morning, some 50 million Americans pop a low-dose aspirin into their mouths with the hope that it will help prevent a heart attack or stroke. For many, taking a daily aspirin is a habit, a no-brainer—a seemingly simple way to protect against cardiovascular disease.

The problem: Aspirin is overprescribed and causes many uncomfortable and possibly dangerous side effects (see the list at the end of this article). In addition, a little-known phenomenon called aspirin resistance means that, for some people, aspirin provides no protection at all.

Good news: There are several natural alternatives to aspirin that have the potential to help more people without the damaging side effects.

ASPIRIN RESISTANCE

For a number of people, aspirin neither prevents blood clots nor reduces inflammation. Aspirin resistance has no symptoms. Sadly, people find out that the daily aspirin they are taking has no effect only when they suffer a heart attack or stroke.

There currently is no single laboratory test for, or accepted definition of, aspirin resistance. Estimates of how many people are aspirin resistant vary widely, from as low as 5.5% to an astonishing 60%, according to a recent study in *Journal of the American College of Cardiology.*

Aspirin is a mild anticoagulant—it reduces the risk of an abnormal blood clot forming that could cause a heart attack or stroke. Stronger anticlotting medication, such as *warfarin* (Coumadin) or *heparin*, generally is given to people who are at higher risk of developing blood clots. Possible side effects from these stronger medications include hemorrhage and hypersensitivity (characterized by chills, asthma, red marks and itchy skin).

NATURAL ANTICLOTTING PROTECTION

Everyone who is concerned with heart health should follow a Mediterranean-style diet, consisting mainly of whole grains, vegetables and olive oil, as well as cold-water fish, such as salmon. This type of diet has been shown to significantly reduce the risk for heart attack and stroke.

Next: Take steps to reduce your risk for cardiovascular disease. Risk is determined by age, gender, family and medical history, smoking, cholesterol levels and other cardiovascular risk markers, blood pressure, weight and whether you have diabetes.

In addition, holistic physicians often use a blood test to track *fibrinogen*, a protein essential to blood clot formation. High fibrinogen levels can indicate a risk of developing a blood clot. I monitor fibrinogen levels and use a laboratory test to measure the time it takes for a patient's blood to clot. I order these tests every few months until the readings are normal.

If you are already taking any anticoagulant medication, including aspirin, check with your doctor before taking any of the supplements below. People who take an anticoagulant are at greater risk for hemorrhage because the medication reduces the body's ability to form a blood clot and stop internal or external bleeding.

My recommendations: Three natural anticoagulants—and one clot-busting enzyme—that can be used in place of aspirin. *These supplements, which are available at health-food stores, can be used as follows...*

• **For those who don't have heart disease and want to prevent it,** take fish oil, vitamin E and bromelain.

• **For those with atherosclerosis (fatty buildup in the arteries),** take *nattokinase* and fish oil.

• **For those with elevated fibrinogen,** take nattokinase and fish oil, and then add vitamin E and bromelain if lab tests indicate fibrinogen has not decreased after two months.

• **Fish oil.** Omega-3 essential fatty acids are necessary for natural cardiovascular disease prevention and treatment. Research has shown that patients with coronary artery disease (plaque in the arteries of the heart) who were given fish oil supplements had a mild-to-moderate regression of atherosclerosis as measured by angiography. This means that even people with existing plaque have a chance to reduce it with fish oil.

The beneficial omega-3 fatty acids in fish oil are combined *eicosapentaenoic acid* (EPA) and *docosahexaenoic acid* (DHA).

Best fish sources: Oily, cold-water fish (salmon, herring, sardines, mackerel, anchovies), either broiled or baked. (Vegetarians can get their omega-3s from flaxseed or hemp seed.) To prevent coronary disease, consume two to three servings of fish weekly or take 1,500 milligrams (mg) daily of combined EPA and DHA. For those who already have atherosclerosis and high levels of fibrinogen, take 3,000 mg daily of combined EPA and DHA (1,500 mg twice daily with meals). Keeping atherosclerosis under control can be a lifelong battle, so patients can take these amounts indefinitely.

• **Vitamin E.** In moderate doses, this antioxidant has natural blood-thinning properties. Vitamin E is a collection of eight related compounds—*tocopherols* and *tocotrienols*. Look for mixed tocopherol and tocotrienol vitamin E—it is better than any single tocopherol formulation. Take 800 international units (IU) to 1,200 IU daily. Ask your holistic doctor or cardiologist about the amount that is right for you based on your cardiovascular health.

• **Bromelain.** Found in pineapples, this enzyme acts as an anticoagulant by helping to break down excess fibrin (a blood protein made from fibrinogen that forms at the site of a blood clot). Take 500 mg three times daily, not around mealtimes. If you have ulcers, don't take bromelain.

• **Nattokinase.** Extracted from the traditional Japanese food natto, this enzyme is made from fermented soybeans. With its strong fibrin-dissolving effect, nattokinase is a more aggressive approach to treatment than other natural therapies. It is recommended for people with elevated fibrinogen or a history of heart disease. Researchers have found that it can effectively and safely prevent blood clots without any side effects. Some holistic practitioners have even been able to help their patients who are taking medications such as warfarin switch to nattokinase.

For people with atherosclerosis or high fibrinogen, take 2,000 fibrinolytic units (FU) to 4,000 FU of a nattokinase supplement twice daily under the supervision of a health-care professional. Supervision is important with all anticoagulants because there is the danger that too much can lead to hemorrhage and too little to heart attack or stroke. Nattokinase should not be taken with other blood thinners, such as aspirin or warfarin.

WHO SHOULD TAKE ASPIRIN

For some people, aspirin is indeed a lifesaver. With few exceptions, anyone who thinks he/she is having a heart attack should chew and swallow 325 mg of aspirin immediately. (Chewing any of the supplements will not have the same effect.) Most heart attack patients also are advised to continue taking this amount daily for one month under a cardiologist's care—because people who survive a heart attack are especially prone to another one in the weeks afterward. After one month, I believe only one group should continue to take aspirin—those at high risk for cardiovascular disease who are unwilling to take supplements and change their diets and lifestyles.

Caution: Don't take aspirin if you are allergic to it...suspect that you are having a stroke...or have been told by your physician not to take it.

If you are on aspirin therapy, keep in mind that regular use can deplete your body of several nutrients. To protect yourself, take the following daily—folic acid (400 micrograms, or mcg), vitamin C (500 mg), vitamin B-12 (100 mcg), zinc (30 mg). When using zinc long-term, also take copper (1 mg).

Best: Don't take these supplements at the same time of day that you take aspirin.

WHO SHOULD DEFINITELY NOT TAKE ASPIRIN

I disagree with the way many doctors routinely put patients with any risk for cardiovascular disease (or no particular risk at all) on a daily aspirin. This includes a wide swath of people—men over age 40...women over age 50 who have atherosclerosis or high cholesterol...people over age 40 who have diabetes...people who have a parent or sibling with heart disease...and others.

In addition, some people should flat-out avoid aspirin (although after a heart attack, a cardiologist would determine use), including...

•**People with active peptic ulcers.** Aspirin erodes the stomach lining.

•**Those with poor kidney or liver function.** Aspirin can do further damage to these organs.

•**Patients taking anticoagulant medications, such as warfarin.** It can increase the risk of bleeding.

•**Asthma patients.** Aspirin can make breathing difficult in some patients whose asthma is triggered by the chemicals in aspirin.

WHAT IS ASPIRIN?

Aspirin-like substances date back to the ancient Greeks, who used a powder made from willow tree back to relieve fever and pain. Aspirin belongs to a class of drugs called non-steroidal anti-inflammatory drugs (NSAIDs). They work by inhibiting the enzymes that make prostaglandins, chemicals that promote inflammation, pain and fever, and are necessary for blood clotting.

ASPIRIN'S SERIOUS SIDE EFFECTS

People often think of aspirin as a completely benign substance. *It is not. In fact, its side effects may surprise you...*

•**Gastrointestinal bleeding.** In the US, about 103,000 hospitalizations and about 16,500 deaths occur annually from gastrointestinal bleeding related to NSAIDs, including aspirin.

•**Dyspepsia.** This condition, which is characterized by pain or discomfort in the upper abdomen, is reported by 12% of users of aspirin and other NSAIDs.

•**Gastroduodenal lesions.** In a study of arthritic patients taking NSAIDs for pain, 30% developed painful gastroduodenal lesions or sores in the stomach and/or small intestine.

•**Cataracts.** Prolonged aspirin use can increase risk for cataracts (hardening and clouding of the lens of the eye) by 55%, according to a study in *Ophthalmology.*

REPORT #28
Natural Remedies That Work Like Drugs Without the Side Effects And High Cost

Tod Cooperman, MD, founder and president of ConsumerLab.com, the leading independent evaluator of nutritional and vitamin/mineral supplements, White Plains, New York. Reports can be found at *www.consumerlab.com* (subscription required). He also is editor of *ConsumerLab.com's Guide to Buying Vitamins & Supplements* (ConsumerLab.com).

Most people assume that prescription medications are stronger and more effective than supplements. But we have found that some supplements can be just as effective—without the side effects that often accompany prescription drugs.

Also, people with chronic conditions who have no insurance or are under-insured or who have been hit with higher co-pays can save hundreds or even thousands of dollars a year by using supplements in place of drugs.

Caution: Always check with your doctor before stopping a prescription drug or taking a supplement.

Here, natural alternatives to commonly prescribed medications. If there are two alternatives, try one. If that doesn't work, try the other. Dosages are those typically prescribed, but always follow directions on the supplement label or from your health practitioner.

HIGH CHOLESTEROL

Statins, the most popular drugs for lowering cholesterol, can reduce LDL (bad) cholesterol by as much as 60%, depending on the drug and dose. Drawback: Some of these drugs can cause liver problems and/or a type of muscle pain known as *myopathy*.

Alternative 1: Red yeast rice. It contains *monacolins*, chemical compounds that inhibit the body's production of cholesterol. One of these compounds, *lovastatin*, is chemically similar to the active ingredient in some statin drugs.

One study found that people taking red yeast rice supplements had reductions in LDL of 23%. When the supplements were combined with healthy lifestyle changes, LDL dropped by 42%.

Other benefits: Because red yeast rice contains a variety of cholesterol-lowering compounds, it may be effective in patients who don't respond to single-ingredient statins. It also appears to be less likely to cause liver problems and muscle pain.

Dose: 600 milligrams (mg) of red yeast rice extract, taken twice daily.

Alternative 2: Phytosterols. These are naturally occurring plant compounds that come in supplement form as well as in cholesterol-lowering margarines, such as Benecol and Take Control. Plant sterols inhibit the absorption of cholesterol in the intestine and can lower LDL by between 10% and 14%.

Dose: 1.3 grams (g) of a plant sterol supplement daily, divided into two doses. Or two tablespoons of a cholesterol-lowering margarine.

OSTEOARTHRITIS

It's the most common form of arthritis, affecting up to 20 million American adults. Osteoarthritis occurs when cartilage in the joints wears and breaks down, causing pain and stiffness. People with frequent or severe symptoms often depend on prescription-strength anti-inflammatory drugs. These drugs reduce symptoms but don't change the outcome of

the disease. They also can cause stomach upset or other gastrointestinal problems.

Alternative 1: Glucosamine. This supplement usually is derived from shellfish, though vegetable-based versions are starting to appear. It helps the body repair and rebuild damaged cartilage. It can help reduce pain as well as subsequent joint damage.

Dose: 1,500 mg, once daily.

Alternative 2: Glucosamine plus chondroitin. This supplement combination is more expensive than glucosamine alone, but it sometimes helps patients who don't respond to glucosamine. Chondroitin, the added ingredient that typically is made from cow or pig cartilage, promotes the absorption of fluids into connective tissue and aids in flexibility and repair.

Dose: 1,500 mg of glucosamine and 1,200 mg of chondroitin, once daily.

Important: Studies have revealed that supplements protect joints better than they relieve pain. Most people who take them still need an occasional anti-inflammatory painkiller.

RHEUMATOID ARTHRITIS

This form of arthritis causes inflammation throughout the body that can damage joints as well as the eyes, lungs and/or heart. Most people with rheumatoid arthritis take prescription drugs, such as *methotrexate* (Rheumatrex) or *hydroxychloroquine* (Plaquenil). Most rheumatoid drugs are expensive, and many have a high risk for side effects, including suppressed immunity.

Supplementation can reduce inflammation and potentially reduce the dosage of prescription drugs.

Alternative: Fish and fish oil. The omega-3 fatty acids in cold-water fish, such as salmon and tuna, have potent anti-inflammatory effects. A study at the University of Pittsburgh School of Medicine found that 59% of patients given supplemental omega-3s had decreased joint pain.

Dose: A total of 1,200 mg to 2,400 mg of EPA and DHA (types of fish oil) daily, or eat three or more fish servings a week. Caution: Fish oil may interact with blood-thinning drugs, such as *warfarin* (Coumadin).

DEPRESSION

Antidepressant medications, including *selective serotonin reuptake inhibitors* (SSRIs), such as *paroxetine* (Paxil), *escitalopram* (Lexapro) and *citalopram* (Celexa), have revolutionized the treatment of depression. Many people who take them, however, experience troublesome side effects, including heightened anxiety and reduced libido.

Alternative 1: St. John's wort. It appears to be as effective for mild-to-moderate depression as SSRIs but with milder side effects. It is not effective for patients with major depression and should not be taken with prescription antidepressants. It also may interact with other medications, including blood thinners, such as *warfarin* (Coumadin).

Dose: 300 mg, three times daily. Look for a product that contains 1% to 3% *hypericin*, the active ingredient.

Alternative 2: Fish oil. It improves a number of emotional and mental disorders, including depression and bipolar disorder. A study found that those who combined EPA with an antidepressant medication did better than those using either treatment alone.

Dose: 1 g of EPA, once daily, or eat three or more fish servings a week. (See fish oil caution on page 30.)

ENLARGED PROSTATE

Starting in their 40s, many men experience a rapid growth of the prostate gland. If the inner part of the gland gets too large, it can press against the urethra. This condition, called *benign prostatic hyperplasia* (BPH), can cause irritation or difficulty urinating.

Some drugs, such as *finasteride* (Proscar), reduce the size of the prostate gland. Others, such as *terazosin* (Hytrin) and *doxazosin* (Cardura), relax the prostate and make it easier to urinate but also may cause dizziness.

Alternative: Saw palmetto. This herbal supplement helps prevent testosterone from fueling the growth of prostate cells. In some but not all studies, it has been shown to be as effective as finasteride for men with mild symptoms of BPH.

Dose: 160 mg, twice daily. It can take several months to a year before saw palmetto is fully effective.

Volume 3
Stroke Damage Cures

REPORT #29

How Brain Scientist Jill Bolte Taylor Came Back From a Stroke

In 1996, Jill Bolte Taylor, PhD, a 37-year-old brain scientist, had a severe hemorrhagic (bleeding) stroke in the left hemisphere of her brain.

Taylor's cognitive abilities degenerated rapidly in the hours following the stroke. Bleeding affected the motor cortex (paralyzing her right arm)…the sensory cortex (making it difficult for her to see or hear)…and the brain's language centers (making it difficult for her to speak).

After struggling to call for help, she was taken to the hospital, where she underwent surgery two-and-a-half weeks later to remove a golf ball–sized blood clot in her brain.

Today, Taylor is completely recovered—all of her physical, cognitive and emotional abilities are intact. Her recovery refutes the widely held belief that if a stroke survivor doesn't regain a particular ability within six months, it will never be regained.

We recently spoke with Taylor, a neuroanatomist (a scientist specializing in the anatomy of the brain) who lectures widely, about her stroke recovery. The strategies she shared also can be used by all those who have had a debilitating ischemic stroke (in which a blood clot stops blood supply to an area of the brain) or any severe brain injury…

STEP 1: MOVE TO RECOVER

People who survive a stroke often experience crushing fatigue due to the damage that occurs to brain cells (neurons)—this affects their energy levels and abilities to process information. Simple tasks, such as changing the position of your body or even opening your

Jill Bolte Taylor, PhD, a neuroanatomist affiliated with the Indiana University School of Medicine in Indianapolis. She is a national spokesperson for the Harvard Brain Tissue Resource Center, which collects human brain tissue for research and author of *My Stroke of Insight: A Brain Scientist's Personal Journey* (Plume).

eyes, are extraordinarily difficult. But the same activities that restore physical strength also force individual neurons to reconnect and communicate with one another—a process that is essential for post-stroke neurological recovery.

Helpful: Any physical activity is beneficial—even basic movements, such as standing up or sitting down.

Important: When you feel rested and capable of expending the necessary energy, you should push yourself to do more and more physically each day. As I gained strength, I progressed to trying more difficult activities, such as standing at the sink and doing dishes.

STEP 2: ESCAPE THE MENTAL NOISE

Neurons that are damaged by a stroke are unable to process normal stimuli, such as bright lights or the sound of a television. As a result, visual or auditory distractions may be interpreted by the brain as mental "noise." Saturating the brain with such stimuli may make it much harder for the neurons to recover and may impede the retention of new information.

Helpful: After any kind of stroke or other brain trauma, alternate periods of sleep with briefer periods (about 20 minutes) of learning and cognitive challenges (such as those described below). Periods of sleep (as much as needed until waking up naturally) allow the brain to assimilate information that is gleaned during periods of wakefulness.

STEP 3: WORK THE MIND

The brain has remarkable "plasticity" (the ability to form new connections between the surviving neurons). After a stroke, if there is damage to the brain areas that control movement, sensory perceptions and cognition, you need to challenge these areas.

Examples…

• **Multiple-choice questions.** My mother, who was my primary caregiver, understood that asking "yes" or "no" questions didn't force me to think hard enough. That's why she asked me multiple-choice questions—for example, did I want minestrone soup or a grilled cheese sandwich? Each question forced me to relearn words.

• **Simple puzzles.** If you've had a serious stroke, putting together a simple jigsaw puzzle may be a huge challenge. You might not recognize shapes or colors. You might not have the dexterity to put the pieces together. But doing such a puzzle is a superb exercise because it forces you to work different parts of the brain at the same time.

• **Reading.** It's among the hardest tasks because, for many stroke patients, the entire concept of letters and words is lost—temporarily for some stroke survivors, but permanently for others. I had to relearn everything from scratch—that the squiggles that make up letters have names…that combinations of letters make sounds…and that combinations of sounds make words.

Helpful: I started with children's picture books, which would be appropriate for most stroke patients who are relearning to read.

STEP 4: THE SIMPLEST STEPS

Healthy people can't begin to comprehend how complicated things seem after a stroke. When I first started walking, for example, I didn't understand the concept of sidewalk cracks. Each time I saw one, I had to stop and analyze whether it was important.

Helpful: Caregivers need to break down tasks to the simplest levels. For example, a stroke patient might not understand how to sit up in bed. He/she might need to spend days just learning how to shift body weight. In my case, I had to learn to simply hold an eating utensil before I could imagine raising it to my mouth.

STEP 5: FOCUS ON ABILITIES

When you've had a stroke, the extent of your disabilities can be overwhelming. It took me eight years before I was fully recovered. Patients can easily get frustrated and quit trying. At that point, if a patient is not aware of what recovery step needs to be taken next, he may never actually take that next step. It's normal for a stroke survivor to reach a recovery plateau, to continue to learn, then hit another plateau. There are many plateaus along the way.

Helpful: Even if progress seems exceptionally slow, remind a person who has had a stroke of the smallest successes—it may be something as simple as once again being able to hold a fork securely.

If you are the stroke survivor, use small triumphs as inspiration. In my case, it was embarrassing to drool in front of strangers, but I reminded myself that I had managed to swallow.

After my stroke, I never imagined that I would regain enough of my abilities to return to a career as a scientist and teacher. I've managed to do both—in fact, at the same level and intensity. My stroke recovery gave me an opportunity to start my life again.

REPORT #30
Hyperbaric Medicine...
The Oxygen Cure

Mark A. Stengler, NMD, licensed naturopathic medical doctor in private practice, La Jolla, California...adjunct associate clinical professor at the National College of Natural Medicine, Portland, Oregon...author of many books, including *The Natural Physician's Healing Therapies* and coauthor of *Prescription for Natural Cures* (both from Bottom Line Books)...and author of the *Bottom Line/Natural Healing* newsletter.

Hyperbaric medicine, the therapeutic use of oxygen at levels higher than are in our atmosphere, has been around for more than a century. It is perhaps best known as a treatment for deep-sea divers who have decompression sickness ("the bends"). This noninvasive therapy, also known as *hyperbaric oxygen therapy* (HBOT), is proving to help a range of other medical conditions, from wound healing to stroke recovery.

To learn more about how HBOT works, we spoke with Robert Sands, an engineer and designer of hyperbaric chambers, who is director of Healing Chambers International (*www. HBOInfo.com*), a center for hyperbaric therapy in San Diego.

THE SCIENCE OF HYPERBARIC THERAPY

During HBOT, the patient breathes 100% oxygen while in an airtight chamber. This is about five times as much oxygen as we typically breathe at sea level. The increased pressure, combined with the pure oxygen, causes the extra oxygen to permeate the body's cells.

Saturating the body's cells in oxygen, HBOT supercharges the body's repair cells (white blood cells and other immune system cells) so that they work more powerfully and effectively. Typically these repair cells require up to 24 times as much oxygen as ordinary cells do. HBOT also increases the number of circulating stem cells, which are critical to injury repair of tissues and organs. That is why wounds become inflamed and swollen—blood vessels are dilating to rush more oxygen-filled red blood cells to the injured tissue. With HBOT, inflammation is reduced because the cells have the oxygen that they need to heal.

FOR SEVERE INJURIES

The history of HBOT has been marked by debate about its benefits. However, its effectiveness at healing injured tissue is no longer disputed. A study from Doctors Medical Center in San Pablo, California, found that patients with soft-tissue infections treated with HBOT had an 88% survival rate and zero amputations, compared with a 66% survival rate and 50% amputations for those who did not receive HBOT. And a Swedish study found that 76% of patients with diabetic foot ulcers completely recovered after HBOT, compared with 48% of those receiving conventional therapy.

Today HBOT is widely used for severe injuries that don't easily heal with conventional medical treatments. Medicare currently provides reimbursements for 15 HBOT treatments, including for gangrene, crush injuries and severe burns.

BEYOND WOUND HEALING

HBOT has the potential to treat other conditions as well...

•**Stroke and other neurological conditions.** HBOT has been shown to regenerate damaged brain and nerve cells. Stroke occurs when blood doesn't reach brain tissue—but the brain damage is due to that tissue being deprived of oxygen. It is believed that HBOT stimulates formation of new blood vessels and helps damaged tissue survive. Studies have shown that it can reduce damage and long-term effects if given a few days after a stroke. Even patients treated 10 years after a stroke have improved cognitive and motor function. HBOT also can help improve motor function in patients with cerebral palsy.

HBOT is currently being tested for the following conditions…

•**Lyme disease.** HBOT may be able to treat nerve damage associated with the disease and to kill the bacteria that causes Lyme disease.

•**Lupus and rheumatoid arthritis.** The extra oxygen shuts down the inflammation process, the root of these autoimmune conditions.

•**Cancer.** HBOT even shows potential for shrinking some cancerous tumors, although this is highly controversial, since there is a counteracting concern that the extra oxygen could spur some cancers to grow more rapidly.

•**Autism.** HBOT may improve the symptoms of autism by reducing inflammation.

HOW HBOT IS ADMINISTERED

Today there are about 600 hospital-based or freestanding hyperbaric facilities in the US. Some are large multichamber units that several people can use at the same time, while others are single-person units in which the patient sits or lies down. In the US, HBOT can be given only with a doctor's prescription. While treatment generally is safe, the pressure and oxygen flow must be carefully monitored at all times. HBOT is not recommended for people with respiratory infections or high fever, because the pressure might harm them.

During HBOT, patients may feel sensations similar to those experienced while flying in an airplane. Some feel pressure in their ears, others feel their ears pop.

Cost varies greatly—from $1,500 to $2,000 per treatment at a hospital-based hyperbaric unit to about $150 to $250 per treatment at a freestanding facility, which is just as safe and effective as a hospital-based HBOT. Regardless of the type of facility, insurance pays for only those conditions that have been approved. Inflatable air chambers for home use are not effective and not recommended.

HBOT sessions last about an hour and a half. Some conditions require just two or three sessions, while others require up to five sessions weekly for one to three months. To find a hyperbaric treatment center near you, contact the Undersea and Hyperbaric Medical Society (877-533-8467, *www.uhms.org*).

REPORT #31
People Who Drink Tea Are Less Likely to Have a Stroke

A recent analysis of nine studies involving nearly 195,000 adults found that for each additional three cups of black or green tea consumed daily, stroke risk dropped by 21%.

Theory: The antioxidant *epigallocatechin gallate* or the amino acid *theanine*, both found in tea, may have anti-inflammatory effects that protect the heart and brain. (Processing that is done for decaffeinated tea may remove these ingredients.)

Lenore Arab, PhD, professor of medicine and biological chemistry, David Geffen School of Medicine, University of California, Los Angeles.

Volume 4
Blood Pressure Cures

REPORT #32
What You're Not Being Told About Hypertension

Getting your blood pressure checked is a routine part of most physical exams. But how the measurement is taken and the treatment your doctor recommends if you have high blood pressure (hypertension) can have a profound effect on your health.

High blood pressure occurs when the force with which blood travels through the arteries is higher than it needs to be. Blood pressure readings consist of two measurements—*systolic pressure* (top number) measures the force as the heart contracts...*diastolic* (bottom number) represents the pressure between beats. Hypertension typically is defined as 140/90 mmHg or above, although readings above 120/80 mmHg are considered higher than optimal.

It's well-known that hypertension is often "silent" (causing no symptoms) and that it can lead to death or disability due to heart attack...stroke...and kidney damage.

What you may not know: One-third to one-half of all patients who take medication for hypertension lower their blood pressure insufficiently...take the wrong drugs...or suffer unnecessary side effects.

Samuel J. Mann, MD, a renowned hypertension specialist at New York-Presbyterian Hospital in New York City shares his insights about these and other dangerous traps...

Trap: Getting inaccurate blood pressure readings. The equipment in doctors' offices and home arm-cuff blood pressure monitors are usually accurate, but how they're used can greatly affect readings. *Three common mistakes...*

Mistake 1: Rushing the test. It takes five to 10 minutes of sitting quietly for blood pressure

Samuel J. Mann, MD, hypertension specialist and attending physician at New York–Presbyterian Hospital and professor of clinical medicine at Weill-Cornell Medical College, both in New York City. He is the author of *Healing Hypertension: A Revolutionary New Approach* (Wiley).

to stabilize. Testing too quickly can produce a reading that's considerably higher than your usual resting blood pressure.

Mistake 2: Using a cuff that's too small. Doctors often use the same blood pressure cuff on all patients—but if you have a large arm, the reading can be artificially high. Ask your doctor whether the blood pressure cuff size is right for you.

Mistake 3: Talking while blood pressure is being measured. It can add 10 millimeters or even more to the systolic (top number) reading.

Trap: Ignoring "white-coat hypertension." Up to 20% of people exhibit elevations in blood pressure in the doctor's office even though their pressure at home is normal. This phenomenon, known as white-coat hypertension, sometimes is due to the anxiety many people experience when they go to the doctor.

We used to think that white-coat hypertension was insignificant. Now, a study published in the *Journal of Human Hypertension* shows that people who exhibit this trait do face higher risks—for both heart attack and true hypertension at some point in their lives—than those whose office blood pressure is normal.

It's not yet clear why these patients have higher risks. Studies of patients who perform home monitoring suggest that their pressure tends to be slightly higher than what's considered optimal even if it's not high enough to be classified as hypertension.

Warning: Some people with white-coat hypertension are undertreated because their doctors tend to ignore elevated office readings while not paying attention to a gradual rise in home readings. Others are overtreated based on the elevated office readings, even though home readings are normal.

Helpful: Patients with hypertension—or those at risk of getting it (due to such factors as family history and being overweight)—should use a home monitor to check their blood pressure two or three times a week. Take three readings each time, waiting about one to two minutes between each measurement.

Trap: Overtreating hypertension because of high readings obtained at times of stress. It's clear that blood pressure rises sharply at moments when people are angry, anxious or stressed. Many people have their blood pressure checked—or check it themselves—at such times, and their doctors increase medication based on these readings.

Helpful: Blood pressure elevation during emotional moments is normal. If your blood pressure is otherwise normal, an increase in medication usually is not necessary.

Trap: Taking the wrong drug. Up to 25% of patients with hypertension take a beta-blocker to lower blood pressure. This type of drug inhibits the kidneys' secretion of the enzyme renin, which results in lower levels of angiotensin II, a peptide that constricts blood vessels.

Beta-blockers also reduce the rate and force of heart contractions. However, most beta-blockers, including the widely prescribed *metoprolol* (Lopressor) and *atenolol* (Tenormin), have the undesirable effect of reducing blood flow.

These effects often result in fatigue. Many patients don't even realize how fatigued they are until they stop taking the beta-blocker and experience a sudden boost in energy.

Fact: The majority of patients with hypertension who suffer from fatigue due to a beta-blocker don't even need to take this drug. For most patients, it's best to start with other drugs or drug combinations, such as a diuretic (sodium-excreting pill) and/or an *angiotensin-converting enzyme* (ACE) inhibitor or an *angiotensin receptor blocker* (ARB).

Exception: Beta-blockers are usually a good choice for patients with hypertension who also have underlying coronary artery disease or who have had a heart attack.

If you need a beta-blocker: Ask your doctor about newer versions, such as *nebivolol* (Bystolic), that dilate arteries. Nebivolol is less likely to cause fatigue.

Trap: Switching to a newer drug—without good reason. Even if people are getting good results with the blood pressure medication they are taking, there's often a temptation to switch to a newer drug. Some newer drugs may have features that are an improvement over older medications, but others may offer little advantage and are not worth the extra cost.

Example: Aliskiren (Tekturna) is the first FDA-approved medication in a new class of blood pressure drugs known as renin inhibitors. Aliskiren inhibits the blood pressure–raising effects of the renin-angiotensin system. However, it is no more effective at lowering blood pressure than older treatments, such as ACE inhibitors or ARBs.

Switching drugs does make sense if you're not achieving optimal control—or if your current treatment is causing side effects. But for most patients, the older drugs are both effective and well-tolerated—and much less expensive.

Trap: Taking medication unnecessarily. It's estimated that only about 40% of patients with hypertension achieve optimal control by taking a single drug (monotherapy). Most patients will eventually need multiple drugs—but monotherapy is effective for some patients, particularly those with mild (stage 1) hypertension (defined as systolic pressure of 140 mmHg to 159 mmHg and/or diastolic pressure of 90 mmHg to 99 mmHg).

Adding drugs invariably increases both the cost of treatment and the risk for side effects. If a drug doesn't work within a few weeks, then switching drugs is an alternative to simply adding drugs. Or if a second drug is added and it normalizes your blood pressure, your doctor may consider reducing the dose of—or stopping—the first drug.

REPORT #33
Skim Milk Lowers Hypertension

A two-year study of 5,880 people found that those who consumed more than two to three servings of skim milk and other low-fat dairy products daily had half the risk of developing high blood pressure of those who rarely or never consumed such foods.

Whole milk products were not found to reduce hypertension risk.

Theory: The calcium, which is highly absorbable in skim dairy products, may decrease blood pressure.

Alvaro Alonso, MD, PhD, assistant professor, division of Epidemiology and Community Health, School of Public Health, University of Minnesota, Minneapolis, Minnesota.

REPORT #34
Hibiscus Tea Curbs Blood Pressure

In a study of 65 adults with prehypertension or mild hypertension, those who drank hibiscus tea had a 7.2-point drop, on average, in systolic (top number) blood pressure, compared with a one-point drop, on average, in the placebo group.

Theory: Antioxidant flavonoids in hibiscus help lower blood pressure.

If you have been diagnosed with prehypertension or hypertension: Three cups daily of hibiscus tea may benefit you.

Diane L. McKay, PhD, assistant professor of nutrition, science and policy, Tufts University, Boston.

REPORT #35
Beet Juice Lowers Blood Pressure

Mark A. Stengler, NMD, licensed naturopathic medical doctor in private practice, La Jolla, California…adjunct associate clinical professor at the National College of Natural Medicine, Portland, Oregon…author of many books, including *The Natural Physician's Healing Therapies* and coauthor of *Prescription for Natural Cures* (both from Bottom Line Books)…and author of the *Bottom Line/Natural Healing* newsletter.

In a British study, 14 healthy participants drank 17 ounces of either water or beetroot (beet) juice. Blood pressure was measured every 15 minutes for one hour before, and three hours after, the beverages were consumed, and again after 24 hours. Results: Among beet juice drinkers, the maximum decreases in blood pressure—10.4 points systolic (top number) and 8.1 points diastolic (bottom number)—occurred two-and-a-half to three hours after ingestion, when blood levels of nitrite, a key element in the juice, peaked. After 24 hours, blood pressure still was somewhat lowered. Water drinkers experienced no significant changes.

My view: Nitrite is converted in the stomach into nitric oxide, which dilates blood vessels, reduces inflammation and combats clotting—improving circulation and lowering blood pressure. Though this study was small, I find it encouraging.

Recommended: If you have high blood pressure, drink four to eight ounces (17 ounces is unrealistic) of beet juice daily. Mix with carrot or celery juice if you desire.

REPORT #36
Sleep More to Lower Blood Pressure

People who get five hours or less of sleep a night were more than twice as likely to develop high blood pressure as people who slept seven to eight hours, according to a recent study.

Theory: Blood pressure drops by 10% to 20% during sleep, so a sleep deficit raises average 24-hour blood pressure and increases the workload on the cardiovascular system. Lack of sleep also boosts stress, which increases appetite for salt and decreases salt excretion—further raising hypertension risk in some people.

James E. Gangwisch, PhD, assistant professor, department of psychiatry, Columbia University, New York City, and leader of a study of 4,810 people, published in *Hypertension*.

REPORT #37
Put Away those Dangerous Drugs…And Try these Natural Alternatives

Mark A. Stengler, NMD, licensed naturopathic medical doctor in private practice, La Jolla, California…adjunct associate clinical professor at the National College of Natural Medicine, Portland, Oregon…author of many books, including *The Natural Physician's Healing Therapies* and coauthor of *Prescription for Natural Cures* (both from Bottom Line Books)…and author of the *Bottom Line/Natural Healing* newsletter.

Isn't it strange when some wholesome-looking actor appears on a TV commercial to promote a pharmaceutical? The ad tells you how great the drug is, then proceeds with a long, rapid-fire list of potential side effects. What a contradiction!

It's hard to believe, but Americans spend close to $200 billion each year on prescription drugs. Now, many people are concerned about the side effects of these medications—and with good reason. Each year, 2.9% to 3.7% of hospitalizations in the US are due to adverse reactions to medications.

The solution is to get healthy—and stay healthy—using natural methods. Many nutritional supplements can be used safely and effectively in place of prescription medications. Whether you're treating heartburn, high blood pressure, elevated cholesterol, depression or any number of other common ailments, there are excellent natural alternatives.

Caution: Do not stop taking a prescription drug or begin using a supplement unless you are being monitored by a health professional. These natural alternatives work best when combined with diet and lifestyle improvements, particularly regular exercise, stress-reduction techniques and adequate sleep.

STOMACH MEDICATIONS

Up to 18% of Americans experience heartburn at least once weekly. Heartburn that occurs more than twice a week may be *gastroesophageal reflux disease* (GERD), a condition in which stomach contents back up into the esophagus. The most commonly prescribed drugs for heartburn and GERD are *esomeprazole* (Nexium), *lansoprazole* (Prevacid), *rabeprazole* (Aciphex), *omeprazole* (Prilosec) and *pantoprazole* (Protonix). Known as *proton pump inhibitors* (PPIs), these drugs block the production of stomach acid. And they carry a hefty price tag—about $4 per dose. Potential side effects include diarrhea, vomiting, headache, rash, dizziness, abnormal heartbeat, muscle pain, leg cramps and water retention.

Natural alternatives: Try them in this order—each one alone—for two weeks at a time until you find what works effectively for you. You can take more than one at a time.

• **Licorice root** (in chewable wafers or powder form) reduces heartburn and irritation of the digestive tract lining. Take 500 mg to 1,000 mg three times daily 30 minutes before meals. A special type of licorice root, known as *deglycyrrhizinated licorice* (DGL), does not elevate blood pressure, as do some varieties of the herb. DGL is widely available at health-food stores and pharmacies. It should relieve your symptoms within two weeks. Take as needed if symptoms recur.

• **Nux vomica,** a homeopathic remedy derived from the seeds of the poison nut tree, has helped many of my patients reduce or eliminate heartburn. It soothes irritation of the digestive lining and is believed to help the upper esophageal valve close more efficiently, thereby preventing reflux. Take two 30C potency pellets three times daily until your symptoms are eliminated. Improvement should occur within two weeks. Resume treatment if symptoms return. Because nux vomica is also used to treat asthma, it is good for asthmatics who suffer from heartburn.

• **Aloe vera,** a cactus-like member of the lily family, soothes and promotes healing of the lining of the digestive tract. Some people who don't respond to DGL get relief from aloe vera. Drink one-quarter cup of aloe vera juice or take a 500-mg capsule three times daily.

ANTIDEPRESSANTS

• ***Sertaline*** (Zoloft), *escitalopram* (Lexapro) and *fluoxetine* (Prozac) are the most popular prescription antidepressants sold in the US. They belong to a class of drugs called *selective serotonin reuptake inhibitors* (SSRIs). Serotonin, a neurotransmitter (chemical messenger) produced by nerve cells in the brain, plays an important role in balancing mood. SSRIs temporarily block serotonin from returning to the neuron that released it, boosting the amount of available serotonin.

Potential side effects of SSRIs include drowsiness, nervousness, insomnia, dizziness, nausea, tremors, loss of appetite, headache, diarrhea, dry mouth, irregular heartbeat, skin rash, weight loss or weight gain, and activation of mania in patients with bipolar disorder (also known as manic-depressive illness). These drugs also can cause sexual side effects, including loss of libido and decrease in the intensity of orgasms. The FDA has warned that children and adults taking antidepressants should be monitored for signs of worsening depression or suicidal thoughts.

Natural alternatives: Try them in this order for six to eight weeks. If effective, continue indefinitely. You can take more than one at a time.

• **S-adenosylmethionine (SAMe),** a nutritional supplement derived from the amino acid *methionine*, is excellent for mild to moderate depression. SAMe is thought to work by increasing the production of mood-boosting neurotransmitters. Some studies have shown SAMe to be as effective as pharmaceutical antidepressants—or, in some cases, even more so. Take 400 mg two or three times daily on an empty stomach. Do not use this supplement if you are taking an antidepressant or antianxiety medication—or if you have bipolar disorder. Like SSRIs, SAMe may activate a manic phase in bipolar patients.

• **5-hydroxytryptophan (5-HTP)** is a quick-acting, mood-enhancing amino acid that I recommend for my patients with mild to moderate depression. In the body, 5-HTP is converted into serotonin, helping to raise levels of this mood-balancing neurotransmitter. Take 100 mg two to three times daily on an empty stomach. Do not take 5-HTP in combination with pharmaceutical antidepressant or antianxiety medication.

• **St. John's wort is an herb that is widely used in Europe to treat depression.** In a review of 23 studies, it was found to be as effective as pharmaceutical therapy for mild to moderate depression. I recommend taking 600 mg of a 0.3% hypericin extract in the morning and 300 mg in the afternoon or evening. St. John's wort should not be used by women who take birth control pills or by anyone taking HIV medication or immune-suppressing drugs. Do not take St. John's wort with antidepressant or antianxiety medication.

• **Fish oil has been shown to help mild to moderate depression.** Take a formula that contains 1,000 mg of combined *docosahexaenoic acid* (DHA) and *eicosapentaenoic acid* (EPA) daily. Nordic Naturals and Carlson both make good formulas that are available at health-food stores. Fish oil can be taken indefinitely.

• **B vitamins improve the efficiency of many functions,** including the conversion of glucose to fuel and the synthesis of neurotransmitters. Deficiencies of B vitamins (notably B-3) can lead to anxiety and agitation. Take a 50-mg B complex daily for as long as you like.

CHOLESTEROL-LOWERING DRUGS

An estimated 11 million Americans take cholesterol-lowering statins. *Atorvastatin* (Lipitor), *simvastatin* (Zocor) and *rosuvastatin* (Crestor) are the most commonly prescribed in the US. One month's supply of one of these drugs costs $80 to more than $120.

Such drugs work by inhibiting a liver enzyme that helps produce the "bad" cholesterol, known as *low-density lipoprotein* (LDL) cholesterol. These drugs also decrease fats in the blood known as triglycerides and increase "good" *high-density lipoprotein* (HDL) cholesterol levels. Possible side effects include abdominal pain and digestive upset, joint pain, and muscle weakness and pain. One of the most frightening side effects is *rhabdomyolysis*. This condition affects only one in 100,000 people taking statins each year, but it results in severe pain and may cause kidney failure.

Natural alternatives: Try red yeast rice extract, then retest cholesterol levels in three months. Continue if effective. If not, try policosanol.

• **Red yeast rice extract** is a supplement that has been shown to reduce total and LDL cholesterol levels by 11% to 32% and triglyceride levels by 12% to 19%. It has been shown to raise HDL by 15% to 30%. Take 2,400 mg of red yeast rice extract (containing 9.6 mg to 13.5 mg total monacolins) daily. Side effects, such as mild gastrointestinal discomfort, are rare. As with many products, red yeast rice extract should be avoided by people with liver disease.

• **Policosanol,** a derivative of sugarcane, is another well-researched cholesterol-lowering supplement. The *American Heart Journal* published a review of placebo-controlled studies, which found that taking 10 mg to 20 mg of policosanol daily lowered total cholesterol by 17% to 21% and LDL cholesterol by 21% to 29%. The supplement raised HDL cholesterol by 8% to 15%. Policosanol does not effectively lower triglyceride levels, so I don't recommend it for people who need to reduce these blood fats. Anyone else with high cholesterol should consider taking 10 mg to 20 mg daily.

Important: If your cholesterol levels are significantly elevated (in the mid-300s or higher), you may need to take a statin before trying these natural alternatives. Statins also may be prescribed to help reduce inflammation following a heart attack.

BLOOD PRESSURE MEDICATION

High blood pressure (hypertension) is estimated to affect one of every four adult Americans. *Tenormin* (Atenolol), *lisinopril* (Zestril) and *furosemide* (Lasix) are the most popular prescription drugs for high blood pressure. These drugs are relatively inexpensive—ranging from $11 to $36 per month.

• **Tenormin** (a so-called beta-blocker) works by blocking nerve impulses of the sympathetic nervous system, a portion of the involuntary nervous system that helps control the body's response to stress (the "fight or flight" reaction). Blood pressure is then lowered by reducing the heart rate and the force of the heart muscle contraction. Possible side effects include digestive upset, fatigue, insomnia, impotence, light-headedness, slow heart rate, low blood pressure (a dangerous condition that can lead to fainting and fatigue), numbness, tingling, sore throat and shortness of breath.

• **Lisinopril is an angiotensin-converting enzyme (ACE) inhibitor.** It triggers the relaxation of blood vessels. Relaxed blood vessels help lower blood pressure. Side effects of lisinopril can include chest pain, cough, diarrhea and low blood pressure.

• **Furosemide is a diuretic that causes water excretion.** By blocking absorption of salt and fluid in the kidneys, the drug causes an increase in urine output. Water excretion helps reduce blood volume, which means less work for your arteries and veins. Potential side effects include irregular heartbeat, dizziness, abdominal pain or diarrhea, low blood pressure and an imbalance of electrolytes (key minerals that are needed for vital body functions), leading to muscle cramps or weakness.

Important: If you have moderate to severe high blood pressure (160/100 and above), you may need prescription medication. You may be able to limit your need for prescription blood pressure drugs if you work with your doctor to incorporate natural therapies.

Natural alternatives: Try the first two extracts below for 30 days. If your blood pressure doesn't improve, try using all of the natural treatments together. You should see improvement within four weeks—and can continue the regimen indefinitely.

• **Hawthorn extract,** derived from the berry of a thorny shrub with white or pink flowers, dilates artery walls, decreasing systolic (top number) and diastolic (bottom number) blood pressure by about 10 points each. Take 250 mg to 500 mg three times daily. Hawthorn extract can have a mild blood-thinning effect, so check with your doctor first if you are taking a blood thinner, such as *warfarin* (Coumadin).

• **Bonito fish extract,** a protein from the muscle tissue of the bonito fish, acts like a natural ACE inhibitor. I recommend a daily dose of 1,500 mg.

• **Coenzyme Q10,** an enzyme found in the energy-producing mitochondria of all cells, has been shown to reduce both systolic and diastolic blood pressure by five to 10 points. You may need to take 200 mg to 300 mg daily for a blood pressure–lowering effect.

Calcium and magnesium relax the nervous system and arteries, lowering blood pressure. I suggest 500 mg of calcium and 250 mg of magnesium twice daily.

REPORT #38
Soybean Protein Lowers Blood Pressure

In a study of 302 adults with a median blood pressure of 135/85 mmHg (normal is below 120/80 mmHg), those who ate one cookie containing 40 g of soybean protein a day for 12 weeks had a 4.31-point drop in systolic (top number) pressure and a 2.76-point drop in diastolic (bottom number) pressure compared with those who ate a placebo cookie.

Theory: Soybean protein may influence the sympathetic nervous system, sodium excretion and insulin resistance, all of which affect blood pressure.

Implication: Soybean consumption may be an effective alternative to medication for lowering blood pressure in otherwise healthy people with mild hypertension.

Jiang He, MD, PhD, professor and chair, department of epidemiology, Tulane University School of Public Health and Tropical Medicine, New Orleans.

Volume 5
Arthritis Cures

Breakthrough Therapy Helps Heal Joints and Orthopedic Injuries

When pitcher Takashi Saito was with the Los Angeles Dodgers, he suffered a ligament tear in his elbow and was told that he would be sidelined for about a year if he had it surgically repaired. Instead, he underwent an innovative natural treatment called *platelet-rich plasma* (PRP) *therapy*. A few months later, he was pitching pain-free.

PRP is an emerging treatment in the growing field of orthobiologics, which combines cutting-edge technology with therapies that work by stimulating the body's healing processes. In PRP, a patient's own platelets—the blood component that contains major growth factors, naturally occurring substances that stimulate cell growth—are injected into an injured or arthritic area, enhancing the repair response of soft tissue. Until recently, orthopedic applications of PRP were mostly reserved for professional athletes, but now it is available to everyone through some family physicians and orthopedic surgeons.

At my clinic, Bronner Handwerger, ND, uses PRP therapy to treat patients like a professional football player who had a minor knee cartilage tear. He was able to resume training just three days after receiving PRP. Knee injuries such as his usually take weeks to heal. James Baum, DO, of Santa Fe, New Mexico, is one of many orthopedic surgeons around the country who offers PRP therapy for a variety of conditions. He has treated scores of patients, including a woman with debilitating spinal stenosis

Mark A. Stengler, NMD, licensed naturopathic medical doctor in private practice, La Jolla, California...adjunct associate clinical professor at the National College of Natural Medicine, Portland, Oregon...author of many books, including *The Natural Physician's Healing Therapies* and coauthor of *Prescription for Natural Cures* (both from Bottom Line Books)...and author of the *Bottom Line/Natural Healing* newsletter.

(narrowing of one or more areas of the spine) who now is symptom-free after four injections. He treated another woman who could barely walk because of an arthritic hip. Now, after receiving several PRP injections, she is walking pain-free.

PRP appears to help many types of injuries. Other applications currently being studied include injecting PRP at the site of bone fractures and using it to help speed healing after connective-tissue surgeries. Although it has not yet been shown definitively whether PRP can regenerate cartilage, Dr. Baum believes that clinical research will mirror his own experience in stimulating cartilage regeneration—and that PRP will be crucial in combating the growing epidemic of osteoarthritis as the American population ages.

HOW IT WORKS

In a doctor's office, a few tablespoons of blood are drawn and run through a machine that separates out the platelets. The resulting fluid contains four to 10 times the blood's normal concentration of growth factors. Along with a local anesthetic, this mixture is injected directly into an injured or arthritic area (ultrasound may be used to guide placement). The procedure takes about an hour.

While there may be some soreness for a few days afterward, patients often have reduced pain and improved movement after just one treatment. Depending on the severity of the condition and an individual's healing response, injections may be repeated up to six times at two- to four-week intervals.

PRP therapy is extremely safe because the patient is injected with parts of his/her own blood. Infection at the injection site is extremely rare. (PRP therapy has not been reviewed by the FDA, which doesn't regulate surgical procedures.) The technique also is safer than many other conventional treatments commonly used to treat joint and connective-tissue injuries, such as cortisone shots, anti-inflammatory medications and surgery. These approaches all have drawbacks—cortisone can weaken tissue over time…anti-inflammatory drugs have potentially dangerous side effects, such as kidney and liver damage…and surgery is expensive and involves a lengthy recovery.

PRP's effectiveness still is being studied, but in one Stanford University study, patients with chronic elbow tendonitis who were given one PRP treatment had a 60% improvement in pain compared to only a 16% improvement in those who received an injection of anesthetic only.

When seeking treatment with PRP, keep these points in mind…

• **Insurance.** Because PRP therapy is new, insurance may not cover it. Check with your insurer before scheduling a procedure. PRP costs about $400 to $600 per injection—based on your injury and the type of equipment used by the doctor—a fraction of what surgery costs.

• **Effectiveness.** This depends in large part on the quality and abundance of the growth factors in a patient's blood. For some people, the results are permanent. Smokers don't respond as well to PRP, because they have reduced platelet activity.

WHAT'S TREATABLE WITH PRP?

PRP therapy can treat the knees, shoulders, elbows, feet, wrist and back for the following…

• **Torn tendons or ligaments**
• **Strained rotator cuff**
• **Arthritic or inflamed joints**
• **Carpal tunnel syndrome**
• **Plantar fasciitis** (an inflammatory condition that affects the tissue under the foot's arch)
• **Torn or strained muscles**

BETTER THAN OTHER NATURAL INJECTIONS

PRP therapy is similar to prolotherapy, another injection technique that stimulates the body's natural healing process and has been found helpful for arthritis and injured cartilage, tendons and ligaments. The difference: Prolotherapy involves injecting an injured joint or tissue with a harmless but mildly irritating substance, such as a dextrose (sugar) solution. This induces inflammation in the injured area, attracting growth factors that stimulate growth of collagen and other connective tissues. PRP therapy involves injecting growth factors themselves into an area that has a very poor blood supply. Prolotherapy is less expensive (starting at about $125 per treatment) than PRP. Of the two treatments, I recommend PRP because it is more effective.

REPORT #40
Natural Remedies for Arthritis Relief

Tod Cooperman, MD, founder and president of ConsumerLab.com, the leading independent evaluator of nutritional and vitamin/mineral supplements, White Plains, New York. Reports can be found at *www.con sumerlab.com* (subscription required). He also is editor of *ConsumerLab.com's Guide to Buying Vitamins & Supplements* (ConsumerLab.com).

Most people assume that prescription medications are stronger and more effective than supplements. But some supplements can be just as effective—without the side effects that often accompany prescription drugs.

Also, people with chronic conditions who have no insurance or are under-insured or who have been hit with higher co-pays can save hundreds or even thousands of dollars a year by using supplements in place of drugs.

Caution: Always check with your doctor before stopping a prescription drug or taking a supplement.

Here, natural alternatives to commonly prescribed medications. If there are two alternatives, try one. If that doesn't work, try the other. Dosages are those typically prescribed, but always follow directions on the supplement label or from your health practitioner.

OSTEOARTHRITIS

It's the most common form of arthritis, affecting up to 20 million American adults. Osteoarthritis occurs when cartilage in the joints wears and breaks down, causing pain and stiffness. People with frequent or severe symptoms often depend on prescription-strength anti-inflammatory drugs. These drugs reduce symptoms but don't change the outcome of the disease. They also can cause stomach upset or other gastrointestinal problems.

•**Alternative 1. Glucosamine.** This supplement usually is derived from shellfish, though vegetable-based versions are starting to appear. It helps the body repair and rebuild damaged cartilage. It can help reduce pain as well as subsequent joint damage.

Dose: 1,500 mg, once daily.

•**Alternative 2. Glucosamine plus chondroitin**. This supplement combination is more expensive than glucosamine alone, but it sometimes helps patients who don't respond to glucosamine. Chondroitin, the added ingredient that typically is made from cow or pig cartilage, promotes the absorption of fluids into connective tissue and aids in flexibility and repair.

Dose: 1,500 mg of glucosamine and 1,200 mg of chondroitin, once daily.

Important: Studies reveal that supplements protect joints better than they relieve pain. Most people who take them still need an occasional anti-inflammatory painkiller.

RHEUMATOID ARTHRITIS

This form of arthritis causes inflammation throughout the body that can damage joints as well as the eyes, lungs and/or heart. Most people with rheumatoid arthritis take prescription drugs, such as *methotrexate* (Rheumatrex) or *hydroxychloroquine* (Plaquenil). Most rheumatoid drugs are expensive, and many have a high risk for side effects, including suppressed immunity.

Supplementation can reduce inflammation and potentially reduce the dosage of prescription drugs.

•**Alternative. Fish and fish oil.** The omega-3 fatty acids in cold-water fish, such as salmon and tuna, have potent anti-inflammatory effects. A study at the University of Pittsburgh School of Medicine found that 59% of patients given supplemental omega-3s had decreased joint pain.

Dose: A total of 1,200 mg to 2,400 mg of EPA and DHA (types of fish oil) daily, or eat three or more fish servings a week.

Caution: Fish oil may interact with blood-thinning drugs, such as *warfarin* (Coumadin).

REPORT #41
Alignment Technique

Structural Integration (SI) is a bodywork technique that focuses on the fascia, the protective connective tissue that surrounds the muscles. Founded by Ida P. Rolf, the technique also is sometimes known as "rolfing." SI therapists use pressure and stretching to lengthen and manipulate fascia to enhance body alignment and balance. SI is based on the theory that through the force of gravity and injury, the body's structure becomes misaligned…and fascia shortens, resulting in pain and stiffness. I find that SI is helpful for those with muscle or spine pain. You can find out about practitioners near you from the International Association of Structural Integrators at 877-843-4274 or *www.theiasi.org*.

Mark A. Stengler, NMD, licensed naturopathic medical doctor in private practice, La Jolla, California…adjunct associate clinical professor at the National College of Natural Medicine, Portland, Oregon…author of many books, including *The Natural Physician's Healing Therapies* and coauthor of *Prescription for Natural Cures* (both from Bottom Line Books)…and author of the *Bottom Line/Natural Healing* newsletter.

REPORT #42
Hyaluronic Acid…Help For Painful Joints and Problem Skin

Mark A. Stengler, NMD, licensed naturopathic medical doctor in private practice, La Jolla, California…adjunct associate clinical professor at the National College of Natural Medicine, Portland, Oregon…author of many books, including *The Natural Physician's Healing Therapies* and coauthor of *Prescription for Natural Cures* (both from Bottom Line Books)…and author of the *Bottom Line/Natural Healing* newsletter.

On her first visit to me, 60-year-old Jenny said, "Every time I hear of a supplement that might reduce my arthritis pain, I try it—but I've gotten very little relief. I've almost given up on finding anything that works." I paid close attention as she named nearly a dozen supplements she had taken for the arthritis in her hips and knees. Then I mentioned one oral supplement that had not been on her list—*hyaluronic acid* (HA). "I've never even heard of it, but it's worth trying," Jenny said. Six weeks later, she walked nimbly into my clinic and reported a dramatic reduction in her pain and stiffness. She was surprised at this success—but I was not.

HA has been so effective for so many of my arthritis patients that I consider it an up-and-coming superstar among nutritional supplements. Bonus: HA also promotes skin health.

WHAT IS HYALURONIC ACID?

A naturally occurring substance in the body, the HA molecule is formed by two sugars strung together in a long chain. HA is an essential component of the joints, skin, eyes and blood vessels (as well as the umbilical cord). HA deficiencies, which develop for reasons that are not well-understood, contribute to premature aging and disease in these tissues. As yet, there is no reliable test to measure HA levels.

HA is a key component of synovial fluid, the lubricating fluid in joint cavities. This fluid, which is secreted by a membrane that forms a capsule around the ends of bones, has two main purposes. First, it helps to minimize friction and prevent breakdown of the joints (like the oil used to lubricate moving car parts). Second, synovial fluid helps with shock absorption within joints. Cartilage is the main shock absorber, but it does not contain blood vessels—so synovial fluid transports the nutrients required for cartilage healing and regeneration, and removes waste products. In addition, HA is an actual component of cartilage and is required for healthy cartilage formation.

•**There are two main types of arthritis.** Osteoarthritis is caused by the normal wear and tear of aging and/or by injury. Rheumatoid arthritis is an autoimmune disease in which the immune system attacks the body's own joint tissue and causes deterioration. As either type of arthritis progresses, the synovial fluid degrades, lessening its lubricating and shock-absorbing abilities…and cartilage breaks down and becomes inflamed. Supplementing with HA helps to counteract both of these effects.

THE FIGHT AGAINST ARTHRITIS

When I mention HA to patients, most say they've never heard of it. I expect this to change as news of HA's effectiveness spreads.

• **HA injections.** In 1997, HA injections were approved by the FDA for patients with osteoarthritis of the knee, and they now are being studied for use in shoulder, hip and ankle joints. Injectable HA products include Hyalgan, Supartz, Orthovisc and Synvisc.

HA injections go directly into the affected joint or joints…are done in a doctor's office using local anesthetic…take just a few minutes… and usually are given three to five times, each one week apart. Side effects include minor swelling, temporary pain, rash and/or bruising at the injection site. While not everyone who receives HA injections finds relief, for many people the painful symptoms of arthritis are noticeably reduced for up to six months (especially in the early stages of the disease), allowing patients to delay or avoid joint-replacement surgery.

For now, only a limited number of rheumatologists and osteopaths provide this therapy. HA shots cost about $230 each and may or may not be covered by insurance, depending on your policy. Fortunately, there is a promising alternative—oral HA.

• **HA oral supplementation.** With regard to HA's use as an oral supplement, the big question is whether it can be absorbed and used by the body when taken in capsule form. Critics of HA supplementation say that its molecular structure is too large to be absorbed in the digestive tract—yet several studies in the past four years have shown otherwise.

One of the first studies to demonstrate that HA is absorbed effectively into the bloodstream and the joints was presented at the Experimental Biology Conference. Researchers gave rats and dogs one oral dose of HA that was radio labeled (chemically joined with a radioactive substance), allowing it to be tracked with diagnostic imaging. Result: HA was absorbed into the animals' bloodstreams and distributed to their joints. Although no similar studies have been done on people, I think it is logical to assume that HA's absorbability in humans may be similar to its action in animals.

Why am I keen on supplemental HA for arthritis? During the past year, several dozens of my patients with osteoarthritis and rheumatoid arthritis have taken nonprescription oral HA with good results. I have found that HA by itself can produce significant results—and in many cases, results are even better when HA is taken in combination with mainstay joint supplements, such as chondroitin, fish oil, glucosamine, methylsulfonylmethane (MSM) and/ or S-adenosylmethionine (SAMe).

This is wonderful news, because HA often allows patients to reduce or discontinue the pharmaceutical nonsteroidal anti-inflammatory (NSAID) drugs, such as *ibuprofen* (Motrin) and *naproxen* (Aleve). These drugs are associated with serious adverse side effects, including bleeding stomach ulcers, liver and kidney damage, and increased risk for heart attack and stroke.

HA is an example of a supplement that works well in the real world but has generated limited published data. Existing research mostly involves a patented HA product called BioCell Collagen II (714-632-1231, *www.bio celltechnology.com*), made from the sternal cartilage of chickens and used as an ingredient in various brands of HA oral supplements. One small study included 16 patients with osteoarthritis of the knee or hand who were taking COX-2 inhibitors or other NSAIDs. Eight patients took 1,000 mg of BioCell daily, while the other eight took a placebo. After two months of treatment, the group receiving BioCell reported significant improvement in pain, range of motion and swelling—whereas the placebo group showed no significant changes. One such product, sold at health-food stores, is BioCell Chicken Sternum Collagen Type II, made by Premier Labs (888-678-7145, *www. premierlabs.com*).

Other oral products contain a type of HA called *sodium hyaluronate*, which is produced during microbial fermentation. While I am not aware of any human studies on this form of HA, animal studies suggest that it is safe and several of my patients have reported positive effects. One such product available in health-food stores is Now Foods Hyaluronic Acid (888-669-3663, *www.nowfoods.com*). The recommended dosage is 100 mg twice daily. The Now Foods capsules, like brands that contain BioCell, can be used indefinitely, generally are safe and only rarely cause mild digestive upset.

HYALURONIC HELP FOR THE SKIN

Another benefit of HA is that it improves the health of the largest human organ—the skin.

Here's how…

One of the most important proteins of the skin is collagen, the "glue" of connective tissue that holds the skin together, thereby maintaining its elasticity and form. HA supports collagen production and also is critical for maintaining moisture in and between skin cells. A lack of HA—typically brought on by illness or aging—may contribute to skin dryness, thinning and wrinkles.

• **HA injections.** Like the better-known collagen injections, HA injections can be used to minimize wrinkles, lines and pitting from acne or scars, and to plump up thin lips. HA and collagen injections both typically need to be repeated after six to nine months—but HA is less likely to provoke an allergic reaction.

FDA-approved HA injectable skin fillers include Hylaform and Restylane. Possible side effects include brief redness, swelling and/or tenderness at the injection site. Health insurance generally does not cover cosmetic treatments.

Caution: Cosmetic HA injections should be administered by an experienced cosmetic surgeon, not a family practitioner.

• **HA oral supplementation.** Recently I spoke with a patient who had thin, easily bruised skin as a result of using oral steroids for several years to treat Crohn's disease (an inflammatory condition of the digestive tract). After various foods and supplements failed to improve her skin condition, I recommended an HA oral supplement called Purity Products Ultimate HA Formula (800-769-7873, *www.purityproducts. com*). Eight weeks after she started to take HA, this patient reported that for the first time in years, she was not covered in bruises. Note: HA oral supplements designed to promote skin

health generally contain the same active HA ingredient as those marketed for joint health.

• **HA topical ointment.** Some evidence suggests that HA skin ointment also may reduce wrinkles and skin pitting. One study I obtained from a private research lab showed that topical HA inhibited production of *hyaluronidase*, an enzyme in the skin and connective tissues that degrades the body's own natural wrinkle-fighting HA. In a separate in vitro (test-tube) study from Pennsylvania State University, topical HA was shown to stimulate production of collagen-producing cells called *fibroblasts*, which potentially could further reduce wrinkles and lines.

One commercially available topical skin product that contains BioCell is Skin Eternal Hyaluronic Serum by Source Naturals (800-815-2333, *www.sourcenaturals.com*). Place one to four drops of serum on your finger and gently massage into the skin where desired. It is generally safe for everyone. Rare side effects may include redness and irritation. I suggest trying it for two months to evaluate its effectiveness. If you are satisfied, topical HA can be used indefinitely to optimize the health and appearance of your skin.

While further studies clearly are needed to confirm the benefits of HA, I am optimistic about its potential. After all, it is not often that so promising a therapy arrives on the health-care scene.

FURTHER RELIEF FROM ARTHRITIS

For maximum relief from arthritis pain and inflammation, combine hyaluronic acid (HA) oral supplements or injections with other natural supplements described below. All are available in health-food stores and, unless noted, generally are safe for everyone. Mild arthritis symptoms may respond to the lower end of the dosage range, while severe symptoms may require the higher dosage.

• **Chondroitin,** a substance derived from cow cartilage.

Dosage: 1,200 mg daily. Lower the dosage or discontinue use if you experience digestive upset, such as nausea.

• **Fish oil** in the form of *docosahexaenoic acid* (DHA) and *eicosapentaenoic acid* (EPA), combined.

Dosage: 1,000 mg to 2,000 mg daily.

Caution: Get your doctor's approval first if you take a blood thinner, such as aspirin or *warfarin* (Coumadin).

• **Glucosamine, a substance derived from shellfish.**

Dosage: 1,500 mg daily. Lower the dosage or discontinue use if you experience digestive upset, such as diarrhea.

Caution: Check with your doctor before using if you are allergic to shellfish...or if you have diabetes, because glucosamine may cause blood-sugar fluctuations.

• **Methylsulfonylmethane (MSM),** an organic sulfur compound.

Dosage: 2,000 mg to 6,000 mg daily.

• ***S-adenosylmethionine* (SAMe),** an amino acid-like substance.

Dosage: 600 mg to 1,200 mg daily.

How to use: For rheumatoid arthritis, take fish oil and MSM. For osteoarthritis, start with glucosamine and MSM...and if symptoms are not adequately relieved within two months, also take chondroitin, fish oil and SAMe.

REPORT #43
7 Must-Have Healing Herbs

Kathy Abascal, RH, registered herbalist who practices in Vashon, Washington. A member of the American Herbalists Guild, she is coauthor of *Clinical Botanical Medicine* (Mary Ann Liebert).

Until recently, if you peeked inside the medicine cabinet of a typical American household, you were likely to find such items as aspirin for headaches...an anti-inflammatory ointment for sore muscles and joints...an antihistamine for colds—and perhaps even a prescription sedative for sleep problems and/or an antidepressant.

Latest development: With the recent economic downturn and rising drug costs, many Americans are turning to medicinal alternatives. Recently, nationwide sales of herbal supplements totaled $4.8 billion, up more than 4% from the previous year. Perhaps due to the recession, Americans now appear to be trying many of the same herb-based products that have been used for generations in other parts of the world as the front-line treatments for many common conditions.

How herbs can help you: Compared with many medications widely used in the US, herbal therapies tend to have fewer side effects, are generally just as effective—if not more so—and are often less expensive.*

Seven of the most useful herbs to have on hand in your home...

ECHINACEA FOR COLDS

A recent study reported that echinacea is not effective for the common cold. Then, another study, found that it does help. Does it or doesn't it?

Echinacea stimulates both white blood cells (which attack viruses) and natural killer cells (which destroy virus-infected cells). Most scientific studies of echinacea involve dosing patients every four to six hours. That's not enough.

How to use: Add about one teaspoon of echinacea tincture to one-half cup of water. Drink it once every waking hour at the first signs of a cold until symptoms subside.

Helpful: Add to the mixture one-half teaspoon of elderberry tincture—which also helps boost immunity—for additional antiviral effects.

EUCALYPTUS FOR CONGESTION

Used as an essential oil, eucalyptus penetrates the mucous membranes and promotes drainage—helpful for relieving symptoms caused by the common cold and/or sinusitis (inflammation of the sinuses). The oil also has antimicrobial properties that can inhibit viruses and bacteria.

How to use: At the first signs of a cold or sinusitis, put five to 10 drops of eucalyptus essential oil in a large bowl. Add one to two cups

*If you have a chronic condition and/or take prescription medication, consult your doctor before taking herbs.

of steaming hot water. (The dose is correct if you can smell the eucalyptus.) Put a towel over your head, and lean over the bowl (with your eyes closed) and breathe in the steam for about 10 minutes. Repeat as needed, using fresh eucalyptus oil each time.

Caution: Keep your head far enough from the steaming water to avoid burning yourself.

TURMERIC
FOR JOINT PAIN

Studies show that this extremely potent anti-inflammatory herb is about as effective as nonsteroidal anti-inflammatory drugs—such as aspirin and *ibuprofen* (Advil)—for easing joint pain. Unlike these and similar drugs, turmeric (taken at the doses recommended below) rarely causes stomach upset or other side effects.

How to use: Take 400 mg to 500 mg, three times daily. For additional benefits, use powdered turmeric when cooking. As little as one-quarter teaspoon per recipe will have anti-inflammatory effects over time.

Important: When cooking, use turmeric and black pepper. This greatly increases absorption of turmeric into the bloodstream.

Also helpful: Look for a turmeric supplement formula that includes black pepper.

VALERIAN
FOR INSOMNIA

Compounds in valerian act on brain receptors to induce drowsiness and relaxation.

How to use: Take one-half teaspoon of valerian tincture, diluted in water according to the instructions on the label, one hour before bedtime and one-half teaspoon at bedtime, as needed. In small doses—about one-quarter to one-half of the insomnia dose—valerian also can help reduce mild anxiety. Most people avoid valerian tea due to its unpleasant odor.

WHITE WILLOW BARK
FOR HEADACHES

It contains salicin, a chemical that's converted in the body into salicylic acid, an aspirin-like substance. Some studies indicate that white willow bark works as well as aspirin (minus the side effects, such as gastrointestinal upset)

for headaches and other types of pain, such as osteoarthritis pain and low-back pain.

How to use: Take 200 mg, twice daily with food for headache and other types of pain (described above).

Caution: If you take a blood thinner, such as *warfarin* (Coumadin), consult your physician before using white willow bark, which also has blood-thinning effects.

ST. JOHN'S WORT
TO LIFT YOUR MOOD

It's thought to inhibit the activity of enzymes that break down serotonin, a neurotransmitter that plays a key role in regulating mood.

Studies have shown that St. John's wort is as effective for mild to moderate depression as some prescription antidepressants.

St. John's wort also is one of the most effective herbs for treating seasonal affective disorder (SAD), a form of depression that tends to occur in winter.

Caution: Consult your doctor before trying St. John's wort if you take a prescription antidepressant or other medication—or drink alcohol.

How to use: The recommended dose is usually 300 mg, three times daily (standardized to 0.3% hypericin). Consult your doctor for advice on treatment duration.

Helpful: If you suffer from SAD, take 1,000 international units (IU) to 2,000 IU of vitamin D along with St. John's wort. A lack of sun and low levels of vitamin D (also associated with infrequent sun exposure) can cause depression.

ALOE VERA FOR BURNS

Like an antibiotic cream, the gel from aloe leaves has antimicrobial properties. It soothes painful burns.

How to use: Keep an aloe plant in your home. For minor burns, slice open an aloe leaf and squeeze the gel over the affected area. Store-bought aloe gel also is effective.

Helpful: Keep several aloe leaves in the freezer. The cold gel will act as a mild anesthetic.

REPORT #44
Looking for Pain Relief? Try Prolotherapy

Allan Magaziner, DO, director of Magaziner Center for Wellness in Cherry Hill, New Jersey, and a clinical instructor at University of Medicine and Dentistry of New Jersey in New Brunswick. His Web site is *www. drmagaziner.com.*

A medical procedure that "tricks" the body into healing itself, prolotherapy treats acute or chronic pain from damaged ligaments, tendons and cartilage. Some studies show significant improvement in patients with injuries or arthritis, especially in the joints, back, neck or jaw. Prolotherapy is used as a first-line therapy or when other treatments fail.

• **How it works.** A physician injects a solution, typically of dextrose (a sugar) and lidocaine (an anesthetic), into the painful area. This provokes minor, temporary inflammation… causing the body to send more blood and nutrients to the spot…which hastens healing.

• **What to expect.** Each session lasts 15 to 30 minutes and includes from one to 20 injections, depending on the areas treated. Patients experience slight discomfort during injection and mild soreness for several days after. Minor pain might need one session…severe pain might require 10 sessions spread over several months.

• **Cautions.** Your doctor may advise you to temporarily reduce or discontinue anti-inflammatory drugs—aspirin, *ibuprofen* (Motrin), *naproxen* (Aleve)—while undergoing prolotherapy. *Acetaminophen* (Tylenol) is okay. If you take blood thinners or other drugs, tell your doctor—extra precautions may be warranted.

• **Finding a practitioner.** Prolotherapy should be administered by a physician trained in the procedure—preferably through the American Association of Orthopaedic Medicine (800-992-2063, *www.aaomed.org*) or Hackett Hemwall Foundation (*www.hacketthemwall.org*). Visit these Web sites for referrals.

Cost: $100 to $400 per session. Because prolotherapy is considered experimental, insurance seldom covers it.

REPORT #45
Sitz Baths…A Water Remedy for Many Ailments

Mark A. Stengler, NMD, licensed naturopathic medical doctor in private practice, La Jolla, California… adjunct associate clinical professor at the National College of Natural Medicine, Portland, Oregon…author of many books, including *The Natural Physician's Healing Therapies* and coauthor of *Prescription for Natural Cures* (both from Bottom Line Books)…and author of the *Bottom Line/Natural Healing* newsletter.

S itz baths—sitting so that your bottom is in water—can be an easy, at-home way to help many health problems, including urinary tract infections, insomnia, even headaches.

Sitz baths promote healing by changing blood flow to the area, reducing pain and inflammation. Warm water increases blood flow to the area, while cold water helps blood move to other body parts.

What you'll need: Purchase a plastic sitz-bath tub that is placed on the toilet (available at drugstores). These are contoured to focus circulation on the buttocks.

Next best: The bathtub. Fill the tub with water high enough to reach just under the navel while you are seated.

How to do it: Use a thermometer to determine water temperature. To alternate between warm and cold water, have two buckets of water ready or use both the purchased sitz bath and the bathtub.

Conditions: Abdominal or uterine pain, low-back pain, insomnia, hemorrhoids, muscle spasms (add 2 cups of Epsom salts).

Warm treatment: Water 106°F – 110°F, 5 to 8 minutes, one to two times daily.

Conditions: Acute bladder infection, itchy rectum, acute urinary tract infection.

Lukewarm treatment: Water 92°F – 97°F, 15 minutes to one hour (depending on your comfort level), one to two times daily.

Conditions: Constipation, prostate enlargement, uterus or rectum prolapse.

Cold treatment: Water 55°F – 75°F, 5 to 8 minutes, one to two times daily.

Conditions: Vaginal infections, prostatitis, headache, postpartum recovery, chronic urinary tract infection.

Alternating treatment: Warm water for 3 to 5 minutes, followed by 30 to 60 seconds in cold. Repeat three times daily.

If you have diabetes, heart disease or high blood pressure, speak to your doctor before taking a sitz bath because it can cause changes in blood pressure, pulse and glucose levels.

REPORT #46
Natural Cures for an Ailing Immune System

Jamison Starbuck, ND, naturopathic physician in family practice and a lecturer at the University of Montana, both in Missoula. She is past president of the American Association of Naturopathic Physicians and a contributing editor to *The Alternative Advisor: The Complete Guide to Natural Therapies and Alternative Treatments* (Time Life).

The immune system is remarkable in its ability to help fight off infections and a wide variety of serious illnesses ranging from flu to staph infections. When our defenses go awry, however, our health can be threatened in a number of ways. For unknown reasons, the body's immune system can attack a part of itself, resulting in autoimmune disease.

Examples: *Systemic lupus erythematosus* (commonly known as lupus) can affect the kidneys, skin and blood vessels. With Crohn's disease, the immune system strikes the bowel. In patients who have rheumatoid arthritis, the joints are assaulted.

When a patient is diagnosed with an autoimmune disease, conventional doctors generally begin treatment with medication. For lupus and Crohn's disease, *prednisone* (a steroid drug) is commonly used. For rheumatoid arthritis, medications typically include nonsteroidal anti-inflammatory drugs (NSAIDs), corticosteroids and, most recently, drugs called *tumor necrosis factor inhibitors*, such as *etanercept* (Enbrel) and *infliximab* (Remicade). While these medications reduce symptoms, they can cause potentially serious side effects, such as liver damage and hypertension. That's why I prefer to treat symptoms naturally whenever possible, reserving strong medications for flare-ups. My advice for people with autoimmune disease…

• **Eat an anti-inflammatory diet.** Limit animal food (meat and poultry) to two meals per day and no more than three to four ounces per meal. Also consume at least five one-half cup servings of vegetables daily…one cup of a whole grain, such as brown rice or millet, and/or legumes, such as lentils or split peas…a small handful of nuts…and two or more pieces of fruit.

• **Take an omega-3 supplement.** For most of my patients with an autoimmune disease, I recommend a daily dose of 2,800 mg of inflammation-fighting omega-3 oils from fish oil, 50% of which should be *eicosapentaenoic acid* (EPA), a fatty acid shown to have strong immune-supportive effects. Omega-3 oils should always be taken with food because they are more readily digested. Check the label to be sure your fish oil source has been tested for heavy metal contamination.

• **Limit your exposure to environmental pollutants and drugs.** Both appear to trigger autoimmune disease in sensitive individuals. Substances that are known to cause this reaction in some people include mercury, cadmium, pesticides, anticonvulsant medications, beta-blockers (taken for heart disease) and estrogens (taken for menopausal symptoms). Talk to your doctor about getting tested for heavy metal toxicity and about taking only those prescription medications that he/she feels are absolutely necessary.

Take a vitamin D supplement daily. An increasing body of scientific evidence links vitamin D deficiency with autoimmune disease.

Researchers theorize that vitamin D helps regulate immune cell activity in the body. My recommendation: A supplement containing 800 international units (IU) to 1,200 IU of vitamin D daily.

REPORT #47
Leeches—A Suprisingly Effective Therapy

From *Bottom Line's Breakthroughs in Drug-Free Healing* by Bill Gottlieb (Bottom Line Books). *www. bottomlinesecrets.com.*

D on't expect your doctor to prescribe them anytime soon (or your local pharmacy to stock them), but European physicians are finding out that leeches*—yes, leeches, the animals detested by Humphrey Bogart in the African Queen but prized by natural healers since antiquity for their power to cure blood clots and disinfect wounds—are adept at reducing arthritis pain…

*www.leechesusa.com, Leeches U.S.A. LTD., 300 Shames Drive, Westbury, NY 11590 (800-645-3569).

New study: Doctors in Germany studied 51 people with osteoarthritis of the knee, treating 24 with leech therapy ("a single treatment of four to six locally applied leeches"), and 27 with four weeks of daily topical application of the NSAID *diclofenac* (Solaraze, Voltaren Topical). After seven days, those receiving leech therapy had a 64% decrease in pain, while those using *diclofenac* had a 16% decrease. The people receiving leech therapy also had less stiffness and more ease performing the tasks of daily living, such as getting dressed—benefits that continued for the next three months, until the end of the study.

"Traditional leech therapy seems to be an effective symptomatic treatment for osteoarthritis of the knee," says Andreas Michalsen, MD, in the *Annals of Internal Medicine*. He also notes that it was "safe and well-tolerated."

Theory: Leech saliva contains anti-inflammatory and other active compounds—factors that reduce blood clotting, improve circulation, anesthetize and cut the production of tissue-damaging proteins.

Latest development: The FDA has formally approved the medical leech—*Hirudo medicinalis*—as a "medical device."

Volume 6

Headache and Pain Cures

REPORT #48
The Wilen Sisters' Home Remedies that Work Better than Drugs

The Wilen sisters have been using home remedies all their lives, and for the last quarter of a century, they've been researching and writing about them as well.

We asked the Wilens to share the remedies they use most often for a variety of health challenges. The sisters may not always be able to explain why the remedies work—but they work. All use ingredients readily available in most kitchens, supermarkets or health-food stores. Of course, always check with your doctor before taking any dietary supplement or herb.

SORE THROAT

At the first sign of a sore or scratchy throat, mix two teaspoons of apple cider vinegar in six-to-eight ounces of warm water. Take a mouthful, gargle with it and spit it out—then swallow a mouthful. Repeat the gargle/swallow pattern until there's nothing left in the glass. Do this every hour until your throat is better. We usually feel better within two or three hours.

COLDS

We eat chicken soup when we feel a cold coming on. Aside from being a comfort food, it helps prevent a cold from becoming full-blown and/or it shortens the duration of one. We either prepare the soup from scratch, adding lots of veggies (carrots, onions, parsnip, celery, string beans), or we do the next best thing—buy packaged soup found in the supermarket's frozen food section, then add vegetables. In either case, we add the most potent and health-restoring ingredient—garlic. To derive the full healing powers of garlic, add

Lydia Wilen and Joan Wilen, folk-remedy experts based in New York City. The sisters are coauthors of many books, including *Bottom Line's Healing Remedies: Over 1,000 Astounding Ways to Heal Arthritis, Asthma, High Blood Pressure, Varicose Veins, Warts and More!* (Bottom Line Books). *www.bottomlinesecrets.com.*

one or two finely minced raw cloves after the warmed soup is in the bowl.

STOP BLEEDING

A simple first-aid procedure to stop a minor cut or gash from bleeding is to cover the cut with cayenne pepper from your spice cabinet. Gently pour on the pepper. Yes, it will sting. And yes, the bleeding will stop quickly.

DIARRHEA

If you must be away from a restroom, prepare slippery elm tea (we use the inner bark powder available at health-food stores). Pour eight ounces of just-boiled water over a heaping teaspoon of the powder. Let it steep for about eight minutes, then strain the liquid into a mug and drink it. It works quickly. For severe cases, do not strain it—just drink this soothing, gloppy tea.

HEARTBURN

We use our mother's remedy. As soon as the burning starts, eat a palmful of almonds—that's about one ounce—and the heartburn stops immediately. Our mom used dry-roasted almonds. We buy raw almond slivers.

STY

A sty is an inflamed swelling on the eyelid. This classic folk remedy sounds ridiculous but has worked for us many times. The minute you feel as though you're getting a sty, take a 14-carat gold ring (wash it first) and rub it several times across your eyelid every 15 minutes or so, until that "sty-ish" feeling disappears… along with the sty. In our experience, it works right away.

BURNED FINGERTIPS

Ever reach for a pot handle that's surprisingly hot? How about grabbing the wrong side of a plugged-in iron? We have a unique way of treating these minor first-degree burns, where the skin is painful and red but unbroken. It's a form of acupressure. Place your thumb on the back side of your earlobe, and the burned fingertips on the front side of the same earlobe. Press firmly. After a minute, the pain is gone.

INSOMNIA

Our new best friends are nuts—in this case, walnuts. They're rich in serotonin, the brain chemical that calms anxiety and allows us to turn off the pressures of the day to get a good night's sleep. Eat a palmful (one ounce) of raw walnuts before going to bed. It's important to chew each mouthful thoroughly, until the nut pieces are ground down.

REPORT #49
Optimism Helps Whiplash Recovery

Whiplash patients were interviewed 23 days after being injured and again six months later. Compared with the most optimistic patients, those who'd had similar injuries yet had the lowest expectations for recovery were four times as likely to suffer serious disability. Optimism may help patients stay active, which aids recovery…a mind/body interaction may promote healing.

Best: If you feel pessimistic after an injury, see a mental-health professional.

Lena Holm, DrMedSc, Institute of Environmental Medicine, Stockholm, Sweden, and leader of a study of 1,032 whiplash patients, published in *Public Library of Science* (PLoS) *Medicine* journal.

REPORT #50
Drug-Free Pain Relief With New Patch Technology

Mark A. Stengler, NMD, licensed naturopathic medical doctor in private practice, La Jolla, California…adjunct associate clinical professor at the National College of Natural Medicine, Portland, Oregon…author of many books, including *The Natural Physician's Healing Therapies* and coauthor of *Prescription for Natural Cures* (both from Bottom Line Books)…and author of the *Bottom Line/Natural Healing* newsletter.

A few months ago, 70-year-old Louise, one of my patients, was in an automobile accident. She wasn't seriously injured, but her back hurt, so her husband took her to a hospital emergency room. She waited for an hour and a half to see a doctor, then gave up and went home. She called me to tell me what had happened. At length, we discussed the nature of her back pain, which sounded like muscle strain. We agreed that her injury was minor and there was no need for immediate medical attention. Relieved that her injury was not severe, Louise went on to mention a new kind of pain patch that she had heard about and recently purchased to ease the occasional ache or pain.

Louise and I had already had several discussions about these pain patches. Called IceWave patches, they were created by a company called LifeWave (*www.LifeWave.com*) for drug-free pain relief.

Patients always are bringing new and interesting products into my office for me to look over. Louise had brought the patches to me, as had several of my other patients, many of whom reported good results after using them.

Louise and I agreed that she should try the patches for her back pain. She called me a few days later—and reported that when she applied the patches to her back, she felt much better in 30 minutes. She continued using the patches during the next several days and went on to make a full recovery without flooding her body with pain medication.

Louise had a phenomenal response to the pain patches. I also have seen a very high percentage of people with arthritis and musculoskeletal problems who respond well to these patches. The patches seem most helpful when used by patients for pain and stiffness related to muscle trauma and for problems such as back spasms or a stiff neck.

INSIDE THE PATCH

There are many types of pain patches on the market. Most release a type of anesthetic into the skin that numbs the area. The IceWave patch is not a medicated patch that contains pain-relieving drugs. It contains no medication, and its ingredients never cross the skin or enter the body. According to the manufacturer, the IceWave patches work by emitting energy frequencies that are stimulated by the body's heat. These frequencies affect the electromagnetic field of nearby cells, reducing pain and inflammation in much the same way that acupressure or acupuncture needles do when applied to various body parts. When the IceWave patches are placed over a painful body part, the area around the patches becomes several degrees cooler as measured by thermography, a type of infrared imaging technique. This indicates that the inflammatory response in that area is being inhibited.

I believe that there is more to learn about how these noninvasive nonmedicinal patches do the job—but there's no question about the good results that my patients have seen.

WHERE TO PLACE THEM

IceWave patches are used in pairs. One patch is placed on the point where the pain is most noticeable. The other is placed a few inches away from it—and is held in place for about 10 seconds to see if there is any noticeable relief. If not, the second patch is moved in a clockwise circle around the other patch (repeating the 10-second test) until the spot that brings maximum pain relief is located.

Some people don't experience any pain relief at all from IceWave patches.

Helpful: Drink plenty of water because being dehydrated seems to prevent the patches from working properly.

There are other ways to place the patches, depending on the nature of the pain. Knee pain, for example, can be treated by placing one patch on the left side of the knee and one on the right. If that doesn't work, the patches can be placed on the same side of the knee, a few inches apart from one another. If you have pain in two different parts of the body, four patches (two sets) can be used at the same time.

LifeWave recommends leaving the patches on for 12 hours, after which they should be discarded. It's generally recommended that users apply the patches in the morning and remove them before going to bed.

Some patients experience immediate relief, while others feel less pain after three to five days of using the patches. The manufacturer claims that the patches can be used safely for longer than five days, but if at any time you feel discomfort, remove them. The patches are nontoxic, and there are no reports of safety issues or side effects from them. The patches are not recommended for use by children or pregnant women, because they have not been tested in these populations.

The IceWave patches are sold through regional distributors and cannot be purchased from LifeWave directly. Prices begin at $19.95 for six patches (three sets). To find a distributor in your area, call 866-420-6288 or go to *www. LifeWave.com* (click on "Customer Service" at the bottom of the page).

I have no financial interest in this company or its products.

REPORT #51
Natural Cures for Back Pain

Jamison Starbuck, ND, naturopathic physician in family practice and a lecturer at the University of Montana, both in Missoula. She is past president of the American Association of Naturopathic Physicians and a contributing editor to *The Alternative Advisor: The Complete Guide to Natural Therapies and Alernative Treatments* (Time-Life).

L ow back pain is a common complaint—especially after age 60, when one of every two people is affected. In a recent issue of the *Journal of the American Medical Association* (JAMA), new research concluded that back surgery and nonsurgical treatment provide similar relief for back pain in patients with lumbar disk herniation (protrusion of a disk out of the normal vertebral space).

Whenever possible, I have always urged my patients to opt for nonsurgical treatment of back pain, so it's nice to see that the study results published in JAMA confirm the wisdom of this approach. Nonsurgical treatment, which helps heal back pain in part by improving circulation, is far less expensive than back surgery and avoids its risks, such as infection.*
My advice…

*Seek medical attention if your back pain is not improving or is getting worse or if you experience numbness in the legs or paralysis.

- **Walk.** Regular walking is by far the best medicine for back pain. Walking uphill is particularly useful because it strengthens muscles that support the low back. Start with very short distances (one-eighth of a block, or about 25 steps). It's fine to start walking at a slow pace. Just keep moving and do the distance three times a day, every day. Wear comfortable, supportive shoes, such as running shoes. Use a walking stick initially, if it helps. As soon as you are able to walk your starting distance without pain, increase the distance.

- **Practice deep breathing.** As you walk, take deep breaths to increase oxygen intake and help relax back muscles. Imagine your back muscles relaxing with each inhalation, strengthening and healing with each exhalation.

- **Try Thai massage.** This ancient, interactive type of massage—which involves "assisted" stretching, yoga, reflexology (massage of pressure points on the feet that correspond to other parts of the body) and acupressure (massage of points on the body that correspond to energy pathways known as "meridians")—reduces back pain. Thai massage increases muscle relaxation, mobility and overall energy. A 60-minute Thai massage, once a week for a month, can significantly improve back health. To find a practitioner, consult Thai Healing Alliance International, *www.thaihealingalliance.com.*

- **Consider trying homeopathic remedies.** *Cuprum metallicum* and *Rhus toxicodendron*, both available at health-food stores, are most widely used for back pain. Cuprum is indicated when the pain is sharp, and the muscles are tight and in spasm. Rhus is useful for stiffness and soreness that improves when you limber up with movement. Take two pellets of the 30-C potency of either remedy, under the tongue, two times a day for no more than two weeks.

- **Soak in Epsom salts.** Add two cups of Epsom salts to a tub of hot water and soak for 20 minutes. Epsom salts reduce back pain by relaxing your muscles. To supplement your pain relief, burn a lavender-scented candle in the bathroom. The aroma of lavender oil helps relax your body and your mind.

REPORT #52
The Buzz About Apis

Mark A. Stengler, NMD, licensed naturopathic medical doctor in private practice, La Jolla, California... adjunct associate clinical professor at the National College of Natural Medicine, Portland, Oregon...author of many books, including *The Natural Physician's Healing Therapies* and coauthor of *Prescription for Natural Cures* (both from Bottom Line Books)...and author of the *Bottom Line/Natural Healing* newsletter.

Apis (pronounced aye-pis) is a remedy that is derived from the honeybee—the stinger as well as the whole bee. Think of the symptoms that a bee sting causes such as stinging, burning, swelling and itching. These are all the symptoms for which apis is beneficial. So a homeopathic doctor may recommend it for bee stings, allergic reactions including hives, arthritis, urinary-tract infections, kidney disease, herpes, sore throat and ovarian pain.

Apis is indicated when symptoms include a lack of thirst, a negative response to heat, and a positive response to cold applications.

Recommendations for...

•**Allergic reactions.** Allergic reactions that cause hives or burning and stinging pains that move around the body can be improved quickly with apis. Apis also improves other symptoms of allergic reaction such as swelling of the throat and eyes. These could be allergic reactions to food or to drugs.

Note: Seek emergency medical treatment for allergic reactions, especially if you start to have trouble catching your breath.

•**Arthritis.** If you have swollen joints that burn or sting—and if your joints feel better after applying cold compresses—then the condition can probably be alleviated with apis.

•**Bee stings.** Apis quickly relieves the pain of a bee sting. This is proof of the homeopathic principle that "like cures like." Take it as soon as possible after getting stung to prevent swelling and other symptoms from getting severe. It is a remedy that should be in your home first-aid kit.

•**Herpes.** Apis is a common remedy for herpes infections. Herpes of the mouth—cold sores that sting and burn and that have a vesicle formation—improves quickly with apis. This also applies to the acute treatment of genital herpes.

•**Kidney disease.** Apis is used in acute kidney disease such as *glomerulonephritis* or *nephritic syndrome* where there is protein loss in the urine and edema of the body.

•**Meningitis.** Symptoms include a stiff neck, high fever and dilated pupils. Homeopathic apis is most effective in patients whose symptoms are made worse when heat is applied. This remedy can be used in conjunction with conventional treatment.

•**Ovarian pain.** Apis is specific for right-sided ovarian cysts where there is burning and stinging pain. It not only reduces the pain, but also stimulates dissolving of the cysts.

•**Shingles.** Apis is one of the primary homeopathic medicines for shingles, especially when there is stinging or burning. Apis helps to relieve the pain and heal the shingles.

•**Sore throat.** Apis is very effective for relieving a sore and swollen throat, especially when the sore throat has specific characteristics. Those characteristics include a burning pain (that feels better when you have a cold drink) and a bright red, swollen uvula (the flap of tissue in the middle of the mouth).

•**Toxemia in pregnancy.** Apis is a good remedy for toxemia in pregnancy where there is protein in the urine, high blood pressure and lots of body swelling.

•**Urinary-tract infections.** Urinary-tract infections can be helped by apis. This is particularly true for bladder infections that cause scalding pain during urination. If you have a right-sided kidney infection, it's another indication that this remedy will probably work well.

Dosage: For acute conditions such as a bee sting or allergic reaction, I recommend taking the homeopathic formulation with a 30C potency every 15 minutes for two doses. Then wait and see if the remedy is helping. The other option is to take one dose of a higher potency such as a 200C.

For skin rashes, sore throats and other conditions that are not so acute, I recommend taking a 6C, 12C, or 30C potency twice daily for three to five days, or as needed for continued improvement.

What are the side effects?: Side effects are not an issue with apis. It either helps or there is no effect at all. It is also safe to use for children.

REPORT #53
What Relief! Natural Ways to Curb Your Pain

Mark A. Stengler, NMD, licensed naturopathic medical doctor in private practice, La Jolla, California…adjunct associate clinical professor at the National College of Natural Medicine, Portland, Oregon…author of many books, including *The Natural Physician's Healing Therapies* and coauthor of *Prescription for Natural Cures* (both from Bottom Line Books)…and author of the *Bottom Line/Natural Healing* newsletter.

Not long ago, a 60-year-old woman came to my office suffering from severe arthritis pain in both hands. I gave her a bean-sized dab of a homeopathic gel that she applied directly to the skin on her hands. After a few applications in the span of 30 minutes, her pain was reduced by 90%. She did not need to apply the gel again for two weeks.

I witnessed a similar result with a retired National Football League player. He had severe chronic hip pain from past injuries. With one application of the gel, his pain was relieved by 70% for two full days.

The relief that these people experienced has given them each a new lease on life. But here's the best news—unlike pharmaceutical pain relievers, which often cause gastrointestinal upset or damage to internal organs, natural therapies can reduce pain without adverse effects.

WHAT ARE YOU TAKING FOR PAIN?

Most Americans take too many pharmaceutical pain relievers. An estimated 175 million American adults take over-the-counter (OTC) pain relievers regularly. About one-fifth of Americans in their 60s take at least one pain-killer for chronic pain on a regular basis.

The life-threatening risks of anti-inflammatory medications such as *rofecoxib* (Vioxx) and *celecoxib* (Celebrex), two pain relievers that had been heavily prescribed by conventional doctors to treat the chronic pain of arthritis and similar conditions have been revealed. Vioxx was pulled off the market by its manufacturer, Merck, following research that linked it to increased risk of heart attack and stroke. Celebrex carries warnings that it may increase the chance of heat attack or stroke, which can lead to death.

Of course, pain-relieving drugs can be a blessing in the event of injury, severe acute migraines or diseases, such as terminal cancer. A number of years ago, when I had a wisdom tooth extracted, I received a local anesthetic. Afterward, I went to an acupuncturist for pain relief so I wouldn't need any painkillers. For about one hour after the acupuncture, I was fine—but then the pain-relieving endorphins wore off. I tried a few natural remedies, but when the pain became excruciating, I resorted to the OTC pain reliever *acetaminophen* (Tylenol). That did the trick.

But many people use painkillers on a regular basis for several months or even years, which increases the risk of dangerous side effects. For instance, people who rely on acetaminophen increase their risk of developing stomach ulcers, liver disease and kidney disease. If you regularly take Celebrex or an OTC nonsteroidal anti-inflammatory drug (NSAID), such as aspirin or *naproxen* (Aleve), you run the risk of kidney and stomach damage. Regular use of NSAIDs also increases risk of heart attack, according to the FDA.

BETTER RESULTS, FEWER RISKS

Before you take any remedy, it's important for your doctor to identify what is causing your pain. Remember, pain is your body's distress signal that something is being irritated or damaged. Sometimes we protect ourselves by reacting instinctively. If you touch something hot, for example, you eliminate the pain by quickly pulling back your hand.

But what if your back hurts? You may need a pain reliever—but back pain also can be a signal that you're harming your body by bending or sitting the wrong way. You may need to address the underlying cause to prevent further injury. Pain receptors are found in the skin, around bones and joints—even in the walls of arteries. If a muscle is torn, for example, a pain signal is released from fibers in the shredded tissue.

In light of the dangers from prescription and OTC drugs, what safe alternatives are available to you? There are many natural supplements that I recommend.

NATURE'S PAIN RELIEVERS

If you take prescription or OTC pain medication, work with a naturopathic physician, holistic medical doctor or chiropractor who will incorporate natural pain fighters into your treatment regimen. With his/her help, you may be able to reduce your dosage of pain medication (natural pain relievers can be used safely with prescription or OTC painkillers)—or even eliminate the drugs altogether.

Natural pain-fighting supplements are even more effective when combined with physical therapies, such as acupuncture, chiropractic, magnet therapy or osteopathic manipulation (a technique in which an osteopathic physician uses his hands to move a patient's muscles and joints with stretching, gentle pressure and resistance). Physiotherapy (treatment that uses physical agents, such as exercise and massage, to develop, maintain and restore movement and functional ability) also is helpful.

Here are—in no special order—the best natural pain relievers, which can be taken alone or in combination…

• **White willow bark extract is great for headaches, arthritis, muscle aches and fever.** In Europe, doctors prescribe this herbal remedy for back pain, and recent research supports this use. One study conducted in Haifa, Israel, involved 191 patients with chronic low-back pain who took one of two doses of willow bark extract or a placebo daily for four weeks. Researchers found that 39% of patients taking the higher dose of willow bark extract had complete pain relief, compared with only 6% of those taking a placebo. The participants who benefited the most took willow bark extract that contained 240 mg of the compound salicin, the active constituent in this herbal remedy. (Aspirin is made from *acetylsalicylic acid*, which has many of the chemical properties of salicin.) However, aspirin can cause gastrointestinal ulceration and other side effects, including kidney damage. Willow bark extract is believed to work by inhibiting naturally occurring enzymes that cause inflammation and pain.

I recommend taking willow bark extract that contains 240 mg of salicin daily. In rare cases, willow bark extract can cause mild stomach upset. Don't take willow bark if you have a history of ulcers, gastritis or kidney disease. It also should not be taken by anyone who is allergic to aspirin. As with aspirin, willow bark extract should never be given to children under age 12 who have a fever—in rare instances, it can cause a fatal disease called Reye's syndrome. Willow bark extract has blood-thinning properties, so avoid it if you take a blood thinner, such as *warfarin* (Coumadin). For low-back pain, you may need to take willow bark extract for a week or more before you get results.

• **Methylsulfonylmethane (MSM) is a popular nutritional supplement that relieves muscle and joint pain.** According to Stanley Jacob, MD, former professor at Oregon Health & Science University who has conducted much of the original research on MSM, this supplement reduces inflammation by improving blood flow. Your cells have receptors that send out pain signals when they're deprived of blood. That's why increased blood flow diminishes pain.

MSM, a natural compound found in green vegetables, fruits and grains, reduces muscle spasms and softens painful scar tissue from previous injuries. A double-blind study of 50 people with osteoarthritis of the knee found that MSM helps relieve arthritis pain.

Start with a daily dose of 3,000 mg to 5,000 mg of MSM. If your pain and/or inflammation doesn't improve within five days, increase the dose up to 8,000 mg daily, taken in several doses throughout the day. If you develop digestive upset or loose stools, reduce the dosage. If you prefer, you can apply MSM cream (per the label instructions) to your skin at the painful area. This product is available at health-food stores and works well for localized pain. MSM has a mild blood-thinning effect, so check with your doctor if you take a blood thinner.

• **S-adenosylmethionine (SAMe) is a natural compound found in the body.** The supplement is an effective treatment for people who have osteoarthritis accompanied by cartilage degeneration. SAMe's ability to reduce pain, stiffness and swelling is similar to that of NSAIDs such as ibuprofen and naproxen, and the anti-inflammatory medication Celebrex. There's also evidence that SAMe stimulates cartilage repair, which helps prevent bones from rubbing against one another. A 16-week study conducted at the University of California, Irvine, compared two groups of people who were being treated for knee pain caused by osteoarthritis. Some took 1,200 mg of SAMe daily, while others took 200 mg of Celebrex. It took longer for people to get relief from SAMe, but by the second month, SAMe proved to be just as effective as Celebrex.

Most patients with osteoarthritis and fibromyalgia (a disorder characterized by widespread pain in muscles, tendons and ligaments) who take SAMe notice improvement within four to eight weeks. Many studies use 1,200 mg of SAMe daily in divided doses. In my experience, taking 400 mg twice daily works well. It's a good idea to take a multivitamin or 50-mg B-complex supplement daily while you're taking SAMe. The vitamin B-12 and folic acid contained in either supplement help your body metabolize SAMe, which means that the remedy goes to work faster.

• **Kaprex is effective for mild pain caused by injury or osteoarthritis.** It is a blend of hops, rosemary extract and oleanic acid, which is derived from olive leaf extract. Rather than blocking the body's pain-causing enzymes, these natural substances inhibit pain-causing chemicals called prostaglandins.

In a study sponsored by the Institute for Functional Medicine, the research arm of the supplement manufacturer Metagenics, taking Kaprex for six weeks reduced minor pain by as much as 72%. I recommend taking one 440-mg tablet three times daily. Kaprex is manufactured by Metagenics (800-692-9400, *www.metagenics.com*), the institute's product branch. The product is sold only in doctors' offices. To find a practitioner in your area who sells Kaprex, call the toll-free number. Kaprex has no known side effects and does not interact with other medications.

• **Proteolytic enzymes,** including bromelain, trypsin, chymotrypsin, pancreatin, papain and a range of protein-digesting enzymes derived from the fermentation of fungus, reduce pain and inflammation by improving blood flow. You can find these natural pain fighters at health-food stores in products labeled "proteolytic enzymes." Take as directed on the label. Bromelain, a favorite of athletes, is available on its own. Extracted from pineapple stems, bromelain reduces swelling by breaking down blood clots that can form as a result of trauma and impede circulation. It works well for bruises, sprains and surgical recovery. If you use bromelain, take 500 mg three times daily between meals.

Repair is a high-potency formula of proteolytic enzymes that I often recommend. It is manufactured by Enzymedica (to find a retailer, call 888-918-1118 or go to *www.enzymedica. com*). Take two capsules two to three times daily between meals. Don't take Repair or any proteolytic enzyme formula if you have an active ulcer or gastritis. Any enzyme product can have a mild blood-thinning effect, so check with your doctor if you take a blood thinner.

Pain Med is the homeopathic gel that gave such quick relief to the patients I described at the beginning of this article. It is remarkably effective for relieving the pain of arthritis, muscle soreness and spasms, sprains, strains, stiffness, headaches (especially due to tension) as well as injuries, including bruises.

Pain Med is a combination of nine highly diluted plant and flower materials, including arnica, bryonia, hypericum and ledum. Like other homeopathic remedies, it promotes the body's ability to heal itself. A bean-sized dab works well for anyone who has pain. It should be spread on the skin around the affected area. Following an injury, use it every 15 minutes, for a total of up to four applications. As the pain starts to diminish, apply less often. Do not reapply the gel once the pain is gone. Pain Med does not sting, burn or irritate the skin. It is clear, has no odor, does not stain and dries quickly.

Because it has so many uses and works so rapidly, Pain Med is a good first-aid remedy to have on hand. To order, contact the manufacturer, GM International, Inc., at 800-228-9850, *www.gmipainmed.com*.

REPORT #54
Most Back Pain Has Emotional Roots

John E. Sarno, MD, professor of clinical rehabilitation medicine at New York University School of Medicine and attending physician at the Howard A. Rusk Institute of Rehabilitation Medicine, NYU Medical Center, New York City. He is the author of *Mind Over Back Pain* and, *Healing Back Pain: The Mind/Body Connection* (Warner Books).

As anyone who routinely gets migraine or tension headaches or upset stomachs will confirm, real pain can originate in the mind.

When tension mounts, any of a wide range of uncomfortable conditions can develop, from spastic colon—to asthma—to eczema. In fact, the mind can use practically any body organ or system as a defense mechanism to sidetrack itself from the awareness of undesirable, negative emotions.

Currently the most popular distraction is pain in the back, neck or shoulders. It has not always been so. Forty years ago no one took these pains seriously.

Now they are costing the American economy somewhere between $60 billion and $70 billion a year.

Forty or 50 years ago ulcers, colitis and tension headache were the best distractors. But people knew they were caused by tension and doctors learned to clear them up with medication so the brain had to look around for a better hiding place.

The back was perfect because no one suspected it and it gradually took over the number-one spot.

What the brain created was something I call the *tension myositis syndrome*, or TMS, in which pain is caused simply by reducing the blood flow a little. I have found it to be the commonest cause of back pain by far. Fortunately—understanding what's going on usually stops the pain.

WHO CAN GET TMS

It is fair to say that everybody is susceptible. I used to think that it was only the "nervous" types who got it but we now realize that anyone who has pressure in his/her life can get TMS. And strangely, the greatest pressure comes from our own personalities because we pressure ourselves to be perfect and to be good. Since the middle years of life (30 to 60) have the greatest pressures, TMS is most common during these years. This is why persistent pain in the back, neck or shoulders is usually due to TMS.

Caution: Never assume you have TMS unless you have seen a doctor and ruled out serious disorders like tumors, cancer, bone disease and the like.

Each person with TMS develops a pattern of what time of the day or night the pain will appear, what part of the body will be involved, what activities will make it better or worse and how severe the pain will be.

One patient may say, "I'm fine when I get up, but as the day goes on, it gets worse. By late afternoon, I can't sit for more than five minutes at a time."

Another patient may have pain-racked nights followed by increasing relief through the day. They both have TMS.

SEEKING TREATMENT

People with back pain understandably want to know what is wrong and how to get better. They go from practitioner to practitioner, often getting a different diagnosis with each visit.

Surgery is commonly done but since structural abnormalities are rarely responsible for the pain, in my experience, this does not solve the problem—the pain returns to the same or another place, or the problem switches to another organ or system.

A very common misconception is that recurrent back pain is due to an old injury.

Example: "I was ice skating 10 years ago and fell on my tailbone, and my back has hurt on and off ever since."

This makes no sense for the body tends to heal itself, quickly and completely. Recurrent attacks are due to TMS.

Another mistaken idea is that if the pain is excruciating there must be a structural abnormality. In fact, such severe pain is due to muscle spasm, a powerful contraction of muscle when it is suddenly deprived of its full complement of oxygen, as occurs with TMS.

Instead of attributing their pain to psychological factors, most people would rather believe it is the result of some structural abnormality that can be treated surgically, with medication or some other kind of therapy. It is my impression that eight out of 10 people are unable to accept the diagnosis of TMS.

Unfortunate: People who would benefit most from a pyschological diagnosis tend to be the least able to accept it.

Am I saying that people consciously induce their own pain? Of course not. It is the stress and pressures of life that bring on the pain because they lead to internal bad feelings, like anger, which the brain then avoids by turning our attention to the pain.

Patients are often told in pain clinics that they are unconsciously making their pain worse in order to gain certain benefits like sympathy, attention, money, etc. I don't believe that is a significant factor in chronic pain.

Why don't more doctors diagnose TMS? Unfortunately, medical teaching still tends to view the body as a magnificent machine and the doctor as an engineer to that machine. There is still very little awareness in the ranks of medicine of the intimate connection of the mind and body. This is a tragedy for the average patient.

How can you prove that TMS exists? It doesn't show up on an X ray or blood test, but if a large number of patients (thousands) get better when treated for that diagnosis, it must exist.

The cure: Repudiate the structural explanation for the pain and acknowledge that it is due to pressure and tension. This is accomplished through teaching and group meetings. In about 10% of cases it is also necessary to work with a psychotherapist who is familiar with the disorder.

Through the years many people have written to me and described how they were cured by carefully studying my book, *Healing Back Pain.* This is logical because information is the primary therapeutic ingredient. It's what I give my patients.

But remember, one must never consider this diagnosis unless all serious disorders have first been ruled out.

REPORT #55
Natural Pain Busters

Mark A. Stengler, NMD, licensed naturopathic medical doctor in private practice, La Jolla, California…adjunct associate clinical professor at the National College of Natural Medicine, Portland, Oregon…author of many books, including *The Natural Physician's Healing Therapies* and coauthor of *Prescription for Natural Cures* (both from Bottom Line Books)…and author of the *Bottom Line/Natural Healing* newsletter.

When something hurts, you want to feel better quickly. Often that means reaching for an over-the-counter or prescription drug. But there are natural pain stoppers that offer the same relief—without the risks.

Aspirin and *ibuprofen* (Advil) can both cause intestinal bleeding…*acetaminophen* (Tylenol) can lead to liver damage…powerful prescription pain relievers, such as *acetaminophen-hydrocodone* (Vicodin) and acetaminophen with codeine, may make you drowsy and can be addictive.

Despite the dangers, these medications are valuable for treating occasional severe (long-lasting) or acute (sudden, but stopping abruptly) pain. But for many chronic conditions that need ongoing relief, such as osteoarthritis, natural pain stoppers work just as well with a much lower risk for side effects.

Caution: Severe pain, or mild pain that gets suddenly worse, can be a sign of a serious injury or other medical problem.

Best: Seek medical attention immediately.

HOW TO USE NATURAL REMEDIES

For each common pain problem discussed here, I give more than one treatment. You may have more success with, or simply prefer, a particular treatment. If something has worked for you in the past, start there. If you don't get much relief from a treatment, try another option. If you get only partial improvement, try adding another supplement. Because natural remedies have a very low risk for serious side effects, it's usually safe to use them in combination with prescription or nonprescription medications, such as for high blood pressure—and over the long run, they can help reduce the need for these drugs entirely. Check with your doctor before starting a natural regimen or changing your drug regimen.

Natural remedies also work well in combination with pain-relieving "body work," such as chiropractic, physical therapy as well as acupuncture.

HELP A HEADACHE

Migraines and other headaches are often set off by food sensitivities—most commonly, to red wine, caffeine, chocolate and food additives, such as *monosodium glutamate*. Other triggers, such as lack of sleep or hormonal fluctuations, can also leave you with headache pain.

Best: Pay attention to patterns and avoid your triggers.

Fortunately, headaches are usually very responsive to natural remedies…

• **Mild (tension) headaches.** First, try acupressure. This ancient Chinese technique uses gentle pressure and light massage on specific points.

In traditional Chinese medicine, *chi* (chee) is the vital energy of all living things. Your chi flows along 12 meridians that run through your body and nourish your tissues. Each meridian is associated with a particular organ, such as the liver or gallbladder. Along each meridian are specific points, designated by numbers, that are the spots where the flow of chi can be affected. For headaches, the standard acupressure points are…

• **Gallbladder 20**—the small indentation below the base of the skull, in the space between the two vertical neck muscles. Push gently for 10 to 15 seconds, wait 10 seconds, then repeat five to 10 times.

• **Large intestine 4**—located in the webbing between the thumb and index finger. Push gently for 10 to 15 seconds (as described above). Do this on one hand, then switch to the other.

• **Yuyao**—the indentation in the middle of each eyebrow (straight up from the pupil). Push gently for 10 to 15 seconds (as described above) on both points simultaneously.

If you don't feel relief within several minutes after trying a particular pressure point, move on to a different one.

Another option for mild headaches: A cup of peppermint tea, or a dab of peppermint oil on the temples, can banish a mild headache quickly.

Note: Peppermint essential oil is highly concentrated—don't take it internally.

To brew peppermint tea, make an infusion using one to two teaspoons dried peppermint leaf in eight ounces of boiling water. Let steep for five minutes. You may find relief after one cup. Drink as much and as often as necessary.

• **Migraine headaches.** The herb feverfew has been used effectively for centuries to treat migraines. Take a feverfew capsule standardized to contain 300 micrograms (mcg) of the active ingredient *parthenolide* every 30 minutes, starting at the onset of symptoms.

Maximum: Four doses daily or until you feel relief.

Prevention: Take a feverfew capsule standardized to contain 300 to 400 mcg of parthenolide—or 30 drops of a standardized tincture, either in a few ounces of water or directly on your tongue, every day. In about three months, you should notice dramatically fewer migraines, and/or less severe symptoms.

Note: Feverfew may thin blood, so consult your doctor if you are taking a blood thinner, such as *warfarin* (Coumadin).

SOOTHE SORE MUSCLES

Natural remedies can help an aching back or sore, cramped muscles. Here, too, acupressure is valuable. Zero in on the points that are most tender and then gently press on them and release, or massage for 10 to 15 seconds, at 10-second intervals, five to 10 times. If you can't reach a spot, have someone do it for you.

For some people, an ice pack on the affected area helps. Others prefer warmth from a hot compress or heating pad. For acute injuries, use cold (within 24 hours). Otherwise, use warmth or alternate warmth and cold. Other remedies that help sore muscles...

• **Herbal arnica cream or tincture** can soothe sore muscles and is also great for bruises. It reduces swelling, which helps lessen pain. Rub a small amount on the affected area. Repeat as needed.

Caution: Don't use on broken skin because it is not intended for internal use.

• **Homeopathic Rhus toxicodendron** is especially helpful in relieving low back pain. Take two pellets of 30C potency twice daily for two or three days.

EASE ARTHRITIC JOINTS

The stiff, swollen joints of osteoarthritis are a major cause of doctors' visits for people over age 45. *But with natural remedies, the pain and joint damage can be kept to a minimum...*

• **Glucosamine sulfate** helps rebuild damaged cartilage in arthritic joints and works as well as or better than many of the drugs doctors recommend. It can take several weeks to feel the benefits. Begin by taking 1,500 to 2,000 mg daily for three months. After that, cut back to 500 to 1,000 mg daily. If symptoms worsen, go back to the higher dose. It's okay to continue with anti-inflammatory drugs, but be sure to tell your doctor if you're using glucosamine.

• **Boswellia,** an herb used in Ayurveda, traditional medicine from India, is a powerful anti-inflammatory that's very helpful for arthritis. Take 1,200 to 1,500 mg of a standardized extract containing 60% to 65% boswellic acids, two to three times daily.

• **Bromelain,** an enzyme derived from pineapple stems, is very effective at reducing pain and swelling. Bromelain supplements come in two designations—MCU (milk-clotting units) and GDU (gelatin-dissolving units). Use either formula, choosing a product that's standardized to either 2,000 MCU per 1,000 mg or 1,200 GDU per 1,000 mg. Take 500 mg three times daily between meals.

Caution: If you take a blood-thinning medication such as warfarin, skip the bromelain—it could thin your blood too much.

Any of these supplements can be used alone or in combination. Natural pain stoppers can be effective alternatives to drugs, but pain is also your body's way of telling you that something is wrong. If your pain is very sudden or severe, and/or accompanied by other symptoms—such as weakness, nausea, redness and swelling in the painful area, shortness of breath or fever—get medical attention immediately.

REPORT #56
Quick Cure for Headaches

Put your feet in a bucket of warm water and put an ice pack around your neck. The strategic use of heat and cold causes blood to move away from your head and toward your feet, relieving headache pain. It takes about five to 10 minutes for the pain to recede. This technique might not help people with poorly controlled diabetes or vascular disease who have diminished blood flow to the feet.

Mark A. Stengler, NMD, licensed naturopathic medical doctor in private practice, La Jolla, California...adjunct associate clinical professor at the National College of Natural Medicine, Portland, Oregon...author of many books, including *The Natural Physician's Healing Therapies* and coauthor of *Prescription for Natural Cures* (both from Bottom Line Books)...and author of the *Bottom Line/Natural Healing* newsletter.

Volume 7
Ulcer and Digestive Cures

REPORT #57
Natural Cures for Heartburn and Ulcers

"**D**octor, I have heartburn, but I don't want to take a prescription drug. What can I do?" Many people have asked me for such advice—especially since the media have publicized risks associated with popular heartburn and ulcer medications called *proton pump inhibitors* (PPIs). These drugs, including *omeprazole* (Prilosec), *lansoprazole* (Prevacid) and *esomeprazole* (Nexium), offer short-term relief by reducing stomach acid, but they do not cure the underlying problem. Even worse, long-term use (more than a year) of PPIs increases risks for hip fracture (because of decreased mineral absorption)...and the bacterial intestinal infection *Clostridium difficile* (because stomach acid is needed to fight bacteria). For my patients, I use a different approach that focuses on improving digestion and healing the lining of the stomach and the esophagus. *My advice...*

If you suffer from heartburn and/or have an ulcer, avoid any foods that may irritate your condition, such as fried foods, citrus, tomato-based foods and spicy meals. Don't overeat. Large meals increase the demand for stomach acid. Chew thoroughly and eat nothing within two hours of going to bed. Avoid smoking and pain relievers, such as aspirin or *ibuprofen* (Advil), that can cause gastrointestinal irritation.

Herbal tea also can be surprisingly effective for heartburn and ulcers. Chamomile and licorice root are two herbs with a long medicinal history for treating the digestive tract lining.* Drink three cups of either tea daily, on an empty stomach. Use two teaspoons of dried plant or one teabag per eight ounces of water.

*If you have high blood pressure, avoid licorice tea.

Philip M. Tierno, Jr., PhD, director of clinical microbiology and immunology at New York University Medical Center, and associate professor, department of microbiology and pathology at New York University School of Medicine, both in New York City. He is author of *The Secret Life of Germs* (Atria).

For heartburn (without ulcer), I suggest that you add stomach acid—which is necessary for good digestion—rather than reduce it with an acid blocker. At the end of your meal, sip on a four-ounce glass of water to which you have added one teaspoon of either apple cider vinegar or fresh lemon juice.

Caution: Do not drink vinegar or lemon water if you have an ulcer or gastritis (inflammation of the lining of the stomach). Discontinue this practice if it causes pain or worsens symptoms.

If you have an ulcer (with or without heartburn), I recommend adding other botanical medicines. The antiseptic herbs echinacea, cranesbill root and Oregon grape root (50 mg each) help reduce bacteria associated with ulcers. The herbs cabbage leaf, marshmallow root and slippery elm bark (200 mg each) help restore the gut's protective lining. Take these herbs three times daily on an empty stomach until the ulcer symptoms have eased, usually for two to eight weeks.

If you take a PPI but want to stop using it, gradually wean yourself off the drug while you add this protocol. Consult your doctor about your plan and schedule a follow-up visit in a month. You can review your condition and discuss what I hope will be good news about your progress.

REPORT #58
Difficult-to-Treat GERD

Mark A. Stengler, NMD, licensed medical doctor in private practice, La Jolla, California...adjunct associate clinical professor at the National College of Natural Medicine, Portland, Oregon...author of many books, including *The Natural Physician's Healing Therapies* and coauthor of *Prescription for Natural Cures* (both from Bottom Line Books)...and author of the *Bottom Line/Natural Healing* newsletter.

I have tried every therapy you can think of," said my new patient Esther, who had suffered from heartburn and bad breath since high school. "I hope you have something that can help me!" This 59-year-old financial adviser had tried pharmaceutical medications and natural remedies—but nothing seemed to stop the constant burning in her chest.

In high school, Esther had been diagnosed with both *gastroesophageal reflux disease* (GERD), a condition in which stomach acids back up into the esophagus, and *irritable bowel syndrome* (IBS), a condition that causes diarrhea, constipation and digestive discomfort. Over the next 40 years, she had taken various acid-blocking medications, such as *esomeprazole* (Nexium) and *omeprazole* (Prilosec). While these medications helped the reflux symptoms (the burning or pressure in her chest), they worsened her IBS symptoms, including diarrhea and abdominal pain.

Esther was especially concerned about the potential long-term side effects of these medications. Her concerns had inspired her to try alternative medicine remedies.

She had already taken many of the classic dietary supplement remedies for GERD that I always first recommend to patients with the condition. These included calcium (which neutralizes stomach acid), *deglycyrrhizinated licorice root* (DGL), probiotics, aloe vera juice and digestive enzymes. Esther was not overweight (which can be a risk factor for GERD) and found that what she ate did not have much impact on her reflux.

For Esther's difficult-to-treat GERD, I suggested a new, less commonly known supplement that has been shown to be effective—orange peel extract. I am using it with more and more patients, and it may become a first-line treatment. Heartburn Free (800-783-2286, *www.enzymatictherapy.com*) contains orange peel extract that is standardized to contain a high concentration of *d-limonene*, a phytochemical found in citrus. The supplement is believed to help the lower esophageal sphincter close more efficiently so that acid doesn't rise up as easily from the stomach. Heartburn Free has no reported side effects. It is safe for all adults except those with gastric ulcers and women who are pregnant or nursing (for whom it has not yet been tested).

I had Esther take one capsule every other day for 10 days. When she followed up with me a month later, she reported that her GERD was 80% better overall and that she had not taken a citrus peel extract capsule in two weeks. Her bad breath, a symptom of GERD, had subsided, as had her IBS, which is not uncommon, because these conditions frequently overlap. This was the best result that she had ever gotten from any treatment. If she experienced any increase in her symptoms, she could start taking the capsules again.

REPORT #59
Natural Therapies for Ulcers

James N. Dillard, MD, DC, in private practice, East Hampton, New York. He is a former assistant clinical professor at Columbia University College of Physicians and Surgeons and clinical director of Columbia's Rosenthal Center for Complementary and Alternative Medicine, both in New York City.

If you've got an ulcer, chances are you're taking an over-the-counter (OTC) antacid and/or prescription medication to neutralize gastric acid or inhibit its production. These medications include *proton pump inhibitors* (PPIs), such as *esomeprazole* (Nexium) and *lansoprazole* (Prevacid), and H2-blocking drugs, such as *cimetidine* (Tagamet) and *ranitidine* (Zantac).

What most people don't realize: There are several natural, complementary remedies that help reduce ulcer symptoms and promote healing while conventional treatment is under way. Some of these treatments also can help prevent ulcers in some patients.

WHAT CAUSES ULCERS

It's been more than 20 years since doctors learned that an infectious disease—rather than emotional stress—was the primary cause of most ulcers.

A screw-shaped bacterium, *Helicobacter pylori*, or H. pylori, burrows through the protective mucous lining in the small intestine and/or stomach, allowing harsh digestive fluids to accumulate and ulcerate the lining. About 50% of Americans over age 60 are infected with H.

pylori. The bacterium doesn't always cause ulcers—but about 60% of patients with ulcers harbor H. pylori.

The remainder of ulcers are caused by regular use of stomach-damaging nonsteroidal anti-inflammatory drugs (NSAIDs), such as aspirin, *ibuprofen* (Advil) and *naproxen* (Aleve)...alcohol...and/or smoking. Excessive alcohol wears down the lining of the stomach and intestines. Nicotine causes the stomach to produce more acid.

Best complementary treatments...*

NONDRUG THERAPIES

●**Probiotics.** The intestine contains up to four pounds of "friendly" bacteria, which aid digestion. There's some evidence that maintaining adequate levels of beneficial bacteria helps create an inhospitable environment for H. pylori and makes it harder for this ulcer-causing bacterium to thrive.

Self-defense: Take a probiotic supplement that contains *Lactobacillus acidophilus* and *Bifidobacterium bifidus*. These organisms create a healthful mix of bacteria and can inhibit the growth of harmful organisms. Probiotics are helpful if you've taken antibiotics, which can kill off some beneficial bacteria.

The optimal dose for probiotics hasn't been determined. Preliminary research cites a daily dose of up to 10 billion organisms—the amount usually included in one to two capsules. Probiotics are available at health-food stores.

●**Cabbage juice.** This folk remedy has some evidence to support it. Cabbage is high in vitamin C, which seems to inhibit growth of H. pylori. It also contains *glutamine*, an amino acid that may strengthen the protective lining in the stomach.

A small Stanford University School of Medicine study found that ulcer patients who drank about a quart of cabbage juice daily healed significantly faster than those who didn't drink it.

Self-defense: If you have an active ulcer, consider drinking a quart of cabbage juice (about the amount in half a head of cabbage) once daily for up to two weeks.

*Check with your doctor before taking supplements. They can interact with prescription medications.

• **Deglycyrrhizinated licorice (DGL).** Herbalists often recommend fresh licorice root to heal ulcers. Licorice contains *mucin*, a substance that protects the stomach lining, as well as antioxidants that may inhibit H. pylori growth.

However, natural licorice can increase the effects of *aldosterone*, a hormone that promotes water retention and can increase blood pressure in some people. DGL supplements (available at health-food stores) are a better option, because the substances that increase blood pressure have been removed.

Self-defense: Take one DGL tablet before meals, and another before bed. DGL may be effective for people with ulcers whose H. pylori has been successfully treated with antibiotics but who still have some stomach irritation.

• **Vitamin A.** Vitamin A helps repair damaged mucous membranes. A report in the British medical journal *The Lancet* suggests that ulcers heal more quickly in patients given supplemental vitamin A.

Caution: High-dose vitamin A therapy can be toxic, so get your vitamin A from dietary sources along with a daily multivitamin—not from a separate vitamin A supplement.

Self-defense: Get 10,000 international units (IU) of vitamin A daily if you're undergoing ulcer treatment. (A multivitamin typically contains 3,500 IU to 5,000 IU of vitamin A.)

Good food sources: Beef liver (one-and-one-half ounces contains 13,593 IU)...carrots (one raw carrot contains 8,666 IU)...and spinach (one cup of raw spinach contains 2,813 IU).

• **Zinc.** Like vitamin A, zinc is involved in tissue healing. In Europe, a drug compound made with zinc plus an anti-inflammatory is often used for treating ulcers. Early studies indicate that zinc alone can speed ulcer healing and possibly even help prevent some ulcers.

Self-defense: Don't exceed the recommended daily intake (15 mg) of zinc. Take a daily multivitamin that includes zinc...and get adequate intake from dietary sources (five medium fried oysters, 13 mg...3/4 cup fortified breakfast cereal, 15 mg...three-ounces lean beef tenderloin, 5 mg).

ANOTHER WAY TO FIGHT ULCERS

NSAIDs alleviate pain by inhibiting the production of pain-causing chemicals called *prostaglandins*. However, the body produces several kinds of prostaglandins, including some that protect the stomach lining. That's why NSAIDs, which block the production of pain-causing and stomach-protecting prostaglandins, make people who regularly use the drugs more susceptible to ulcers.

Self-defense: If you require regular pain relief, start with *acetaminophen* (Tylenol). It relieves pain without depleting stomach-protecting prostaglandins.

Caution: Taking more than the recommended dosage or drinking alcohol with acetaminophen can cause liver damage.

Also helpful: Ask your doctor about taking *Arthrotec*, a prescription drug combination that includes the NSAID *diclofenac* along with *misoprostol*, which protects the stomach and intestinal lining. One study found that patients taking Arthrotec experienced up to 80% fewer ulcers than those taking an NSAID alone.

REPORT #60
Treatment for Colitis

Mark A. Stengler, NMD, licensed naturopathic medical doctor in private practice, La Jolla, California...adjunct associate clinical professor at the National College of Natural Medicine, Portland, Oregon...author of many books, including *The Natural Physician's Healing Therapies* and coauthor of *Prescription for Natural Cures* (both from Bottom Line Books)...and author of the *Bottom Line/Natural Healing* newsletter.

After five years of suffering, 31-year-old Ann was at her wit's end. She experienced constant severe nausea, intermittent vomiting and diarrhea, and frequent bloody stools. She was down to a skeletal 88 pounds...she hadn't menstruated in almost two years...and her hair and nails had basically stopped growing. Digestive tract bleeding had necessitated two blood transfusions. "The pain is unbearable," she told me tearfully, "and most days, I'm too weak to even get out of bed."

Unable to tolerate solid food, Ann largely subsisted on juice. Her medical doctor had prescribed numerous pills, plus injections of morphine and the steroid prednisone. She had become depressed, anxious and prone to panic attacks.

While taking her medical history, I learned that Ann had been infected five years earlier with *Clostridium difficile*. This bacterium has emerged in recent years in especially virulent forms and is a known cause of colitis (inflammation and ulcers in the lining of the large intestine). Ann had been treated first with a standard antibiotic and then with the more potent antibiotic *metronidazole* (Flagyl). Afterward her stool had tested negative for C. difficile—yet her symptoms had continued to worsen.

I repeated a comprehensive stool test and found no C. difficile infection. However, I did find that Ann had very low levels of beneficial digestive bacteria, such as *Lactobacillus acidophilus* and *Bifidobacterium*. To make her more comfortable, I prescribed the homeopathic remedy *Arsenicum album* (sold in health-food stores), which eases nausea and abdominal pain and also reduces anxiety. In addition, I prescribed a powdered herbal formula that contained turmeric, ginger, quercetin and other anti-inflammatory nutrients...plus the amino acid glutamine, which promotes healing of the digestive tract...and suggested she mix it with almond milk and drink it twice daily. I also recommended that Ann increase her nutrient intake by adding soups and stews to her diet, and I added a probiotic supplement to replenish her beneficial digestive bacteria.

With these changes, Ann slowly improved, day by day. After one month, she reported that her abdominal pain was greatly reduced and that she required less morphine. She had diarrhea far less often and was no longer vomiting. In addition, Ann was sleeping better and her emotional state had improved.

In about four months, Ann's hair and nails started to grow again and she got her period. Her bowel movements normalized, and she could eat most foods without trouble. Her

weight increased to a healthy 128 pounds, and she felt strong and energized. "This is the first time in five years that I haven't been in the hospital during Thanksgiving and Christmas," she told me with obvious delight. Now, a year and half later, Ann takes a lesser dose of the almond-milk herbal formula, plus my high-potency probiotic, and continues to do well.

REPORT #61
My Natural Cure for Constipation

Jamison Starbuck, ND, naturopathic physician in family practice and a lecturer at the University of Montana, both in Missoula. She is past president of the American Association of Naturopathic Physicians and a contributing editor to *The Alternative Advisor: The Complete Guide to Natural Therapies and Alternative Treatments* (Time Life).

So-called herbal "bowel cleansers" are touted as a healthy and effective treatment for chronic constipation. In my clinical experience, this claim simply is not true. Bowel-cleansing formulas typically contain strong laxative herbs, such as aloe resin (sometimes listed as "aloe leaf"), buckthorn, cascara, rhubarb and senna. These herbs increase peristalsis, the wave-like movement of the bowel that facilitates elimination of stool, but they also irritate the gut wall. Like any good laxative, these herbs will promote a bowel movement, but repeated or large doses create cramping, diarrhea and blood in the stool.

I define constipation as having less than one bowel movement per day. Common causes of constipation include irregular bowel habits (ignoring the urge to go or not allowing enough time)...inadequate fiber and/or water...lack of exercise...and poor digestive function (due to low secretion of digestive enzymes). Medications such as antihypertensives, tricyclic antidepressants, antacids and opiate pain relievers (such as codeine) can cause constipation. Unless your constipation is temporary (caused, for example, by the use of opiate medication following surgery), avoid strong laxatives—even if they are natural or herbal products. The bowel becomes reliant on laxatives, which can worsen your constipation and create inflammation and irritation in your intestinal tract.

Rather than seeking a temporary solution, people who are constipated should slowly retrain their bowels to work correctly. This process usually takes about four weeks. *Here's how…*

1. Eat fiber. Fiber helps retain water in the colon, which promotes softer and larger stool. While a healthy, toned bowel will respond to a moderate amount of fiber, a bowel that has become slack and weak (due to the effects of insufficient fiber) will need much more fiber.

Start with five half-cup servings of vegetables and four half-cup servings of fruit per day. Have at least one cup daily of a whole grain, such as brown rice, oatmeal, quinoa or millet.

2. Exercise. Physical activity improves peristalsis. Get at least 20 minutes each day. My favorite exercises are yoga and aerobic activity, such as brisk walking, cycling or swimming.

3. Drink lemon water. To expand stool size and encourage elimination, drink 64 ounces of water daily.

Twice a day, before meals, drink 16 ounces of water that contains the juice from half a fresh lemon (bottled lemon juice also can be used, but it is not as healthful).

Lemon water encourages the secretion of bile, a digestive fluid that acts as a laxative.

4. Use small doses of herbs. A tea made with equal parts dandelion, yellow dock, burdock and licorice root has a mild laxative effect.

What to do: Mix one-half ounce of each dried herb. Use two teaspoons of the mix per eight ounces of water, simmer for eight minutes, strain and drink.

Start with one cup four times daily during the first week of bowel retraining. Reduce by one cup per week until you are able to eliminate regularly without the tea.

REPORT #62
Wormwood: This Controversial Herb Deserves Another Look

Mark A. Stengler, NMD, licensed naturopathic medical doctor in private practice, La Jolla, California…adjunct associate clinical professor at the National College of Natural Medicine, Portland, Oregon…author of many books, including *The Natural Physician's Healing Therapies* and coauthor of *Prescription for Natural Cures* (both from Bottom Line Books)…and author of the *Bottom Line/Natural Healing* newsletter.

The herb *wormwood* (*Artemisia absinthium*) has a long history of use in Europe and China as a remedy for digestive disorders. But wormwood has been dogged by controversy. That's because it is a flavoring and color agent in *absinthe*, an alcoholic beverage that was banned in the US and Europe in the early 1900s because it was thought to cause hallucinations and even insanity. A component of wormwood—the chemical *thujone*—was believed to have these mind-altering properties. But some experts have since questioned the science behind this belief, and in the 1990s, Europe lifted the ban on the manufacture and consumption of absinthe…without any related increase in mental illness. In 2007, the US government began allowing *thujone-free absinthe* to be imported into the country, and herbal wormwood is widely available in health-food stores. *Recent research shows that this controversial herb may be helpful in fighting some insidious health conditions…*

•**Crohn's disease.** A study published recently by doctors at Yale University School of Medicine found that wormwood significantly reduced symptoms of Crohn's disease, a form of inflammatory bowel disease that is difficult to treat. Forty patients were given either 750 mg of wormwood extract (*brand name:* Seda-Crohn) or placebos twice daily for 10 weeks. After eight weeks, 13 of the 20 patients (65%) taking wormwood had almost a full remission of symptoms. As a result, they were able to reduce their use of corticosteroid drugs. For most of the patients taking placebos, symptoms worsened.

•**Malaria.** A very close relative of wormwood called sweet wormwood (*Artemisia annua*) has been found beneficial in treating malaria, which is caused by a mosquito-borne parasite. Although most Americans are not likely to contract malaria, the disease is still a major problem in Africa and throughout the developing world.

The World Health Organization has approved the use of wormwood-based compounds in the treatment of malaria—a sign of the herb's efficacy and safety.

•**Parasitic infections.** Wormwood has a long history of use in traditional Chinese medicine and in Western naturopathic medicine for treating a variety of parasitic infections.

I have found that a wormwood tincture (10 drops three times daily) or capsule (200 mg) helps rid the body of parasites in the digestive tract.

•**Cancer.** Some research suggests that extracts of wormwood might have anticancer benefits. However, the research has been limited to small-scale cell and mouse studies.

Some companies are hyping wormwood as a potential cancer fighter, but at this point, I do not believe there is enough evidence to justify its use in treating cancer.

What about the risk? The amount of thujone in herbal preparations is extremely small—I have never found a problem with its use.

In fact, thujone also is found in the culinary herb sage, commonly used as a rub for Thanksgiving turkeys.

Important: Work with a physician if you suspect that you have any of the conditions mentioned here, and ask about wormwood as a possible treatment.

My patients have not experienced any hallucinations or other side effects as a result of the doses I prescribe.

REPORT #63
The All-Purpose Remedy—Licorice Root

Mark A. Stengler, NMD, licensed medical doctor in private practice, La Jolla, California…adjunct associate clinical professor at the National College of Natural Medicine, Portland, Oregon…author of many books, including *The Natural Physician's Healing Therapies* and coauthor of *Prescription for Natural Cures* (both from Bottom Line Books)…and author of the *Bottom Line/Natural Healing* newsletter.

In my experience, licorice root is the most versatile of all the herbs. Native to both Asia and the Mediterranean, it has been used by practitioners of Ayurvedic and Chinese medicine for over 5,000 years.

In fact, close to 50% of all Chinese herbal formulas contain licorice root. The ancient Chinese texts say it can suppress coughs and moisten the lungs, relieve spasms, and soothe the digestive tract. It is also called a "harmonizing" herb. This means that it helps other herbs to work more effectively to reduce their toxicity when used in a formula.

Licorice also helps detoxify the liver, supports the adrenal glands (your body's major guardians against stress), balances the hormones and has powerful anti-inflammatory effects.

IMMUNITY BOOSTER

Licorice contains two substances, *glycyrrhizin* (pronounced gle-sir-heh-zin) and *glycyrrhetinic* (pronounced gle-sir-heh-ti-nic) acid, that have been shown in animal studies to increase the body's supply of one of nature's most powerful antiviral agents—interferon. Interferon helps to keep viruses from reproducing and stimulates the activity of other beneficial immune cells, as well. That's probably why licorice root is found in so many Western, Chinese, Japanese and Ayurvedic formulas for treating infectious disease.

Licorice root is highly regarded among European physicians as one of the top herbal medicines for combating viral hepatitis. They use the intravenous form for the treatment of both Hepatitis B and C.

DELICIOUS DETOXIFIER

The Chinese have found through many centuries of using licorice that it reduces the toxicity of other herbs, so they add it to many of their remedies. For example, traditional Chinese herbal formulas containing Ma Huang (containing the chemical ephedrine, which helps open respiratory passageways but can also cause stimulant effects, such as fast heartbeat, sweating, and anxiety), almost always contain licorice root, which helps to prevent these unwanted side effects.

Note: The Chinese species of licorice root is *Glycyrrhiza uralensis*. I find it works very similar in action to the kind used in North America—*Glycyrrhiza glabra*.

Dosage: For most conditions, I recommend taking licorice in tincture, capsule, or tablet form. As a tincture, take 10 to 30 drops two to three times daily. As a capsule, take 1,000 to 3,000 milligrams daily.

DGL extract comes in tablet form. Chew one or two tablets (380 milligrams per tablet) 20 minutes before meals or take between meals.

What are the side effects?: High dosages of licorice root (3,000 milligrams daily of the powdered extract or more than 100 milligrams of the constituent glycyrrhizin) taken over many days can have effects similar to those associated with the hormone aldosterone. These include sodium and water retention, and potassium loss, which can lead to high blood pressure. We saw this problem occur when practitioners began recommending very high dosages of licorice root for adrenal burnout and chronic fatigue (which it can help).

Overall, I feel the risk of developing high blood pressure from using licorice is greatly exaggerated. Historically, herbalists have used this root in formulas for thousands of years. The trick is to use it in small amounts.

I do hear the occasional story of someone who feels that taking small amounts of licorice root has caused an increase in his or her blood pressure. This is possible for people who are very sensitive to licorice root or who have low levels of potassium. As a matter of fact, anyone concerned about high blood pressure should increase his or her intake of potassium-rich foods (bananas, orange juice, vegetables, etc.) and decrease the intake of sodium-containing foods (table salt, canned foods and restaurant foods). Using table-salt substitutes, which usually contain potassium, can help reduce sodium intake. Multivitamins also contain potassium.

Unless instructed to do so by a natural health-care practitioner, people who have kidney failure and hypokalemia (low potassium blood levels) should avoid using licorice root. Likewise, pregnant women and people with high blood pressure should use it with caution and under medical supervision. Whole licorice extract should not be combined with digitalis and diuretic medications. Taking only the DGL extract (for ulcers) eliminates most of the potential risk for high blood pressure.

Recommendations for…

• **Coughs.** Licorice is an excellent herb to use for coughs, both wet and dry. Licorice has a moistening and soothing effect for dry coughs. It also has a direct cough suppressant effect and is a common ingredient in throat lozenges.

• **Detoxification.** Licorice is one of the herbs to consider when undergoing a detoxification program. As I mentioned, it helps support the liver and should be considered along with herbs like milk thistle and dandelion root. It also works well to heal a damaged digestive tract, which is key to long-term detoxification success.

• **Eczema and psoriasis.** Creams containing glycyrrhetinic acid are used to treat inflammatory skin conditions such as eczema and psoriasis. Its effect is similar to that of topical cortisone, and some studies have found it more effective. However, I do not recommend topical treatments (whether natural or pharmaceutical) as the main therapy for skin conditions, as they can simply mask a symptom without treating its underlying cause (e.g., food sensitivities, poor digestion, nutritional deficiencies, etc.). Topical treatments are fine, so long as you also address the internal imbalances that are creating the symptom.

• **Fatigue.** People who experience high levels of stress for long periods of time can suddenly find that their adrenal glands can no longer produce balanced levels of stress hormones, such as DHEA, pregnenolone and cortisol. As a result, fatigue, poor memory, blood-sugar problems, decreased resistance to illness and hormonal imbalance can occur.

Some doctors immediately recommend using hormone replacement, and in some cases this is necessary. However, it is worth trying a gentler approach, using supplements such as licorice root, especially to balance out cortisol levels. A typical adult dosage would be 1,000 to 2,000 milligrams of licorice root extract taken daily for two months or longer.

Other supplements that work synergistically to treat this condition include adrenal glandular, ginseng, pantothenic acid, vitamin C, beta carotene and zinc. In more serious cases, hormones such as DHEA, pregnenolone, and even cortisol may need to be used.

• **Hormone imbalance.** Licorice is one of the better hormone-balancing herbs. It appears to have a balancing effect between estrogen and progesterone, and reduces excess testosterone levels. It is commonly included in formulas for PMS and menopause.

• **Infections.** As mentioned earlier, licorice root is very good for the immune system. The soothing and anti-inflammatory effect of licorice makes it especially good for respiratory tract infections.

• **Inflammation.** Licorice has potent anti-inflammatory properties. Glycyrrhizin is an important constituent that improves the effects of cortisol in the body (powerful anti-inflammatory and antiallergy effects), without the side effects seen with pharmaceutical anti-inflammatory agents such as prednisone. It also inhibits the formation of prostaglandins, which are substances in the body that cause inflammation.

• **Inflammatory bowel disease.** Licorice root is often included in formulas designed to heal conditions such as Crohn's disease and ulcerative colitis.

• **Mouth sores.** Mouth sores, also called *aphthous ulcers*, can be helped by licorice root. One study of 20 people found that a DGL mouthwash improved the symptoms of 15 of the participants by 50% to 75% within 1 day, and complete healing of the sores within 3 days.

• **Ulcers.** One of the most popular uses of licorice extract is for ulcers of the digestive tract. The recommended form is DGL.

It has an interesting mechanism of action: It stimulates cell growth of the stomach and intestinal linings, increases the natural mucous lining of the stomach, increases blood flow to the damaged tissues and decreases muscle spasms.

In a single-blind study of 100 people with peptic ulcers, participants took either DGL (760 milligrams three times daily) or the medication *Tagamet* (cimetidine). Both groups showed equally significant healing of ulcers after 6 and 12 weeks, demonstrating that DGL is as effective as pharmaceutical medications for this condition. Another study of 874 people also demonstrated that DGL was as effective as antacids and the antiulcer drug *cimetidine* in persons with duodenal ulcers.

More important, DGL actually works to heal ulcerated tissues instead of simply suppressing stomach acid in the way antacids and drug medications do. Remember, with insufficient stomach acid, you cannot digest proteins, minerals and other nutrients very efficiently. Stomach acid also acts as a natural barrier that keeps bacteria, parasites and other microbes from penetrating the digestive tract.

REPORT #64
Natural Remedies for Celiac Disease

Jamison Starbuck, ND, naturopathic physician in family practice and a lecturer at the University of Montana, both in Missoula. She is past president of the American Association of Naturopathic Physicians and a contributing editor to *The Alternative Advisor: The Complete Guide to Natural Therapies and Alternative Treatments* (Time Life).

The next time a waiter puts a basket of fresh bread on your restaurant table, think twice before you eat it. Experts believe that at least one out of every 100 American adults has celiac disease, a condition that can make sufferers ill after eating even a single slice of bread. The culprit is gluten—a type of protein found in wheat, barley, rye and, in some cases, oats that creates an autoimmune, inflammatory reaction in the small intestine. The usual symptoms are bloating and diarrhea, but some people also experience abdominal pain and/or constipation. In some cases, celiac disease causes only a blistery, itchy skin condition (*dermatitis herpetiformis*) or fatigue.

If you think you might have celiac disease, discuss it with your doctor. A diagnosis requires specific blood tests and, in some cases, an intestinal biopsy. If you do have celiac disease, your medical doctor will tell you to completely avoid gluten. This may sound like hard work, since gluten is in all sorts of things you might not suspect, such as many kinds of soy sauce, creamed soups and salad dressings. But it is definitely doable and gets easier as you learn where gluten-free products (even bread and pasta) are available—for example, in many health-food stores and a growing number of restaurants.

Payoff: Once you start avoiding gluten, your celiac symptoms will disappear over a period of weeks and months. *Other steps to consider...* *

•**Take supplements.** Inflammation in the small intestine interferes with the absorption of key nutrients. I advise my celiac patients to take a daily regimen that includes 5 mg of folic acid...800 international units (IU) each of vitamins E and D...25,000 IU of vitamin A...and 2 mg of vitamin K.

Note: Vitamin K supplements should be avoided by patients taking *warfarin* (Coumadin) or another blood thinner. I also recommend taking a botanical formula that contains one or more of these herbs (in powdered form)—deglycyrrhizinated licorice root, slippery elm and marshmallow root. Follow label instructions and take until inflammatory bowel symptoms abate.

•**Eat healthful fats daily and fish twice a week.** Olive oil, avocado, soy milk and small portions of unsalted nuts (eight to 12) are

*To minimize inflammation, follow the dietary advice indefinitely—and also continue to take the vitamin supplements to guard against a nutritional deficiency.

good sources of healthful fat. (However, celiac patients should avoid peanuts, which can be hard for them to digest.) Fatty fish, such as salmon or halibut, is an easily digested protein source.

Warning: In people with celiac disease, high-fat dairy products, as well as fried foods, tend to worsen diarrhea.

•**Use plant-based enzymes.** Enzyme supplementation helps break down food and reduces post-meal bloating. Plant-based enzymes (available at natural-food stores) are usually derived from pineapple or papaya, and they are safe for just about everyone unless you have ulcers or you are allergic to pineapple or papaya.

Typical dose: One or two capsules per meal.

•**Get support.** Avoiding gluten isn't easy, but you'll feel much better if you do. For more advice, consult the Celiac Sprue Association/USA, 877-272-4272, *www.csaceliacs.org.*

REPORT #65
Natural Ways to Improve Digestive Health

Jamison Starbuck, ND, naturopathic physician in family practice and a lecturer at the University of Montana, both in Missoula. She is past president of the American Association of Naturopathic Physicians and a contributing editor to *The Alternative Advisor: The Complete Guide to Natural Therapies and Alternative Treatments* (Time Life).

Though sometimes overlooked by doctors, gastrointestinal (GI) health is fundamental to overall wellness. The GI tract, also known as the "gut," allows us to draw nourishment from our food and eliminate toxins. A variety of medications claim to promote intestinal health, but I prefer my own eight-step natural approach, which is both inexpensive and easy to follow. Add one new step each day. If you're like most people, your GI tract will be healthier within two weeks. *My advice...*

1. Avoid foods that cause indigestion. Indigestion is your body's way of telling you that a certain food is not readily digestible. Instead of trying to make a food digestible by taking drugs, choose foods that you can easily digest, such as fish, brown rice and steamed vegetables.

2. Shortly after awakening in the morning, drink an eight-ounce glass of room-temperature water. This "wakes up" the GI tract, preparing you for both digestion and elimination. Repeat this step five to 10 minutes before each meal. Avoid iced beverages, including water, with meals and 15 minutes before and afterward. Some research suggests that cold beverages decrease the secretion of digestive enzymes.

3. Squeeze fresh lemon or sprinkle vinegar on your food. For most people, one-half teaspoon of lemon or vinegar per meal fights indigestion by increasing stomach acidity and improving the digestion of fats.

4. Take a 15-minute walk after meals. Doing so will improve your digestion and elimination. If you can't do this after every meal, do so following the largest meal of the day.

5. Practice simple home hydrotherapy. This practice increases blood flow to your intestines, which helps them function properly.

What to do: Finish your daily shower or bath with a 30-second spray of cool or cold water to your entire abdomen. Towel dry with brisk strokes immediately after the cool water spray.

Caution: If you have a history of stroke, check with your doctor before trying hydrotherapy.

6. Drink chamomile or peppermint tea after dinner. These herbs soothe the lining of the stomach and intestines. Add one tea bag or two teaspoons of loose herb to eight ounces of water.

7. Use foot reflexology to relieve intestinal pain. Massaging reflexology points on the feet is thought to help increase blood flow to and improve the function of corresponding organs or body parts.

What to do: Whenever you have GI discomfort, firmly massage (for five to seven minutes)

with your thumb and forefinger the outside portion of the middle one-third of the soles of the feet. According to reflexologists, this area corresponds to the colon. Your strokes should move toward the heel.

8. Never eat when you are stressed. Our bodies are not designed to simultaneously manage both stress and digestion. Studies show that just a few moments of relaxation, such as deep breathing or prayer, before a meal will improve the digestive process.

REPORT #66
Nature's Detox Program

Jamison Starbuck, ND, naturopathic physician in family practice and a lecturer at the University of Montana, both in Missoula. She is past president of the American Association of Naturopathic Physicians and a contributing editor to The Alternative Advisor: The Complete Guide to Natural Therapies and Alternative Treatments *(Time Life).*

Cleansing the liver with so-called "detox" products is becoming more and more popular these days. Such products are theoretically designed to help the liver more efficiently perform its many functions that are crucial to your daily health. For example, the liver makes bile, a substance stored in the gallbladder and used in digestion and elimination. But the liver also synthesizes nutrients, including hormones and proteins, and plays an important role in the metabolism of fats and carbohydrates. In addition, the liver breaks down potentially dangerous compounds, including most medications, turning them into particles that the body can excrete via urine or stool.

But anyone who considers using one of these detox products should remember "buyer beware" and proceed only with the advice of a doctor. I see many patients each year who experience ill effects from over-the-counter "liver detox" pills. They typically suffer liver or gallbladder pain, diarrhea, constipation and/or gastrointestinal cramping. Instead of liver detox pills, I recommend trying the time-tested foods and liver "tonic" described below to promote optimal functioning of this vital organ...

Root vegetables—especially carrots and beets—have a long tradition as liver "medicine." They are rich in antioxidant vitamins and minerals that help the liver remove toxins from the body.

My advice: Eat two raw carrots daily...or add one-quarter cup each of shredded carrots and beets to a salad. As an alternative, eat a baked beet salad (bake fresh beets 25 to 45 minutes at 400°, slice and add olive oil, vinegar and any seasoning you like) and include steamed carrots in your diet several times a week.

"Bitter" leafy greens, such as dandelion, mustard, kale and beet tops, also promote good liver health. Leafy greens assist with fat metabolism and bile production and are high in folate, a nutrient that is essential for healthy cell development.

My advice: Include at least one portion (one-half cup cooked or one cup raw) of these bitter greens (steamed or added to soup or stew or finely chopped raw in a salad) in your daily diet.

Caution: People who take a blood thinner, such as *warfarin* (Coumadin), should not add more greens to their diet—the vitamin K in greens can interfere with the drug.

Milk thistle. Research has shown that this herb can help reduce elevated liver enzymes in people recovering from such conditions as viral hepatitis, alcoholism and medication-induced liver damage.

For a short-term liver tonic: Add one teaspoon of ground or powdered milk thistle seeds to your food each day for one month. You can buy the whole seeds in natural-food grocery stores and grind or powder them at home in a coffee mill. If you find it to be more convenient, you also can buy ground or powdered milk thistle at most natural-food stores. Ground and powdered milk thistle are equally effective. Use this tonic daily for two weeks—it will do its job by then—and repeat once every six months.

Volume 8
Anxiety and Depression Cures

REPORT #67
Soothe Anxiety with Probiotics

You already know that chocolate can do wonders for a dark mood —but...yogurt? If you buy the kind that contains active probiotics, it may indeed brighten your spirits. A new study from Canada demonstrated that probiotics can help modulate anxiety.

The study involved 35 patients with *chronic fatigue syndrome* (CFS) who experienced a host of gastrointestinal problems, including *irritable bowel syndrome* (IBS) and constipation. Participants were divided randomly into two groups, one taking a probiotic drink containing *Lactobacillus casei strain Shirota* (LaS), and the other taking a placebo that was identical in taste and appearance but had no probiotics. Results: After two months, the probiotic group had a significant decrease in anxiety symptoms, while the placebo group did not.

The probiotic group also showed a significant increase in *Bifidobacteria*, which are beneficial for gastrointestinal health, compared with the placebo group.

INTESTINAL FLORA AND YOUR BRAIN

A. Venketeshwer Rao, BSc, MSc, PhD, the study author and professor emeritus of nutritional science at University of Toronto, says that there has been skepticism in the medical world about the role intestinal flora plays in the system of gut-brain communication (the enteric nervous system, often called "the second brain"). He said that this study provides evidence that through their metabolism in the gut, probiotic bacteria can boost levels of the mood-elevating chemicals *tryptophan* (an amino acid) and *serotonin* (a neurotransmitter). He added that the regions of the brain affected by CFS also house anxiety and depression. "These parts of the brain seem to respond to changes in the microflora, and most of our

---

A. Venketeshwer Rao, BSc MSc, PhD, professor emeritus of nutritional science, University of Toronto.

behavior patterns are controlled by these areas," he says.

Dr. Rao says there still is much to learn about the role of gut flora. But many, if not most people, could improve their health by taking probiotics. The study used a probiotic drink, but Dr. Rao says that probiotic supplements may be even more effective, depending on what types and how many of the live microbes they contain. He advises looking for a product that contains *Lactobacillus Shirota* and *Bifidobacteria*, with 100 to 120 billion live probiotic bacteria.

REPORT #68
Six Self-Help Ways to Ease Anxiety

Michael McKee, PhD, cognitive-behavioral therapist in private practice in Scarsdale, New York, and research scientist at the Anxiety Disorders Clinic, New York State Psychiatric Institute, New York City.

Here are six simple ways to ease anxiety on your own—without help from a therapist…

- **Exercise.** Research shows that all kinds of exercise will make you feel more confident and at ease. Aerobic exercise stimulates release of endorphins, neurotransmitters that are the body's natural "feel good" drug. Yoga can calm nerves.
- **Deep breathing.** Slow breathing from deep in the diaphragm (belly breathing) slows racing thoughts and restores a sense of control.
- **Progressive muscle relaxation.** To remove tension from your muscles, clench them tightly for a full five seconds, then slowly release. Do this for individual body parts starting with your toes and working all the way up to your face.
- **Cut back on coffee.** The caffeine in coffee is a stimulant, so if you are nervous, it will make you more so. Switch to green tea—it has much less caffeine. Green tea also contains amino acids that researchers believe have a calming effect on the brain.

- **Limit alcohol consumption.** It stimulates stress hormones, so have no more than one alcoholic beverage a day.
- **Keep a "joy journal."** Write down on a piece of paper a list of all the good things in your life. Take notes during the day of any funny, entertaining or rewarding things that occur. By consciously thinking about them, they will become more meaningful than stressful parts of your life.

REPORT #69
Bananas Fight Depression, Heartburn And More

Ara DerMarderosian, PhD, professor, Department of Biological Sciences and research professor of pharmacognosy (the study of natural products used in medicine) at the University of the Sciences in Philadelphia. He also is the scientific director of the University's Complementary and Alternative Medicines Institute. Dr. DerMarderosian has published more than 100 scientific papers and chapters in books as well as two books.

Most people know that bananas are an excellent source of potassium (one ripe banana supplies more than 10% of an adult's daily requirement of the mineral). That's important because people with a low dietary intake of potassium are 28% more likely to suffer a stroke than those who consume higher levels, according to a study conducted at Tulane University.

Lesser-known medicinal uses of bananas…

- **Depression.** Bananas are a good source of tryptophan (a precursor to serotonin, a brain chemical that helps regulate mood).
- **Diarrhea.** Unripe bananas and plantains (high-starch, green bananas that are typically cooked) are a rich source of tannins, astringent plant compounds that help stop water accumulation in the intestines, thus diminishing diarrhea.
- **Heartburn and ulcers.** Bananas neutralize acidity and soothe and coat esophageal tissue with pectin (a substance used as a thickener and stabilizer in jellies).

Important: In rare cases, bananas may cause an allergic reaction. Bananas with blackened skin can increase blood sugar levels. Because bananas have high levels of potassium, people with kidney problems should check with their doctors before eating this fruit.

REPORT #70
Ear Seeds Help Weight Loss, Insomnia, Depression, Pain and More

Jeffrey Zimmerman, OMD, LAc, once a classical musician, is a Doctor of Oriental Medicine, licensed acupuncturist, martial artist and Qigong master in Westport, Connecticut.

At a family picnic a few months ago, my cousin raved about a form of acupuncture that brought her almost immediate relief from the depression, anxiety and insomnia she'd wrestled with for months. Called *auricular* (ear) *therapy*, this sub-type of acupuncture involves insertion of very small needles or taping tiny metal "seeds" onto various places in the ear. Auricular therapy can be useful in beating back demons like smoking, alcohol or drug addiction...helpful for people seeking to lose weight...soothing for chronic pain, as with arthritis...useful for treating nausea and high blood pressure...and for numerous other problems, including those related to mood. My cousin told me that the night after her first treatment, she slept soundly and woke up feeling free from the sense of doom that had long engulfed her.

HOW DOES IT WORK?

Acupuncture of the ear has been popular in China for centuries, but what's been known as auricular therapy was developed in the 1950s when a French doctor named Paul Nogier, MD, mapped specific sites, called points, on the ear based on the shape of a fetus (or *homunculus*). Take a careful look at a human ear, probably someone else's, and see if you can detect the outline of an inverted fetus. This may challenge your imagination, but the concept is important—it is the key to understanding how auricular therapy works. This "ear map" is how the acupuncturist finds the particular points that correspond to the problem area of the patient's body.

Though the exact mechanism that makes auricular therapy effective isn't clear, a possible explanation is that stimulating certain nerves sends signals to the brain, generating a reflex response that sends soothing sensations to the targeted body part.

EXPERT INSIGHTS INTO AURICULAR THERAPY

To find out more about this unusual therapy, we spoke with Jeff Zimmerman, OMD, LAc, a doctor of Oriental medicine and licensed acupuncturist in Westport, Connecticut. He told me he likes to use auricular therapy in conjunction with other types of acupuncture, though many practitioners treat certain types of problems with ear therapy alone. Most practitioners begin a session with a discussion of your motivation for wanting to, say, cut back on or stop drinking alcohol. You may be asked what obstacles have presented challenges in previous efforts, since treatment is tailored not just to your problem but also to how it interacts with your life. Depending on the specific way you experience the problem (e.g., drink until you pass out versus become a loud and angry drunk), different points will be used.

How many seeds or needles a practitioner uses varies—Dr. Zimmerman says he secures about five to seven seeds per ear under a small adhesive dressing (like tape), which should stay in place until the next treatment. Patients learn how to massage the points where the seeds are, thereby activating their effect at least three times a day and/or when they need relief from pain or anxiety or have an urge for the forbidden substance. This massaging may even help them when the seeds are removed.

Dr. Zimmerman says some of his patients have triumphed over a bad smoking habit after just one session, but that the general routine for an addiction treatment is six weekly sessions and then perhaps continuing another month or two after those. Some patients need "tune-up" therapy from time to time, and he noted that patients who seek auricular therapy for chronic pain or depression may want to return for a treatment every few months or so to keep their energy flowing freely.

PRACTICAL POINTERS

Auricular therapy is not covered by all health insurance plans, but may be paid for as part of acupuncture. However, even insurers who won't cover the primary cost of treatments may allow you to deduct them from a flexible spending account—check your policy. Prices vary considerably, depending on where you live and the kind of training your practitioner has had, with $50 or $60 per half-hour session a good ballpark estimate.

When looking for a practitioner, Zimmerman says to check for certification by the NC-CAOM (National Certification Commission for Acupuncture and Oriental Medicine, *www.nccaom.org*) and licensing by your state specifically for acupuncture. Before you book, inquire about his/her experience in treating your particular problem. He adds that it is important to be an educated consumer—ask around for information about the person you are considering and trust your instincts when you meet.

REPORT #71
Depression Prevention Diet

In a study of more than 10,000 men and women without depression, those who most closely adhered to the Mediterranean diet (rich in fruits, vegetables, legumes, nuts, olive oil, fish and whole grains) over an average 4.4-year period were about half as likely to develop depression.

Theory: The diet enhances function of the *endothelium* (the blood vessels' inner lining), which is needed to support the brain-cell development that helps prevent depression.

If you are at risk for depression (due to family history or recent stressful life events):

Try the Mediterranean diet. Learn more at *www.OldWayspt.org/mediterranean-diet-pyramid*.

Miguel A. Martínez-Gonzalez, MD, PhD, professor and chair, department of preventive medicine, University of Navarra, Pamplona, Spain.

REPORT #72
Dr. Joy Browne on Getting The Help You Need

Joy Browne, PhD, licensed clinical psychologist in New York City and host of a daily syndicated radio show. She is author of several books, including *Getting Unstuck: 8 Simple Steps to Solving Any Problem, Dating Disasters and How to Avoid Them* (both from Hay House). *www.drjoy.com*.

As a psychologist, I am struck by the way people tend to isolate themselves during painful times. Whether dealing with losing a job, the end of a relationship or any major disappointment, it seems that when we most need other people, we find it most difficult to ask for help.

One reason is that people believe—erroneously—that they should be able to handle problems themselves. They don't want to impose or be a burden.

The truth is that most people like being asked for help. Think about how you feel when a friend needs your help. It's flattering. It means that your friend is taking the relationship seriously. Giving and receiving make friendships stronger.

BE SPECIFIC

Some people feel it's up to friends and loved ones to recognize distress and offer help without being asked, but it's unrealistic to expect others to read your mind or catch your hints. *Here are ways to ask for the help you need…*

•**Problem solving.** "I can't figure out what to do. Would you mind brainstorming options with me?"

•**A sympathetic ear.** "It's been a tough week. Can I tell you about it?"

●**Reassurance.** "I'm discouraged. I'd love it if you could remind me of the things I'm doing right in my life."

●**Perspective.** "I'm not sure if the problem is me or him. Can I get your take on the situation?"

●**Sympathy.** "My boss is on a rampage. I don't need to hear about how I should handle him—I just want someone to take my side for a few minutes."

●**Affection.** "I could use a hug."

●**Company.** "Would it be OK if I came over for a few hours? I don't want to be alone this afternoon."

●**Suggestions.** "My computer crashed. Can you recommend a good repair service?"

●**Physical assistance.** "I'm too sick to go out. Could you stop by the deli and pick up some soup for me?"

●**Practice.** Don't wait until you're in a crisis to ask for help. Practice in situations that aren't so traumatic.

Example: When your car is in the shop, call a friend and say, "Would you be able to give me a ride to work?"

SHOW APPRECIATION

Helping isn't something you contract for. Treating your request as a quid pro quo ("If you do X for me, I'll do Y for you") is likely to offend. Instead, be generous with your thanks.

Examples: Send a thank-you note...flowers...or a small gift.

REPORT #73
Depressed? Give New Eyeglasses a Try

Eyeglasses can ease depression among the elderly.

Recent finding: After two months, seniors who received properly prescribed eyeglasses had higher scores for activities, hobbies and social interaction—and fewer signs of depression—than seniors with similar visual acuity who were not given new eyeglasses.

Cynthia Owsley, PhD, professor, department of ophthalmology, University of Alabama at Birmingham, and leader of a study of 78 nursing home residents, published in *Archives of Ophthalmology*.

REPORT #74
How I Calm Down

Joy Browne, PhD, licensed clinical psychologist in New York City and host of a daily syndicated radio show. She is author of several books, including *Getting Unstuck: 8 Simple Steps to Solving Any Problem*, *Dating Disasters and How to Avoid Them* (both from Hay House). *www.drjoy.com.*

In prehistoric times, if you failed to feel enough anxiety to trigger a fight-or-flight response, you got eaten by a saber-toothed tiger. Even today, the body's instant reaction to danger includes a surge of the stress hormone adrenaline—causing rapid breathing, pounding heart, tingling hands and nausea. This floods large muscles with energy-giving oxygen by increasing breathing and heart rate and by diverting blood from the extremities and digestive tract.

Problem is, this also occurs in situations that aren't physically dangerous—such as being caught in traffic on your way to an appointment. It's tough to focus on the task at hand during an anxiety attack. Worse, repeated adrenaline surges and other anxiety responses can contribute to hypertension, digestive disorders, weakened immunity and depression.

To ease anxiety: A technique called *square breathing* helps me regain control over my body and mind by reestablishing the proper ratio of oxygen to carbon dioxide in my system. I inhale deeply for a count of four...hold for four...exhale slowly for four...hold for four...and repeat until anxiety subsides. It's like giving my body a mini-vacation. You can use it any time—when preparing to make a toast, waiting for test results—because it is inconspicuous.

REPORT #75
Drug-Free Depression Treatments

David Mischoulon, MD, PhD, assistant professor of psychiatry at Harvard Medical School and director of Research and Alternative Remedy Studies at the Depression Clinical and Research Program, Massachusetts General Hospital, Boston.

Depression remains stubbornly intractable for many of the estimated 20-plus million Americans who suffer from it. Many of these people have difficulties with the pharmaceutical drugs so often prescribed for depression, finding them either ineffective or to cause disagreeable side effects including lowered libido and weight gain. Also several of these drugs have been associated with an increased risk for suicide, though this remains a controversial issue. All this has opened the door to a growing interest in natural solutions for depression. Research into CAM (complementary and alternative medicine) treatments for depression is active in some very mainstream academic medical centers, and several natural substances have earned a respected position on the list of depression treatment alternatives.

A chief researcher in this area is David Mischoulon, MD, PhD, assistant professor of psychiatry, Harvard Medical School, and director of Alternative Remedy Studies at the Depression Clinical and Research Program, Massachusetts General Hospital. We spoke with Dr. Mischoulon recently to get an update on alternative treatments for depression.

THE "BIG THREE"

Depression researchers refer to the "big three" in natural substances for treating depression. One well-studied natural treatment is SAM-e (*S-adenosyl methionine*), a synthetic form of a chemical produced naturally in the body with numerous functions including influencing moods and emotions. Research on SAM-e and depression has been encouraging, showing that it works better than placebo and that it is as effective as *tricyclics*, a class of older antidepressants that dates back to the 1950s

and is still very popular today. Dr. Mischoulon's research group is now studying SAM-e against the newer antidepressant drugs, SSRIs (*selective serotonin reuptake inhibitors*) such as *fluoxetine* (Prozac) and *sertraline* (Zoloft). The typical prescribed dosage of SAM-e is 800 to 1,600 mg a day, and SAM-e seems to be well-tolerated, with few if any immediate side effects.

Next, perhaps surprisingly, comes omega-3 fatty acids. We have known for some time that omega-3 fatty acids help treat many physical conditions, including cardiovascular disease. But Dr. Mischoulon says there have been numerous studies on omega-3 fatty acids and their impact on mental health, including bipolar disorder as well as depression, with many suggesting that these fatty acids are indeed effective. The types of omega-3 fatty acids that help with depression are EPA and DHA, found in cold-water fish and fish oil supplements. Psychiatric benefits are commonly obtained with about 1,000 mg a day of combined EPA/DHA.

And then there is our old friend, St. John's wort (*hypericum perforatum*). Dr. Mischoulon says that it has tested well in a number of studies, including against older antidepressant drugs. Studies have shown that this substance is calming while at the same time it seems to work in part like SSRIs. Recommended doses are on the order of 900 to 1,200 mg per day, but because of subtleties regarding dosage and the fact that St. John's wort is known to interact with many other medications, it's imperative to take this supplement under the supervision of a medical professional experienced in its use.

OTHER NATURAL TREATMENTS

Yet another substance that Dr. Mischoulon says may be helpful is Valerian (*valeriana officinalis*). It has primarily been studied as a sleep aid, but Dr. Mischoulon says it may also be useful for anxiety. It's important to keep in mind that Valerian requires several weeks to work, whether for sleep purposes or for anxiety relief, although many report feeling positive effects fairly quickly. The usual dose administered is 400 mg to 600 mg of extract in capsule form, but there is considerable variety among brands as to purity and active ingredients. Different brands may achieve different results in different people, so Dr. Mischoulon says not to give up if a particular one doesn't work for you.

A number of physical treatment modalities are being incorporated in depression treatment, though research remains limited. Acupuncture is one that studies have found promising, says Dr. Mischoulon. Curiously, acupuncture studies have an unusually high placebo-effect rate (subjects on placebo showing improvement), so how much acupuncture actually helps is unclear. On the other hand, most people find acupuncture to be neither painful nor harmful, so it may be worth a try.

Exercise has also been studied with regard to potential benefits for depressed people, with new studies suggesting beneficial mood-elevating effects. However, because depression tends to cause a decrease in energy and motivation, it can be difficult to get depressed people to engage in exercise programs, Dr. Mischoulon acknowledged. But if they can push past the lethargy, they may be pleasantly surprised by how good exercise makes them feel—including the sense of accomplishment.

DEPRESSION IS MANAGEABLE

Anyone who experiences depression for more than a few weeks should seek professional treatment, says Dr. Mischoulon. Though it may take a while to find the treatment that works for you, it is important to remember that depression is usually manageable. Left untreated, it can become chronic and difficult to treat.

When choosing to treat depression with natural substances, always work under the supervision of a naturopathic physician or other health care professional who can help identify the best solution for you. To find such a doctor, seek referrals from your primary care physician and consult the database of the AANP (American Association of Naturopathic Physicians) at *www.naturopathic.org*. Click on "Find a Doctor." Then speak with the doctors to find one that seems to be a good fit for you.

Patience is in order—just as with pharmaceutical drugs for depression, natural treatments often require time to take effect, from three to six weeks, says Dr. Mischoulon. Finally, some of these therapies have been found effective in treating mild to moderate depression. While some may be of help for severe depression, the evidence to date relates only to the milder forms—treatment of more serious cases may require a different strategy.

REPORT #76
Lies and Half-Truths About Herbal Supplements

Mark A. Stengler, NMD, licensed naturopathic medical doctor in private practice, La Jolla, California…adjunct associate clinical professor at the National College of Natural Medicine, Portland, Oregon…author of many books, including *The Natural Physician's Healing Therapies* and coauthor of *Prescription for Natural Cures* (both from Bottom Line Books)…and author of the *Bottom Line/Natural Healing* newsletter.

I have exposed some of the lies and half-truths about nutritional supplements, including vitamins. Herbal supplements also have gotten an undeserved bashing in recent years. Yet millions of people benefit from these safe natural remedies. Also, many prescription drugs are based on plant molecules. Herbs often work as well as, or better than, medications—and they are much gentler on the body.

Lie: St. John's wort doesn't help severe depression.

Truth: A study published in the *Journal of the American Medical Association* (JAMA) claimed that St. John's wort did not help severe depression, which is difficult to treat even with pharmaceutical drugs. As a result, many headlines stated that St. John's wort was ineffective for all types of depression. At that time, the herb was most often used to treat mild-to-moderate depression—it worked well, caused few side effects and was less expensive than antidepressants. In a later study, an analysis of 29 studies in which St. John's wort was used to treat major depression was published in the *Cochrane Database of Systematic Reviews*. The article concluded that the herb worked just as well as drugs, although the dose to treat severe depression was higher than that needed to treat milder forms. Yet the impression left by the earlier study remained.

Note: St. John's wort should not be taken with an antidepressant or by women who are pregnant, breast-feeding or taking birth control pills.

Lie: Garlic does not reduce blood pressure.

Truth: There's evidence that garlic supplements can reduce blood pressure in people who have high blood pressure. Analyses of studies in *Annals of Pharmacotherapy* and *BMC Cardiovascular Disorders* confirmed that garlic lowered systolic blood pressure (the top number in a blood pressure reading) or both systolic and diastolic blood pressure (bottom number). Despite this evidence, conventional medical doctors typically don't prescribe garlic to lower blood pressure.

Brand to try: Kyolic Healthy Heart Formula 106, which provides 300 milligrams (mg) of aged garlic extract (800-421-2998, *www.kyolic. com*).

Lie: Echinacea does not help fight the common cold.

Truth: An analysis of 14 studies published in *The Lancet Infectious Diseases* found that echinacea supplements reduced the risk of catching a cold by 58% and reduced the length of colds by 1.4 days, on average. This herb's effectiveness may be in question because not all echinacea products are of the same quality or strength, which means dosages vary.

Brand to try: Nature's Way Echinacea (800-962-8873, *www.natureswey.com* for a store locator).

Lie: Black cohosh makes breast cancer spread.

Truth: Many women use this herb to reduce hot flashes. An old theory is that black cohosh contains weak estrogen-like plant compounds that attach to estrogen receptors on the surface of the cell that could raise the risk for breast cancer. Concern increased when research published in *Cancer Research* found that mice bred

to develop aggressive breast cancer were more likely to have the cancer spread to their lungs when given this herb. Other studies published in *Maturitas* and *BMC Pharmacology* demonstrated that black cohosh reduces estrogen levels and does not contain phytoestrogens (estrogen-like plant compounds). Also, a National Institutes of Health sponsored study published in *International Journal of Cancer* that compared the supplement use of women with and without breast cancer found that women who took black cohosh had a 61% lower risk for breast cancer. I believe that black cohosh is safe for all women, even those who have a history of breast cancer.

Lie: Saw palmetto is not effective for benign prostate enlargement.

Truth: Enlargement of the prostate gland, known as *benign prostatic hypertrophy* (BPH), commonly affects men age 50 and older. The main symptom is reduced or erratic urinary flow. One study found that saw palmetto did not help men who had severe BPH. But many other studies reviewed in the *Cochrane Database of Systematic Reviews* have found that it does help men with mild-to-moderate BPH, which is the more common condition. For men with this condition, saw palmetto works just as well as prescription drugs, with fewer side effects—and it is less expensive.

Half-truth: Licorice root raises blood pressure.

Truth: In very large amounts, licorice root can increase blood pressure and deplete potassium, so if you have heart disease, diabetes or high blood pressure, you should not have licorice root tea or black licorice candies frequently. But these warnings about licorice don't apply to people who don't have these conditions or to multi-ingredient formulas that contain very small amounts of the herb. Most licorice supplements, which help to improve digestion, heartburn and ulcers, are *deglycyrrhized*, which means that the sweet-tasting ingredient that raises blood pressure has been removed.

Lie: Ginseng increases blood pressure.

Truth: Conventional medical physicians and organizations often advise patients who have high blood pressure against taking certain types of ginseng. Studies published in *Hypertension* found that different types of ginseng, including Asian ginseng (Panax ginseng), did not increase blood pressure—and a study published in *Annals of Pharmacotherapy* found that Panax ginseng actually reduced it. I believe that ginseng can safely be used by those with high blood pressure.

REPORT #77
Natural Remedies a Pharmacist Has in Her Own Medicine Cabinet

Suzy Cohen, RPh, registered practicing pharmacist for over 20 years and author of *The 24-Hour Pharmacist* (Collins). Her syndicated newspaper column, "Dear Pharmacist," reaches more than 24 million readers. Based in Florida, she is a member of the American College for Advancement in Medicine, American Academy of Anti-Aging Medicine, and American Pharmacist's Association.

As a pharmacist for almost two decades, Suzy Cohen knows the importance of medication—but she also has learned to "think outside the pill" and recommend natural options that often are just as good or better at promoting health without the risk of dangerous side effects.

Here are the remedies she recommends most often. All are free of significant side effects unless otherwise noted, but always talk with your doctor before using any supplements.

TEA TREE OIL FOR WOUNDS

This oil kills germs, reduces pain and helps wounds heal more quickly. You can use it in place of antibiotic ointment for minor cuts, scratches and burns…to treat toenail fungus… and, when diluted, as a gargle to kill the germs that cause sore throat.

How it works: It's a strong antiseptic that kills bacteria as well as fungi.

How to use: Moisten a cotton ball or swab with one or two drops of the oil, and apply it to the area two to three times daily until it heals.

For a gargle for sore throat: Mix a few drops in a cup of water, gargle and spit it out.

Caution: Do not swallow it.

GINGER FOR NAUSEA

Studies have shown that ginger can relieve nausea—due to pregnancy, seasickness, etc.—as well as or better than over-the-counter drugs.

How it works: Ginger increases the pH of stomach acid, reducing its acidity. In one study, published in *The Lancet*, volunteers were given either ginger or Dramamine (a nausea-preventing drug), then were seated in a chair designed to trigger motion sickness. Those given ginger were able to withstand the motion 57% longer than those given the drug.

How to use: Put one teaspoon of peeled, grated fresh gingerroot in a cup of boiling water. Let it steep for 10 minutes, then drink (you can filter out the ginger if you want). Or chew and swallow a piece of crystallized ginger, sold in health-food stores.

Caution: Ginger can increase the risk of bleeding when taken with blood-thinning drugs, such as *warfarin* (Coumadin).

RHODIOLA ROSEA FOR STRESS

This herb acts like a natural form of Valium by reducing physical and emotional stress. The supplement is made from the root of the Siberian plant.

How it works: Herbalists classify Rhodiola as an adaptogen, a class of herbs that "sense" chemicals in the body and either raise or lower them. It normalizes levels of brain chemicals that affect mood, such as monoamines and beta-endorphins, which help counter the effects of stress. Rhodiola also may increase serotonin, which enhances feelings of well-being.

How to use: During times of stress, take 100 milligrams (mg) of rhodiola rosea in capsule form, two to three times daily. It's best taken on a cyclical basis—two months on, two weeks off.

CALCIUM PLUS MAGNESIUM
FOR CRAMPS

People who experience frequent and/or painful menstrual or muscle cramps often have a deficiency of calcium and magnesium.

How it works: Calcium and magnesium regulate the contraction and relaxation of muscles.

How to use: Before going to bed, take 500 mg to 600 mg of calcium, along with 150 mg to 200 mg of magnesium (using the chelate or glycinate forms—check the label). Combination formulas are easy to find and fine to use.

For menstrual problems, start 10 days before you expect your period to begin each month and continue until your period is complete.

GABA FOR INSOMNIA

Gamma-aminobutyric acid (GABA) is a neurotransmitter (mood-related brain chemical) that is naturally present in the body. It's taken in supplement form to reduce insomnia, as well as anxiety and depression.

How it works: GABA is an inhibitory neurotransmitter that slows activity in the brain and makes it easier to fall asleep.

How to use: Take 500 mg to 1,000 mg one hour before bedtime if you have trouble getting to sleep. If your problem is that you wake in the middle of the night and can't get back to sleep, take it then. Don't exceed recommended doses on the package. Do this for two weeks. If it doesn't help, talk to your doctor.

Caution: Combining GABA with prescription or over-the-counter sleep aids can cause excessive sedation.

CAPSAICIN CREAM
FOR PAIN

Capsaicin is the chemical compound that puts the "hot" in chili peppers. It is effective for easing muscle aches, back and joint pain and nerve pain caused by the herpes virus (*post-herpetic neuralgia*).

How it works: When applied as a cream, it causes nerve cells to empty their reservoirs of substance P, a pain-causing chemical. This results in less pain from the underlying disorder.

How to use: Start with a 0.025% concentration. Apply it two to three times daily—the initial burning sensation diminishes with continued use. If needed, you can always buy the stronger 0.075% concentration—but it's best to work your way up to this strength.

Caution: Wear latex gloves when applying capsaicin—and wash your hands thoroughly after using to prevent residual cream from getting into the eyes, nose, etc.

PROBIOTICS FOR
DIGESTIVE DISCOMFORT

A healthy digestive tract contains trillions of bacteria, many of which have beneficial effects. These so-called "good" (probiotic) organisms promote digestive health, improve immunity and aid in the synthesis of B vitamins, among many other functions.

How they work: Probiotic supplements replenish beneficial bacteria and crowd out harmful organisms that can cause gas, bloating, diarrhea and other digestive problems.

How to use: Take a daily supplement of at least 10 billion organisms that contains a variety of living organisms, such as *L. bulgaricus*, *L. bifida* and *B. longum*. Some yogurts contain these live active cultures, but avoid those that contain sugar or artificial sweeteners.

BIOTIN
FOR CRACKED NAILS

The B vitamin biotin is the only nutrient that has been shown to improve nail health in generally healthy adults. People with a deficiency of biotin often have fragile nails that crack easily.

How it works: Biotin is absorbed by the nail matrix, the part under the fingernail where nail cells are generated.

How to use: Take 2,000 micrograms (mcg) to 4,000 mcg of biotin daily, as well as a B-complex supplement. Most people will notice an improvement in nail strength and thickness in one to two months.

REPORT #78
Meditation for Women Who Hate to Sit Still

Judith Boice, ND, naturopathic physician and acupuncturist in private practice in Montrose, Colorado. She conducts wellness seminars nationwide and is author of eight books, including *Menopause with Science and Soul: A Guidebook for Navigating the Journey* (Celestial Arts). *www.drjudithboice.com.*

Meditation is good for us—it can relieve tension by shifting brain activity away from the stress-prone right frontal cortex and into the calmer left frontal cortex. But some people have trouble finding time to meditate—or just can't seem to sit still.

Solution: Combine exercise and meditation through rhythmic, repetitive motions, such as walking, swimming or rowing, so you simultaneously strengthen the body and soothe the mind.

Bonus: "Meditation in motion" makes exercise easier, because while you do it, you won't be thinking about tired muscles or tasks that await after your workout. *Begin with walking meditation...*

• **Pick a spot.** Find a secluded outdoor area where you won't feel self-conscious...or an empty hallway where you won't bump into furniture.

• **Begin walking.** Start slowly, focusing on the rhythm of your heels striking the ground and your toes pushing off. Keep your eyes open for safety, but don't get distracted by the sights around you.

• **Recite a mantra.** Choose or invent a rhythmic chant, such as "I am one with the world, I am filled with peace." Repeat it over and over, out loud or in your mind, melding its rhythm with the movement of your feet. I recommend not listening to music—it may distract you from your mantra.

• **Try to stay focused.** At first you may succeed for only a few minutes before thoughts of daily life intrude. Work your way up to a 30-minute session daily.

• **Meditate at the gym.** Once you've mastered walking meditation, try the technique while using a treadmill or elliptical machine or while swimming laps.

REPORT #79
Saffron, the Happiness Spice

From *Bottom Line's Breakthroughs in Drug-Free Healing* by Bill Gottlieb. (Bottom Line Books). *www.bottomlinesecrets.com.*

Think saffron, and you probably think of the world's most expensive spice, and the golden-yellow color of saffron-containing dishes, such as Spanish paella or Indian biryani. What you probably don't think of is depression. But some psychiatrists do.

BREAKTHROUGH STUDIES

Doctors at the Psychiatric Research Center at the Tehran University of Medical Sciences in Iran (the country that produces 80% of the world's saffron) studied 40 people with depression, dividing them into two groups. One group received the antidepressant *fluoxetine* (Prozac). The other group received saffron capsules.

Result: After six weeks, both groups had the same level of relief from depression.

"The results of this study indicate the effectiveness of *Crocus sativus* [saffron] in the treatment of mild to moderate depression," say the researchers, in the *Journal of Ethnopharmacology.*

In another study by the same team of researchers, saffron matched the depression-ending power of *imipramine* (Tofranil), a drug in the tricyclic class of antidepressants.

Suggested intake: The researchers used 30 mg a day.

• **EXIR Saffron Dietary Supplements** are available at *www.amazon.com.*

REPORT #80
Natural Remedies for Depression

Tod Cooperman, MD, founder and president of ConsumerLab.com, the leading independent evaluator of nutritional and vitamin/mineral supplements, White Plains, New York. Reports can be found at *www.consumerlab.com* (subscription required). He also is editor of *ConsumerLab.com's Guide to Buying Vitamins & Supplements* (ConsumerLab.com).

Most people assume that prescription medications are stronger and more effective than supplements. But some supplements can be just as effective—without the side effects that often accompany prescription drugs.

Also, people with chronic conditions who have no insurance or are under-insured or who have been hit with higher co-pays can save hundreds or even thousands of dollars a year by using supplements in place of drugs.

Caution: Always check with your doctor before stopping a prescription drug or taking a supplement.

Here, natural alternatives to commonly prescribed medications. If there are two alternatives, try one. If that doesn't work, try the other. Dosages are those typically prescribed, but always follow directions on the supplement label or from your health practitioner.

DEPRESSION

Antidepressant medications, including *selective serotonin reuptake inhibitors* (SSRIs), such as *paroxetine* (Paxil), *escitalopram* (Lexapro) and *citalopram* (Celexa), have revolutionized the treatment of depression. Many people who take them, however, experience troublesome side effects, including heightened anxiety and reduced libido.

Alternative 1: **St. John's wort.** It appears to be as effective for mild-to-moderate depression as SSRIs but with milder side effects. It is not effective for patients with major depression and should not be taken with prescription antidepressants. It also may interact with other medications, including blood thinners, such as *warfarin* (Coumadin).

Dose: 300 mg, three times daily. Look for a product that contains 1% to 3% *hypericin*, the active ingredient.

Alternative 2: **Fish oil.** It improves a number of emotional and mental disorders, including depression and bipolar disorder. A study found that those who combined EPA with an antidepressant medication did better than those using either treatment alone.

Dose: 1 g of EPA, once daily, or eat three or more fish servings a week.

Caution: Fish oil may interact with blood-thinning drugs such as *warfarin* (Coumadin).

Volume 9
Diabetes Cures

REPORT #81

Cures from the Kitchen— Common Foods that Help Stave Off Serious Diseases

If we could reduce the incidence of diabetes, high blood pressure and osteoporosis, we'd slash medical expenses in this country by tens—maybe hundreds—of billions of dollars. What's especially compelling about these three illnesses is that the cost of prevention is virtually nothing, while the cost of treatment is exorbitant...but obvious as it is, people are resistant. We recently spoke with nutritionist Joy Bauer, MS, RD, the author of *Joy Bauer's Food Cures* (Rodale) and nutrition expert for the *Today* Show about how eating the right foods can significantly reduce the incidence and effects of diabetes, high blood pressure and osteoporosis, among other maladies. She shared with me her favorite food fighters to help keep these particularly common age-related medical problems at bay.

DIABETES

It's not news. Type 2 diabetes is a serious disease and one that's skyrocketing in the US, yet it can often be controlled through closer attention to diet and exercise. This is especially true among younger people, in whom the greatest number of new cases are seen, and who can still reverse damage, which gets harder as people age. Two-thirds of Americans are now overweight, and research has shown that losing just a few of those extra pounds —say, 10 pounds over two years—can reduce your risk of diabetes by up to 30%. Even people who already need medication to manage their blood sugar and insulin levels can improve their diabetes and overall health by eating the right foods—ones that successfully

---

Joy Bauer, MS, RD, CDN, nutritionist and author of *Joy Bauer's Food Cures* (Rodale) and *The Complete Idiot's Guide to Total Nutrition* (Alpha Books). Bauer is the nutrition expert for the *Today* Show and Yahoo.com, and monthly weight-loss columnist for *SELF* magazine.

control blood sugar and weight—to ward off common and dangerous complications such as heart disease, nerve damage and illnesses of the eye. *Your best bets...*

• **Ground flaxseed.** Flaxseed contains a high percentage of soluble fiber, a component of plant cell walls that slows the absorption of glucose from food in the stomach, reduces the glycemic index and keeps blood sugar on an even keel. Other excellent sources of soluble fiber are beans (kidney, lima, black, navy, pinto), legumes (peas, lentils), oatmeal and vegetables.

Tip: A good way to eat flaxseed is to sprinkle a handful, ground, along with a few berries over a bowl of whole-grain cereal.

• **Broccoli, peppers as well as cauliflower.** These, along with a host of other high-quality, low-glycemic index foods contain many vitamins, minerals and fiber. This attribute is particularly important for diabetics, because it means these foods raise blood sugar slowly. Other healthful carbs include not just fiber-rich veggies but also unsweetened oatmeal, chickpeas, lentils, blueberries, strawberries, apples, etc., all of which are better than high-glycemic snacks like soft drinks, candy, cakes and "white" carbs such as white bread, pretzels, donuts, etc. Empty carbohydrates will not only make you fat, they also raise blood sugar quickly, leading to spikes and crashes in energy that aggravate diabetes.

• **Meat, seafood as well as fish.** For optimal blood sugar control, eat high-quality protein with those high-quality carbs as it slows their absorption, Bauer explains. Good choices include organically raised poultry and wild salmon, herring or mackerel—but not king mackerel, which like other large ocean fish is prone to mercury contamination.

HIGH BLOOD PRESSURE

High blood pressure, or hypertension, is often called "the silent killer," since many have it without experiencing obvious symptoms. But don't make the mistake of thinking the lack of symptoms means all's well inside your body—high blood pressure damages healthy blood vessels and causes inflammation. According to Bauer, you can help control high blood pressure by making sure you get enough calcium, vitamin D, magnesium and potassium in your diet. (Look for good sources of calcium and vitamin D below under osteoporosis.) *Your best bets...*

• **Unsalted pumpkin seeds, sunflower seeds, almonds and cashews.** Research shows that these magnesium-rich foods bring a variety of cardiovascular benefits. They can reduce high blood pressure, lower blood fats known as triglycerides and lower "bad" LDL cholesterol.

Tip: Instead of reaching for chips or candy, snack on a daily handful of healthful seeds or nuts.

• **Bananas, avocados and sweet potatoes.** Potassium-packed foods help your body maintain a normal balance between sodium and potassium, which in turn helps regulate blood pressure. There are plenty of foods rich in potassium including beans, lentils, split peas, kale, Swiss chard, radicchio, arugula, papaya, pistachio nuts, butternut squash, mushrooms, cantaloupe and carrots.

Tip: Make a batch of lentil, split pea, mushroom or other tasty homemade soup each week, and refrigerate or freeze individual portions for quick and healthful snacks and meals.

OSTEOPOROSIS

When it comes to fighting osteoporosis, the key nutrients to focus on are calcium and vitamin D in order to help maintain bone strength and density. *Your best bets...*

• **Kale, broccoli and white beans.** Everyone knows that milk and other dairy products such as yogurt and cheese are good sources of calcium, but these three non-dairy sources can also help you meet your daily requirements.

Tip: For bone support, enjoy a vegetable salad tossed with raw broccoli, white beans and salmon or sardines with bones, drizzled with a teaspoon of olive oil and a squeeze of fresh lemon.

• **Shiitake mushrooms.** Calcium is ineffective without vitamin D, notes Bauer, which it requires for efficient absorption. While the sun is the primary source of vitamin D, there are food sources as well. Shiitake mushrooms are one rich source, and others include canned sardines and wild salmon (no bones are needed for vitamin D...but include the bones and you'll get a two-in-one bonus for both calcium and vitamin D), shrimp, egg yolks and vitamin D-fortified whole grain cereals or soy milk.

Bauer notes that it is important to remember that eating healthful foods will go a long way toward supporting optimal health—but if you have or suspect you have a medical problem, be sure to see your physician. As the old saying goes, "You are what you eat," so therefore, the healthier you eat, the healthier you'll be.

REPORT #82
Whole Grains to The Rescue

Joanne Slavin, RD, PhD, food science and nutrition professor at the University of Minnesota in St. Paul. She is author of dozens of medical articles on dietary fiber.

Everyone knows that if you eat ample amounts of fruits and vegetables you can lower cholesterol, promote weight control and help prevent heart attack, stroke, diabetes and some types of cancer. But few people realize that whole grains are just as good as fruits and vegetables—and sometimes even better—at fighting many of these serious illnesses.

Fiber gets most of the credit for the healthful properties of whole grains, but studies have found that the phytochemicals, antioxidants, vitamins and minerals found in whole grains, which contain all parts of the grain, are just as important. The whole grains described below can be found at most health-food stores and many grocery stores...*

AMARANTH
What it's good for: This tiny grain with an earthy, faintly grassy taste may protect against heart disease and cancer. It is also an excellent source of complete protein—that is, one that contains all eight essential amino acids.

Major effective ingredients: Vitamins E and B. Amaranth is also rich in calcium, phosphorus and iron.

How to add it to your diet: As it cooks, amaranth releases a glutinous starch that adds body to soups and stews.

BROWN RICE
What it's good for: Helps fight eye disease (macular degeneration) and certain cancers, including lung cancer.

Major effective ingredients: Vitamin E and other antioxidants.

How to add it to your diet: Season brown rice as you would white rice, or it can be added to soups, casseroles, stir-fry dishes as well as salads.

CORN
What it's good for: Helps fight heart disease and cancer...and may guard against cataracts.

Major effective ingredients: Of all the grains, whole-grain corn is the richest source of antioxidants. It's also a good source of insoluble fiber, which cannot be digested but adds bulk to the stool.

How to add it to your diet: Choose whole-grain corn-based cereals, whole-grain cornmeal breads and cornmeal tortillas.

OATS AND BARLEY
What they are good for: Lowering your cholesterol.

Major effective ingredient: Soluble fiber. When soluble fiber is digested, it changes to a gummy consistency that lowers blood cholesterol. The exact mechanism of this effect is not yet known.

How to add oats to your diet: Choose an oat cereal or oatmeal or you can make oatmeal cookies.

How to add barley to your diet: Use it to thicken soups and make creamy risottos, or cook it with carrots.

---

*For recipes using whole grains, read *Whole Grains Every Day Every Way* (Clarkson Potter) by Lorna Sass or visit the Web site of the Whole Grains Council, *www.wholegrainscouncil.org*.

RYE

What it's good for: Protects against heart disease and hormone-dependent cancers, such as breast and prostate malignancies.

Major effective ingredient: Rye is a rich source of lignans, a class of phytoestrogens (plant compounds that help protect against the harmful effects of excess estrogen).

How to add it to your diet: Use whole-grain rye bread or whole-grain rye crackers.

WHEAT

What it's good for: It has a laxative effect that aids digestion and also is high in vitamins, minerals and antioxidants.

Major effective ingredient: Insoluble fiber.

How to add it to your diet: Replace white bread with whole-wheat bread...and highly processed cereals with whole-grain cereals.

Helpful: To ensure that a bread product contains whole grain, the label must include the word "whole."

Example: For whole wheat, look for whole-wheat flour or whole-wheat grain. Breads that contain seven, 12 or even 15 grains are not necessarily whole-grain breads.

REPORT #83
Get More Legumes

Eating legumes may lower diabetes risk. In a recent finding, women who consumed the most peanuts, soybeans and other legumes had significantly lower risk for type 2 diabetes. Legumes are good sources of magnesium, isoflavones and fiber, and they have a low glycemic index, which may explain why they help lower diabetes risk. Of all legumes, soybeans (though not most processed soy products) appear to be the most beneficial. Women who consumed the most soybeans were 47% less likely to develop diabetes than women who consumed the least.

Raquel Villegas, PhD, assistant professor of medicine, School of Medicine, Vanderbilt University, Nashville, and lead author of a study of 64,227 women, published in *The American Journal of Clinical Nutrition.*

REPORT #84
Chamomile Tea May Fight Diabetes

An animal study suggests that chamomile tea can help prevent diabetic complications, such as blindness, nerve damage and kidney failure, by lowering blood glucose levels and reducing levels of enzymes linked to nerve, eye and kidney damage.

Atsushi Kato, MD, department of hospital pharmacy, University of Toyama, Japan, and coauthor of a study published in *Journal of Agricultural and Food Chemistry.*

REPORT #85
Black Tea Helps Treat Diabetes

When researchers compared concentrations of *polysaccharides* (a type of carbohydrate) in black, green and oolong teas, the polysaccharides in black tea were the best blood sugar (glucose) inhibitors.

Theory: Polysaccharides in black tea block an enzyme that converts starch into glucose.

If you have diabetes or prediabetes: Consider drinking three cups of black tea daily to better control blood sugar.

Haixia Chen, PhD, associate professor, School of Pharmaceutical Science and Technology, Tianjin University, Tianjin, China.

REPORT #86
Coffee and Green Tea Cut Diabetes Risk

In a study of 17,413 adults, those who reported drinking six or more cups of green tea or at least three cups of caffeinated coffee daily were one-third less likely to develop type 2 diabetes than those who drank less than one cup of green tea or coffee a week.

Theory: Caffeine stimulates oxidation (burning) of fat.

Caution: High caffeine intake—more than 500 mg daily—has been linked to arrhythmia (irregular heartbeat). One eight-ounce cup of coffee contains about 100 mg of caffeine... green tea, about 35 mg. Ask your doctor how much caffeine is appropriate for you.

Hiroyasu Iso, MD, PhD, MPH, professor of public health, Osaka University Graduate School of Medicine, Osaka, Japan.

REPORT #87
Milk Thistle Improves Diabetes

Mark A. Stengler, NMD, licensed naturopathic medical doctor, La Jolla, California...adjunct associate clinical professor at the National College of Natural Medicine, Portland, Oregon...author of many books, including *The Natural Physician's Healing Therapies* and coauthor of *Prescription for Natural Cures* (both from Bottom Line Books)...and author of the *Bottom Line/Natural Healing* newsletter.

A recent study reported that milk thistle, an herbal supplement, reduced blood sugar levels in people with type 2 diabetes. Along with their regular diabetes medication, 51 men and women (ages 40 to 65) took either 200 mg of *silymarin* (the active ingredient in milk thistle) three times daily before meals or a placebo. After four months, the average fasting blood glucose level (the amount of sugar in the blood eight hours after a person's last meal) fell by 15% in the silymarin group, while rising 13% in the placebo group.

My view: Milk thistle has long been used to treat liver conditions, such as hepatitis. Now it appears to be useful in treating type 2 diabetes, too—perhaps because its antioxidant properties help to control the metabolic abnormalities of diabetes. It is safe for everyone.

REPORT #88
Moderate Drinking May Cut Diabetes Risk

In a recent finding, people who consume one or two standard alcoholic drinks per day are about 30% less likely to develop type 2 diabetes than people who don't drink at all. The risk reduction is the same whether a person has one or two drinks.

Caution: Drinking more than three alcoholic beverages a day raises diabetes risk. Ask your doctor if daily alcohol is right for you.

Lando L.J. Koppes, PhD, researcher at VU University Medical Center, EMGO Institute, Amsterdam, the Netherlands, and leader of a meta-study analyzing data from 15 studies involving alcohol use and diabetes risk in nearly 370,000 people, published in *Diabetes Care*.

REPORT #89
Indian Herb Fights Diabetes

Mark A. Stengler, NMD, licensed naturopathic medical doctor, La Jolla, California...adjunct associate clinical professor at the National College of Natural Medicine, Portland, Oregon...author of many books, including *The Natural Physician's Healing Therapies* and coauthor of *Prescription for Natural Cures* (both from Bottom Line Books)...and author of the *Bottom Line/Natural Healing* newsletter.

Salacia oblonga is an herb commonly used in traditional Ayurvedic medicine to treat diabetes and obesity. Researchers fed 66 people with type 2 diabetes test meals on three separate occasions. Study participants were given a high-carbohydrate liquid meal or the liquid meal plus *Salacia oblonga* (S. oblonga) at a dosage of either 240 milligrams (mg) or 480 mg.

Result: Compared with the control meal alone, the 240-mg dose of S. oblonga lowered blood sugar by 14%...and the 480-mg dose lowered it by 22%. The amount of insulin, a hormone that regulates blood sugar, produced in response to the meal was reduced by 14% and 19%, respectively (high insulin contributes to inflammation in the body). These reductions were especially impressive given the high-carb meal (carbs raise blood sugar and insulin).

This herb prevents carbohydrates from being broken down in the digestive tract, allowing less glucose into the bloodstream—and resulting in lower blood glucose and insulin levels. Studies have shown it to be safe, and side effects are uncommon. People with mild-to-moderate elevation in glucose levels, as well as those with diabetes, should talk to their doctors about S. oblonga.

Note: Three of the study authors are employed by Abbott Laboratories, which funded the research. However, two other studies with humans also have shown the benefits of S. oblonga.

REPORT #90
How to Help Your Diabetic Heart Naturally

Seth Baum, MD, medical director of Integrative Heart Care in Boca Raton, Florida, and author of *The Total Guide to a Healthy Heart* (Kensington). *www.vital remedy.com.*

Kenneth Madden, MD, assistant professor of geriatric medicine at the University of British Columbia.

Robb Wolf, owner of NorCal Strength and Conditioning, Chico, California and author of *The Paleolithic Solution* (Victory Belt Publishing).

If you have type 2 diabetes, you've already had a heart attack—whether you've had one or not!

"The guidelines for physicians from the American Heart Association are to treat a person with diabetes as if that individual has already had a heart attack," says cardiologist Seth Baum, MD, medical director of Integrative Heart Care in Boca Raton, Florida, and author of *The Total Guide to a Healthy Heart* (Kensington).

HOW DOES DIABETES HURT YOUR HEART?

As excess sugar careens through the bloodstream, it roughs up the linings of the arteries.

Insulin resistance (the sub-par performance of the hormone that moves glucose out of the bloodstream and into muscle and fat cells) raises blood pressure, damaging arteries.

Diabetes also injures tiny blood vessels called capillaries, which hurts your kidneys and nerves—damage that in turn stresses the heart.

The end result—an up to seven-fold increase in the risk of heart disease and stroke, the *cardiovascular diseases* (CVD) that kill four out of five people with diabetes.

But recent studies show there are several natural ways for people with diabetes to reverse the risk factors that cause heart disease…

RECENT RESEARCH

It's never too late to exercise—and a little goes a long way. Researchers at the University of British Columbia in Vancouver, Canada, studied 36 older people (average age 71) with type 2 diabetes, high blood pressure, and high cholesterol, dividing them into two groups.

One group walked on a treadmill or cycled on a stationary bicycle for 40 minutes, three days a week. The other group didn't.

To find out if the exercise was helping with CVD, the researchers measured the elasticity of the arteries—a fundamental indicator of arterial youth and health, with arterial stiffness increasing the risk of dying from CVD.

Results: After three months, the exercisers had a decrease in arterial stiffness of 15 to 20%.

"Aerobic exercise should be the first-line treatment to reduce arterial stiffness in older adults with type 2 diabetes, even if the patient has advanced cardiovascular risk factors" such as high blood pressure and high cholesterol, conclude the researchers, in *Diabetes Care.*

WHAT TO DO

Kenneth Madden, MD, the study leader, and assistant professor of geriatric medicine at the University of British Columbia, says "You can improve every risk factor for diabetes and heart disease—and you can do it in a very short period of time."

Dr. Madden recommends that older people with diabetes and cardiovascular disease see a doctor for a checkup before starting an exercise program.

Once you get the okay from your physician, he says to purchase and use a heart monitor during exercise, so you're sure that you're exercising at the level used by the participants in his study—60% to 75% of maximum heart rate.

Example: An estimate of your maximum heart rate is 220, minus your age. If you're 60, that would be 220 – 60 = 160. Exercising at between 60% to 75% of your maximum heart rate means maintaining a heart rate of between 96 and 120 beats per minute.

Finally, Dr. Madden advises you exercise the amount proven to improve arterial elasticity—a minimum of three sessions of aerobic exercise a week, of 40 minutes each.

•**Maximize magnesium.** Researchers in Mexico studied 79 people with diabetes and high blood pressure, dividing them into two groups. One group received a daily 450 milligrams (mg) magnesium supplement; one didn't.

Results: After four months, those on magnesium had an average drop of 20 points systolic (the higher number in the blood pressure reading) and 9 points diastolic (the lower number). Those on the placebo had corresponding drops of 5 points and 1 point.

"Magnesium supplementation should be considered as an additional or alternative treatment for high blood pressure in people with diabetes," says Fernando Guerrero-Romero, MD, the study leader.

What to do: "Magnesium acts as a natural vasodilator, relaxing arteries and lowering blood pressure," says Dr. Baum. "People with diabetes should incorporate a magnesium supplement into their regimen."

He suggests a daily supplement of 400 mg, about the level used in the study.

"People with diabetes and high blood pressure should also be encouraged to increase their dietary intake of magnesium, through eating more whole grains, leafy green vegetables, legumes, nuts and fish", says Dr. Guerrero-Romero.

•**Eat like a Neanderthal.** Researchers in Sweden tested two diets in 13 people with type 2 diabetes—the diet recommended by the American Diabetes Association (ADA), a generally healthful diet limiting calories, fat and refined carbohydrates; and a "Paleolithic" diet, consisting of lean meat, fish, fruits, vegetables, root vegetables, eggs and nuts—and no dairy products, refined carbohydrates or highly processed foods, whatsoever.

In terms of lowering risk factors for heart disease, the Paleolithic diet clubbed the ADA diet.

Results: After three months, it had done a better job of decreasing…

•**High LDL "bad" cholesterol,**

•**High blood pressure,**

•**high triglycerides (a blood fat linked to heart disease) and**

•**Too-big waist size** (excess stomach fat is linked to heart disease).

The diet was also more effective at increasing HDL "good" cholesterol.

And it was superior in decreasing *glycated hemoglobin* (A1C), a measure of long-term blood sugar control.

"Foods that were regularly eaten during the Paleolithic, or 'Old Stone Age', may be optimal for prevention and treatment of type 2 diabetes, cardiovascular disease and insulin resistance," concludes Tommy Jönsson, MD, in *Cardiovascular Diabetology*.

What to do: "Eating a Paleolithic Diet is far easier than most people think," says Robb Wolf, owner of NorCal Strength and Conditioning in Chico, California and author of *The Paleolithic Solution* (Victory Belt Publishing).

THE BASIC DIET

Eat more—lean meat, fish, shellfish, fruits, vegetables, eggs and nuts.

Eat less (or eliminate)—grains, dairy products, salt, refined fats and refined sugar.

Resource: You can order pre-packaged Paleolithic snacks and meals at *www.paleo brands.com.*

• **Have a cup of hibiscus tea.** Researchers in Iran studied 53 people with type 2 diabetes, dividing them into two groups. One group drank a cup of hibiscus tea twice a day; the other drank two cups a day of black tea. (The hibiscus tea was made from Hibiscus sabdariffa, which is also known as red sorrel, Jamaican sorrel, Indian sorrel, roselle and Florida cranberry.)

Results: After one month, those drinking hibiscus had…

• **Higher HDL "good" cholesterol,**

• **Lower LDL "bad" cholesterol,**

• **Lower total cholesterol and**

• **Lower blood pressure.**

The black tea group didn't have any significant changes in blood fats or blood pressure.

The findings were in *The Journal of Alternative and Complementary Medicine* and the *Journal of Human Hypertension.*

What to do: Consider drinking a cup or two of hibiscus tea a day, says Hassan Mozaffari-Khosravi, PhD, an assistant professor of nutrition, Shahid Sadoughi University of Medical Sciences, Yazd, Iran and the study leader.

REPORT #91
Apple Cider Vinegar

Mark A. Stengler, NMD, licensed naturopathic medical doctor, La Jolla, California…adjunct associate clinical professor at the National College of Natural Medicine, Portland, Oregon…author of many books, including *The Natural Physician's Healing Therapies* and coauthor of *Prescription for Natural Cures* (both from Bottom Line Books)…and author of the *Bottom Line/Natural Healing* newsletter.

Patients often tell me that apple cider vinegar has helped them with a variety of ailments. This intrigued me because, until recently, there was little research to back up these claims.

CURE-ALL?

Apple cider vinegar has been singled out as beneficial for a variety of conditions, including leg cramps, stomach upset, sore throat, sinus problems, high blood pressure, obesity, osteoporosis and arthritis. It also has been used to help rid the body of toxins, improve concentration, slow aging, reduce cholesterol and fight infection.

It is used topically to treat acne, sunburn, shingles and insect bites…as a skin toner…and to prevent dandruff. Many women add it to bathwater to treat vaginitis. Two of its most common uses are for weight loss and arthritis.

THE SCIENTIFIC EVIDENCE

Recent studies have found that consuming apple cider vinegar can improve insulin resistance, a condition in which muscle, fat and liver cells have become resistant to the uptake of the hormone insulin and the blood sugar glucose needed to provide fuel for energy.

This is common among people who have diabetes as well as in some people we consider prediabetic—that is, their blood glucose and insulin levels are approaching the numbers that define diabetes.

People with insulin resistance are more likely to be overweight and have increased cholesterol and triglyceride levels as well as high blood pressure.

A study at the University of Arizona examined the effects of apple cider vinegar on 29 participants (10 had type 2 diabetes, 11 had signs that they could become diabetic and eight were healthy but "insulin sensitive"). All participants fasted and were randomly asked to drink either a vinegar solution (two tablespoons or 20 g of apple cider vinegar, some water and a bit of saccharin for flavor) or a placebo drink. The drinks were followed by a high-carbohydrate meal of one white bagel, butter and orange juice.

Researchers found that postmeal spikes of insulin and glucose in the vinegar group were significantly lower in those who had insulin resistance and slightly lower in those who had diabetes, compared with those in the placebo group. Other research has shown that apple cider vinegar helps control insulin and glucose spikes in healthy people.

HOW IT WORKS

Researchers theorize that the acetic acid in any vinegar, including apple cider vinegar, interferes with the enzymes that digest carbohydrates, so carbs pass through the digestive tract without being absorbed.

Acetic acid also has been shown to affect enzymes that alter glucose metabolism in liver and muscle cells, reducing insulin spikes.

Because high levels of insulin promote inflammation, taking vinegar to maintain better insulin levels will control any inflammatory response in the body. This may explain why vinegar eases arthritis pain.

DOSAGE

People can try apple cider vinegar for weight loss, blood sugar balance and other traditional uses, including arthritis relief.

Dilute one to two tablespoons (some people use as little as two teaspoons to start with) in an equal amount of water, and drink it at the beginning of a meal.

Sometimes it is more convenient to take it in supplement form. A good product is Apple Cider Vinegar Plus, which is made by Indiana Botanic Gardens (800-644-8327, *www.botanicchoice.com*).

Take one capsule with each meal for a total of three capsules a day. Ninety capsules cost $12.99.

Apple cider vinegar can cause digestive upset in some people. If you have active ulcers, use caution when taking apple cider vinegar.

REPORT #92
Banaba—Ancient Herb, Modern Success

From *Bottom Line's Breakthroughs in Drug-Free Healing* by Bill Gottlieb (Bottom Line Books). *www.bottomlinesecrets.com.*

I t's called *banaba* in the Philippines, *banglang* in Cambodia, *bungor* in Malaya and *jalal* in India. For thousands of years, folk healers in these southeast Asian countries have used the many-named plant to lower blood sugar. Scientists are catching on.

BREAKTHROUGH STUDIES

Japanese researchers in the Department of Diabetes and Clinical Nutrition at Kyoto University gave 31 people with diabetes and other blood sugar problems either *corosolic acid* (the active ingredient of banaba) or a placebo. Then they gave them a big dose of dietary sugar, in what's called a glucose tolerance test. An hour later...90 minutes later...and 2 hours later...those taking the banaba had much lower blood sugar levels.

In a similar study* conducted in the United States, 10 people with diabetes were given banaba for 2 weeks—and their high blood sugar dropped by 30%.

Why it works: Corosolic acid stimulates cells to absorb glucose, say the researchers.

Suggested intake: 32 to 48 mg a day of a banaba extract standardized to 1% corosolic acid (CRA), the active ingredient.

*The US study used Glucosol, a soft-gel formulation found in many products, including Glucotrim from NSI, Gluco Trim from NOW Foods and Glucosol/Rx-Blood Sugar from Nature's Plus.

Volume 10
Memory Loss Cures

REPORT #93
Natural Ways to Power Up Your Brain

You can improve your memory, your energy, your productivity and your general well-being throughout your entire life by developing everyday habits that are very good for your brain...

•**Get exercise that requires quick movements.** Exercise increases blood flow to the brain, ensuring a healthy supply of oxygen and the nutrients on which the brain depends. Insufficient blood flow can lead to poor coordination and difficulty processing complex thoughts.

Exercise also increases the supply of *brain-derived neurotrophic factor* (BDNF), a protein that helps with the creation of new cells.

A recent study of people in their 70s found that those who exercised moderately or vigorously at least once a week were 30% more likely to maintain their cognitive skills than people who exercised less often.

Any type of exercise is good, but the ideal exercise for a healthy brain combines an aerobic workout with complex movements requiring quick reactions.

Examples: Dancing, tennis, table tennis, racquetball and juggling.

•**Eat berries, beans and salmon.** Be sure that your diet includes...

•Fruits as well as vegetables. Antioxidants in fruits and vegetables fight damage from free radicals—unstable molecules that damage cells, contribute to aging and promote inflammation, which is a factor in Alzheimer's disease. Berries are particularly rich in antioxidants.

Daniel G. Amen, MD, distinguished fellow of the American Psychiatric Association and CEO and medical director of Amen Clinics, Inc., headquartered in Newport Beach, California, *www.amenclinics.com.* He is assistant clinical professor of psychiatry and human behavior at University of California, Irvine, School of Medicine, and his work has been the basis of several PBS specials. Dr. Amen is author of many books, including *Change Your Brain, Change Your Body* (Three Rivers).

• Complex carbohydrates—such as cooked dried beans and whole grains. The brain uses sugar as its main energy source. Complex carbohydrates release sugar slowly. In contrast, white bread and other refined starches and sugars cause dramatic spikes and drops in blood sugar, leading to concentration problems and fatigue.

• Cold-water fish. Any lean protein, including chicken and lean pork, helps build neurons. Salmon, cod and other cold-water fish have the added benefit of providing omega-3 fatty acids, which play an important role in maintaining nerve cell membranes. Other sources of these healthy fats are avocados, nuts and olive oil.

• **Boost vitamin D.** Vitamin D is believed to play a role in mood and memory. A recent study published in *Journal of Geriatric Psychiatry* and *Neurology* found a possible association between dementia and low levels of vitamin D.

The best source of vitamin D is sunlight—at least 15 minutes a day without sunscreen. If you spend most of the day indoors or live in a northern latitude, take a supplement with 400 international units (IU) of vitamin D daily.

• **Avoid food additives, such as mono-sodium glutamate, and artificial sweeteners, such as aspartame.** Though studies are inconclusive, anecdotal evidence suggests that these additives may have a hyperstimulating effect, causing confusion and/or mood swings.

• **Limit caffeine and alcohol.** Caffeine and alcohol reduce blood flow to the brain, depriving cells of nutrients and energy. Both can interfere with sleep, which is essential to healthy brain activity.

Both also can be dehydrating—the brain is 80% water, so anything that dehydrates has the potential to cause problems in thinking.

One or two cups of coffee or tea a day are harmless and enhance alertness, but heavy caffeine consumption—more than 500 milligrams (mg) to 600 mg a day, or about four to seven cups of coffee—should be avoided.

Alcohol has additional dangers—it blocks oxygen from reaching cells' energy centers and reduces the effectiveness of neurotransmitters involved in learning and memory. Heavy drinkers—people who consume four or more alcoholic drinks a day—have a higher risk for dementia.

Some people drink wine daily because of evidence that it may be good for the heart. However, there are other ways to help the heart—such as exercise and diet—that don't put the brain at risk. If you are accustomed to having a drink every day, consider cutting back to one or two drinks a week.

• **Avoid airborne toxins.** Fumes from paint, pesticides and other chemicals have been associated with brain damage. If you are exposed to strong fumes—for example, while painting the interior of your house or having your nails done—be sure that the area is well-ventilated.

• **Don't smoke, and avoid being in rooms where others are smoking.** Oddly, smoking can make you feel smarter by stimulating the release of neurotransmitters that improve reaction time, but nicotine constricts blood vessels, reducing blood flow and depriving the brain of nutrients.

• **Don't overdo your electronic interaction.** Computers, mobile devices and other electronic tools can interfere with optimal brain function in several ways. They have an addictive quality, stimulating release of the neurotransmitter *dopamine*, which acts on the brain's pleasure centers. Over time, greater amounts of dopamine are required to get the same pleasurable feeling.

E-mail and text-messaging can interfere with concentration, encouraging a state of mind that is alert to the next distraction, rather than focused on the task at hand. One study at London University found a temporary IQ loss of 10 points in people who constantly checked for messages during the day.

Best: Process e-mail and text messages at set times of day, not as each message comes in. Take frequent breaks that are away from the computer.

• **Protect your skull.** The brain is very soft. The hard skull that covers it has many ridges that can damage the brain during trauma. Yet people are astonishingly careless with this precious organ.

Take precautions to protect yourself from head injury. Stabilize ladders carefully. Use nonslip mats in the bathtub and shower. Keep the floor in your house and the pathways outside it clear of debris that could cause you to trip and fall. If you bicycle or ski, be sure to wear a helmet.

• **Manage stress.** Long-term exposure to high levels of the stress hormone cortisol is associated with a smaller-sized hippocampus—the brain area involved with memory—and with poor performance on memory tests.

Cope with stress by finding daily activities that calm you, such as exercise, meditation, prayer or yoga. During difficult times, focus on what you are grateful for and talk things out with someone who can help you keep an optimistic perspective.

REPORT #94
Dr. Gary Small's Secrets For Getting Your Memory Back in Gear

Gary Small, MD, professor of psychiatry and biobehavioral sciences, and director, University of California, Los Angeles, Center on Aging. Dr. Small is one of the world's leading physician/scientists in the fields of memory and longevity. He is author of *The Memory Bible* and *The Longevity Bible* (both from Hyperion). *www.drgarysmall.com.*

Age is the biggest factor for memory loss. We all have memory problems of some sort by age 60, such as momentarily forgetting someone's name, or briefly wondering why we just walked into a room. We can't stop the effects of aging, but we can slow them down.

At the University of California, Los Angeles, Center on Aging, where I am director, we find that using very simple techniques and lifestyle changes—such as reading regularly and playing board games—can have a positive impact on memory retention. Scientific research shows that whenever we push ourselves to solve problems in a new way, we may be strengthening the connections between our brain cells.

MEMORY TECHNIQUES

Some people are so good at memorizing things that they test their talent in competitive matches involving knowledge of trivia or the recall of remarkably large numbers. Scientists have found that those people are no different from the rest of us. There is nothing out of the ordinary in their brain structure nor are there any indications of unusual intelligence. They simply often tap into a memory technique used since antiquity called the Roman Room method.

This method is simple. Visualize yourself walking a familiar route, such as the rooms of your home. Mentally place images of the items to be remembered on specific points on the route. It may be helpful to place items where they may logically be—if you want to remember to buy coffee beans, perhaps they're best mentally placed on the kitchen counter. When you want to recall them, mentally retrace your steps.

Over time, you can add more objects to the rooms. If one day you want to remember to pick up the newspaper, add it next to the coffee beans on the counter. If it's airline tickets, visualize them taped to the fridge door. You can also extend your route or even add other familiar locations for certain kinds of memory tasks.

The Roman Room method is a very useful technique. Orators back in Ancient Rome would remember lengthy speeches this way, imagining each progression of a speech by mentally walking through rooms where they had placed objects to remind themselves of lines. Yet since today we have much more clutter coming at us, I also teach my patients an additional memory technique that I call Look, Snap, Connect…

• **Look reminds us to focus our attention.** The most common explanation for memory loss is that the information never gets into our minds in the first place. Because we are distracted, we don't take in the information or don't allow ourselves to absorb it. Simply reminding ourselves to focus our attention will dramatically boost memory power.

• **Snap stands for creating a mental snapshot or visual image in your mind's eye**

of the information to be remembered. For most people, visual images are much easier to remember than other forms of information.

• **Connect means we need to link up the visual images from snap in meaningful ways.** These associations are key to recalling memories when we want them later. When linking your mental images, create a story that has action and detail.

Example: Say that you want to remember five words on your "to do" list: Mail, gasoline, grandson, sweater, airline. Come up with a story linking them. For instance, I imagine a grandson knitting a sweater on a plane, then mailing it at the airport, when the plane lands to refuel.

Whatever the story ends up being, having detail, action and, for me, humor, all help to imprint the information.

This linking technique works very well with everyday memory tasks, such as grocery lists or errands to run.

When trying to remember faces and names, create an image either linked to the person whose name you need to remember or a distinguishing feature of his/her face. A redhead named Lucy could be remembered by noting that the red hair reminds you of Lucille Ball. You could remember the last name of a woman named Potvin by imagining that she landscaped her yard with pots full of vines.

MENTAL AEROBICS

It's never too late to improve your memory. Recent studies show that even people in the early stages of Alzheimer's can be taught significant face and name retention under the guidance of a professional. For those of us looking to overcome the common forgetfulness in daily life, we can tackle much of that ourselves by doing activities that involve lateral thinking.

Lateral thinking means that we are trying to solve a problem from many angles instead of tackling it head on. Here are some mental aerobic exercises to get you started and, hopefully, suggest further how to invoke lateral thinking in your life.

QUIZ TIME

A lot of memory loss is simply being too busy to absorb what people are saying. These exercises are meant to remind you to slow down, pay attention and consider what is at hand. *In doing so, your memory will improve...*

1. Brush your hair using your nondominant hand. You may find it awkward at first, but over a few days notice how much easier it gets. This and other exercises don't directly help your memory (after all, how often will any of us need to remember to brush with the opposite hand?). What these mental aerobics do is challenge your mind to think differently and examine tasks we often do without thinking, and which lead to our minds getting "flabby."

2. Fill in a grid so that every row, column and two-by-two box contains the numbers 1, 2, 3 and 4.

3. Say "silk" six times. Then answer the following question: What do cows drink?

This exercise will help you be more thoughtful about things, which in turn is conducive to better memory.

4. See how many words you can spell from these letters:

LIGOBATE

No letter may be used twice in any given word, and each word must contain the letter L.

5. How many months have 28 days?

6. All of the vowels have been removed from the following saying. The remaining consonants are in the correct sequence, broken into groups of two to five letters. What is the saying?

STRK WHLTH RNS HT

How well did you do? Regardless, this is just a start to remembering more and living better.

ANSWERS TO QUIZ

Q2: Across row 1: 1, 2, 3, 4 or 1, 2, 4, 3. Row 2: 4, 3, 1, 2. Row 3: 2, 1, 4, 3 or 2, 1, 3, 4. Row 4: 3, 4, 2, 1.

Q3: Cows drink water. If you said "milk," you need to focus your attention.

Q4: agile, ail, aale, bagel, bail, bale, blog, boil, el, Gail, gale, gel, glib, glob, globe, goal, goalie, lab, lag, lea, leg, lib, lie, lob, lobe, log, loge, oblige.

Q5: All of them. (If you say only one month has 28 days, it's an example of not paying attention to the matter at hand—all months have 28 days, after all.)

Q6: Strike while the iron is hot.

B-12 levels. Loss of brain volume is associated with memory loss and other cognitive problems.

What to do: After age 55, it may be a good idea to take B-12 supplements to avoid risk of deficiency of the vitamin.

A. David Smith, MD, founding director, Oxford Project to Investigate Memory and Ageing, University of Oxford, Britain.

REPORT #95
Antioxidant Improves Memory

In a study of 6,000 men, half took pills containing 50 mg daily of the antioxidant beta-carotene (roughly the amount in four carrots), and the others took a placebo.

Result: Those who took beta-carotene for at least 15 years scored higher on memory tests than those who took a placebo.

Theory: Beta-carotene protects against oxidative stress, which can lead to brain aging.

If you're concerned about memory loss: Ask your doctor about taking 50 mg daily of a beta-carotene supplement.

Francine Grodstein, ScD, associate professor of medicine, department of epidemiology, Brigham and Women's Hospital, Boston.

REPORT #96
Vitamin B-12 May Prevent Brain Shrinkage Among Seniors

Recent study: Individuals ages 61 to 87 who initially had no cognitive problems were followed for five years.

Finding: Participants among the one-third who had the lowest blood levels of vitamin B-12 were six times more likely to lose brain volume, as measured by MRI scans, than were those among the one-third with the highest

REPORT #97
Green Tea Boosts Brain Power

In a recent Japanese study of cognitive function in people age 70 or older, participants who drank two or more cups of green tea daily had a 54% lower prevalence of cognitive decline—measured via memory, attention and language-use tests—than those who drank three cups or less weekly. Theory: Antioxidants in green tea may reduce the buildup of a type of plaque in the brain that is responsible for memory loss in Alzheimer's disease. Self-defense: Drink two or more cups of green tea daily to help promote brain health.

Shinichi Kuriyama, MD, PhD, associate professor of epidemiology, Tohoku University Graduate School of Medicine, Sendai, Japan.

REPORT #98
Green, Leafy Vegetables Protect Memory

Recent finding: People who eat about three servings of vegetables a day have a 40% slower rate of cognitive decline than people who eat less than one serving a day. All vegetables provide protection, but green, leafy ones, including spinach, provide the most protection.

Surprising: Fruits don't help slow memory loss, but researchers are not yet sure why.

Theory: Vitamin E is believed to prevent cognitive decline. Vegetables contain high amounts of it and are typically eaten with added fats, such as salad dressing, which increase vitamin E absorption.

Bottom line: Eat at least three servings of green, leafy vegetables every day.

Martha Clare Morris, ScD, associate professor, department of internal medicine, Rush University Medical Center, Chicago, and leader of a study of 3,718 people, age 65 and older, published in *Neurology*.

REPORT #99
Memory Busters

Mark A. Stengler, NMD, licensed medical doctor in private practice, La Jolla, California...adjunct associate clinical professor at the National College of Natural Medicine, Portland, Oregon...author of many books, including *The Natural Physician's Healing Therapies* and coauthor of *Prescription for Natural Cures* (both from Bottom Line Books)...and author of the *Bottom Line/Natural Healing* newsletter.

A number of environmental and health factors can contribute to short- and long-term memory loss. *Among the most common...*

• **Prescription drugs can adversely affect memory.** If you are taking any medications, ask your doctor whether memory loss is a known side effect.

• **Low thyroid function also can cause poor memory and concentration.** With a simple blood test, your doctor can check thyroid levels. If they are low (hypothyroidism), he/she can prescribe medication.

• **Toxic metals, such as lead, mercury and aluminum, can lead to brain degeneration.** A holistic doctor can test your urine levels of these metals and recommend treatment, such as chelation therapy, if necessary.

REPORT #100
Strengthen Your Brain, Naturally—What You Can Do to Stay Sharp and Healthy

Dharma Singh Khalsa, MD, one of the world's leading experts in integrative or complementary medicine, Alzheimer's disease and memory loss. Dr. Khalsa is an associate fellow of the University of Pennsylvania Medical School, and has formulated a holistic medicine program for the prevention and treatment of Alzheimer's disease and memory loss (The Brain Longevity Program). He is author of numerous books including *The Better Memory Kit* (Hay House) and *Brain Longevity* (Grand Central) and is president and medical director of the Alzheimer's Research and Prevention Foundation (*www.alzheimersprevention.org*). Visit his Web site at *www.drdharma.com*.

Recent headlines have trumpeted the exponential growth in the number of people with Alzheimer's disease—according to one report we read, someone in this country develops the disease every 72 seconds. It is estimated that within a few decades, that rate will more than double, with Alzheimer's striking a new victim every 33 seconds. Researchers are working to isolate the causes and develop effective treatments... but more important is finding ways to prevent the disease—and certainly those who already have it would benefit from avoiding or minimizing side effects caused by treatments.

Keeping memory sharp with brain teasers and other mental activities won't stave off Alzheimer's disease altogether (if only it were so simple) but, we recently learned, it actually can help decrease the intensity and persistence of symptoms and help maintain functionality.

Wondering whether there were particular foods we should eat, supplements we could take or exercises to do to fortify memory, we called Dharma Singh Khalsa, MD, a leading expert in integrative medicine, Alzheimer's disease and memory loss. An Associate Fellow of the University of Pennsylvania Medical School and the medical director of the Alzheimer's Research and Prevention Foundation, Dr. Khalsa has created a program for avoidance and treatment of Alzheimer's disease and memory loss, called the Brain Longevity Program. Understanding that age-related memory loss (normal forgetfulness that occurs with advancing years) and full-out Alzheimer's exist on a continuum, it's important for all people to work to keep their memory skills sharp and strong. "Just like your muscles, the brain gets weak as we age—but it doesn't have to be that way," he said.

INVESTING IN THE MEMORY BANK

As opposed to dementia, Dr. Khalsa believes that mild cognitive impairment is something of a "disease of lifestyle." He said that some intriguing new research is focused on a concept called cognitive reserve, which he likened to a savings account for your brain in that its capacity can be built up over time. "By building up your cognitive reserve through healthy diet and mental and physical exercise, you will not only have better brainpower now, you'll have better ability to resist challenges to the brain later in life," he said.

The three basic strategies Dr. Khalsa recommends to accomplish this aren't exactly new—but they bear repeating...

• **Eat well and take supplements.** Research shows that people eating plenty of vegetables each day (around three or four servings or more) seem to have a slower rate of cognitive decline. Interestingly studies suggest that fruits are not as protective as vegetables in this regard—Dr. Khalsa speculates that since vegetables are so loaded with natural anti-inflammatories, they reduce inflammation, which is known to figure in cognitive impairment and Alzheimer's. Basic supplements, including a multivitamin, and B vitamins (including folic acid), vitamin C and vitamin E, are also helpful.

• **Manage stress.** Stress causes the release of cortisol into the bloodstream, which in chronic and excessive amounts can cause cell death in the brain's memory center, Dr. Khalsa told me. He said that meditation and other relaxation techniques are excellent ways to reduce damagingly high levels of stress hormones.

• **Exercise.** Can you walk and talk at the same time? According to Dr. Khalsa, "for optimal impact on the brain, both physical and mental exercise need to happen—preferably at the same time." For instance, he suggests taking a walk—but instead of daydreaming, sing a song or talk aloud, mindfully. "Say, 'I'm walking up a hill, the tree over there is green with a brown trunk, and there goes Dave driving his new Ford,'" he suggests. "This kind of mental involvement literally lights up the brain." You could also just walk with a friend, discussing current events or anything else you find interesting.

Though we hear an awful lot about mental exercise nowadays, Dr. Khalsa explained that it does not have to be sophisticated or difficult to be effective. "You don't need to do Sudoku puzzles or crosswords to benefit. Going to a museum with friends and talking about what you've just seen is great. Many recent studies have shown that merely being mentally engaged, no matter what the topic, actually increases blood flow, leading to the building of new brain cells along with enhanced cognitive function. You're literally increasing your cognitive reserve!"

FORTIFY YOUR MEMORY WITH SUPPLEMENTS

Finally, Dr. Khalsa closely follows research on dietary supplements and cognitive function, and told me he believes that certain ones are quite helpful. *He likes...*

• **Phosphatidylserine.** This naturally occurring molecule, known as a *phospholipid*, is important for the integrity and maintenance of the brain cell membranes. Because it is depleted by stress hormones like cortisol, it is often deficient in people with chronic stress.

• **Fish oil.** The anti-inflammatory properties of fish oil are very helpful in reducing inflammation in the brain which many scientists believe increases vulnerability to Alzheimer's. Interestingly, the National Institutes of Health has begun to study omega-3 oils and their effect on cognitive function, though no conclusive findings are yet available.

• **Ginkgo biloba.** "A recent study showed that patients taking gingko performed no differently on standard memory tests than a matched group of patients taking *donepezil* (Aricept), a common medication for Alzheimer's," said Dr. Khalsa.

• **Turmeric/curcumin.** This spice is a significant anti-inflammatory and therefore thought to be helpful to all brain function. Take in supplement form or simply use the spice when cooking as much as possible.

• **L-Alpha Glycerylphosphorylcholine (Alpha-GPC).** Naturally present in all cells, this molecule can also be taken as a supplement. It is a pro-phospholipid, used by the body to build cell membranes. Numerous studies have shown that, used as a supplement, it benefits attention, mental focus, recall and other higher mental functions.

While there is no proven way to prevent Alzheimer's, employing some or all of these strategies may help you stay sharper and more functional longer. Who among us wouldn't benefit from doing that?

REPORT #101
The Truth About Brain Food...and Supplements that Keep Your Memory Intact

Mark A. Stengler, NMD, licensed medical doctor in private practice, La Jolla, California...adjunct associate clinical professor at the National College of Natural Medicine, Portland, Oregon...author of many books, including *The Natural Physician's Healing Therapies* and coauthor of *Prescription for Natural Cures* (both from Bottom Line Books)...and author of the *Bottom Line/Natural Healing* newsletter.

Everyone forgets something from time to time. Some people have trouble remembering names. Others can't keep track of their car keys. Whether we suffer everyday absentmindedness or moments of real memory loss, all of us are concerned about keeping our brain power intact.

In recent years, a great deal of research has focused on the most severe kinds of memory loss—senile dementia and Alzheimer's disease. In the US, these closely related conditions affect up to 10% of people over age 65 and nearly half of those over age 85.

Many studies have identified ways to lower risk of these age-related problems. Popular methods include stress-reduction strategies, such as daily exercise, positive mental imagery, biofeedback and close personal relationships, to prevent spikes in the memory-draining stress hormone cortisol..."brain workouts," including crossword puzzles, word games and challenging card games...and eight to nine hours of sleep each night. Good nutrition— and the right kind of supplementation—also can help protect our brains and safeguard our memories at any age. The sooner you get started with a brain-protecting regimen, the more you'll benefit.

For optimal brain function, your diet should be well-balanced with carbohydrates (40%), protein (30%) and fats (30%). You can accomplish this by eating meals that include whole grains, fruits and vegetables (for complex carbohydrates)...fish, poultry, lean meats, legumes, nuts and seeds (for protein)...and fish oil, olive oil, avocados, almonds, walnuts and ground flaxseed (for fats). Steer clear of dairy products and packaged and processed foods, such as cookies, white bread and pasta, which are packed with simple carbohydrates that wreak havoc on glucose levels, contributing to diabetes, stroke/vascular disease and dementia.

THE VALUE OF FISH

Fish provides *docosahexaenoic acid* (DHA) and *eicosapentaenoic acid* (EPA), the most plentiful fatty acids in the brain. DHA, an omega-3 fatty acid, is found in abundance in cold-water fish such as mackerel, sardines, salmon and herring. You also can get it from fish-oil supplements, egg yolks, DHA-enriched eggs and some algae supplements, such as Neuromins, a product that is available at most health-food stores. Foods such as walnuts... leafy, green vegetables...and supplements including flaxseed and hemp oil contain *alpha-linolenic acid*, an omega-3 fatty acid that can be converted by the body into DHA and EPA.

How essential is DHA to memory? It has been known for some years that people have a higher risk of Alzheimer's if they have low blood levels of DHA. A study in *Archives of Neurology* revealed that people who ate fish one to three times a month had a 40% lower risk of Alzheimer's than those who never ate fish. Those who consumed fish once a week or more had a 60% lower risk. Fish may be baked, broiled or grilled.

It also makes sense to take a fish-oil supplement daily. I suggest 1,000 mg of combined DHA and EPA. Good brands are Nordic Naturals (800-662-2544, *www.nordicnaturals.com*) and Carlson Laboratories (888-234-5656, *www.carlsonlabs.com*), both available at health-food stores.

Caution: Fish oil can thin blood, so check with your doctor before using it if you take blood-thinning medications such as *warfarin* (Coumadin).

GLA IS ESSENTIAL

Omega-6s make up another class of essential fatty acids that are necessary for good brain function. Omega-6 is found in vegetable oils, including safflower, sunflower and corn oils. Most American diets contain too much of these oils due to consumption of packaged and fried foods. However, the most important omega-6 fatty acid is linoleic acid, which is converted in the body to *gamma-linolenic acid* (GLA). This essential fatty acid plays a big role in the formation of healthy brain-cell membranes, the part of the cell that stores information. Taking borage oil or evening primrose oil are healthful ways to increase GLA intake—hempseed and hempseed oil also are good sources. Another way to get GLA in the diet is by consuming flaxseed (with water to prevent constipation) or flaxseed oil.

COUNT ON CHOLINE

Just as a car needs spark plugs, an active brain needs quick-firing neurotransmitters. As the name implies, a neurotransmitter sends a signal that jumps from one brain cell to another. Substances that act as neurotransmitters—the most important of which is a brain chemical called *acetylcholine*—are vital components of the brain's communication system.

There's one hitch. In order for your body to manufacture enough acetylcholine, you need to get a closely related nutrient called *choline*. The best source of choline is *phosphatidylcholine* (PC), which occurs naturally in fish, egg yolks, legumes, nuts, meat and vegetables. It

also is found in breast milk. To help prevent memory problems, you can boost your PC intake by taking a 1,500-mg to 2,000-mg PC supplement daily. (Doses of more than 3,000 mg can cause digestive upset, including diarrhea, nausea and stomachache.)

PC is only part of the neurotransmitter equation. To turn PC into brain-friendly choline, you also need to get healthy doses of vitamin C and certain B vitamins. You can get plenty of these vitamins in your diet by eating red, yellow and green peppers, citrus fruits and cantaloupe for vitamin C and sweet potatoes, tuna and avocados for B vitamins. Also, I recommend taking a balanced daily multivitamin/mineral supplement.

Deficiencies of folic acid and other key B vitamins have been associated with an increased risk of Alzheimer's disease. These nutrients help to lower levels of homocysteine, a harmful by-product of protein metabolism that is increased in people who are genetically susceptible. That's why it is important to have your blood levels of homocysteine, folic acid and B-12 tested by your doctor to see if you need additional supplementation of folic acid and/or B-12.

THE EUROPEAN CURE

For years, European doctors have recommended a supplement called *L-alpha-glycerylphosphorylcholine* (GPC) to promote mental acuity (the ability to respond quickly and appropriately to mental challenges). GPC actually is used by the brain more effectively than PC to form acetylcholine—but it costs twice as much and is less widely available in the US. A good GPC supplement by Source Naturals is sold in some health-food stores under the brand name Alpha GPC (to find a retailer, go to *www.sourcenaturals.com*). Take two 300-mg capsules twice daily for the first four weeks, then two 300-mg capsules once daily as a maintenance dosage. Side effects are rare, but take GPC with a meal if it seems to interfere with your digestion.

PS: BE SURE TO GET MORE

Phosphatidylserine (PS) is a fat that the brain needs to preserve the key brain chemicals serotonin and dopamine. It also has been shown to reduce levels of the stress hormone cortisol. PS is found in fish, soy and leafy, green vegetables. As we age, PS levels in the body start to decline, so most people need to take a supplement once they're past age 50.

A normal daily diet has about 70 mg of PS. You need about four times that much if you have memory problems. Nearly anyone can benefit from a 300-mg daily supplement of PS. You're likely to notice improvements in mental alertness after four to eight weeks. A small percentage of people have digestive upset, such as bloating and diarrhea, but you can reduce the dosage if this is a problem. PS is available at health-food stores and pharmacies. Make sure you buy a product that lists "*phosphatidylserine*" on the label. (Some supplements contain "phosphorylated serine," a nutrient complex that doesn't provide the same benefits as PS.) A high-quality PS supplement is made by Jarrow Formulas (to find a retailer, call 800-726-0886 or go to *www. jarrow.com*).

HELP FROM ALC

When taken as a supplement, a nutrient known as *acetyl-L-carnitine* (ALC) has been shown to improve cognitive function and memory in older adults. Researchers also have found that ALC slows the progression of early-stage Alzheimer's disease. By improving communication between the two main hemispheres of the brain, ALC helps enhance the interplay of creative and cognitive brain activity.

For people with mild memory problems, I recommend taking 500 mg of ALC daily on an empty stomach. For those with more severe problems such as dementia, I suggest the same dose three times daily. Cut back if you have digestive upset. Most health-food stores carry a reliable ALC formula produced by Now Foods (888-301-1336, *www.nowcatalog.com*).

ADD ANTIOXIDANTS

In all likelihood, Alzheimer's disease and other types of dementia are related to excessive damage by free radicals (normal by-products of metabolism that can destroy cells, organs and tissues). Free radicals irreversibly injure our cells and contribute to accelerated aging, but studies have shown that this damage can be warded off by getting enough antioxidant nutrients to help guard our brain-cell membranes.

There's ample evidence that a daily dose of 2,000 international units (IU) of the powerful antioxidant vitamin E can slow the decline of cognitive function in people who have moderate to severe Alzheimer's disease. There have been controversial vitamin E studies that seemed to show a link to worsening chronic disease. However, I don't have much confidence in those studies because they were performed on unhealthy people. When it comes to Alzheimer's, results of vitamin E studies have been quite good.

All fresh fruits, vegetables and other plant foods provide multiple naturally occurring antioxidants. Juices are an especially concentrated source of antioxidants. In fact, a study of nearly 2,000 Japanese Americans found that those who reported drinking fruit and vegetable juices at least three times a week had a 75% lower risk of developing dementia than those who drank juices less than once a week. The most nutritious fruit juices include cranberry, pomegranate, apple and blueberry. I also like mixed vegetable juices containing any combination of spinach, celery, lettuce, parsley, watercress, carrot and tomato.

If there is a strong family history of dementia or you have beginning signs of it, take up to 2,000 IU of vitamin E daily. Green tea also is an excellent source of antioxidants. I recommend drinking two to four cups of green tea daily and eight ounces of fresh juice.

GINKGO—THE BRAIN PLEASER

Ginkgo biloba is an herbal remedy that has been shown to improve memory and cognitive processing by promoting blood flow to the brain. I recommend a 24% *flavoglycoside* extract. Start with a dose of 120 mg to 240 mg daily, and increase to 360 mg daily over a four-week period. Some people begin to see results in four to eight weeks. If you're already taking a blood-thinning medication such as aspirin or warfarin, consult your doctor before taking ginkgo.

REPORT #102
Exercise Rejuvenates Your Brain

John J. Ratey, MD, associate clinical professor of psychiatry at Harvard University, Boston, *www.johnratey. com*. He is author of *Spark: The Revolutionary New Science of Exercise and the Brain* (Little, Brown).

Staying active is a key to a vigorous, healthy body as we grow older. But exercise is just as important for mental health. Walking, biking or swimming helps keep your memory and reasoning ability sharp and your mood bright while it strengthens your heart, arteries—and muscles.

Like every organ, the brain requires a steady supply of oxygen and nutrients to maintain vigor. A sound mind needs a healthy body, and a healthy body needs exercise. Heart disease, diabetes and other illnesses can have a devastating effect on the brain, and exercise cuts the risk that you'll get them.

In recent years, scientists have learned a lot about what happens inside the brain when we think, form memories and learn new things… and what determines whether our moods are up or down. They've found solid evidence that exercise—even a modest amount—can have a positive effect on biological events within the brain cells themselves.

YOUR GROWING BRAIN

Not that long ago, everyone believed that after maturity, no new brain cells were born—your supply of several hundred billion declined gradually but inexorably with advancing years. Now we know that like other parts of the body, the brain constantly renews itself, generating blank cells that, under the right circumstances, can turn into thinking, functioning tissue.

At work are naturally occurring chemicals called growth factors. They are produced by the brain itself and by blood vessels and muscles. They act like fertilizer on a flowerbed, stimulating new brain cells to grow and new blood vessels to support them.

Brain cells are constantly dying, succumbing to a mix of toxins and overstimulation called molecular stress. With age, the balance shifts—growth factors decline, along with the cells' ability to withstand stress. After age 40, we lose 5% of our brain cells per decade, on average. The network of capillaries feeding the brain withers.

Nothing can stop the effects aging has on the brain, but exercise can dramatically slow it down. Animal experiments have shown that exercise boosts growth factors and the number of new brain cells produced. Other studies found that when animals were active, their brains worked better—exercise increased their ability to learn new things.

KEEP YOUR MENTAL EDGE

There's evidence that just a modest amount of exercise can have a powerful anti-aging effect on the human brain.

A study at the University of Illinois divided 59 sedentary people aged 60 to 79 into groups that did one hour of stretching three times a week, or had sessions of aerobic exercise (activity that gets your heart rate up and keeps it up) for the same amount of time. After six months, magnetic resonance imaging scans found that brain volume had increased in the aerobic exercisers—the frontal and temporal lobes, which are involved in thinking, decision-making and learning, had actually grown bigger.

These results "suggest a strong biological basis for the role of aerobic fitness in maintaining and enhancing central nervous system health and cognitive functioning in older adults," the researchers concluded.

Looking at actual performance on tests of mental ability, scientists have found that a regular aerobic program can apparently push back age-linked decline in brain function by seven to 10 years.

Exercise also protects against the worst brain-killers of all—diseases such as Alzheimer's and Parkinson's. Besides generally strengthening brain circuits, it helps keep arteries healthy and blood sugar under control, cutting the risk for dementia.

IMPROVE YOUR MOOD

Low moods can strike no matter how old you are, but the stresses and losses that frequently come with age—illness, ending a career, retiring to an unfamiliar place—make depression a special danger. Biology also plays a role. The neurotransmitters that carry messages between brain cells dwindle as the years pass. Low levels of these chemicals—*serotonin, dopamine* and *norepinephrine*—are associated with depression, and antidepressants appear to work by raising them.

Exercise stimulates neurotransmitter production and can battle depression as effectively as medication. In a Duke University study, an aerobic program proved as potent as the antidepressant Zoloft in relieving depressive symptoms.

You needn't be clinically depressed to benefit. The neurotransmitter boost of exercise raises mood, increases motivation and can charge up anyone's zest for life.

AEROBICS AND BEYOND

Your goal should be to get some physical activity nearly every day. But, especially if you've been sedentary, get there slowly. The good news is that noticeable benefits start at a much lower level—with as little as an hour a week of exercise.

Important: Check with your doctor before starting any exercise program.

Aerobic exercise appears to be the most beneficial to the brain. Swimming, biking and jogging are good, but for most, brisk walking is perfect.

How hard you should work out: To calculate your "maximum heart rate," subtract your age from 220. Your goal is walking (or doing another activity) strenuously enough to get your pulse up to 60% to 65% of maximum. Vary your workouts from 30 minutes to an hour, four days a week.

After you've become used to exercising, pick up the pace—go for 70% to 75% of maximum for 20 to 30 minutes, then back down to 60% to 65%—during two of the four workouts.

Keep it interesting. Many find that walking is more stimulating out of doors. Team up with a friend so that you can motivate each other and add the pleasures and benefits of social interaction. Variety spices up routine. If you

have access to a health club or gym, try the treadmill, exercise bike or elliptical trainer.

Strength training: The brain benefits of strength training (with weights or resistance machines) haven't been researched as thoroughly as those of aerobics, but it's well worth the effort anyway—to counter the muscle deterioration that otherwise comes with age. Try to include strength training in your workouts twice a week. If you're new to it, have a personal trainer design a program for you.

FEED YOUR BRAIN

The same diet recommended for general good health maintains the strong circulation and metabolic balance that protect your brain—lots of fruits, vegetables and whole grains, abundant fiber and limited fats. *Particularly beneficial…*

• **Berries, broccoli, spinach, beets, garlic and onions, green tea and red wine.** These contain antioxidants and other nutrients that activate cellular repair.

• **Omega-3 fatty acids**—the kind found in fish—have been linked to a host of health benefits and seem especially vital for brain vigor. The Framingham Heart Study found that a diet with the omega-3s found in three servings of fish weekly cut dementia risk in half. If you don't like fish, take a daily supplement that includes EPA and DHA, the key fatty acids.

REPORT #103
Brain-Boosting Nutrients Women Need

JoAnn E. Manson, MD, DrPH, is a professor of medicine and women's health at Harvard Medical School and chair of the division of preventive medicine at Brigham and Women's Hospital, both in Boston. She is one of the lead investigators for two highly influential studies on women's health—the Harvard Nurses' Health Study and the Women's Health Initiative. Dr. Manson is author, with Shari Bassuk, ScD, of *Hot Flashes, Hormones & Your Health* (McGraw-Hill).

Certain foods may help ward off subtle age-related cognitive decline or even full-blown dementia, recent research suggests. *Nutrients linked to a clear mind and sharp memory...*

•**Folate.** In studies of people age 70 and older, those with low blood levels of folate had about twice the risk for Alzheimer's disease as those with normal levels.

Folate reduces homocysteine, a dietary by-product linked to inflammation, blood clots and small blood vessel damage.

Best: Each day, eat two or more servings of folate-rich dark green leafy or cruciferous vegetables, such as spinach, romaine lettuce, broccoli and brussels sprouts.

As insurance, consider taking a daily multivitamin that provides 400 micrograms of folic acid (synthetic folate). Many doctors recommend up to 1,000 mcg.

•**Marine omega-3 fatty acids.** Fish provide the omega-3s *eicosapentaenoic acid* (EPA) and *docosahexaenoic acid* (DHA). Studies show that people who eat fish five or more times weekly are 30% less likely to suffer a stroke than those who rarely eat fish.

Frequent fish consumption also is associated with fewer "silent" (symptomless) brain lesions, as seen on imaging tests...and may reduce Alzheimer's risk.

Fish oil also improves function of nerve cell membranes and boosts the production of brain chemicals that allow nerve cells to communicate.

Wise: Eat salmon, tuna, herring, sardines or mackerel at least twice weekly...or take daily fish oil supplements with 400 mg to 1,000 mg of combined EPA and DHA.

Important: Watch consumption of large fish such as tuna and salmon. These may have higher levels of mercury and PCBs.

•**Flavonoids.** Oxidation, a chemical reaction that can damage blood vessels, may be a key contributor to brain aging.

Antioxidant plant pigments called flavonoids may counteract this—particularly the *anthocyanins* in deep-colored fruits such as berries, cherries and Concord grapes. In animal studies, berry extracts reversed age-related declines in spatial learning and memory as measured by how quickly the animals learned to navigate a maze.

Goal: Eat berries or deep-colored fruit at least two to three times per week.

•**Coffee.** In a study of 7,017 people age 65 and older, women who drank at least three cups of caffeinated coffee or six cups of caffeinated tea per day experienced less decline in memory over four years than those who drank one cup or less.

However, caffeine can trigger digestive upset, insomnia and migraine.

Advised: Have no more than four eight-ounce cups of coffee daily.

The alcohol question: Moderate alcohol intake is linked with less cognitive decline—though this may simply reflect that people who already have cognitive problems are less likely to imbibe.

Recommended: Do not start drinking alcohol specifically to prevent cognitive decline. If you already drink, limit consumption to no more than one alcoholic beverage daily.

REPORT #104
Cinnamon Can Help You Stay Focused

It speeds the rate at which the brain processes visual cues. Try chewing cinnamon-flavored gum before doing something that will require quick responses, such as playing tennis. To make cinnamon a regular part of your diet, sprinkle one teaspoon of it on oatmeal or cereal at breakfast.

Daniel G. Amen, MD, Amen Clinics, Newport Beach, California, writing in *AARP*, 601 E St. NW, Washington, DC 20049.

REPORT #105
The Most Powerful Brain-Building Nutrients And Herbs

Mao Shing Ni ("Dr. Mao"), PhD, DOM (doctor of oriental medicine), LAc (licensed acupuncturist), chancellor and cofounder of Yo San University in Los Angeles, and codirector of Tao of Wellness, a clinic in Santa Monica, California. He is author of numerous books, including *Second Spring: Dr. Mao's Hundreds of Natural Secrets for Women to Revitalize and Regenerate at Any Age* (Free Press). *www.taoofwellness.com.*

You open your cupboard but then can't recall what you wanted…you're introducing two friends and suddenly draw a blank on one's name.

Such instances of "brain fog" are common, but they are not an inevitable part of aging. Many people remain remarkably sharp all their lives—and the right nutritional strategies can help you be one of them.

Cognitive declines can result from hormonal changes and reductions in neurotransmitters, chemicals that help brain cells communicate with each other. Increasing your intake of certain nutrients helps balance hormones and protect neurotransmitters. *You can get these nutrients from…*

• **Foods.** Eating brain-boosting foods is an ideal way to get needed nutrients.

Reasons: The body is designed to absorb nutrients from foods rather than from isolated or manufactured chemicals (such as in supplements)…and foods contain complementary components that enhance nutrient absorption.

• **Herbs.** The healthful aromatic oils are most active when herbs are fresh, but dried herbs also will do.

• **Supplements.** These are an option if you cannot find the foods that provide certain nutrients, or if you need specific nutrients in quantities beyond what you typically get from food. Unless otherwise noted, the following supplements generally are safe, have few side effects and may be used indefinitely. All are sold at health-food stores.

Important: Ask your doctor before supplementing, especially if you have a health condition…use medication…or are pregnant or breast-feeding. To reduce the risk for interactions, do not take supplements within 30 minutes of medication…and limit your use of these supplements to any four of the following.

NUTRIENTS YOUR MIND NEEDS

For the foods recommended below, one serving equals four ounces of meat, poultry, fish, or soy products…eight ounces of milk…two ounces of nuts…two eggs (with yolks)…one-half cup of vegetables or fruit…and one cup of leafy greens.

• **Choline.** The neurotransmitter *acetylcholine* plays a key role in learning and memory. Choline is a precursor to acetylcholine that is produced in the liver. Production of choline declines with age, as does the body's ability to efficiently use the choline that remains.

Brain boost: Eat one or more servings daily of choline-rich broccoli, cauliflower, eggs, kidney beans, navy beans, liver, milk or even peanuts.

Supplement option: 1,200 milligrams (mg) daily.

• **DMAE (2-dimethylaminoethanol).** The body uses fatty acids to create brain cells and neurotransmitters. DMAE, a chemical in fatty acids, helps produce acetylcholine.

Brain boost: Have two servings weekly of DMAE-rich anchovies or sardines. If fresh fish is not available, have canned water-packed sardines or anchovies and rinse before eating to reduce salt.

Supplement option: 500 mg twice daily after meals.

• **L-carnitine.** Mitochondria are the engines of cells. The amino acid L-carnitine transports fatty acids to mitochondria for use as fuel and provides nutrients to brain cells.

Brain boost: Have two weekly servings of lamb or poultry, which are rich in L-carnitine.

Supplement option: 500 mg to 1,000 mg before breakfast and again in the afternoon.

• **Vitamin B-12.** This is key to red blood cell formation and nerve cell health. The body's ability to absorb vitamin B-12 diminishes with age—about 10% to 15% of people over age 60 are deficient in it.

Brain boost: Have two servings weekly of beef or lamb…halibut, salmon, sardines or sea bass…eggs…or vitamin B-12–enriched soybean products (miso, tempeh).

Supplement option: 500 micrograms (mcg) to 1,000 mcg daily.

THE MOST HELPFUL HERBS

An easy way to get the benefits of mind-sharpening herbs is to brew them into a tisane, or herbal infusion—more commonly called herbal tea.

To brew: Pour eight ounces of very hot water over one heaping tablespoon of fresh herbs or one teaspoon of dried herbs. Steep for five minutes, strain and drink.

Convenient: To reduce the number of cups needed to meet the daily recommendations below, brew two or more herbs together.

• **Chinese club moss.** This herb contains the chemical *huperzine A*, which helps conserve acetylcholine.

Brain boost: Drink one to two cups of Chinese club moss tea each day.

Supplement option: 50 mcg of huperzine A twice daily (discontinue if supplements cause gastric upset or hyperactivity).

• **Ginkgo biloba.** This herb increases blood flow to the brain's tiny capillaries and combats DNA damage caused by free radicals.

Caution: Do not use ginkgo if you take blood-thinning medication, such as *warfarin* (Coumadin).

Brain boost: Drink three cups of ginkgo tea daily.

Supplement option: 120 mg daily.

• **Kitchen herbs.** Oregano, peppermint, rosemary and sage have oils that may increase blood flow in the brain and/or support neurotransmitters, promoting alertness.

Brain boost: Use any or all of these herbs to brew a cup of tea for a pick-me-up in the morning and again in the afternoon.

Also: Use herbs liberally when cooking.

Supplement option: About 150 mg each of any or all of these herbs daily, alone or in combination.

• **Mugwort (wormwood).** This herb improves circulation, aiding delivery of nutrients to brain cells.

Brain boost: Twice a week, drink one cup of mugwort tea…add a half-dozen leaves of fresh mugwort to salad…or sauté leaves with garlic or onions.

Supplement option: 300 mg daily.

Caution: Avoid mugwort during pregnancy—it may stimulate uterine contractions.

Don't forget: Green Tea

Strictly speaking, an herb is a flowering plant whose stem above ground does not become woody. In that sense, the leaf of the Camellia sinensis shrub—otherwise known as tea—is not an herb. Yet green tea (which is less oxidized than black) is so helpful that it must be listed among the top brain boosters.

Along with antioxidant polyphenols, green tea provides the amino acid *theanine*, which stimulates calming alpha brain waves and improves concentration. Green tea also has been linked to a reduced risk for Alzheimer's disease.

To brew: Pour eight ounces of very hot water over one teaspoon of loose, fresh green tea leaves (or a tea bag if fresh is not available) and steep for three to five minutes. You needn't strain the tea. As you empty your cup, you can add more warm water to the remaining leaves—as long as the water turns green, the tea still contains polyphenols.

Brain boost: Drink three cups of green tea (caffeinated or decaffeinated) daily.

Supplement option: 350 mg of green tea extract daily.

REPORT #106
Breakthrough Jellyfish Treatment Makes You Smarter Within Days

Mark A. Stengler, NMD, licensed medical doctor in private practice, La Jolla, California…adjunct associate clinical professor at the National College of Natural Medicine, Portland, Oregon…author of many books, including *The Natural Physician's Healing Therapies* and coauthor of *Prescription for Natural Cures* (both from Bottom Line Books)…and author of the *Bottom Line/Natural Healing* newsletter.

Scientists have found that a naturally occurring protein in one of the planet's oldest sea creatures—the jellyfish—might hold the key to improved memory and comprehension. The substance, *apoaequorin* (a-poh-ee-kwawr-in), found in the Aequorea victoria jellyfish species, has a unique way of working in the brain that is different from other natural memory enhancers. Many of my patients already are benefiting from it. Apoaequorin not only seems to reverse some of the effects of aging on the brain but also might help alleviate the effects of serious neurodegenerative diseases such as Alzheimer's disease, Parkinson's disease and ALS (Lou Gehrig's disease).

THE JELLYFISH CONNECTION

Scientists first discovered apoaequorin and its companion molecule, green fluorescent protein (GFP), in the Aequorea jellyfish, found off the west coast of North America, in the 1960s. The natural glow of GFP enables researchers to observe microscopic processes within cells that were previously invisible, such as how proteins are transported or how viruses enter cell membranes. Apoaequorin, which binds to calcium and becomes luminescent once it does, has been used since the 1990s in a similar way to track the activity of calcium in the body's cells. In 2008, three researchers who played key roles in developing these chemical markers were awarded the Nobel Prize in Chemistry. Apoaequorin's value as a memory-boosting supplement also depends on its calcium-binding properties but in a different way. In the brain, calcium plays an important role

in the chemical process that allows nerve cells to recharge before firing. It has to be present in just the right amounts. If too much calcium builds up inside a nerve cell, it interferes with the nerve-firing process and causes the cell to die. One of the key roles of calcium-binding proteins is to prevent the toxic buildup of calcium by removing excess calcium from the nerve cells. In the normal course of aging, beginning at around age 40, the number of calcium-binding proteins in our brain cells starts to decline, resulting in the gradual buildup of toxic calcium inside these cells. This leads to impaired cellular function and eventually brain damage as the toxic calcium kills off brain cells. The symptoms of this age-related deterioration start slowly but then accelerate as we get older. Because apoaequorin is similar to the naturally occurring calcium-binding proteins in the brain, the theory is that by taking daily supplements, you can replace the calcium-binding proteins that are lost through the aging process—allowing your brain cells to function optimally again while also preserving them from the long-term toxic effects of excess calcium.

A "EUREKA" MOMENT

The jellyfish protein went from "scientific" discovery to "supplement for the brain" because of the efforts of Mark Underwood, cofounder of the biotech firm Quincy Bioscience, the company that makes Prevagen (888-814-0814, *www.prevagen.com*), the only commercially available form of apoaequorin. Underwood's "eureka" moment came when he was reading about an Australian swimmer who developed multiple sclerosis–like symptoms after being stung by a jellyfish. Underwood wondered what protected the jellyfish from its own venom…and whether apoaequorin's calcium-binding abilities could have neuroprotective properties.

His company conducted a number of studies in conjunction with the University of Wisconsin–Milwaukee that found that apoaequorin did seem to have a powerful protective effect on brain cells. In one study, 56 people ranging in age from 20 to 78 showed significant improvements in memory after taking 10 mg of Prevagen daily for 30 days. More than half the group reported gains in general memory and information retention…two-thirds did better at word recall…and 84% showed improvement in their ability to remember driving directions. Most of my patients and others report that taking Prevagen helps them feel mentally sharper, improves their memory and gives them more mental energy. Some even say that their mood is enhanced and that they sleep more soundly.

HOW TO USE IT

Prevagen is best taken in the morning (because cognitive function is more important during the day than at night), with or without food. I recommend it for anyone over age 40 who wants to improve memory and focus. While 10 mg daily is the recommended starting dose, apoaequorin also is safe at higher doses. I recommend that my own patients who have suffered a noticeable decline in cognitive function start out with 10 mg daily for four weeks. If they don't notice an improvement in memory and focus, they can increase to 20 mg daily. Most of my patients benefit from taking 10 mg or 20 mg daily. Research has shown that Prevagen is safe to take with other memory-enhancing supplements, such as omega-3 fish oils, or medications, such as *donepezil* (Aricept). People with allergies to fish or shellfish can use it because jellyfish is neither. The manufacturer of Prevagen is exploring apoaequorin's potential as a medical treatment for conditions such as Alzheimer's disease and Parkinson's disease. It's a good choice for those who need safe, natural memory support.

REPORT #107
Rejuvenate Your Mind With Acupressure

Applying pressure to certain areas of the body opens energy pathways by increasing blood circulation.

How to do it: Gently place your thumb and middle finger of one hand on your forehead above each eyebrow, making a bridge. Meanwhile, with your other hand, reach around to the back of your head and apply firm pressure just below the base of the skull on either side of the spine. Use light pressure in front and firm pressure in back for three minutes to refresh your mind.

More information: *www.tensionrelief.info* and *www.acupressure.com*.

Michael Reed Gach, PhD, founder, Acupressure Institute, Berkeley, California.

REPORT #108
Exercise Your Brain by Using the Internet

Brain scans show that searching the Internet for information may take more brain power than reading and can be a great mental exercise. Activities that keep the mind engaged may help preserve brain health and cognitive ability with advancing age. Traditionally, these activities include reading, games and puzzles, but now Internet use may be among the best.

Gary Small, MD, professor, Jane & Terry Semel Institute for Neuroscience and Human Behavior, University of California, Los Angeles, and coauthor of *iBrain: Surviving the Technological Alteration of the Modern Mind* (Harper).

Volume 11
Fatigue Cures

REPORT #109
Feeling Tired All the Time? How to Get Your Energy Back

All too often, conventional medical practitioners mistakenly assume that fatigue is a red flag for depression—especially if the patient complains only of a vague yet constant tiredness. But fatigue typically results from a complex constellation of physical and emotional issues. That's why treatment should be based on an assessment of the patient's physical health and lifestyle. *Before you see your doctor with a complaint of fatigue, spend two weeks completing this checklist...*

•**Monitor your breathing.** Shallow breathing, which is commonly caused by anxiety, fear and poor posture, reduces your oxygen supply and, as a result, often leads to fatigue. To monitor your breathing, pay attention to your breathing patterns throughout the day.

In addition, practice deep breathing for five minutes several times a day.

What to do: As you inhale deeply, allow your lungs to fully expand (your belly should rise if you're doing this correctly), then exhale to a count of five. If you have trouble taking a deep breath, or if you cough or wheeze during deep breathing, discuss this with your physician. These reactions could be signs of disease or injury.

•**Note your caffeine intake.** If you need more than 20 ounces of a caffeinated beverage to get through the day, ask your doctor to order blood tests to check your levels of blood sugar (glucose) and the adrenal hormones *dehydroepiandrosterone* (DHEA) and cortisol as well as your thyroid function (TSH, T3 and T4). Each may be linked to fatigue.

Jamison Starbuck, ND, naturopathic physician in family practice, Missoula, Montana. She is past president of the American Association of Naturopathic Physicians and a contributing editor to *The Alternative Advisor: The Complete Guide to Natural Therapies and Alternative Treatments* (Time Life).

• **Do a media and computer "fast" for the weekend.** Keeping up with media reports is enough of a job. When you add in the deluge of information most of us receive via the computer, it can be a tremendous energy drain. A time-out will tell you if you need to cut back on these activities.

• **Keep a diet diary for one week.** Each day, write down what you eat and drink and a description of your energy levels in the morning, afternoon and evening. Look for patterns. Skipping meals and consuming foods that can trigger allergic reactions, such as wheat, dairy, eggs or soy, are common causes of fatigue. Not drinking enough plain water, which is important to overall physiological function, also may be a culprit.

My advice: Drink one-half ounce of plain water for every pound of body weight—for example, if you weigh 150 pounds, drink 75 ounces of water daily.

• **Assess your emotional state.** Fatigue can result from painful emotions, such as grief or anger, but some doctors are too quick to prescribe an antidepressant. It's often better to first try keeping a journal, talking to a close friend and/or meeting with a counselor.

Of course, fatigue can be caused by medical conditions, such as diabetes, anemia and even cancer. That's why you should see a doctor if your fatigue does not improve after trying these steps. If you experience extreme fatigue accompanied by pain, fever or disorientation, see your doctor immediately.

REPORT #110
Energy Drinks

Energy drinks can raise blood pressure, cause faster heartbeat and lead to irritability, nervousness and nausea. Many contain as much caffeine as one or two cups of coffee and as much sugar as one can of soda. Some also include herbal stimulants. An occasional energy drink may be a useful stimulant—but regularly drinking several energy drinks a day can damage health.

Also: It is dangerous to consume energy drinks with alcohol or when you are dehydrated. The caffeine and other ingredients can increase risk for fainting and even a heart attack.

Mayo Clinic Health Letter, 200 First St. SW, Rochester, Minnesota 55905. *www.healthlettermayoclinic.com.*

REPORT #111
10 Quick Energy Boosters

Jon Gordon, best-selling author of *Energy Addict: 101 Physical, Mental and Spiritual Ways to Energize Your Life* (Perigee) and *The 10-Minute Energy Solution* (Putnam). His performance-energy consulting firm The Jon Gordon Companies, is based in Ponte Vedra Beach, Florida. Clients include the PGA Tour, the Jacksonville Jaguars football team, General Electric, State Farm Insurance and Wachovia Bank. *www.jongordon.com.*

Three-quarters of the people I meet complain of tiredness during the day. This epidemic of exhaustion is brought about by mental and physical stress, including too much caffeine and sugar as well as too little sleep and exercise.

Here are easy ways to feel more alert and energetic…

• **Stop hitting the snooze button on your alarm clock in the morning.** Your brain goes through periods of light and heavy sleep. Falling back to sleep for just five more minutes can cut short a new sleep cycle, leaving you groggier when you do arise.

Better: Set your clock for when you really have to get up. Open your shades right away, and get as much light as possible—bright light wakes you up and invigorates you. Raise your heartbeat for at least five minutes in the morning by running in place or doing sit-ups, push-ups or jumping jacks.

• **Eat a power breakfast.** It will energize you as you start the day.

My favorite power breakfast: Mix low-fat plain yogurt and one-half cup of old-fashioned raw oatmeal when you first get up. The yogurt will soften the oats while you shower and dress. Add a few chopped walnuts, one-half cup of pineapple or one-quarter cup of blueberries.

• **Sit up straight.** Bad posture can decrease your oxygen intake, and slouching exhausts your neck, shoulders and upper-back muscles.

Correct posture for sitting: Your back should be aligned against the back of the chair, so that you can work without leaning forward. Your knees should be a bit higher than your hips. Keep both feet flat on the floor and your arms flexed at a 75- to 90-degree angle

• **Replace coffee with green tea.** The rich taste of coffee and the mental alertness it imparts make coffee drinking a tough habit to break. But coffee raises stress hormones, and just a few cups a day creates an energy roller coaster that increases overall fatigue. I have found that people who have the most success giving up coffee switch to green tea. It contains one-third the amount of caffeine (20 mg to 25 mg per six-ounce cup), so you get an energy boost without feeling irritable or experiencing a slump later on.

Bonus: Green tea is loaded with disease-fighting antioxidants.

If you have no intention of giving up your daily coffee, at least try cutting back to half regular/half decaffeinated.

• **Consume protein with meals.** It helps your body absorb sugar at a slower rate, so your energy levels don't fluctuate so much during the day.

Examples: Fish, eggs, hummus, skinless poultry breast, lean red meat.

• **Go for a 10-minute walk after lunch.** It raises your metabolism and prevents you from falling into the familiar, post-meal "coma."

If it's inconvenient to go outside, try chair squats.

How to do that: With a chair behind you, stand with your feet positioned shoulder-width apart. Keep your back straight and your chin up. Squat down, and push out your rear as if you were going to sit in the chair behind you. Just as your rear touches the chair, return to your starting position. Repeat five to 30 times—or until you feel your muscles have had enough.

• **Take a short nap, no more than 25 minutes.** Longer than that and you move into a deeper phase of sleep, which, if interrupted, can leave you groggier than before your nap. The optimal time to take a nap is eight hours after you wake up.

• **Eat an energy snack, such as a banana or a handful of walnuts or almonds.** Avoid commercial energy drinks and energy bars—they often work by introducing caffeine and/or sugar into your system.

Helpful: I do recommend a caffeine-free, multivitamin energy powder that I use myself each day—Fatigued to Fantastic! from Enzymatic Therapy, available at health-food stores.

Cost: About $30 or more for a month's supply.

• **Try peppermint.** It boosts mood and motivation. Have a cup of peppermint tea, or dab peppermint oil (available at health-food stores) on your wrists.

• **Breathe.** We tend to hold our breath when we work intensely or are under stress—and this contributes to fatigue.

To practice energy-boosting breathing: Stand up straight with your arms at your sides. Inhale for two seconds as you raise your arms slowly over your head with your palms open. Continue lifting your arms until they are directly over your head with fingertips touching. Exhale for three seconds as you bring your arms down. Repeat 10 times.

REPORT #112
12 Powerful Ways to Boost Your Energy

Kenneth H. Cooper, MD, MPH, pioneer in the fields of preventive medicine and physical fitness. He is founder and chairman of Cooper Aerobics Center, Dallas, and author of 18 books, including *Regaining the Power of Youth at Any Age* (Nelson). His books have sold more than 30 million copies worldwide. *www.cooperaerobics.com.*

As we get older, we often complain that we're "running on empty." I call this age-related loss of energy youth drain—but we don't have to be victims of it. At 74 years of age, I work 60 hours a week, travel widely and still feel energetic.

Youth drain can be caused by a variety of factors, including obesity...chronic medical problems, such as anemia, diabetes, emphysema or an under-active thyroid gland...depression... cancer...use of sedatives and sleeping pills... menopause...poor diet...inadequate sleep...and stress. These factors batter us over the years and drain our vitality—unless we learn how to respond to them and counter their effects.

Here, 12 revitalizing strategies for us all...

1. Eat less but more frequently. Consuming large meals (more than 1,000 calories per sitting) makes you feel sluggish, as your body's resources are directed toward digesting all that food.

Instead, graze on small meals and snacks that contain a mix of carbohydrates and protein (but little fat) to provide a steady stream of fuel.

Examples: Yogurt smoothie (one cup light nonfat yogurt, one-half cup fat-free milk, one-half peach, blended)...peanut butter and banana sandwich (one slice wholewheat bread, one-half tablespoon peanut butter, one-half banana, sliced)...fruity cottage cheese (one-half cup 1% low-fat cottage cheese, one-half cup pineapple chunks in juice, drained).

2. Exercise. The health benefits of exercise are well-known, but many people tell me they continue to exercise year after year because it makes them feel good and gives them more energy. I recommend at least 30 minutes of sustained activity five times a week. The best activities for most people tend to be brisk walking, jogging, swimming, cycling and aerobic dance.

3. Take a multivitamin. In a clinical trial, people who took multivitamins daily not only had improved immunity against infectious diseases but also had more energy. In general, it is best to get vitamins from food, but many people don't get the necessary amounts, so I suggest taking a multivitamin/mineral supplement daily.

4. Prevent dehydration. Consuming an inadequate amount of fluids, particularly if it's hot outside or you're exercising, can deplete energy and lead to weakness, dizziness and headaches. Drink at least six to eight eight-ounce glasses of water daily. On days that you exert yourself to the point of perspiring, increase that to up to 13 glasses.

5. Watch what you drink. Drink no more than one caffeinated beverage a day. Coffee, tea, cola and other caffeinated beverages provide a temporary energy boost, but energy levels plunge when the stimulant's effects wear off.

Caffeinated drinks also have a diuretic effect, which may cause you to lose fluids because you urinate more frequently.

Also, limit alcohol consumption to no more than one drink a day—any more can lead to fatigue.

6. Practice the "relaxation response." This technique, developed by Herbert Benson, MD, of Harvard University, has been shown to reduce blood pressure and heart rate. For me, doing this for just five minutes in the middle of the day is rejuvenating.

How to do it: Sit in a chair in a quiet room. Close your eyes. Starting with your feet, begin to relax your muscles, progressively moving up the body to the top of the head. While you do this, breathe in slowly and naturally through your nose and out through your mouth. As you exhale, silently repeat a focus word or phrase that has meaning for you, such as "peace." Push away distracting thoughts by focusing on your breathing and the word you have chosen to repeat.

For more information, read *The Relaxation Response* by Herbert Benson, MD (Harper-Torch).

7. Take naps. Surveys show that most Americans don't get as much sleep as they need (most of us require seven to eight hours a night). Daily naps of 15 to 20 minutes are energizing—and longer naps can help you catch up if you are sleep-deprived. I sleep only five to six hours a night, so I often take a two-hour nap on Saturdays.

8. Don't immerse yourself in bad news. The glut of negative information coming our way from TV, radio, newspapers, the Internet, etc. can hurt the psyche, causing stress and fatigue. Reduce the amount of time you spend watching, listening to or reading the news, and focus on things that bring you joy.

9. Be social. Studies show that isolation can lead to depression and early death. We gain energy by being with others (both humans and animals). Make time for family, friends and pets.

10. Explore your creativity. Boredom leads to a lack of motivation and energy. Finding a creative outlet that absorbs you is invigorating. Developing your creativity also teaches you new skills…challenges your brain…and leads to the release of endorphins, feel-good brain chemicals. Take up a new hobby…learn a musical instrument…take on an unusual project at work.

Added benefit: Mentally stimulating activities such as the ones mentioned above, can lower your risk of Alzheimer's disease.

11. Laugh. Laughter appears to release endorphins just as creative pursuits do. By improving your outlook, you'll feel more energetic and ready to tackle life.

Helpful: Watch funny movies…read cartoons…share humorous stories and jokes with friends.

12. Think young. To a large extent, your mindset dictates how much energy you have as you age. If you expect the worst, you're likely to feel tired and unwell. If you expect to stay vital, you'll fight off disease that can sap energy and well-being—and you'll add years to your life.

REPORT #113
Boost Your Energy in Eight Minutes or Less

Evangeline R. Lausier, MD, director of clinical services at Duke Integrative Medicine and assistant clinical professor of medicine at Duke University School of Medicine, both in Durham, North Carolina.

When you feel drowsy or droop with fatigue, every task you undertake seems monumental—and even fun activities you normally enjoy feel like work.

Helpful: Take a double-pronged approach to invigoration—including on-the-spot techniques for an immediate energy burst…plus simple strategies that take just minutes to do, yet give you long-lasting stamina day after day.

For An Instant Energy Surge…

• **Wake up your nose—and the rest of you will follow.** Aromatherapy stimulates the brain's olfactory center and heightens awareness of your surroundings. Dab a drop of therapeutic-grade rosemary essential oil (sold at health-food stores) on the pulse points behind both ears, as you would perfume…or dampen a cloth with cool water, sprinkle it with four drops of therapeutic-grade lemon essential oil, then place it on your forehead or the back of your neck for five minutes. Do not dab full-strength essential oil directly under your nose—it could be too strong.

To Refuel Energy Reserves…

• **Eat a stamina-boosting breakfast—one cup of fortified, whole-grain cereal.** Whole grains are complex carbohydrates that enter the bloodstream slowly, providing sustained energy by keeping blood sugar levels stable. Avoid starting your day with simple carbohydrates, such as white toast or a doughnut, which cause blood sugar and energy levels to spike and then plummet by mid-morning.

Also: With your cereal, have one-half cup of low-fat milk or fortified soy milk. Its calcium and vitamin D nourish your bones…its protein is used to build and repair muscle and other tissues.

• **For snacks, go nuts.** A handful of almonds, cashews, walnuts or other type of nut provides a sustained energy boost, thanks to blood sugar–stabilizing complex carbohydrates and tissue-building protein.

More benefits: Though relatively high in calories at about 160 per ounce, nuts tend not to cause energy-depleting weight gain because they promote long-lasting satiety and stave off hunger. Nuts also are rich in unsaturated fats that promote cardiovascular health.

Volume 12
Insomnia Cures

REPORT #114
New and Natural Sleep Aids

Oh for a sweet sleep—and, goodness, how Americans are clamoring to get one. Naturopathic physician Chris D. Meletis, ND says that if this is a new situation, first consider what may be causing it. Is there something in your life that has increased stress—perhaps conflicts at work or a problem with your child—anything, in fact, causing anxiety that might interfere with sleep? Maybe the problem is something less apparent, for instance, your sleep environment. A mattress that has become uncomfortable or a pillow that is too hard or soft can be just enough of an irritant to intrude on good sleep. Is the bedroom dark enough and the temperature just right for you? Also consider—have you started any new medications (or changed dosages) that might impact the quality of your sleep?

Dr. Meletis also reminds people that food and drink can impact sleep. Caffeine, of course, is often a culprit. Some people must avoid having caffeine after 2:00 pm, but supersensitive types should stay away from caffeine completely. Only by eliminating or vastly reducing it for a few weeks will you know if you are in that group. Remember, too, that caffeine lurks in chocolate, colas and tea as well as coffee. As to food, Dr. Meletis recommends having the last meal of the day provide a balance of protein and complex carbs—vegetables (except tomatoes and peppers)...whole grains and the like. This will fill you enough that hunger won't wake you up. Avoid spicy, fried and fatty foods and mint, all of which may increase acid reflux, and don't eat or drink liquids for two or three hours before bed to avoid middle-of-the-night treks to the bathroom. The ban includes alcohol, which also interferes with the quality of sleep.

Chris D. Meletis, ND, executive director and officer of Academic Affairs for the Institute of Healthy Aging, Beaverton, Oregon.

Anyone who is taking sleeping pills may need to be careful when weaning off of them, he says.

The reason: You can become dependent on the drug and need time to recover. Under supervision of the prescriber, gradually decrease dosage until you are off the medication completely. This process often takes several weeks. Dr. Meletis says that drinking green tea (during the day since it also has caffeine) will help in this process because it has *L-theanine*, an amino acid that potentially helps induce relaxation. He adds that B-complex vitamins also combat stress and, as a bonus, often make dreams more vivid. (Although necessary to take at least twice daily, unduly high B vitamin supplementations can contribute to sleeplessness because they can be energizing.) Certain herbs are also calming and can help produce a more restful sleep, including valerian, Passion Flower and chamomile tea.

Dr. Meletis says there are also herbal formulas that some people find helpful for occasional sleeplessness.

He likes Herbal Sleep by Vitamin Research Products (*www.vrp.com*) that contains the following…

- **L-theanine (150 mg)**
- **Hops (133 mg)**—Humulus lupulus extract, (strobiles)
- **Lemon Balm (133 mg)**—(Melissa officinalis extract, leaf)
- **Valerian (100 mg)**—(Valeriana officinalis extract, root with 0.8% valerianic acid)
- **Passion Flower (133 mg)**—(Passiflora incarnata, arial)

Consult a knowledgeable physician before you take any of the herbs or supplements above, as all botanicals can have side effects or interact with other pharmaceuticals or other supplements.

OTHER IDEAS

Some nights, though, you may need other ways to quiet a mind that continues to churn. Dr. Meletis suggests keeping a note pad and pen next to your bed so that you can jot down a few words that capture the worry or great idea so that you can relax knowing you have a reminder for the morning. He also suggests the following self-healing techniques, based in part on existing sleep-inducing methods. Studies show a stressful experience during the day can inhibit sleep at night and so it is important to combat one with relaxation techniques right away.

Try this for a brief mid-day meditation: Sitting up, close your eyes and observe your breathing without changing the way you breathe in any way. How much time do you spend breathing in and how much time breathing out? Pay attention to where the breath goes inside of you and what parts of you don't participate in the breath process. Again, don't change the way you breathe, merely observe it until you feel completely relaxed.

For soothing yourself into sleep, try these techniques, both of which you should do slowly, gently and in bed…

- **On your back, rest your palms on either side of your belly.** As you breathe in, notice how your fingers go along for the ride as your belly gently swells on breathing in and recedes as you exhale. After many breaths, begin to gently, minimally lift one set of fingers, such as your thumbs, then switch to index fingers, just slightly so that ultimately the tips are barely off your skin as you finish breathing in. Allow them to return to the belly as you exhale and your belly recedes. The idea is not to breathe bigger or differently in any way, which is enough to induce stress. Instead simply observe what you do and repeat as necessary.

- **On your back, rest your arms at your sides and bend your elbows so that one forearm is now perpendicular to the bed with your hands in a soft-fist position.** Keeping your forearm upright, gently bend your wrist so that the palm faces the bed. Do this slowly enough that you can feel that pull of gravity on your hand. (Your forearm position does not change.) You will see that your fist gradually and naturally unfolds as you do this. Gently, slowly, return your hand to its original position where it will return to a soft fist, again, naturally. Repeat as necessary.

REPORT #115
Better Insomnia Relief

In a study of 46 people with chronic insomnia, one group was trained in *cognitive-behavioral therapy* (CBT) techniques, including relaxation practices and stimulus (noise, light) control. Two other groups took either the sleeping pill *zopiclone* (Imovane) or a placebo every night.

Result: After six weeks, time spent awake dropped 52% in the CBT group compared with 4% in the zopiclone group and 16% in those taking a placebo.

Theory: CBT helps patients identify and change negative thoughts, which can be an underlying cause of insomnia.

Børge Sivertsen, PhD, researcher and psychologist, department of clinical psychology, University of Bergen, Norway.

have been used for generations in other parts of the world as the front-line treatments for many common conditions.

How herbs can help you: Compared with many medications widely used in the US, herbal therapies tend to have fewer side effects, are generally just as effective—if not more so—and are often less expensive.*

An herb to have on hand in your home...

VALERIAN FOR INSOMNIA

Compounds in valerian act on brain receptors to induce drowsiness and relaxation.

How to use: Take one-half teaspoon of valerian tincture, diluted in water according to the instructions on the label, one hour before bedtime and one-half teaspoon at bedtime, as needed. In small doses—about one-quarter to one-half of the insomnia dose—valerian also can help reduce mild anxiety. Most people avoid valerian tea due to its unpleasant odor.

*If you have a chronic condition and/or take prescription medication, consult your doctor before taking herbs.

REPORT #116
Healing Herb for Insomnia

Kathy Abascal, RH, registered herbalist who practices in Vashon, Washington. A member of the American Herbalists Guild, she is coauthor of *Clinical Botanical Medicine* (Mary Ann Liebert).

Until recently, if you peeked inside the medicine cabinet of a typical American household, you were likely to find such items as aspirin for headaches...an anti-inflammatory ointment for sore muscles and joints...an antihistamine for colds—and perhaps even a prescription sedative for sleep problems and/or an antidepressant.

Latest development: With the recent economic downturn and rising drug costs, many Americans are turning to medicinal alternatives. Recently, nationwide sales of herbal supplements totaled $4.8 billion, up more than 4% from the previous year. Perhaps due to the recession, Americans now appear to be trying many of the same herb-based products that

REPORT #117
Insomnia Remedy

Certain aromas have a calming effect that can help bring on sleep.

Helpful: Make a sachet to place under your pillow. You'll find most of the items you need at natural-food stores.

In a bowl, toss together two tablespoons of corncob chips (sold as bedding at pet shops) and four drops each of lavender essential oil and lemon essential oil...cover and let stand overnight. Uncover and stir in one-half cup of dried hops...and one-quarter cup each of dried lavender buds and lemon verbena leaves. Place mixture inside a small fabric drawstring sack (about six inches square). Refill the sack with a fresh batch of herbal stuffing every two to three weeks or when the aromas start to fade.

Dorie Byers, RN, master gardener and herbalist, Bargersville, Indiana, and author of *Natural Beauty Basics: Create Your Own Cosmetics and Body Care Products* (Vital Health).

REPORT #118
The Hidden Risks of Sleep Problems

Lawrence J. Epstein, MD, instructor in medicine at Harvard Medical School in Boston, medical director of Sleep HealthCenters, based in Brighton, Massachusetts and author of *The Harvard Medical School Guide to a Good Night's Sleep* (McGraw-Hill).

Most people assume that lack of sleep is more of an annoyance than a legitimate threat to their health. But that's a mistake. Lack of sleep—even if it's only occasional—is directly linked to poor health. If ignored, sleep problems can increase your risk for diabetes and heart disease.

About two out of every three Americans ages 55 to 84 have insomnia, but it is one of the most underdiagnosed health problems in the US. Even when insomnia is diagnosed, many doctors recommend a one-size-fits-all treatment approach (often including long-term use of sleep medication) that does not correct the underlying problem.

Everyone should have a comfortable mattress...keep the bedroom cool (about 68°F to 72°F)...and dim or turn out the lights (production of the sleep hormone melatonin can be inhibited in the presence of light). Keep TVs and computers out of the bedroom—both can be stimulating, rather than relaxing. But these basic steps may not be enough.

To treat specific sleep problems...

IF YOU WAKE UP TOO EARLY IN THE MORNING

Early risers often have *advanced sleep phase syndrome* (ASPS), which is seen most commonly in older adults. With this condition, a person's internal body clock that regulates the sleep-wake cycle (circadian rhythm) is not functioning properly. ASPS sufferers sleep best from 8 pm to 4 am.

My solutions: To be able to reset your circadian rhythm, try a light box (a device that uses lightbulbs to simulate natural light). Light boxes don't require a doctor's prescription and are available for $100 to $500 online or from retailers, such as Costco. Most people use a light box for 30 minutes to an hour daily at sundown. (Those with ASPS may need long-term light therapy.) If you have cataracts or glaucoma or a mood disorder (such as bipolar disorder), consult your doctor before trying light therapy. Patients with retinopathy (a disorder of the retina) should avoid light therapy.

Also helpful: To help regulate your internal clock so that you can go to bed (and get up) later, take a 3-mg to 5-mg melatonin supplement each day. A sleep specialist can advise you on when to use light therapy and melatonin for ASPS.*

IF YOU CAN'T STAY ASLEEP

Everyone wakes up several times a night, but most people fall back to sleep within seconds, so they don't remember waking up.

Trouble staying asleep is often related to sleep apnea, a breathing disorder that causes the sufferer to awaken repeatedly during the night and gasp for air. Another common problem among those who can't stay asleep is *periodic limb movement disorder* (PLMD), a neurological condition that causes frequent involuntary kicking or jerking movements during sleep. (Restless legs syndrome, which is similar to PLMD, causes an uncontrollable urge to move the legs and also can occur at night.)

My solutions: If you are unable to improve your sleep throughout the night by following the strategies already described, consult a sleep specialist to determine whether you have sleep apnea or PLMD.

Sleep apnea patients usually get relief by losing weight, if necessary...elevating the head of the bed to reduce snoring...using an oral device that positions the jaw so that the tongue cannot block the throat during sleep...or wearing a face mask that delivers oxygen to keep their airways open. PLMD is usually treated with medication.

IF YOU CAN'T GET TO SLEEP

Most people take about 20 minutes to fall asleep, but this varies with the individual. If your mind is racing due to stress (from marital strife or financial worries, for example) or if you've adopted bad habits (such as drinking

*To find a sleep center near you, consult the American Academy of Sleep Medicine (630-737-9700), *www. sleepcenters.org*.

caffeine late in the day), you may end up tossing and turning.

My solutions: Limit yourself to one cup of caffeinated coffee or tea daily, and do not consume any caffeine-containing beverage or food (such as chocolate) after 2 pm. If you take a caffeine-containing drug, such as Excedrin or some cold remedies, ask your doctor if it can be taken earlier in the day.

Helpful: If something is bothering you, write it down and tell yourself that you will deal with it tomorrow—this way, you can stop worrying so you can get to sleep.

Also helpful: When you go to bed, turn the clock face away from you so you don't watch the minutes pass. If you can't sleep after 20 to 30 minutes, get up and do something relaxing, such as meditating, until you begin to feel drowsy.

IF YOU CAN'T GET UP IN THE MORNING

If you can't drag your head off the pillow, sleep apnea or a *delayed sleep phase* (DSP) disorder might be to blame. DSP disorder makes it hard to fall asleep early, so you stay up late at night and then struggle to get out of bed in the morning.

My solutions: To treat DSP disorder, progressively stay up for three hours later nightly for one week until you reach your desired bedtime. By staying up even later than is usual for you, you'll eventually shift your circadian rhythm. Once you find your ideal bedtime, stick to it. Also consider trying light-box therapy each morning upon arising. Light helps advance your body clock so that your bedtime should come earlier. Taking 3 mg to 5 mg of melatonin one hour before bedtime should also make you sleepy at an earlier hour.

IF YOU CAN'T STAY AWAKE DURING THE DAY

If you're getting ample rest—most people need seven and one-half to eight hours a night—and still are tired, you may have narcolepsy. This neurological disorder occurs when the brain sends out sleep-inducing signals at inappropriate times, causing you to fall asleep and even temporarily lose muscle function.

Sleep apnea or periodic limb movements also can leave people feeling exhausted.

My solutions: Figure out how much sleep you need by sleeping as long as you can nightly (perhaps while on vacation) for one to two weeks. At the end of that period, you should be sleeping the number of hours you need. Give yourself that much sleep time nightly. If you remain sluggish, ask your doctor about tests for sleep apnea, PLMD or narcolepsy, which is treated with stimulants, such as *modafinil* (Provigil), that promote wakefulness.

REPORT #119
Can't Sleep? Surprising Causes of Insomnia

Andrew L. Rubman, ND, medical director, Southbury Clinic for Traditional Medicines, Southbury, Connecticut. *www.southburyclinic.com.*

Every night, millions of Americans have trouble falling asleep or staying asleep. Quite often this is caused by stress, anxiety, caffeine or overstimulation before bed. But there is another common cause that few people even know to consider—a nutritional deficiency of one kind or another. If you have such a deficiency, once it is identified you can easily correct it—and start enjoying peaceful slumber once again.

This is a far superior approach to prescription sleeping pills, which not only fail to address the underlying reason for sleeplessness but often are also addictive and have side effects such as disorientation and next-day fatigue and sluggishness.

One example: My usually bubbly and energetic colleague Kathryn suddenly started dragging at work, even nodding off during meetings. At night she would awake with unpleasant and uncontrollable urges to move her legs. The surprising cause turned out to be related to Kathryn's new vegetarian diet, which she had started several months before—without meat, her diet no longer included the iron she needed. As a result, she had developed restless legs syndrome, which makes sleeping a real challenge.

The simple solution: Her doctor prescribed iron supplements and began monitoring her levels. Now Kathryn sleeps like a baby and is once again bursting with energy at the office.

NUTRITIONAL DEFICIENCIES INTERFERE WITH SLEEP

Iron and restless legs syndrome is just one of the hidden dietary deficiencies affecting sleep. For more insight on potentially sleep-disturbing dietary deficiencies and how to address them, we turned to our nutrition guru, contributing medical editor Andrew L. Rubman, ND. If you suffer from insomnia, he recommends consulting a doctor who is knowledgeable about nutritional biochemistry to assess your nutrient levels and offer diet advice and/or supplements to support your body's natural sleep processes.

Dr. Rubman told me that the following nutrients are strongly related to sleep...

CALCIUM: NATURE'S SEDATIVE

When you run short on calcium, you are apt to toss and turn and experience frequent awakenings in the night. This mineral has a natural calming effect on the nervous system. It works by helping your body convert *tryptophan*—an essential amino acid found in foods such as turkey and eggs—into the neurotransmitter *serotonin*, which modulates mood and sleep. Serotonin, in turn, is converted into *melatonin*, a hormone that helps regulate the sleep cycle.

Dr. Rubman suggests: It's always better to get the nutrients you need from food rather than supplements. Milk and dairy products are the most common dietary sources of calcium, but Dr. Rubman notes that many people have trouble digesting cow's milk, especially as they grow older. Excellent nondairy sources of calcium are leafy green vegetables such as kale and collard greens, canned sardines, sesame seeds and almonds. The Recommended Dietary Allowance (RDA) for adults over age 18 is 1,000 to 1,200 mg/day. For those not getting enough from dietary sources, Dr. Rubman often prescribes the calcium-magnesium supplement *Butyrex* from T.E. Neesby. Take it half an hour before going to bed.

RELIEVE LEG CRAMPS WITH MAGNESIUM

Nighttime leg cramps, often due to a magnesium deficiency, are a common cause of sleeplessness. Magnesium helps your body's cells absorb and use calcium, so this mineral pair works hand in hand to relax muscles, relieve painful cramps or spasms and bring on restful slumber.

Dr. Rubman suggests: Leafy green vegetables are the best source of dietary magnesium, followed by artichokes, nuts, legumes, seeds, whole grains (especially buckwheat, cornmeal and whole wheat) and soy products. The Butyrex Dr. Rubman prescribes for calcium deficiency contains magnesium, so it helps solve this problem too. (The RDA for magnesium for adults is 400 mg/day for men and 310 mg/day for women.)

VITAMIN B-12 FOR SEROTONIN PRODUCTION

Vitamin B-12 supports the production of neurotransmitters that affect brain function and sleep, helping to metabolize calcium and magnesium and working with them to convert tryptophan into the neurotransmitter serotonin. Insufficient B-12 may be a factor if you have trouble falling or staying asleep.

Dr. Rubman suggests: Foods rich in vitamin B-12 include liver and other organ meats, eggs, fish and, to a lesser degree, leafy green vegetables. For B-12 deficiency, Dr. Rubman sometimes prescribes B-12 tablets taken sublingually (dissolved under the tongue) one hour before bedtime—but notes that it's important to take a multivitamin that contains B vitamins twice daily as well, since it helps your body use the B-12 efficiently. Note: Most B multivitamins contain B-12 but only a minimal dose, Dr. Rubman said, so further supplementation is usually necessary.

VITAMIN D MODULATES CIRCADIAN RHYTHMS

Again with the vitamin D! We can't hear enough about the importance of this vital nutrient, it seems—and indeed, vitamin D turns out to be essential to support your body's up-take and usage of calcium and magnesium. Its role in sleep involves modulating your circadian rhythm (the sleep/wake cycle that regulates your 24-hour biological clock).

Dr. Rubman suggests: Pointing out that most Americans have less than optimal levels of vitamin D, Dr. Rubman said he commonly prescribes daily supplements of D-3, the form most efficiently used by the body. He noted that 10 to 20 minutes of sunshine daily helps your body manufacture vitamin D, and foods such as fish and fortified milk are rich in this nutrient.

HERBS: SOME HELP, SOME INTERFERE WITH SLEEP

Although they do not specifically address nutritional deficiencies, Dr. Rubman also recommends relaxing herbal supplements such as chamomile, hops or valerian to gently nudge you toward sleep. Try them in teas, capsules or tinctures from reputable manufacturers such as Eclectic (*www.eclecticherb.com*), taken half an hour before retiring.

Though many people swear by melatonin, Dr. Rubman said that there is not enough scientific evidence yet to demonstrate that this popular sleep supplement works efficiently and without long-term ill effects. He does not prescribe it.

It's also important to be aware that a number of supplements are stimulating and may cause sleep irregularities in some individuals.

The biggest stimulators: Ginseng, ginkgo, St. John's wort, alpha lipoic acid and Sam-e. If you take any of these, do so early in the day, take the lowest dose that seems effective for you or discuss alternatives with your physician. These are all best used under professional guidance.

A SOOTHING BEDTIME SNACK

Dr. Rubman said that his favorite sleep inducer is to head upstairs each evening with a soothing bedtime beverage—either a cup of herbal tea with honey or a glass of warm milk (though not everyone's digestive system easily tolerates milk). He generally advises against late-night snacking, which can disturb sleep, but if you must have something keep it light. A high-protein, low-glycemic snack, such as a banana with peanut butter or half a turkey sandwich on whole-grain bread, can help encourage serotonin production...and sweet dreams.

Volume 13
Cold and Flu Cures

REPORT #120
Fighting Winter Bugs

The holidays bring together families and friends...and unfortunately, all those hugs, kisses and handshakes can spread cold and flu germs. That's one major reason why the incidence of wintertime infections usually peaks in January.

And it turns out that the flu shot is not as protective as doctors have believed. Researchers recently reported that while flu shots can prevent people from contracting specific strains of influenza, they do not decrease flu-related deaths, according to the *American Journal of Respiratory* and *Critical Care Medicine*. Why not? Those who survive the flu tend to be healthier to begin with, so the shot may not be the lifesaving factor.

Luckily, you can bolster your defenses and, if necessary, ease your symptoms with the help of natural remedies. In my experience, it's easy to reduce a cold to about two and a half days with comparatively mild symptoms. The same regimen also can minimize flu symptoms and keep them from lingering.

THREE TIPS FOR PREVENTION

Of course, it is always best to avoid getting sick in the first place. *These suggestions—challenging as they may be during the holiday season—can so effectively prevent a bug from catching hold that they are worth trying...*

• **Don't indulge in a lot of sweets.** Sugary foods reduce the ability of white blood cells to fight germs. Allow yourself a small treat or two on any given day—no more.

• **Watch your stress.** People often overcommit during the holidays. Don't overdo...get lots of rest.

Mark A. Stengler, NMD, licensed naturopathic medical doctor in private practice, La Jolla, California...adjunct associate clinical professor at the National College of Natural Medicine, Portland, Oregon...author of many books, including *The Natural Physician's Healing Therapies* and coauthor of *Prescription for Natural Cures* (both from Bottom Line Books)...and author of the *Bottom Line/Natural Healing* newsletter.

• **Wash your hands often.** It's easy to pick up germs from handshakes and doorknobs, utensils and other objects. Wash with soap for at least 20 seconds, or use a hand sanitizer if you can't get to a lavatory.

BE PREPARED TO ACT QUICKLY

If you do start to feel sick but act quickly—as soon as you notice a slight runny nose and before sniffles turn into sneezes—you may prevent cold and flu germs from taking hold. You'll need to have a "nutritional first-aid kit" handy. Stock it with these supplements, available at drugstores and health-food stores. *You can take them all at the same time…*

• **N-acetylcysteine (NAC).** In one of the many studies on this potent antioxidant and immune-system booster, Italian researchers found that people taking 600 mg twice daily developed few if any flu symptoms, even though blood tests confirmed infection. I recommend taking 500 mg to 600 mg of NAC daily throughout the year—and doubling this dose during the cold and flu season. At the first sign of symptoms, increase your intake to 2,000 mg to 3,000 mg daily for two to three days. If you are fighting a full-fledged cold or flu, maintain this higher dose for a week.

• **Vitamin C.** Take at least 1,000 mg daily throughout the year. Consider doubling this amount during the winter. I recommend 3,000 mg to 5,000 mg during the first few days of symptoms. Warning: If you develop loose stools, you're taking too much.

• **Vitamin D.** Vitamin D boosts levels of *cathelicidin*, a powerful germ-killing agent produced by your body's immune cells. Some researchers propose that colds and flu are related to low seasonal levels of vitamin D. Take 1,000 IU of vitamin D3 daily, and increase it to 5,000 IU daily for the first five days of a cold or flu.

• **Zinc.** Studies show that zinc lozenges can reduce the duration of colds in adults (zinc must be dissolved in the mouth in order to exert its antiviral properties). Take a zinc lozenge every two hours for three days, after which you can reduce the frequency—and stop when you are symptom-free. Be sure the lozenges are made with *zinc gluconate, zinc gluconate-glycine* or *zinc acetate*—which allow the best delivery into cells for fighting colds. I recommend the Cold-Eeze brand, which contains 13.3 mg of zinc gluconate-glycine.

EXTRA AMMUNITION

I also recommend that you begin taking one or more of the following supplements on the first day you feel cold or flu symptoms. (You can take them all if you wish.)

• ***Oscillococcinum* (pronounced os-sil-uh-cox-see-num).** One study found that this homeopathic remedy reduced the duration of cold symptoms by about one-fourth. A review published by the *Cochrane Collaboration* described the treatment as "promising." Follow label directions.

• **Elderberry.** Extract of elderberry (*Sambucus nigra)* rapidly reduces the aches, fatigue, coughing and fever commonly associated with flu. In one study, Israeli researchers found that 14 out of 15 people taking elderberry extract had a significant reduction in symptoms after just two days…and 13 of the patients were symptom-free after three days. I recommend the brand Sambucol, a syrup—take according to label directions.

• **Andrographis.** This Chinese herb (*Andrographis paniculata*) can reduce symptoms of upper respiratory infections, such as flu. For extra benefits, take Siberian ginseng (*Eleutherococcus senticosus*) at the same time. Stop when symptoms go away. Because herbal products vary, follow label directions.

Good brand: Nature's Way (800-962-8873, *www.natureway.com*).

• **North American ginseng.** In a study of 323 adults with a history of catching colds, supplements of North American ginseng (also known as *Panax quinquefolium*) cut the duration of colds by one-third. I recommend the COLD-fX brand, available at many pharmacies. Take one or two capsules a day if symptoms are just beginning…increase to six to nine capsules if you already have a pronounced cold or flu symptoms.

Caution: In rare cases, Panax ginseng may increase blood pressure.

• **Echinacea.** This herb enhances the body's ability to fight infections. It is readily available in tablets, capsules and alcohol-based tinctures. In an analysis of 14 studies, University of Connecticut researchers found that echinacea supplements reduced the length of a typical seven-day cold by about a day and a half. I recommend Nature's Way Echinacea capsules and Natural Factors Echinamide. Take according to label directions.

Extra defense: If you fly on commercial aircraft between November and February, assume that you will be exposed to cold and flu germs. As a safeguard, double your dose of NAC and vitamin C starting two days before and ending two days after your flight...and take vitamin D and zinc lozenges with you. As added protection, carry antibacterial wipes to keep your hands clean, and twice daily use Xlear nasal rinse, which has antimicrobial properties and helps moisturize nasal passages. All of these products are available at drugstores and health-food stores.

•**What about Airborne?** People frequently ask me what I think of this popular product, which claims to prevent winter bugs if you start taking it at the first sign of symptoms but has not been shown in studies to do so. My view: Take my list of supplements instead—they are proven cold and flu fighters.

I do not recommend that healthy children and adults get an annual flu vaccination. There is no guarantee that it will prevent the bug from striking...and the vaccines may contain traces of the toxin mercury. However, if you are at a higher-than-average risk of contracting the flu or you live with someone who is at high risk, a vaccination is worth considering. Your risk is higher than average if you are pregnant... have suppressed immunity...live with or care for others at high risk of contracting the flu (including health-care workers)...and/or have a lung condition, such as asthma or emphysema. If you do get vaccinated, I strongly recommend thimerosal-free (mercury-free) products, such as the FluMist nasal spray (for ages two to 49) or the Fluzone single-dose, prefilled syringe. Talk to your doctor about which is best for you.

REPORT #121
Eat Just One a Day...And Fight Colds, Flu and More

Carol Johnston, PhD, RD, professor and director, chair, department of nutrition, Arizona State University in Mesa, Arizona. She has published more than 75 research papers and book chapters on nutrition subjects and received the 2004 Grace A. Goldsmith Award from the American College of Nutrition in recognition of her research.

Wouldn't it be nice if you could add one simple item to your diet each day to help your body fight colds, flu, fatigue and other ailments related to a weakened immune system?

You can, according to recent research conducted at the University of California at Los Angeles. The six-year study of 17,688 men and women, published in the *Journal of the American Dietetic Association*, found that people who eat at least a one-cup portion of salad, including raw vegetables and salad dressing, every day have high blood levels of vitamins C and E as well as folic acid, all of which help promote a healthy immune system.

But some salads provide more disease-fighting nutrients than others. *Here's how to make sure your salad is as healthful as possible...*

1. Use salad dressing. In an effort to reduce fat and calories, many people sprinkle salad greens with just lemon juice or vinegar. That's a mistake.

A small amount of fat actually helps promote the absorption of fat-soluble vitamins, such as vitamins A, E, D and K. In addition to the health benefits these vitamins themselves provide, they also aid in the absorption of certain other nutrients—for example, vitamin D helps facilitate the absorption of calcium. Aim to include about two tablespoons daily of olive oil or another healthy oil, such as canola, in your salad dressing.

Smart idea: To ensure that your salad dressing is healthful, make your own. An easy recipe: Combine one-half cup of balsamic vinegar, one-quarter cup of olive oil, two tablespoons each of finely grated Parmesan cheese and sugar, one teaspoon of oregano and one-half teaspoon of garlic salt.

Calories: About 80 per two-tablespoon serving.

Sodium: 60 mg.

Fat: 7.5 g.

If you want the convenience of a bottled salad dressing, shop carefully. Many brands contain as much as 700 mg of sodium per serving (the recommended daily allowance is 1,500 mg for people age 50 and older) as well as partially hydrogenated or hydrogenated oils—code words for trans fat, which has been shown to raise blood cholesterol and heart disease risk—and 100 calories per tablespoon. If your salad contains healthful fat from avocado or nuts, consider using a low-fat dressing.

2. Don't overdo the fat content. Even though a certain amount of healthful fat is good for you, people who try to make a meal of their salad often end up adding too much fat by piling on processed meats, fried chicken, creamy salad mixtures, such as egg salad, tuna salad or macaroni salad, and high-fat cheeses.

Smart idea: Use low- or nonfat cheeses, cubed tofu, poultry (except fried or breaded versions) or fish (salmon and tuna are good choices because of their omega-3 fats).

3. Choose lettuce that is dark green or reddish. The majority of Americans make their salads with iceberg lettuce. However, this is the least nutritious type of lettuce because it contains mostly water.

Smart idea: Select romaine lettuce for your salad, then for variety, add any combination of dandelion greens, arugula, endive, chicory, butterhead lettuce or spinach, all of which are rich in folic acid, a vitamin that is important to cardiovascular health.

In general, the darker the color of the lettuce leaf, the more vitamins and minerals the lettuce contains.

4. Choose a variety of richly colored vegetables. Americans tend to pile their salads with celery and cucumbers. Even though these vegetables make good snacks—they are very low in calories—they are also relatively low in nutrients, compared with some other vegetables.

Smart idea: Add tomatoes, broccoli, snow peas and bell peppers to your salad. They are excellent sources of vitamin C and other key nutrients.

Rule of thumb: The brighter the vegetable's color, the more vitamins and minerals it contains.

5. Get your phytochemicals. These chemicals are antioxidants or enzyme inhibitors that protect our bodies from disease-causing free radicals and help to slow down the aging process.

Smart idea: Add white, yellow or red onions, garlic (crushed or chopped) and mushrooms (such as shiitake or maitake)—all are loaded with healthful phytochemicals.

6. Add nuts. Many people like to top their salads with croutons or bacon bits to add flavor, but croutons often are high in calories and most bacon-bit products contain nitrates—which have been linked to cancers of the digestive tract and the pancreas—as well as harmful fats and sodium.

Smart idea: Add a tablespoon or two of unsalted nuts, such as almonds, pistachios, cashews, walnuts, hazelnuts or peanuts. All of them contain healthful fats and are excellent sources of vitamin E. As an alternative, add unsalted sunflower seeds, which are high in fiber, potassium, phosphorus and other nutrients.

REPORT #122
Echinacea—The Best-Selling Immune Booster

Mark A. Stengler, NMD, licensed naturopathic medical doctor in private practice, La Jolla, California…adjunct associate clinical professor at the National College of Natural Medicine, Portland, Oregon…author of many books, including *The Natural Physician's Healing Therapies* and coauthor of *Prescription for Natural Cures* (both from Bottom Line Books)…and author of the *Bottom Line/Natural Healing* newsletter.

I t's not unusual to get calls at my office from patients wondering what to do about the cold or flu that just hit them.

My first thought is: What natural supplements can they get quickly, right off the shelf?

Well, just about anyone can find *echinacea* (pronounced eck-in-ay'-sha) at a nearby store. It's one of the five top-selling herbs in North America. In fact, it's a worldwide best-seller, as herbalists and doctors in Europe have been prescribing echinacea for decades. Carrying the popular name of purple coneflower (so-called because of its beautiful, purple, daisy-like petals), echinacea is renowned as an herb that enhances the immune system. It's commonly used to treat a number of conditions from flu and the common cold to a range of other infectious diseases.

THE SNAKEBITE CONNECTION

Native Americans of the Plains are believed to be the first to use echinacea. As today, it was a remedy for colds, coughs and sore throats, but also toothaches, battle wounds and even rattlesnake bites.

During the latter part of the 1800s, Plains settlers adopted the purple coneflower as a common remedy; and by the 1920s, echinacea was being sold as a commercial product and prescribed by the many physicians who were comfortable with herbal medicines.

Dr. H.C.F. Meyer of Pawnee, Nebraska, was a keen commercial promoter. Adding his own recommendations to what he had learned from Native Americans, Dr. Meyer sold echinacea as a "cure all" for various ailments. His reputation was considerably enhanced by the claim that he had successfully treated 613 cases of rattlesnake poisoning. One doctor gave the following candid account of Dr. Meyer's own, personal echinacea experiment…

"With the courage of his convictions upon him, he injected the venom of the *crotalus* (rattlesnake) into the first finger of his left hand; the swelling was rapid and in six hours up to the elbow. At this time he took a dose of the remedy, bathed the part thoroughly, and laid down to pleasant dreams. On awakening in four hours, the pain and swelling were gone."

INFECTION FIGHTER TO THE RESCUE

I can't say I have had any patients come to me for the natural treatment of rattlesnake bites. (If I did, I would quickly hurry them off to a hospital emergency room for a dose of up-to-date antivenom.) But it's interesting to note that echinacea does have the special property of preventing the spread of infectious substances to tissues.

Echinacea as a healing remedy was introduced to Europe during the 1930s. Since then the preponderance of scientific research on echinacea has been done in Western Europe, especially Germany, where the government plays an active role in funding natural-medicine research. But Canadian and American researchers have recently made similar strides in echinacea research, with clinical studies and biochemical analysis of the healing herb.

Over 400 studies to date have looked at the pharmacology and clinical uses of echinacea. Not all studies have shown efficacy of the herb, but most of the research indicates that echinacea helps reinforce the immune system.

Echinacea is consistently one of the best-selling herbs in North America and Europe. Over 10 million units are sold annually in Germany alone.

Though there are nine species of echinacea, *Echinacea purpurea* and *Echinacea angustifolia* are the two most often used commercially. Most clinical studies are done with these species, especially purpurea.

TONGUE-TINGLING CHEMICALS

Scientists have not reached a consensus about the active ingredients in echinacea. Though researchers acknowledge the herb has many immune-boosting properties as well as anti-inflammatory and antimicrobial effects, they're not sure what chemicals or combination of chemicals are responsible.

It's known, however, that echinacea contains caffeic acid derivatives such as *cichoric acid* and *polysaccharides*. The plant also has compounds known as *alkylamides* that are thought to be important. (Alkylamides are the substances that make your tongue tingle and go numb if you take a hefty dose of straight echinacea.)

Some of these compounds are water-soluble and some are alcohol-soluble. When tinctures, pills, or tablets are being created from echinacea, the manufacturer must go through an elaborate process to extract the compounds.

Recent research done at the University of British Columbia in conjunction with the University of Alberta has shown that the ratio of the actives in echinacea is important for optimal immune response. So in other words, not only is it important to have active constituents in echinacea products, but to also have them in a specific ratio or blend.

AROUSING IMMUNE CELLS

Echinacea doesn't work like the pharmaceutical antibiotics that "kill" microbes like bacteria. Instead, echinacea arouses the immune cells that patrol and defend the body against these invaders. It increases the number and activity of disease-fighting white blood cells, and it activates antiviral chemicals such as interferon. Echinacea can even activate the immune cells that fight tumors. In addition, research has shown that the chemicals in echinacea have the power to inhibit an enzyme released by bacteria, called *hyaluronidase*. Bacteria normally produce this enzyme to penetrate into human tissue. Echinacea prevents this from happening.

Researchers in a German study found clear evidence that echinacea helps to promote good immune cells, called *phagocytes*. One group of people were given 30 drops of echinacea three times daily for five days, while people in the control group were given a placebo. The level of phagocytes was measured at the beginning and throughout the study. At day three, the phagocyte activity of those taking echinacea increased by 40 percent. By the fifth day, phagocyte activity had increased 120 percent. When people stopped taking echinacea, immune-cell activity dropped off sharply. After three days, there was no difference in immune-cell activity between the group taking echinacea and the control group.

Leading researchers now feel that echinacea may actually be more of an immune-modulating herb, meaning it has a balancing effect on the immune system. As research continues, this may mean that echinacea may be more valuable than just boosting immune function.

VIRUS SLAYERS

While there are a host of modern antibiotics for killing bacteria, modern medicine has a limited arsenal of weapons to defeat viral infections. This presents a problem for the many doctors who rely on conventional pharmaceuticals in their medical practice. Over 65 million people in the U.S. each year "catch" the common cold, while another 108 million get the flu—and these are just two of the infectious diseases caused by viruses. Others include genital herpes, which affects an estimated 45 million people, as well as hepatitis C, which afflicts 170 million people in the world. Even a simple viral infection like a viral sore throat poses a challenge for any doctor who relies exclusively on antibiotics and other conventional prescription medications.

Echinacea, like some other immune-enhancing herbs, has a direct antiviral effect. Even better, it seems to summon all the resources of the immune system to help destroy the viral invaders.

It also works well in combination with other antiviral plants and herbs. I like to prescribe echinacea in a formula called the "virus cocktail," which is comprised of echinacea, lomatium, astragalus, reishi and licorice root. The synergistic blend of these herbs tends to be more effective than any one herb by itself.

BACTERIA AND FUNGUS

Since echinacea enhances the action of your immune cells, it is also effective against bacterial, fungal and yeast infections. This is especially helpful if you're fighting a bacterial infection, because many bacteria are now resistant to antibiotics (because they're over-prescribed by doctors for things like viral infections). If needed, there is no problem using echinacea in combination with antibiotics. As a matter of fact, I find when people are on antibiotics for a bacterial infection and use echinacea simultaneously, they recover more quickly.

At least one study—which included 4,190 patients—confirmed this observation. Researchers divided the patients into two groups and gave about half of them an antibacterial formula that included echinacea (along with two other herbs—*thuja* and *baptisia*). Along with that formula, the patients received antibiotics that were chosen by the doctors. For comparison, the rest of the patients received only antibiotics, with no herbal formula.

The results showed the effectiveness of taking herbal antibacterial agents along with antibiotics. In the group that got an echinacea-based formula plus an antibiotic, people were cured significantly faster and there was a lower incidence of recurring infection than in the group of people who just got an antibiotic. Also, the symptoms of "sore throat" and "difficulty in swallowing" were improved much more efficiently in the first group than in the second group.

Dosage: Echinacea is generally available as a tincture, capsule, tablet or cream in the U.S. It's also possible to take it in the form of an injection, though this method is mainly used in Germany.

Glycerine (alcohol-free) tinctures are available. These are good for kids, who especially enjoy the berry-flavored varieties.

• **Tincture.** I recommend 20 to 60 drops of the tincture every two to three hours for acute infections or twice daily for long-term use.

• **Capsule.** I recommend 500 to 1,000 milligrams every two to three hours for acute infections or twice daily for long-term use.

Note: High-potency, quality echinacea products are standardized to contain active ingredients such as *alkylamides, cichoric acid* and *polysaccharides.*

Some controversy surrounds the length of time one can use echinacea. Many authors state that echinacea should not be used on a long-term basis. However, there are no studies showing that long-term use is harmful or that echinacea loses its effectiveness.

I generally recommend patients use echinacea for acute infections until they are completely over the illness. For those who are very susceptible to infections, especially during the winter, and do not want to change their lifestyle, echinacea can be used on a long-term basis (although it is not so effective as improving diet, reducing stress and exercising). Long-term use of echinacea throughout the winter season is common in European countries.

REPORT #123
Feed a Cold, Starve A Fever and Other Nutrition Myths

Edward Saltzman, MD, chief of the division of clinical nutrition and medical director of the Obesity Consultation Center at Tufts–New England Medical Center, and a scientist at the Jean Mayer USDA Human Nutrition Research Center on Aging at Tufts University, both in Boston.

Many commonly held beliefs about the health impact of certain foods are based on hearsay, not on scientific research. *Here are the realities behind some often-cited nutrition myths...*

Myth: Feed a cold, starve a fever.

Reality: Both a cold and a fever—and you can have both at once—are associated with inflammation, which increases metabolic rate, allowing you to burn calories at rest more quickly. However, eating more or less will have no real effect on how long you remain sick. There is no evidence that food shortens a cold's duration or reduces symptoms.

It's often believed that vitamin C can help a cold, but there's no firm evidence to back that claim. Recently, researchers reviewed 55 previous studies. Most showed that taking vitamin C did not prevent colds—a few showed that colds were slightly shorter with vitamin supplementation, but usually by only one day or so.

Zinc may reduce a cold's duration, but it must be taken early on—before full-blown symptoms strike. The benefit comes from zinc gluconate lozenges (see the label for the correct dosage). Zinc acetate lozenges or zinc-rich foods, such as oysters and beef, have no impact on a cold's severity or duration.

Bottom line: The real goal is to stay hydrated and loosen mucus by increasing your intake of liquids, such as water, clear soups and tea.

Myth: Fiber prevents colon cancer.

Reality: A high-fiber diet keeps your bowel movements regular and can lower cholesterol and reduce risk of insulin resistance, a precursor to diabetes. But there is no consistent evidence that fiber protects against colon cancer.

A study in *The Journal of the American Medical Association* reviewed data on 726,000 people over 20 years and found that high-fiber diets did not reduce the risk of colon cancer. Another study determined that people eating 33 grams of fiber per day—roughly 6.5 servings of fruits and vegetables—had no fewer polyps (benign growths in the colon that may become cancerous) than those eating roughly half as much fiber. Even high-fiber cereals seem to strike out when it comes to protecting against colon cancer, although they may have benefits for cardiovascular health and prevent constipation.

Bottom line: Continue to eat fiber-rich foods, such as fruits, vegetables and whole grains, for their proven health benefits, including cardiovascular health and weight control. Also, while fiber-rich foods do not protect against colon cancer, they do protect against other types of cancer—including those of the breast, mouth, throat and esophagus—probably because of their phytochemicals, protective compounds found in some foods.

Myth: Soy relieves hot flashes.

Reality: Most scientific studies have not found that soy-rich foods or supplements offer relief from hot flashes. While soy is a good source of phytoestrogens (chemicals occurring naturally in plants that act like the hormone estrogen), it provides an extremely weak estrogenic effect. Some menopausal women may benefit from a soy-rich diet, but most do not—at least not on a consistent basis.

Bottom line: Soy-rich foods are nutritious, low in fat and may help lower cholesterol and improve prostate health (so far, studies have produced mixed results). And a recent analysis of 18 previous studies found that soy may slightly lower the risk of breast cancer. To control hot flashes, however, you're better off adjusting room temperature...wearing "breathable" fabrics, such as cotton...and drinking cool beverages when a flash starts. At this time, there are no dietary supplements known to be both safe and effective for hot flashes.

Myth: Eating after 8 pm causes weight gain.

Reality: It's not when you eat that causes weight gain—it's how much. There is no evidence that calorie "burn" is slower at night. Weight gain results from overeating and lack of activity, whether that occurs in the morning, afternoon or night.

This myth likely stems from the fact that many people eat little during the day but then overeat at night, when they're relaxing at home—but these people won't gain any more weight than those who overeat earlier in the day. Some research has suggested that people who eat breakfast are less likely to gain weight or become obese—though the reason for this is unclear.

Bottom line: Watch portion sizes more than the clock. Don't go for long periods without eating, because you are more likely to overeat when you are ravenously hungry.

Myth: Olive oil is the healthiest oil.

Reality: This foundation of the Mediterranean diet is among the healthiest cooking oils—and certainly gets the best publicity—but other oils may be just as good. For example, the FDA decreed that canola oil, like olive oil, can carry a health claim for its ability to reduce the risk of coronary heart disease due to its unsaturated fat content. The important thing is to limit saturated fats, which are most often found in animal products, such as red meat, poultry, butter and whole milk.

Bottom line: Choose oils high in mono- or polyunsaturated fat, such as olive, canola, safflower, flaxseed and walnut oils. If you choose olive oil, select extra-virgin. Extra-virgin olive oil comes from the first pressing of olives, so it's less processed and contains higher levels of antioxidants, substances that slow down the natural process that leads to cell and tissue damage.

Myth: Honey is more healthful than sugar.

Reality: Honey contains more fructose than sugar—and fructose is becoming public enemy number one among some cardiologists. Some studies suggest that high-fructose diets are linked to weight gain and metabolic syndrome, a group of health problems that includes excess abdominal fat, high blood pressure, high triglycerides (a type of fat in the blood), low "good" cholesterol and high blood sugar.

Bottom line: Go easy on sugar and honey. Both offer "empty calories"—a tablespoon of honey has 64 calories and a tablespoon of sugar has about 45 calories. Neither is a good source of any nutrient. You would need to overeat honey to an unhealthy level in order to benefit from its micronutrients or other purported health benefits.

REPORT #124
Amazing Folk Remedies For Colds, Coughs, Flu And More

Joan Wilen and Lydia Wilen are folk-remedy experts based in New York City. The sisters are coauthors of many books, including *Bottom Line's Healing Remedies: Over 1,000 Astounding Ways to Heal Arthritis, Asthma, High Blood Pressure, Varicose Veins, Warts and More!* from which this article is adapted. *www.bottomline secrets.com.*

Not every winter illness requires a trip to the doctor's office. The following time-tested folk remedies offer effective, inexpensive treatments for minor health complaints.

Important: Consult your doctor if your condition persists or grows worse.

COLDS

The average adult contracts between two and four colds each year, mostly between September and May. Medical science has no cure for these highly contagious viral infections, but the following folk remedies can help ward off colds, ease symptoms and possibly shorten a cold's duration…

• **Garlic.** Garlic contains *allicin*, which has been shown to reduce the severity of a cold. Eat four cloves of freshly crushed raw garlic three times a day until you have recovered.

• **Cinnamon, sage and bay.** Cinnamon contains compounds believed to reduce congestion. Sage can help sooth sore throats. Some Native American cultures have used bay leaves to clear breathing passages. Steep one-half teaspoon each of cinnamon and sage with a bay leaf in six ounces of hot water. Strain and add one tablespoon of lemon juice. Lemon helps reduce mucus buildup. If you like your tea sweet, add honey.

• **Chicken soup.** The Mayo Clinic has said in its health newsletter that chicken soup can be an excellent treatment for head colds and other viral respiratory infections for which antibiotics are not helpful.

FLU

• **Influenza is a potentially serious viral infection.** People often mistake colds for the flu. Colds take hold gradually and are not usually accompanied by severe aches or a fever. The onset of the flu is sudden, and symptoms include fever, severe muscle aches and fatigue.

• **Garlic and cognac.** A shot of cognac is a popular flu remedy in Germany, where it's thought to ease symptoms and help the body cleanse itself. Garlic helps clear mucus, among other potential benefits. Peel and dice a half-pound of garlic. Add one quart of 90-proof cognac, and seal the mixture in an airtight bottle. Store in a cool, dark place for two weeks. Strain out the garlic, and reseal the liquid in the bottle. Prepare a new batch each year.

To treat the flu: Add 20 drops to eight ounces of water. Drink three glasses a day, one before each meal.

For prevention: Use 10 to 15 drops, instead of 20, per glass in flu season.

Important: This treatment is not advisable for people who have drinking problems or for children.

• **Sauerkraut.** Sauerkraut's concentration of lactic acid bacteria may weaken infections. Have two tablespoons of sauerkraut juice or about one-half cup of sauerkraut each day during flu season to reduce the chances of getting an infection.

SORE THROATS

Experiment with these remedies until you find what works best for you…

137

•**Apple cider vinegar.** Vinegar is a powerful anti-inflammatory, and its acidity might help kill the bacteria that cause some sore throats. Add two teaspoons of apple cider vinegar to six ounces of warm water. Gargle with a mouthful, spit it out, then drink a mouthful. Continue this until the mixture is gone. Rinse your mouth with water to prevent the vinegar from eroding your teeth. Repeat the vinegar gargle every hour for as long as your sore throat persists.

•**Sage.** Sage is an anti-inflammatory. Add one teaspoon of dried sage to one six-ounce cup of boiling water. Steep for three to five minutes, strain, then gargle and swallow.

•**Lemon and honey.** Honey coats the throat, while lemon can temporarily reduce the mucus buildup that often accompanies a sore throat. Squeeze one lemon, add a teaspoon of honey and drink. Repeat every two hours.

•**Tongue stretching.** Stick out your tongue for 30 seconds, relax it for a few seconds, then repeat four times. This is believed to increase blood flow to the throat, speeding the healing process.

COUGHS

Try these folk remedies to figure out which works best for you…

•**Lemon, honey and olive oil.** Honey and olive oil coat and soothe, while lemon reduces mucus. Heat one cup of honey, a half cup of olive oil and the juice of one lemon over a medium flame for five minutes. Turn off the heat, and stir for two minutes to blend the ingredients. Consume one teaspoon of the mixture every two hours.

•**Vinegar and cayenne pepper.** Cayenne pepper contains capsaicin, a proven painkiller, while vinegar serves as an anti-inflammatory. Add a half cup of apple cider vinegar and one teaspoon of cayenne pepper to one-half cup of water. Add honey if desired. Take one tablespoon when your cough acts up and another tablespoon before bed.

•**Horseradish and honey.** Horseradish can help loosen mucus, while honey coats the throat. Grate one teaspoon of fresh, peeled horseradish into two teaspoons of honey. Consume one teaspoon every two to three hours.

•**Ginger.** Ginger is an anti-inflammatory that contains gingerols, which provide pain-reducing and sedative benefits. Chew a piece of fresh, peeled gingerroot when you feel the cough acting up, usually in the evening before bed. Chew until the ginger loses its kick.

•**Licorice root tea.** Licorice relieves the pain of irritated mucous membranes. Drink licorice root tea as long as your cough persists.

Note: Don't try licorice root if you have high blood pressure or kidney problems.

REPORT #125
Relief at Your Fingertips

Michael Reed Gach, PhD, founder of the Acupressure Institute in Berkeley, California and author of self-healing instructional DVDs and CDs and many books, including *Acupressure's Potent Points* (Bantam), *Acupressure for Lovers* (Bantam), *Arthritis Relief at Your Fingertips* (Warner). *www.acupressure.com.*

Y ou've probably heard of acupuncture, but there's something similar that you can do yourself—no needles involved—called *acupressure*. Acupressure can alleviate many physical, mental and emotional problems in only a few minutes—and it is free.

Acupressure involves stimulating acupoints on the body with fingertips or knuckles and is based on the principles of acupuncture, an ancient healing technique used by practitioners of *Traditional Chinese Medicine* (TCM). The acupoints often have ancient descriptive names, such as "Joining the Valley" and "Mind Clearing." Acupressure increases blood flow to the treated area and triggers the release of *endorphins*, pain-relieving brain chemicals.

Here are the acupressure techniques for various health problems. Unless otherwise noted, daily acupressure sessions, three times a day, are the best way to relieve a temporary or chronic problem.

ARTHRITIS PAIN

Joining the Valley is a truly amazing acupoint because it can relieve arthritis pain anywhere in the body.

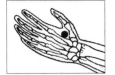

Location: In the webbing between the thumb and index finger, at the highest spot of the muscle when the thumb and index finger are brought close together.

What to do: Rhythmically squeeze the acupoint. As you're squeezing, place the side of your hand that is closest to the little finger on your thigh or a tabletop. Apply pressure in the webbing as you press downward. This allows you to angle more deeply into the point, increasing the benefits.

Also good for: Headache, toothache, hangover, hay fever symptoms, constipation.

Caution: This point is forbidden for pregnant women because its stimulation can cause premature contraction in the uterus.

MEMORY PROBLEMS

The *Mind Clearing* acupoints are for improving recall instantly—for example, when you have forgotten a name or gone to the supermarket without your shopping list.

Location: One finger width (about one-half inch) directly above the center of each eyebrow.

What to do: Gently place your right thumb above your right eyebrow and your middle fingertip above the eyebrow on the left side. Hold very gently. You should feel a slight dip or indentation in the bone structure—the acupoints on both sides are in the dip. Press the indentation very lightly, hold and breathe deeply. After a minute or two, you'll experience more mental clarity and sharper memory.

LOWER BACK PAIN

To help prevent and relieve lower back pain, practice this exercise for one minute three times a day. You can do it standing or sitting.

Location: Place the backs of your hands against your lower back, about one inch outside the spine.

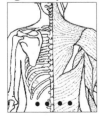

What to do: Briskly rub your hands up and down—about three inches up and six inches down—using the friction to create heat in your lower back.

If you're doing the technique correctly, you'll need to breathe deeply to sustain the vigorous rubbing, and you'll break out in a slight sweat.

Also good for: Food cravings, especially sugar cravings, chronic fatigue, sexual problems, chills, phobias and fibromyalgia symptoms.

EMOTIONAL UPSET

The *Inner Gate* acupoint can reduce emotional upset—such as anxiety, depression and irritability—in two to three minutes.

Location: On the inner side of the forearm, three finger widths up from the center of the wrist crease, in between two thick tendons.

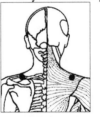

What to do: Place your thumb on the point and your fingers directly behind the outside of the forearm between the two bones. Squeeze in slowly and firmly, hold for two to three minutes, breathing deeply. Repeat on the other arm for the same amount of time.

Also good for: Carpal tunnel syndrome, insomnia, indigestion and nausea.

COLDS AND FLU

If you think you're about to get a cold or

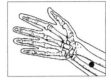

flu, stimulating the *Heavenly Rejuvenation* acupoint may prevent infection.

Location: On the shoulders, midway between the base of the neck and the outside of the shoulders, one-half inch below the top of the shoulders, just above the tip of the shoulder blades.

What to do: There are two ways to stimulate this point…

Curving your fingers, hook your right hand on your right shoulder and your left hand on your left shoulder. You also can use your fingers on your opposite shoulder, which may be easier. With your fingertips, firmly press the point and take three slow, deep breaths.

If you don't have the flexibility to perform the first technique…lie down on your back, on a firm mattress or carpeted floor, with your knees bent and feet on the floor as close to your buttocks as possible. Bring your hands above your head, and rest the backs of your hands on the floor beside or above your head. Inhale and lift up your pelvis, pressing your feet against the floor to assist the lift. The higher your pelvis, the more weight will be transferred onto your shoulders, stimulating the acupoint. Hold this posture for one minute, taking long, slow, deep breaths, with your eyes closed. Lower your pelvis, and rest for three minutes.

Also good for: Nervous tension, stiff neck, high fever, chills, shoulder aches as well as irritability.

INSOMNIA

The acupoints *Calm Sleep* and *Joyful Sleep*—on the outer and inner ankles—can help relieve insomnia. Use these acupressure points whenever you want to deeply relax and sleep better.

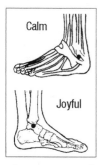

Location: *Calm Sleep* is in the first indentation below the outer anklebone. *Joyful Sleep* is directly below the inside of the anklebone, in a slight indentation.

What to do: Place your thumb on one side of your ankle and your fingers on the other, and press firmly. If you're on the right spot, it will be slightly sore. Hold for two minutes, breathing deeply. Repeat on the other ankle. Do this again if you still are having trouble sleeping or if you wake up.

HEADACHES

The acupoints *Gates of Consciousness* relieve a tension headache or migraine.

Location: Underneath the base of your skull to either side of your spine, about three to four inches apart, depending on the size of your head.

What to do: Using your fingers, thumbs or knuckles, press the points under the base of your skull.

At the same time, slowly tilt your head back so that the angle of your head relaxes your neck muscles. Press forward (toward your throat), upward (underneath the base of your skull) and slightly inward, angling the pressure toward the center of your brain. Continue to apply pressure for two minutes, breathing.

Also good for: Neck pain, insomnia, high blood pressure.

ACUPRESSURE BASICS

Unless otherwise noted, use your middle finger, with your index and ring fingers for support. Firmly and gradually, apply stationary pressure directly on the acupoint for three minutes.

• **Firmly means using an amount of pressure that causes a sensation between pleasure and pain—pressure that "hurts good."** If the pressure is applied too fast or too hard, the point will hurt. If the pressure is too soft, you won't get the full benefit.

• **Gradually means moving your finger into and out of the point in super-slow motion.** Applying and releasing finger pressure allow the tissue to respond and relax, promoting healing.

• **Stationary means you are not rubbing or massaging the area.**

• **Directly means at a 90-degree angle from the surface of the skin.** If you are pulling the skin, the angle of pressure is incorrect.

• **When you apply pressure, lean your weight toward the point.** If your hands are weak or it hurts your fingers when you apply pressure, try using your knuckles. You also can use a tool, such as a golf ball or pencil eraser.

• **Breathe slowly and deeply while you apply pressure.** This helps release pain and tension.

Illustrations courtesy of Michael Reed Gach, PhD.

REPORT #126
Exercise Fights Colds

Researchers studied 160 overweight, sedentary women ages 18 to 85. Half walked for 45 minutes five days a week for 12 to 15 weeks, while the other half remained sedentary.

Result: The walkers who got colds had 40% to 50% fewer days of illness than nonwalkers who got colds.

Theory: Thirty to 60 minutes a day of moderate exercise, such as walking at a 15-minute-per-mile pace, spurs production of germ-killing cells called *neutrophils.*

Caution: Ninety minutes or more of high-intensity daily exercise, such as long-distance running, has the opposite effect, increasing stress hormones and immune dysfunction.

David C. Nieman, MD, DrPH, professor of health and exercise science, Appalachian State University, Boone, North Carolina.

REPORT #127
Eat Turkey to Prevent Colls

Turkey is a good source of *glutamine*, an amino acid used by cells to protect against infection. And, like other protein sources, it boosts immunity. Eat turkey often during cold season to keep protective cells functioning at their peak.

Elizabeth M. Ward, MS, RD, nutrition consultant, Boston, and author of *The Low-Carb Bible* (Publications International).

REPORT #128
Homeopathic Help for Colds and Flu

Richard Mann, ND, chair of the department of homeopathic medicine at Bastyr University School of Naturopathic Medicine and a faculty member in clinical practice at Bastyr Center for Natural Health, both in Seattle. He is a diplomate of the Homeopathic Academy of Natural Physicians.

You may never have tried homeopathy, a form of alternative medicine that boosts the body's own healing responses. But if you get sick this winter, chances are that homeopathy can bring relief—if you pick the appropriate homeopathic remedy for your specific symptoms. *What you need to know...*

HOW HOMEOPATHY WORKS
Like vaccination, homeopathy seeks to stimulate the immune system. A vaccine contains a tiny amount of the pathogen that causes a certain disease.

Principle of homeopathy: Substances of plant, animal or mineral origin that can cause symptoms of disease also can cure symptoms when given in the form of very highly diluted remedies.

Homeopathy is not a one-size-fits-all therapy. Rather, the remedy must be carefully matched to a particular person's specific symptoms and his/her physical and mental reactions to these symptoms. This individualization makes it difficult to devise clinical studies that accurately reflect homeopathy's effectiveness.

What is known: For more than 200 years, homeopathy has helped people heal.

People who have colds or flu often respond to self-treatment using nonprescription homeopathic remedies sold in health-food stores and online.

Key: Match the right remedy with your symptoms.

What to do: Follow directions on product labels, taking 6C, 12C or 30C potency remedies. "C" stands for centesimal and indicates that one part of the active substance was mixed with 99 parts of alcohol...the numbers reflect how many times the mixture went through a dilution process. Paradoxically, the more dilute the potency, the greater the effect.

Remedies usually are sold as tiny pellets that dissolve under the tongue. Oils or other substances on your hands can inactivate pellets, so use a spoon to remove them from the container and place them in your mouth. Do not put anything else in your mouth for 30 minutes before or after taking a remedy.

Homeopathic remedies generally work quickly. *Unless otherwise directed by your practitioner or product labels, follow these instructions...*

• **If there is no change in symptoms after several hours, repeat the dose once more.** If symptoms still do not change after several hours, try a different homeopathic remedy that corresponds to your symptoms.

• **If you feel somewhat better after taking a homeopathic remedy,** repeat it at four-hour intervals until you feel significantly better, for a maximum of four doses in total.

• **Once you feel significantly better, do not take another dose.** If symptoms return, repeat dosing according to the instructions above.

When to seek help: In some cases, patients need prescription-potency homeopathic remedies and/or conventional medical treatment. *See a homeopathic physician or your primary care practitioner if…*

• **None of the remedies below seem appropriate for your specific symptoms.**

• **You have tried three or four of the homeopathic remedies below without result.**

• **You are over age 65 or have a chronic health problem.**

• **You are pregnant or breast-feeding.**

Important: The flu can be deadly, so if your symptoms are severe—for instance, you have a very high fever, have trouble breathing and/or feel extremely weak—seek immediate medical care.

THE RIGHT REMEDY FOR YOU

The following homeopathic remedies are among those most commonly indicated for colds or flu. Choose the remedy that most closely correlates to your symptoms.

Use *Arsenicum album* if you…

• **Have alternating chills and fever.**

• **Are thirsty and prefer warm drinks to cold ones.**

• **Have a runny nose or burning sensation in the nose.**

• **Feel extremely weak.**

• **Are anxious or restless.**

• **Feel worse from 10 pm to 3 am.**

Use *Belladonna* if you…

• **Spike a sudden fever.**

• **Cough a lot.**

• **Have a hot, red face (though hands and feet may be cold).**

• **Have glassy eyes or dilated pupils.**

• **Have a throbbing headache.**

• **Cannot tolerate light.**

• **Feel slightly delirious.**

Use *Gelsemium* if you…

• **Ache all over (particularly if this comes on gradually).**

• **Feel exhausted and weak.**

• **Have a trembling sensation running up and down the spine.**

• **Sneeze and/or have a runny nose.**

• **Develop a sore throat.**

• **Get dizzy.**

• **Feel apathetic or antisocial.**

Use *Hepar sulphuricum* if you…

• **Have a thick nasal discharge.**

• **Develop a sore throat.**

• **Cannot tolerate cold drafts.**

• **Are extremely sensitive to touch.**

• **Perspire heavily.**

• **Feel bothered by everything and everybody.**

Use *Nux vomica* if you…

• **Are shivering.**

• **Sneeze frequently or feel a tickle in the nose.**

• **Have a backache or headache.**

• **Have stomach cramps, nausea or constipation.**

• **Get more congested at night.**

• **Have trouble sleeping.**

• **Are sensitive to noise.**

• **Feel irritable or anxious.**

Use *Pulsatilla* if you…

• **Have had symptoms for several days.**

• **Have a thick green or yellow nasal discharge.**

• **Must blow your nose often.**

• **Have an upset stomach.**

• **Crave cool, fresh air.**

• **Feel worse at night.**

• **Feel weepy or want attention.**

To find a homeopath: Contact the Homeopathic Academy of Naturopathic Physicians

(206-941-4217, *www.banp.net*) or the National Center for Homeopathy (703-548-7790, *www. nationalcenterforhomeopathy.org*).

REPORT #129
Nature's Virus Killers for Colds and Flu

Mark A. Stengler, NMD, licensed naturopathic medical doctor in private practice, La Jolla, California…adjunct associate clinical professor at the National College of Natural Medicine, Portland, Oregon…author of many books, including *The Natural Physician's Healing Therapies* and coauthor of *Prescription for Natural Cures* (both from Bottom Line Books)…and author of the *Bottom Line/Natural Healing* newsletter.

D o you have to get a cold or the flu this coming season? No! This year can be different. With the right preparation, quick intervention and a lineup of powerful, natural virus fighters, there's a good chance that you can enjoy fall and winter without getting sick. *Here's how…*

KNOW YOUR ENEMY

Colds and flu are both caused by viruses. They are spread through the air by coughs and sneezes and through contact with contaminated objects, such as a doorknob or a hand that has been used to cover a cough. A virus is little more than a clump of genetic material (DNA or RNA) inside a packet made of protein. Stray viruses constantly land on your body. The trouble starts when they attach to cell receptors and get inside your cells. Viruses use the cells' own reproductive equipment to duplicate themselves—damaging more and more cells as they churn out millions of lookalikes.

It actually is a good sign when you begin to get a stuffy head or a runny nose. Your body is fighting back. Your immune system picks up signals from the by-products of viral activity—pain, redness, swelling, heat, fever and rash are results of your immune system launching a counterattack. Mucus is produced to help expel viral intruders.

Flu viruses are a lot more powerful than typical cold viruses. Cold symptoms are mainly confined to the head, neck and chest. Flu causes more generalized symptoms, such as fever, body aches, nausea, cramping, vomiting and severe fatigue. Flu also can develop into bronchitis. In the worst cases, it can lead to pneumonia and other severe respiratory diseases that are sometimes fatal, especially in the elderly or others with weakened immune systems.

START WITH PREVENTION

I'll tell you about great ways to feel better if you get a cold or flu, but prevention should be your first line of defense…

• **Avoid spending time around people who already are sick,** particularly if they're coughing or sneezing. If you live with someone who is sick, sleep in separate rooms. Wash your hands frequently during cold-and-flu season, and don't share towels—assign one to each family member or use paper towels. Keep your hands away from your face, especially your nose, mouth and eyes.

• **Take vitamins.** A good multivitamin/mineral supplement provides a base of nutrients to support a healthy immune system. A formula that I recommend as a preventive against viral infections is Source Naturals Wellness Formula (to find a retailer near you, call 800-815-2333 or go to *www.sourcenaturals.com*). It contains vitamins A and C, which are involved in the formation of antibodies…the minerals zinc and selenium…and immune-supportive herbs, such as garlic, echinacea and astragalus, which increase the activity of virus-fighting white blood cells. The dosage used to prevent infection is two capsules daily during cold-and-flu season, taken in conjunction with your year-round multisupplement.

• **Reduce exposure to toxins.** You are more vulnerable to viral infection when your body is "distracted" by having to deal with toxins that can damage or suppress the immune system. Toxins aren't necessarily exotic—they could include sugars and alcohol consumed to excess, fast food and other unhealthy food laced with artificial preservatives and/or pesticides. Toxins also include small but significant amounts of metals—mercury, arsenic and lead—that you can get from food, water and air pollution.

It is even more vital to eat healthfully during cold-and-flu season because you're indoors more and are exposed to higher concentrations of germs. Go easy on holiday sweets and other treats, and you will be less likely to get sick.

Many people cut back their exercise regimens in winter months—a big mistake, since exercise strengthens your immune system. Also consider sitting in a dry sauna once or twice a week for 20 to 30 minutes…or a wet sauna for 10 to 15 minutes. Saunas increase sweating, which excretes toxins. Be sure to check with your doctor first if you have diabetes or heart disease.

For those who get colds or the flu every year, I recommend taking a super-greens formula in the fall to remove toxins from the colon, liver and lymphatic system. It also can be taken year-round for gentle continuous detoxification. One good product is Greens (800-643-1210, *www.greensplus.com)*, which contains chlorella, wheat grass, super-green foods and detoxifying herbs such as milk thistle. The dosage is one scoop a day dissolved in water or juice.

Don't forget the impact that toxic emotions have on your immune system. Anger, anxiety, resentment, loneliness and other chronic emotional difficulties trigger the release of hormones that suppress immune function. Seek support to overcome these problems if they linger.

DO CONVENTIONAL THERAPIES HELP?

At the first sign of a runny nose or scratchy throat, some people head straight to the drugstore for cold and flu remedies. However, there are no conventional drugs—available either by prescription or over the counter—that help cure the common cold. Nasal decongestants and pain medications may make you feel better, but they don't address the actual viral infection. Natural remedies also can help you feel better—with fewer potential side effects—and they simultaneously improve immune function.

For flu, on the other hand, a number of effective prescription antiviral drugs are available that may reduce the flu's severity and duration (by one or two days) if taken within 48 hours of the first signs of illness. Such medicines include *amantadine* (Symmetrel), *rimantadine* (Flumadine), *zanamivir* (Relenza) and *oseltamivir* (Tamiflu). Possible short-term side effects range from central nervous system problems, including anxiety and light-headedness, to decreased respiratory function and digestive upset. These antiviral drugs are not approved for children under age one.

All of these antiviral drugs except zanamivir also are approved for preventing the flu during outbreaks. These may benefit individuals who are immunocompromised—for example, those who have AIDS or have had organ or bone transplants. I prefer to have my otherwise healthy patients focus on effective natural therapies since they work so well and rarely cause side effects.

RELY ON NATURE'S VIRUS KILLERS

If you start to come down with a cold or the flu, my first recommendation is to change your diet. Eat lightly so that your body can focus on healing. For the first 24 hours, consume filtered water, broths and soups with lots of garlic, onions and spices, such as turmeric and cayenne, which relieve congestion, promote circulation and have a natural anti-inflammatory effect. Herbal teas (especially ginger, cinnamon and peppermint) and steamed vegetables also are good choices. When you're feeling better, move toward a more normal diet.

I have found several supplements to be effective for treating colds and flu. Consider taking these when people around you are sick or when you first feel symptoms. You can use one or any combination until you feel better. These also are safe for children when given in dosages of one-quarter to one-half of what I recommend for adults. The bigger the child, the higher the dose you can use.

•**Lomatium dissectum** is a plant once used by Native Americans to fight Spanish flu. Preliminary research shows that *lomatium* has the ability to prevent viruses from replicating and to stimulate white blood cell activity. With colds and flu, I often see improvement within 24 hours. In my experience, the only side effect has been an allergic reaction in the form of a measles-like rash in a small percentage of users. This rash disappears a few days after lomatium is discontinued.

Eclectic Institute makes a potent product called *Lomatium-Osha* (800-332-4372, *www.eclecticherb.com*), which soothes the respiratory tract. This product is 50% alcohol, so take only the dosage recommended on the label. For children, add one-quarter of the adult dosage to hot water and let it sit for five minutes so that the alcohol evaporates. Women who are pregnant or nursing should not use lomatium.

• **Elderberry,** as shown by research in Israel, can stimulate the immune system, enhance white blood cell activity and inhibit viral replication. Flu patients have reported significant improvement within 48 hours of taking elderberry. It also helps with colds. The elderberry used in research studies is Sambucol Black Elderberry Extract from Nature's Way (to find a retailer, call 800-962-8873 or go to *www.naturesway.com*). Adults should take two teaspoons four times daily…children, one teaspoon four times daily.

• **Echinacea.** Contrary to recent media reports, extracts from this plant can be effective for treating colds and flu. Echinacea makes the body's own immune cells more efficient in attacking viruses. The key is using a product that has been processed to contain a high level of active constituents. Ground-up echinacea root or leaves won't do much. The use of alcohol and water by the manufacturer to extract active components is critical to the product's potency. Also, be sure to use enough (many people don't).

Two potent, well-researched products are Echinamide: Fresh Alcohol-Free Echinacea Extract, Natural Berry Flavor, and Echinamide Anti-V Formula Softgels, both by Natural Factors (to find a retailer, call 800-322-8704 or go to *www.naturalfactors.com*). This echinacea has been shown to reduce the length and severity of the common cold.

If you feel a cold or the flu coming on, take 20 drops of liquid extract or two capsules every two waking hours for 24 hours, then cut back to every three waking hours until the illness has passed.

The same company makes a liquid preparation called Anti-V Formula, which contains Echinamide, lomatium and other virus fighters. It is the most aggressive product for cold and flu from the Natural Factors line and can be used instead of the other supplements. Take 1.5 ml every two waking hours for the first 48 hours and then every three waking hours until the illness is gone.

• **Homeopathic influenzinum** is an intriguing remedy that I have used with success. Made from active flu strains, it stimulates the body's own defense system to resist infection. It works along the same lines as an oral vaccine, but since it is homeopathic, none of the flu particles are left in the preparation. It can be used for prevention or treatment of flu and has no side effects.

Take two 30C-potency pellets twice daily for two weeks at the beginning of flu season (in early November). Take two pellets four times daily when exposed to flu sufferers or if you start to have symptoms. It is available from health-food stores and The Vitamin Shoppe (800-223-1216, *www.vitaminshoppe.com*).

• **Oscillococcinum** is another great homeopathic remedy for flu, which is also available from The Vitamin Shoppe, health-food stores and pharmacies or by calling 800-672-4556 or visiting *www.oscillo.com*. It can be taken at the first sign of flu and is the number-one-selling homeopathic flu remedy in the US.

• **N-acetylcysteine (NAC).** This nutrient helps thin the mucus that may accompany a cold or the flu. In addition to making you feel better, NAC helps to prevent sinus and more serious chest infections. A study at University of Genoa, Italy, showed that NAC, when taken as a supplement, could help prevent as well as treat flu. The nutrient increases levels of the powerful antioxidant *glutathione* in the body, which, in turn, improves immune function. NAC is available at any health-food store and many pharmacies. If you tend to get the flu every year, take 600 mg twice daily when you are around people who have the flu or if you start feeling sick yourself.

• **Vitamin C enhances the activity of white blood cells.** I have found that taking 3,000 mg to 5,000 mg daily helps fight viral infections.

However, some people get diarrhea from this amount. For immediate treatment of symptoms, start with 5,000 mg in divided doses. If loose stools occur, cut back to 3,000 mg (or even less).

REPORT #130
Chamomile Tea Is Great For Colds and Other Ailments

Drinking at least five cups a day increases *phenolics*, which help the body fight colds...and boosts levels of *glycine*, which helps soothe muscle spasms and fights stress. Chamomile tea also may help relieve menstrual and other cramps.

Caution: Chamomile can cause a severe reaction in people who are allergic to ragweed.

Andrew L. Rubman, ND, medical director, Southbury Clinic for Traditional Medicines, Southbury, Connecticut.

REPORT #131
Drug-Free Ways to Fight Colds

Effie Poy Yew Chow, PhD, RN, founder and president of East West Academy of Healing Arts in San Francisco, *www.eastwestqi.com*. She is a licensed acupuncturist, qigong grandmaster and registered psychiatric and public health nurse. Dr. Chow is coauthor of *Miracle Healing from China: Qigong* (Medipress).

When a cold makes you miserable, you want relief fast. But drugs designed to ease cold symptoms can have side effects—increased blood pressure and heart rate, gastric upset, blurred vision, trouble concentrating, insomnia.

Instead, I recommend the practices of traditional Chinese medicine, which have been used for thousands of years. These practices may ease inflammation...fight infection...boost the immune system...and promote the healthful flow of qi (energy) through the body.

YIN OR YANG?

According to traditional Chinese medicine, two seemingly opposing yet interdependent natural forces called yin and yang must be in balance for a person to maintain good health. When one force predominates, illness results.

Colds can be characterized as either yin or yang. With a yin cold, you have chills...feel exhausted...and want to crawl into bed. With a yang cold, you have a fever...perspire...and feel agitated. *To reestablish the body's natural balance...*

•**Feed a yin cold—primarily with yang foods.** Yang foods are warming. Generally, they include meat, chicken and fish...and vegetables that grow in the earth, such as carrots, beets, jicama, turnips and yams. Eat as much as you comfortably can. Drink three six-ounce cups of ginger tea daily—ginger has anti-inflammatory and antiseptic effects.

Also soothing: Submerge yourself up to your earlobes in a bathtub of comfortably hot water mixed with Epsom salts.

•**For a yang cold, eat lightly.** Avoid yang foods, and instead focus on cooling yin foods—especially green vegetables, sprouts, fruits and other foods that grow in the open air. Drink eight to 10 cups of water daily. Also drink two or three cups of garlic tea daily—garlic is an antibacterial, antiviral and anti-inflammatory agent.

To make garlic tea: Boil a cup of water... add a clove of garlic cut in half...steep five to 10 minutes...remove garlic...add honey and lemon juice to taste.

Also helpful: Use garlic liberally cooking.

TIME-HONORED REMEDIES

Many traditional treatments may be helpful no matter what type of cold you have. Products mentioned below are sold at health-food stores, Asian markets and/or online. Check with your health-care provider before taking supplements, especially if you have a chronic health condition or take any medication. *Consider...*

•**Loquat syrup.** Made from the yellow pear-shaped loquat fruit, this syrup quiets coughs and soothes sore throats. Try a brand called

Nin Jiom Pei Pa Koa cough syrup or a natural loquat extract. See product labels for specific dosage guidelines.

•**White Flower Analgesic Balm.** This brand-name product combines essential oils of wintergreen, menthol, camphor, eucalyptus, peppermint and lavender.

To relieve nasal congestion: Put a drop of White Flower on your palm, rub palms together, then bring your hands up to your nose (avoiding the eyes) and inhale for four to eight breaths. You can repeat up to four times daily as needed.

To ease headache or body aches: Massage a few drops into achy areas up to four times daily.

•**Acupressure.** This practice stimulates certain points along the body's meridians (energy channels) to eliminate qi blockages. To open sinuses, squeeze the acupressure point on the fleshy area between your thumb and index finger, near the thumb joint. The more blocked your qi is, the more tender this spot may feel. Apply enough pressure to cause mild discomfort. Hold for several minutes, then switch sides. Repeat as needed.

•**Acupuncture.** This can clear even serious sinus congestion, sometimes in a single session. The acupuncturist inserts one or more very fine needles at specific points on the body, depending on the individual's needs, to restore qi flow.

Referrals: American Association of Acupuncture and Oriental Medicine (866-455-7999, *www.aaaomonline.org*).

•**Cupping.** Some acupuncturists and massage therapists provide this treatment. A small glass or bamboo cup is heated and then placed on the person's back for about five minutes. The heat creates a vacuum that pulls on the skin and underlying muscle, improving qi flow and blood circulation to bring healing nutrients to the body's tissues. Cupping sometimes leaves a red mark on the skin—not a burn, just a result of the suction—which fades within a few days. If the practitioner opts to leave the cup on the back for a longer period of time, slight bruising may result—but again, this soon fades.

•**Diaphragmatic breath work.** This technique uses the diaphragm as a piston to improve oxygen flow and blood circulation and relieve congestion. Sit or stand up straight to allow lungs to fill…gently draw in air through your nose (if you're not too congested), letting your abdomen expand outward…then pull your abdomen in so that it pushes the air out through your mouth. Continue for one minute. Consciously repeat several times daily, aiming for this to become the way you automatically breathe throughout the day.

•**Tui na massage.** This Chinese system of massage vigorously stimulates acupressure points and manipulates muscles and joints to promote qi flow. To find a practitioner, contact the National Certification Commission for Acupuncture and Oriental Medicine (904-598-1005, *www.nccaom.org*), and check for practitioners certified in "Asian bodywork." Other types of massage also can be helpful.

HOW TO NOT CATCH A COLD

The best defense against colds is to avoid getting them in the first place. That requires a strong immune system—and certain nutrients can help.

Advised: In addition to a daily multivitamin, take any or all of the following supplements. For maximum effect, use year-round.

•**Coenzyme Q10 (CoQ10).** This vitamin-like substance boosts cellular energy.

Recommended dosage: 100 mg to 200 mg twice daily.

•**Fish oil.** This is rich in the omega-3 fatty acids *eicosapentaenoic acid* (EPA) and *docosahexaenoic acid* (DHA), which reduce disease-promoting inflammation. Take fish oil liquid or capsules at a dosage that provides 3,000 mg daily of combined EPA and DHA.

•**Vitamin D.** This is a fat-soluble vitamin that benefits the body in many ways, including by strengthening the immune system. I recommend taking 2,000 international units (IU) daily of vitamin D3 (*cholecalciferol*).

Alternative: Take one teaspoon of cod-liver oil daily for each 50 pounds of body weight.

REPORT #132
What Is Most Effective Against the H1N1 Flu?

Chemical compounds in a plant called *ferula asafoetida* were more effective against the H1N1 (swine) flu virus than an antiviral drug in laboratory studies. Ferula asafoetida has been used in folk medicine for many years, including during the 1918 Spanish flu epidemic. Compounds in the plant could become the basis for new antiviral medicines.

Fang-Rong Chang, MD, and Yang-Chang Wu, MD, researchers, Kaohsiung Medical University, Taiwan, and correspondent authors of a study published in the *American Chemical Society's Journal of Natural Products.*

REPORT #133
Healing Herbs for Colds And Congestion

Kathy Abascal, RH, registered herbalist who practices in Vashon, Washington. A member of the American Herbalists Guild, she is coauthor of *Clinical Botanical Medicine* (Mary Ann Liebert).

A recent study reported that echinacea is not effective for the common cold. Then, another study, found that it does help. Does it or doesn't it?

Echinacea stimulates both white blood cells (which attack viruses) and natural killer cells (which destroy virus-infected cells). Most scientific studies of echinacea involve dosing patients every four to six hours. That's not enough.

How to use: Add about one teaspoon of echinacea tincture to one-half cup of water. Drink it once every waking hour at the first signs of a cold until symptoms subside.

Helpful: Add to the mixture one-half teaspoon of elderberry tincture—which also helps boost immunity—for additional antiviral effects.

EUCALYPTUS FOR CONGESTION

Used as an essential oil, eucalyptus penetrates the mucous membranes and promotes drainage—helpful for relieving symptoms caused by the common cold and/or sinusitis (inflammation of the sinuses). The oil also has antimicrobial properties that can inhibit viruses and bacteria.

How to use: At the first signs of a cold or sinusitis, put five to 10 drops of eucalyptus essential oil in a large bowl. Add one to two cups of steaming hot water. (The dose is correct if you can smell the eucalyptus.) Put a towel over your head, and lean over the bowl (with your eyes closed) and breathe in the steam for about 10 minutes. Repeat as needed, using fresh eucalyptus oil each time.

Caution: Keep your head far enough from the steaming water to avoid burning yourself.

Volume 14
Menopause and Women's Cures

REPORT #134
All-Natural Beauty Products You Can Make at Home

Skin is porous—so when you use synthetic personal-care products on your hands, face and scalp, artificial ingredients may be absorbed into your bloodstream.

Better: Create your own beauty products using all-natural ingredients available at supermarkets and health-food stores. Unless noted, products do not require refrigeration and can be stored for up to one year in a resealable plastic or glass container (new or recycled).

• **Peppermint hand smoother.** This removes dead skin and stimulates cell regeneration.

1 cup extra virgin olive oil
1 cup coarse salt
10 drops peppermint essential oil

Place all ingredients in a clean container (such as a mason jar), and mix thoroughly.

Daily: Gently massage a grape-sized dollop onto hands for two minutes...rinse with warm water.

• **Beeswax lip balm.** This soothes and protects chapped lips. For color, add a bit of leftover lipstick from the bottom of a used-up tube.

4 teaspoons castor oil
1 teaspoon beeswax
½ teaspoon honey
¼ teaspoon lipstick (optional)
5 drops sweet orange essential oil

Place all ingredients except orange oil in a small saucepan. Stirring, warm over low heat until melted. Remove from heat. Add orange oil and mix well. Fill a casserole dish with two inches of ice water and set the saucepan in the ice-water bath. Whisk the balm rapidly for

Andrea R. Frayser, ND, award-winning cosmetics formulator and founder of All Natural Diverse Eco-Friendly (ANDE) Cosmetics based in Hagerstown, Maryland.

one minute. Spoon balm into a clean, shallow container (such as a baby food jar), cap and refrigerate 30 minutes or until balm solidifies.

Several times daily: Apply to lips with fingertips or a lip brush.

• **Five-oil hair therapy.** This soothes an itchy scalp and makes dry, damaged hair silkier.

¼ cup extra virgin olive oil

¼ cup grapeseed oil

4 tablespoons jojoba oil

10 drops lavender essential oil

10 drops rosemary essential oil

In a small saucepan, combine all ingredients and warm over low heat for three minutes (do not boil). Let cool, then pour into a clean plastic container with a small-hole cap (such as an empty liquid soap bottle).

Weekly: Leaning over a sink, squeeze mixture onto dry hair, using enough to coat all strands. Cover hair with a shower cap for 30 to 60 minutes. Shampoo to remove oil.

• **Two-tea shampoo.** This gentle formula is good for all hair types.

2 cups distilled water

1 chamomile tea bag

1 green tea bag

1 organic orange peel, grated

2 teaspoons chopped fresh rosemary

1 teaspoon chopped fresh sage

½ teaspoon jojoba oil

¾ cup liquid castile soap

In a small saucepan, combine water, tea bags, orange peel and herbs. Bring to a boil, then remove from heat. Let stand, covered, for 30 minutes. Strain liquid into medium-sized bowl. Add jojoba oil and castile soap, stirring until well blended. Pour into a clean, unbreakable container with a tight-fitting lid.

Daily or as needed: Wash hair using ¼ cup to ½ cup of mixture. This also makes an excellent all-over body wash.

Note: Store in the refrigerator, and use within one month for best aroma.

For containers: Check in a drugstore or a dollar store.

REPORT #135
Herbal Aphrodisiacs

Laurie Steelsmith, ND, author of *Natural Choices for Women's Health* (Three Rivers). Her private practice in naturopathic and Chinese medicine is in Honolulu. *www.naturalchoicesforwomen.com.*

If your libido is lagging, rekindle the spark with herbs used by practitioners of *traditional Chinese medicine* (TCM). Try them one at a time, in the order presented (*epimedium* and *rehmannia* can be taken together). If you don't see results with one herb after two months, discontinue it and try the next. Typically an herb corrects the underlying problem within six months and is then discontinued. These herbs are sold in health-food stores. Do not use while pregnant or breastfeeding. If you have any health problems, talk to your doctor before beginning herbal therapy.

Cordyceps (a mushroom) improves kidney health, according to TCM, by supporting *kidney qi* (vital energy)—and abundant qi is necessary for a strong libido. Take 500 mg in tablet form two to three times daily. Do not use if you have a fever because it could worsen symptoms.

Ginseng contains compounds called ginsenosides, which may boost enzymes that help to break down or otherwise dispatch stress hormones, such as cortisol. Stress dampens libido, so decreasing stress helps to increase desire. Ginseng "modulates" the nervous system, boosting sexual energy if you are lethargic and helping you relax if you are tense. Using an extract labeled "standardized to 4% ginsenosides," take 100 mg in pill form or 50 drops in tincture form, two or three times daily. Do not use if you have hot flashes, insomnia, dry mouth or dry skin—ginseng could exacerbate symptoms.

Epimedium (horny goat weed) stimulates the nervous system, especially nerves in the genitalia, by increasing the flow of qi to the pelvis. It usually is sold in a combination herbal formula. Choose a brand that provides 800 mg of epimedium per day. Do not use if you have a fever, hot flashes or insomnia.

Rehmannia is an herb that draws energy into the reproductive organs through the body's meridians (energy pathways). Usually it is sold in combination with other herbs. Select a brand that has 300 mg of rehmannia per tablet, and take three times per day. Do not use if you have diarrhea, because it can loosen stool.

Bonus: Rehmannia eases anxiety and hot flashes—making it even easier to get into the mood for love.

REPORT #136
Better Bones

Recent finding: In a study of 1,500 healthy women (ages 70 to 85), hip-bone density was 2.8% higher in those who drank caffeinated or caffeine-free black tea, compared with people who did not drink tea. Tea drinkers consumed an average of three cups daily.

Theory: Flavonoid antioxidants in black tea may stimulate production of new cells that build bone.

Self-defense: Drinking black tea daily may help protect your bones as you age. If your doctor has advised you not to drink caffeine, opt for caffeine-free black tea.

Amanda Devine, PhD, senior lecturer, nutrition program, Edith Cowan University, Joondalup, Australia.

REPORT #137
Natural Remedies That Really Work to Ease Hot Flashes

Andrea Sikon, MD, board-certified internist and director of primary care/women's health for the Medicine Institute at the Cleveland Clinic in Cleveland. She is certified as a menopause practitioner by the North American Menopause Society.

As many as 75% of menopausal women experience the sudden waves of body heat known as hot flashes. Episodes can be mild, causing just a few moments of discomfort...or intense enough to make a woman drip with perspiration.

Hot flashes and night sweats (which come on during sleep) are triggered by fluctuating levels of the hormone estrogen, affecting a woman's inner thermostat and causing blood vessels near the skin's surface to dilate. Typically, a hot flash ends after several minutes, though it can last a half-hour or more. Episodes generally abate after a few years—but some women continue to have hot flashes for the rest of their lives.

Here's what you should know about which remedies help...which are of questionable value...and which are downright dangerous.

Important: Before beginning any kind of therapy, talk to your doctor about its pros and cons and how they relate to your individual risk factors.

PRESCRIPTION DRUGS

Estrogen is the only prescription medication currently FDA-approved specifically for hot flashes, but others can be prescribed "off-label."

Most effective...

• **Estrogen therapy.** This reduces hot flashes by making up for a woman's own diminishing production of the hormone. It also eases other menopausal symptoms, such as mood swings, vaginal dryness, thinning skin and bone loss...and may reduce risk for hip fracture and colon cancer.

Caution: Estrogen therapy can increase risk for heart disease, stroke, blood clots, breast cancer and possibly Alzheimer's disease. The more time that has passed since a woman reached menopause and/or the longer she takes estrogen, the greater the risks may be.

Consider estrogen if: Hot flashes reduce your quality of life...you have additional menopausal symptoms...and your doctor says that you have no increased cardiovascular or breast cancer risk. If you have not had a hysterectomy, you also must take progestogen (a drug similar to the hormone progesterone) to guard against uterine cancer.

Sometimes helpful...

• **Antidepressants.** Selective serotonin reuptake inhibitors (SSRIs), such as *paroxetine*

151

(Paxil), and serotonin/norepinephrine reuptake inhibitors (SNRIs), such as *venlafaxine* (Effexor), may relieve hot flashes by stabilizing the body's temperature-control mechanism.

New: The manufacturer of the SNRI *desvenlafaxine* (Pristiq) has been given for FDA approval of the drug as a treatment for hot flashes.

SSRIs can cause weight gain, dry mouth and decreased sex drive...and may interfere with the breast cancer drug tamoxifen in some women. SNRIs can cause insomnia, dry mouth, constipation or diarrhea, and perhaps high blood pressure.

Consider an antidepressant if: You cannot or do not want to use estrogen therapy and/or hot flashes are accompanied by mood swings.

•*Gabapentin* (Neurontin). In one study, this antiseizure drug was as effective against hot flashes as estrogen. Side effects may include sedation, dizziness and mild or widespread swelling.

Consider gabapentin if: You also have insomnia and do not have additional symptoms better treated by estrogen or antidepressants.

•*Clonidine* (Catapres). This blood pressure drug affects the central nervous system. In some small studies, it reduced hot flashes. Clonidine can cause dizziness, fatigue, dry mouth and constipation.

Consider clonidine if: Other therapies have failed to relieve hot flashes, and you also require treatment for high blood pressure.

ALTERNATIVE THERAPIES

The FDA does not test herbs or dietary supplements. Nonprescription products labeled "natural" are not necessarily effective or even safe. If you try them, choose brands that have the United States Pharmacopeia (USP) seal to ensure purity.

Perhaps helpful...

•**Supplements of soy and black cohosh.** These have phytoestrogens, plant compounds with estrogen-like effects. Theoretically, they could ease hot flashes via the same mechanism as estrogen—but they also may carry similar risks.

Caution: Women who ought not take prescription estrogen (for instance, due to elevated

risk for heart disease or breast cancer) should use these products only when they have their doctors' approval.

•**Flaxseeds.** One small Mayo Clinic study found that hot flash frequency was reduced by half in women who consumed two tablespoons of ground flaxseeds twice daily for six weeks.

Possible reason: Flaxseeds contain lignans, antioxidants with estrogenic effects. Get your doctor's approval before using. Drink lots of water with flaxseeds to prevent gas and constipation.

•**Acupuncture.** A few studies suggest that this is somewhat effective for hot flashes.

Best: Use an acupuncturist certified by the National Certification Commission for Acupuncture and Oriental Medicine (904-598-1005, *www.nccaom.org*).

Probably not helpful...

•**Evening primrose oil...ginseng...vitamins B, C and E.** These fared no better than placebos in studies.

Ginseng should not be used with blood thinners, stimulants or antidepressant MAO inhibitors...vitamins C and E can cause bleeding in people who take blood thinners.

•**Magnets.** Supporters claim that magnetic fields have healing powers. However, in an Indiana University study, sham magnets eased hot flashes better than real magnets.

Dangerous...

•**Over-the-counter topical progestogen cream.** Absorption varies dramatically from woman to woman—so using these without a doctor's supervision can lead to hormone imbalances.

•**Dong quai.** This herb can interfere with medications and may contain a potential carcinogen.

•**Kava.** This herb is intoxicating and can damage the liver.

•**Licorice extract.** In large doses, it can cause leg edema (swelling), high blood pressure and dangerously low potassium levels.

REPORT #138
Hot Flashes May Signal Blood Pressure Problem

Linda M. Gerber, PhD, professor of public health and director of the biostatistics and research methodology core in the Department of Public Health at Weill Medical College of Cornell University.

Andrew L. Rubman, ND, medical director, Southbury Clinic for Traditional Medicines, Southbury, Connecticut.

Most of us women know that simply reaching midlife puts us at greater risk for heart disease, since we tend to lose the protective effects of estrogen. While previous research has linked menopause to high blood pressure (a major risk factor for heart attack), a new study links one of its most irksome symptoms—hot flashes—to high blood pressure. With hot flashes—defined as being sudden feelings of intense heat that may include sweating and a rapid heartbeat, and lasting usually from two to 30 minutes—being one of the major hallmarks of menopause and perimenopause, this study may be a "red alert" to identify a danger signal for women at risk of future heart problems.

Researchers at Weill Medical College of Cornell University found that women who had hot flashes tended to have higher systolic (top number) blood pressure compared with the lucky ones who didn't have hot flashes. In the study, 154 women aged 18 to 65 with no previous cardiovascular disease and who either had normal blood pressure or mild hypertension (high blood pressure) wore portable monitors that recorded their blood pressure while they were awake and asleep. Women who reported having hot flashes were found to have an age-adjusted average systolic blood pressure of 141 while awake, and 129 while they were asleep, compared with 132 and 119, respectively, for women who did not report hot flashes. The blood pressure differences between these two groups remained statistically significant after controlling for high blood pressure risk factors including race/ethnicity, age and body mass index (BMI).

"One-third of the women we studied reported having had hot flashes two weeks prior to wearing a BP monitor," said Linda M. Gerber, PhD, the study's lead author, who is a professor of public health and director of the biostatistics and research methodology core in the Department of Public Health at Weill Medical College of Cornell University. "Among these women, systolic blood pressure was significantly higher—even after adjusting for whether they were pre-menopausal, menopausal or post-menopausal."

DO WOMEN WITH HOT FLASHES HAVE TO WORRY?

So if you are experiencing hot flashes, even only once in a while, should you worry that you may be at risk for high blood pressure? "You should keep your eye on it, but not be unduly concerned," said Dr. Gerber. "It's important to get an accurate representation of your blood pressure, but that is often difficult to get. Blood pressure varies over the course of the day. Some people get the white coat effect, in which your blood pressure is high when you go to see your doctor. I don't want people to rush to see their doctors. One way to keep an eye on it would be to get a home monitor and check it on a frequent basis."

And what about those pesky hot flashes? "You can do things that might be beneficial to limit the severity and frequency of your hot flashes," said Dr. Gerber. "Keep your weight down, exercise regularly and eat a healthy diet."

Andrew L. Rubman, ND, adds that the association between estrogen reduction and both hot flashes and increased systolic blood pressure may be due to concentrations of calcium within the tissue responsible for both. There are effective natural ways to modulate this, including black cohosh and soy isoflavones, but it's important to work with an experienced expert, such as a naturopathic physician, to ensure safety.

Most important, adds Dr. Gerber: "Be aware that if the frequency of hot flashes increases suddenly and if you have a lot of severe flashes when you didn't have them before, you should get your blood pressure checked."

REPORT #139
Acupuncture for Female Problems

Yi Chan, DPM, LAc, The Bendheim Integrative Medicine Center, Memorial Sloan-Kettering Cancer Center, New York City. *www.yourdrchan.com*.

Gynecological complaints like pelvic pain, infertility, menstrual cramps and the mood swings and hot flashes of menopause are often highly responsive to acupuncture—we've heard this anecdotally from friends and, interestingly, also from doctors, both mainstream and integrative. And we are seeing more and more published research backing this up as well—most recently, a 12-week study of breast cancer patients compared acupuncture treatment to use of an antidepressant, *venlafaxine* (Effexor), for relief of severe hot flashes and other menopausal symptoms. Both treatments were effective, but with some important differences. The women in the acupuncture group reported no side effects, while the drug group suffered many unpleasant ones. The acupuncture group also reported improved energy, clarity of thinking, sexual desire and overall sense of well-being. Finally, improvement among the acupuncture patients lasted much longer—from three to four months after finishing treatment, compared with the Effexor group, in which symptoms resumed within two weeks after they stopped the drug.

WHY IT WORKS
FOR WOMEN'S ISSUES

We are not surprised by this, given our many stories about acupuncture, but it prompted us to look into the therapy's use for a wider range of gynecological issues. We called acupuncturist Yi Chan, DPM, LAc, who is on staff at The Bendheim Integrative Medicine Center at Memorial Sloan-Kettering Cancer Center in New York and in private practice in West Orange, New Jersey. Dr. Chan says the basic philosophy of Chinese medicine is to maintain proper balance of energy flow (chi) in the body and that when the flow is disrupted, it creates disorders and discomfort. He likens this to the

New York City subway where a breakdown of even a single train will cause widespread disruptions in the system. Acupuncture, he says, is a way to locate and correct the disruption of the chi.

Dr. Chan reports that acupuncture helps 80% of his patients—bringing "great improvement" to 60%. With acupuncture, most patients can tell by about the sixth treatment if it is helping their problem—if nothing has changed by then (as is true for about 20%), the challenge may be too great for acupuncture alone to resolve.

WHAT CAN
ACUPUNCTURE HELP?

•**Menstrual cycle problems (flow, regularity, pain).** Sometimes stress, diet or excessive exercise can disrupt normal functioning of the menstrual cycle, by sending energy to the wrong places, explains Dr. Chan. Acupuncture can help repair and "smooth out the bumpy ride," whether the flow is too heavy or too little, or the cycle is shortened, delayed or irregular. Typically, the practitioner treats the patient through several cycles, with about eight to 12 weeks of treatments.

•**Fertility issues.** Acupuncture can be helpful for women having trouble conceiving, and new research shows that it improves the success rate of in-vitro fertilization. Dr. Chan suggests not waiting many months to seek acupuncture to help fertility, urging women who don't get pregnant to use acupuncture sooner rather than later, as it can "free up" their energy flow. But such women should always first have a complete physical exam by a gynecologist to be sure that everything is anatomically functional.

•**Endometriosis and uterine fibroids.** These particular problems can be stubborn and complex. While acupuncture can help ease pain and excessive bleeding, women with endometriosis and/or fibroids often require conventional treatment as well, sometimes including surgery. In those cases, acupuncture can help soothe post-surgery discomfort, supporting healing and re-establishment of the cycle. Again, it is crucial to have a gynecological examination to determine the nature and extent of the problem—if symptoms are mild to moderate, Dr. Chan says acupuncture can help right away, but for severe symptoms, he says women should first see a medical doctor and then seek out an acupuncturist.

•**Hot flashes.** As mentioned above, acupuncture can ease the frequency and severity of hot flashes as well. Dr. Chan advises his patients to keep a notebook, writing down frequency and intensity of the flashes as they occur. With acupuncture, "the frequency may abate, but the intensity remains the same—or vice-versa," he says. "By observing this carefully you will know if acupuncture is working for you." Dr. Chan also has a list of "cooling" foods advised in Chinese medicine for such patients—watermelon, mung bean, mustard greens, bitter melon and grass jelly.

**FIND AN
ACUPUNCTURIST**

To find an acupuncturist near you, go to the Web site of the National Certification Commission for Acupuncture and Oriental Medicine at *www.nccaom.org*, which lists board certified practitioners. Word of mouth is also good, says Dr. Chan. Insurance covers treatment in many cases, though not always. Perhaps this too will change as Western medicine begins to fully embrace the benefits of acupuncture.

REPORT #140
Natural Therapies for Endometriosis...No Surgery Needed

Victoria Maizes, MD, associate professor of medicine, family and community medicine and public health and executive director of the Arizona Center for Integrative Medicine at University of Arizona in Tucson. She is coeditor of *Integrative Women's Health* (Oxford University). *www.integrativemedicine.arizona.edu.*

With endometriosis, tissue from the endometrium (uterine lining) migrates outside the uterus via the fallopian tubes, then grows on the ovaries, fallopian tubes, rectum, bladder and/or pelvic lining.

During menstruation, this displaced tissue behaves as it would if it were in the uterus—it thickens, breaks down and bleeds. Trapped blood inflames surrounding tissues, which can lead to internal scarring. Resulting pain ranges from mild to incapacitating...scarring can impair fertility. Symptoms usually ease after menopause, though hormone therapy may lead to flare-ups.

Conventional treatment typically involves oral contraceptives, which block the effects of natural hormones on the growths outside the uterus...or the drug *leuprolide* (Lupron), which stops menstruation.

Downside: These drugs can cause weight gain and mood swings. When medication does not bring sufficient relief, patients may be advised to have endometriosis tissue surgically removed or to have a hysterectomy—but all surgery carries risks for infection and complications.

Natural approaches may help you avoid drugs and surgery. *Try...*

•**Anti-inflammatory diet.** This reduces the inflammation caused by trapped menstrual blood. To increase intake of anti-inflammatory omega-3 fatty acids, eat more fatty fish (herring, mackerel), flaxseeds and walnuts... and take a daily fish oil supplement. Every day, eat several servings of vegetables and fruits, which are rich in antioxidants. Avoid inflammation-promoting refined carbohydrates (white bread, doughnuts)...eat more whole grains (brown rice, bulgur).

•**Pelvic floor physical therapy.** Chronic muscle tension in the abdomen, legs and pelvic floor may result from a conditioned response to pelvic pain, exacerbating discomfort. Pelvic floor physical therapy from a specially trained therapist can reduce muscle tension and improve day-to-day functioning.

Also helpful: Yoga, stretching.

•**Botanical supplements.** Black cohosh, black haw and/or ginger may help by reducing the effects of inflammatory enzymes and proteins, boosting antioxidants or reducing sensitivity to painful stimuli. Supplements can cause side effects or interact with medications, so consult a holistic doctor for dosage and usage guidelines. Do not take black cohosh or black haw if you have a history of breast cancer. Do not take ginger if you have a bleeding disorder or gallstones.

•**Acupuncture.** Various studies suggest that this can ease the pain of endometriosis, though the exact mechanism is not known.

Find a practitioner: Contact the American Association of Acupuncture and Oriental Medicine (866-455-7999, *www.aaaomonline.org*).

Simplest: Use a heating pad...or take a warm bath to ease discomfort.

REPORT #141
Reducing Breast Cancer Risk After Menopause

JoAnn E. Manson, MD, DrPH, professor of medicine and women's health at Harvard Medical School and chair of the division of preventive medicine at Brigham and Women's Hospital, both in Boston. She is one of the lead investigators for two highly influential studies on women's health—the Harvard Nurses' Health Study and the Women's Health Initiative. Dr. Manson is author, with Shari Bassuk, ScD, of *Hot Flashes, Hormones & Your Health* (McGraw-Hill).

Many postmenopausal women think their primary risk factor for breast cancer is genetics. Yet most breast cancers occur in women with no family history of the disease, and the major breast cancer genes (BRCA1 and BRCA2) account for only 5% to 10% of cases. *The primary risk factors...*

•**Age.** Average age at diagnosis is 61, and rates are highest after age 70.

•**Estrogen.** This hormone stimulates growth of breast tissues—including abnormal cells. Estrogen levels are highest during the childbearing years, so the earlier you started menstruating and the later you reached menopause, the higher your risk.

To help prevent breast cancer...

•**Guard against vitamin-D deficiency.** Vitamin D may fight formation of blood vessels that nourish tumors and inhibit division of cells that line the breast. Many experts now recommend that all adults get 1,000 international units (IU) daily.

Sources: Sunlight (from which skin synthesizes vitamin D)...cod liver oil, fatty fish (mackerel, tuna), fortified milk and cereals...and supplements of vitamin D3 (*cholecalciferol*).

•**Get adequate folate, a B vitamin involved in DNA synthesis and repair.** Eat three one-cup servings daily of folate-rich foods—leafy green vegetables, garbanzo beans, peas, citrus fruits.

•**Avoid unnecessary hormone therapy.** Consider taking estrogen (plus progestin to guard against uterine cancer, if you have not had a hysterectomy) only if hot flashes and night sweats significantly disrupt your sleep or quality of life. Use the lowest effective dose... try to limit use to less than four or five years.

•**Watch your weight.** Obesity after menopause may double breast cancer risk, perhaps because fat cells take over the ovaries' job of producing estrogen. Nearly one-quarter of postmenopausal breast cancers in the US are due to excess weight.

•**Exercise 30 minutes or more per day.** Exercise lowers blood levels of insulin and estrogen, both of which are risk factors for breast cancer.

•**Eat less saturated fat.** In a study of 48,835 postmenopausal women, those who were accustomed to a high-fat diet reduced their breast cancer risk by adopting a diet in which less than 25% of daily calories came from fat.

•**Limit alcohol intake.** Even moderate drinking raises breast cancer risk by increasing estrogen and decreasing folate absorption. Also, alcohol can be metabolized into *acetaldehyde*, a potential carcinogen, so have no more than one drink daily.

If you're at high risk: The drugs *tamoxifen* and *raloxifene* can reduce breast cancer risk—but increase the odds of blood clots, hot flashes, uterine cancer and perhaps stroke. Ask your doctor if these drugs are right for you.

REPORT #142
A Midwife At Menopause?

Angela Deneris, PhD, certified nurse-midwife and associate professor in the Nurse-Midwifery and Women's Health Nurse Practitioner Programs at the University of Utah, Salt Lake City.

Why would you want to see a midwife at menopause? Because they offer a uniquely personal and holistic perspective on the journey. Though historically their role has been to help women through childbirth, many modern midwives now focus on helping women to feel better and be healthier at the other end of the reproductive cycle.

It's an intriguing concept, so we spoke with Angela Deneris, PhD, a certified nurse midwife and associate professor in the Nurse-Midwifery and Women's Health Nurse Practitioner Programs at the University of Utah. According to Dr. Deneris, who has been in practice for nearly 30 years and whose clients range in age from teens to a woman in her 80s, Certified Nurse-Midwives (CNMs) and Certified Midwives (CMs) are fully qualified to partner a woman through perimenopause, menopause and the postmenopausal years—and some actually specialize in caring for older women. All midwives are trained to provide the full spectrum of routine gynecological care—including pap smears and pelvic examinations and referrals for screening and diagnostic tests, such as mammograms and sonograms, as well as routine primary care, including annual physicals and screening for conditions such as diabetes, heart disease and declining bone health.

A MORE PERSONAL RELATIONSHIP

Midwives are trained in "whole woman care," emphasizing natural treatments and lifestyle adjustments over pharmaceutical drugs. For instance, said Dr. Deneris, for a woman complaining about hot flashes, a midwife will start by trying to ascertain whether specific situations trigger them and will also discuss dietary and lifestyle measures that might help reduce their severity or frequency. A midwife will coach patients in how to take more responsibility for the aspects of her health that she can control by eating right, exercising and keeping track of medical history and records. And for those women who really need something more, midwives are qualified to prescribe medication and hormone replacement therapy if appropriate.

MIDWIFE VS. MD— WHAT'S THE DIFFERENCE?

Education for midwives varies from state to state, with some requiring a bachelor of science and others requiring a degree in nursing prior to midwifery training. Accreditation requirements (for both Certified Midwives and Certified Nurse-Midwives) are standardized by The American College of Nurse Midwives (ACNM). An accredited midwife is able to do just about all aspects of routine care (and childbirth, of course) up to but not including surgery.

For older women in particular, midwives work closely with doctors when trying to determine whether symptoms and discomfort a patient is experiencing are caused by aging or disease—especially if serious illness, such as cancer, is suspected. In that case, the doctor will take over the patient's care, but the midwife often remains very involved.

For instance, Dr. Deneris told me she continues to provide gynecological and other care for her patients who have had breast cancer, including screening for heart disease, diabetes and depression as well as counseling for diet and exercise. "Staying involved while a woman is receiving care for a serious, chronic health issue enables us to continue to treat our patients as whole, complete women," she said.

PATIENTS GET MORE TIME

As part of their holistic perspective, Dr. Deneris said women can also expect that a midwife will devote much more time to each patient. She told me she spends about an hour with women over 40 for their annual visits. "We discuss lifestyle, diet, exercise routines, and the particular stressors in their lives, and then put the pieces together," she said. "Rather than immediately prescribing something for mood swings or insomnia, we'll look beyond such symptoms to examine the broader picture." Dr. Deneris said she routinely discusses

157

sexuality with her patients…asks about quality of life…screens for depression…and makes it a point to explore whether there are possible issues around abuse or addiction. It's all intended to provide context for understanding what is happening with a woman's health.

Most insurers cover midwife services. To locate a qualified midwife, Dr. Deneris suggested visiting *www.midwife.org*, the Web site for the American College of Nurse Midwives, which offers a search option for locating a midwife by entering a Zip code or town.

REPORT #143
How to (Finally!) Get Rid of Acne

Mary Ellen Brademas, MD, clinical assistant professor of dermatology at New York University School of Medicine and a dermatologist in private practice, both in New York City.

It's frustrating to battle pimples and wrinkles simultaneously—yet up to 15% of women do have acne breakouts in midlife and beyond.

Possible reason: Production of the hormone estrogen, a natural pimple suppressor, decreases at menopause—and may leave a relatively high ratio of acne-provoking hormones called androgens. Acne develops when pores get blocked with natural skin oils.

Acne develops when pores get blocked with natural skin oils. Products that helped when you were younger now may make acne worse because they're too drying for mature skin—and excessive dryness prompts the sebaceous glands to pump out even more pore-clogging oil. *What does help…*

• **Use anti-acne skin-care products.** Wash your face thoroughly with cold cream or a soapless product, such as Cetaphil Gentle Skin Cleanser. Exfoliate with a cream or gel containing *salicylic acid*, *azelaic acid* and/or *glycolic acid* to slough off dead skin cells that trap oil. Follow with oil-based moisturizer and makeup —water-based products are too drying.

• **Listen to your gut.** Stress activates the nervous system, which in turn triggers reactions in the digestive tract and skin. A churning stomach is a signal that you need to reduce stress if you want to protect your complexion.

Best: Do whatever relaxes you—listen to music, phone a friend, meditate.

• **Identify your personal pimple-provoking foods.** Chocolate doesn't cause breakouts—but the iodine in seafood may irritate pores, and some people are sensitive to dairy products and/or tree nuts (walnuts, cashews, almonds). Keep a food log for a few weeks, and look for patterns. If you discover that you always break out a day or two after eating strawberries, for instance, avoid them.

• **Try natural remedies.** Soak one-third of an ounce of witch hazel bark or white oak bark (sold in health-food stores) overnight in one cup of water. Strain liquid, then saturate a cotton ball and wipe it over your entire face. Let the skin dry before putting on your makeup.

Before bed: Beat an egg yolk, smooth it onto your face, let dry for 10 minutes, then remove it with cold water and a washcloth.

If your acne continues, see a dermatologist. *You may need to…*

• **Try prescription medication.** *Isotretinoin* (Accutane), derived from vitamin A, reduces the oil secreted by the skin…changes the shape and texture of cells that line pores so oil is less easily trapped…and restores collagen and elastin, proteins that give skin its structure. After five months, as many as three out of four patients are cured of acne.

Caution: Accutane can cause severe birth defects, so don't use it if you have any chance of getting pregnant. Accutane can raise levels of cholesterol and triglycerides (blood fats) and cause fluctuations in blood sugar—so your doctor should conduct frequent blood tests to monitor these.

• **Consider hormone therapy.** This may combat acne (and other menopausal symptoms) by raising the body's levels of estrogen. However, it can increase the risk for breast cancer and heart disease, so talk with your doctor about the potential risks and benefits.

REPORT #144
Fight Bone Loss—And Look Better, Too

Karena Thek Lineback, certified Pilates fitness instructor and rehabilitation therapist. She is president of Pilates Teck in Santa Clarita, California and author of *OsteoPilates: Increase Bone Density, Reduce Fracture Risk, Look and Feel Great!* (New Page).

Menopause and the use of steroid drugs are common causes of the bone-thinning disease known as osteoporosis. *But few people are aware of other osteoporosis risk factors, including...*

• **Hypertension,** which can increase the amount of calcium excreted in urine, possibly resulting in loss of bone mineral density.

• **Gastrointestinal disorders,** such as colitis and irritable bowel syndrome (IBS), all of which reduce absorption of dietary calcium.

It's also a big mistake to overlook bone loss in men. While eight million American women have been diagnosed with osteoporosis, two million American men also suffer from the condition—and several million additional women and men are at risk for the disease.

Both women and men can help prevent osteoporosis with a variety of bone-protecting strategies. Among the most important are eating a well-balanced diet (including calcium-rich foods, such as low-fat dairy products ...almonds...and green, leafy vegetables, including broccoli and kale) and taking mineral and vitamin supplements (for example, calcium, vitamin D, magnesium, potassium, zinc and vitamin K).

WHAT IS OSTEOPILATES?

Most doctors recommend weight-bearing exercise, such as walking, stair-climbing and/or strength-training with hand weights, as part of an osteoporosis prevention program.

After eight years of working with women and men at risk for osteoporosis, I have developed a specialized form of the exercise technique known as Pilates to help fight bone loss. Pilates concentrates on strengthening the "core muscles" (in the abdomen and the back) that stabilize and support the spine, as well as the small muscles throughout the body.

I call my version *OsteoPilates*. The exercises of OsteoPilates are designed to stimulate bone growth in areas that are especially vulnerable to thinning (the spine, wrists and hips), while also providing the overall toning benefits of Pilates.

OsteoPilates is generally safe for people with low bone density (including those with osteoporosis) and those with normal bone density, as measured by a *dual energy X-ray absorptiometry* (DEXA) scan. Ask your doctor before starting the program.

The following basic workout, which takes about 15 minutes to complete, should be performed three times weekly, with at least one day of rest between sessions. (The floor exercises can be performed on a thin mat, such as a yoga mat.)

TOE TOUCHES

Purpose: Builds bone mass in the spine, thighs and knees.

What to do: Lie on your back with your bent legs in the air. Your knees should be positioned directly above your hips and your lower legs extended slightly higher than your knees. Point your toes. Next, while keeping your spine pressed to the floor and your legs slightly bent, move your feet forward and downward in a rainbow-like arc until the tips of your toes touch the floor. Then slowly return to the starting position. Repeat four to 12 times.

SWAN

Purpose: Builds bone mass in the spine and wrists.

What to do: Lie on your stomach with legs squeezed together and arms crossed under your head so that your forehead rests on your hands. Keeping your forehead on your hands, lift your head, shoulders and arms off the floor. As you lower them again, lift your legs off the floor, being careful to keep them straight. Imagine that you're a seesaw—as one-half of your body goes down, the other half goes up. Repeat six to 10 times.

Next, lie on your stomach with your hands under your shoulders and your palms flat on the floor. Slowly straighten your arms to lift your head and torso off the floor, while at the same time pulling your navel in toward your spine. Return slowly to the starting position. Repeat four to eight times.

MERMAID

Purpose: Builds bone mass in the spine.

What to do: While sitting on a firm chair, reach your right hand toward the ceiling, being careful to keep your shoulders level. Looking straight ahead, lean your raised arm, head and torso to the left, keeping your right hip firmly pressed down. When you've bent as far as you can, pause, then return to the starting position. Repeat three to six times on each side.

SIDE KICK

Purpose: Builds bone mass in the hips, thighs and knees.

What to do: Lie on your right side with your torso straight and your legs angled forward, so that your body is bent in a slight "L" shape. Fold your right arm under your head, rest your head on your forearm and place your left palm on the floor for support. Keeping your left hip directly above your right hip, lift your left leg about four inches. Flex your left foot and swing your left leg forward as far as you can (stopping when you feel your torso moving), giving a little extra kick at the end of the forward swing. Now swing the leg behind you, giving two small kicks at the end of the backward swing. Repeat eight times on each side.

REPORT #145
Have Much Better Sex As You Age

Dagmar O'Connor, PhD, sex therapist in private practice in New York City. She is creator of a self-help sex book: *How to Make Love to the Same Person for the Rest of Your Life—and Still Love It* (Virgin Black Lace). *www. dagmaroconnor.com.*

Most older Americans grew up not talking about sex. Through others' silence, they were taught to believe that sex was shameful and taboo. Any men-

tion of sex between "old folks," in particular, made people shudder.

Sexual activity is a natural and healthy part of life. In fact, you can get better at sex and enjoy it more—at any age. I treat couples in their 80s and 90s who wouldn't dare tell their children or grandchildren that they're seeing a sex therapist. Typically, whatever the state of their sex life, therapy improves it.

With retirement's gift of time, you can learn how the aging body works differently from its younger self, what pleases you individually and how to please each other in new ways.

PRACTICAL MATTERS

Yes, bodies change with age. Many women start to feel old and asexual at menopause. Men may develop erectile problems. But most difficulties can be overcome.

Physical change: Chronic conditions, such as diabetes, thyroid disease, cancer, Parkinson's disease and depression, can affect sexual function. With heart disease, sex can cause chest pain, and with asthma, breathlessness.

Remember, intercourse is the equivalent of walking two city blocks. Check with your doctor first.

Physical change: Joint pain and stiffness from arthritis makes sex difficult.

Solution: Relax in a Jacuzzi or bath before sex...vacation together in a warm climate... find new positions that won't stress your sore spots.

Physical change: Many drugs—antidepressant, hypertension, heart disease and some cancer medications, as well as alcohol—can affect sexual function.

Solution: If your sex drive is down or you're having other sexual problems, ask your doctor whether your medications could be the cause and if switching might help.

Physical change: After menopause, vaginal tissue becomes less elastic, the vaginal opening becomes smaller and lubrication decreases.

Result: Discomfort during intercourse.

Solution: Don't avoid sex—increase it. The more tissue is exercised, the more it stretches and the more you relax your muscles. Using your finger or a dildo, gently widen the vaginal opening every day. If the problem persists for more than two months, see a gynecologist or sex therapist.

Meanwhile, smooth the way with a nonprescription water-based lubricant, such as Astroglide or K-Y Jelly.

Not as good: Oil-based lubricants or petroleum products such as Vaseline. They may linger in the vagina and irritate it.

Bonus: Applying lubricant may get you in the mood for sex. Or let your partner apply it as part of lovemaking. Good foreplay makes lubrication flow naturally.

Physical change: With age, men require more manual stimulation for erections, take longer to ejaculate and have a longer refractory period—the amount of time between an orgasm and the next erection.

Solution: Patience. These changes are an invitation to discover the slow, loving sex that many women, in particular, have always wanted but haven't received.

Erectile problems can be treated medically, too. Discuss the situation with your doctor. You may be referred to a urologist for medication or other treatment.

BEYOND INTERCOURSE

Couples in their 60s and 70s and older often ask me what to do about erectile problems and other issues that interfere with intercourse. I tell them to slow down—expand their sexual horizons, develop new sexual habits and start all over again. The goal is simply to feel more.

Our society fears low-level arousal—pleasurable excitement that doesn't lead to penetration or orgasm. But those who have always resisted "just touching" become gluttons for such physical connection once they realize how great it is.

Exercise: During the day or with a light on at night, one partner lies back and is touched by the other—but not on the breasts or genitals—for 15 minutes to an hour. The person being touched stipulates what's wanted in a non-verbal way. If you would like your partner to touch more slowly, put your hand over your partner's and slow it down. When the "touchee" is finished, switch places.

Simple interludes set a loving, sensual tone and encourage you both to overcome shyness about requesting what pleases you. Prolonged sensual touching without genital contact removes sexual anxieties...helps you become relaxed, sensitized and responsive...revives a sense of trust and well-being that you may not have experienced since you were stroked as a child.

You'll emerge from the interlude feeling wonderful about each other. Resentments and recriminations will evaporate. Making sensual, uninhibited love often follows naturally. If not, there's always next time.

LOVE YOUR BODY AS IT IS

Our society presumes that only the young and skinny are (or should be) sexually active. As a result, many older people avoid sex out of embarrassment about spotted skin, a protruding stomach, wrinkles and flab. (Do remember that while you are ashamed of your wrinkles and protruding belly, your partner's eyesight has probably also diminished!) A mastectomy or other surgery can interfere with self-esteem, too, especially with a new partner.

Your body is miraculous. Learn to love it the way it really looks. One woman attending my sexual self-esteem workshop said, "I did not learn to love my body until I lost it." But your body at any age is a gift. Value it for itself...not as it compares with anyone else's or to how you looked when younger.

Exercise: Stand together before a full-length mirror. Say what you like about your own body out loud. Do this exercise alone first, before sharing it with your partner. Then try the exercise with your partner, taking turns. Listen, but don't respond.

To learn to appreciate your body, admire it often. Come away from this event loving five things about your body.

If you look better, you'll feel better. I recommend exercise—walking, swimming, Pilates—to couples of all ages. Getting stronger makes both women and men look better and feel more powerful...more sexual.

EDUCATE YOUR PARTNER

The young body works without thought. As you grow older, you can—and may need to—benefit from learning more about your body and your lover's. The key to intimacy is to express your needs—once you have learned what they are—and to insist on knowing the needs of your partner so that you can try to fulfill them.

Special note to women: If you rarely initiated sex but would like to, take baby steps. Try asking for different ways of being touched, or take his hand and show him how you like to be touched.

Exercise: Turn up the thermostat, and hang out nude together. Sleep nude in the same bed even if you haven't done so for years.

REPORT #146
Natural Ways to Ease Menopause Symptoms

Ann Louise Gittleman, PhD, nutritionist based in Post Falls, Idaho, and author of 25 books, including *Hot Times: How to Eat Well, Live Healthy, and Feel Sexy During the Change* (Avery).

For decades, women relied on *hormone replacement therapy* (HRT) to relieve symptoms of menopause—hot flashes, sleep disturbance, anxiety and mood swings. But several large studies have linked long-term HRT with increased risk of breast cancer, dementia, heart attack and stroke.

Fortunately, there are safer, natural alternatives to HRT.

MORE THAN JUST ESTROGEN

People typically attribute menopausal symptoms to declining production of the female hormones estrogen and progesterone. But poor eating and lifestyle habits also play a role, by overtaxing the adrenal glands. For women who are going through menopause, the adrenal glands are nature's backup system. When the ovaries decrease their production of estrogen and progesterone, the adrenals have the ability to produce hormones to compensate. Poor diet and lifestyle choices put stress on the adrenals, creating an imbalance in body chemistry and contributing to the uncomfortable symptoms that we associate with menopause.

If you are a woman with menopausal symptoms, adopting healthier habits can help to even out these imbalances.

If you are a man and the woman you love is going through menopause, you can help by understanding that she is experiencing a profound physiological change. Your kindness and patience can ease her transition through a time that is confusing—for her as well as for you.

Common symptoms and natural solutions...

HOT FLASHES

As many as 80% of women experience hot flashes during menopause. One theory is that the hypothalamus, which controls body temperature, is triggered in some way by hormonal fluctuations.

• **Avoid spicy foods.** Foods containing cayenne or other peppers have a thermogenic effect, meaning that they raise your body temperature.

• **Cook with garlic, onion, thyme, oregano and sage.** These seasonings contain very small amounts of phytoestrogens (plant-based estrogens such as lignans and isoflavones that occur naturally in certain foods) and can help restore hormone balance.

• **Cut down on caffeine.** Caffeine stimulates the adrenal glands, leading to a spike in blood sugar levels followed by a plunge in blood sugar to even lower levels than before. This stresses the body and aggravates menopause woes.

If you don't want to give up coffee completely, have one cup a day with food. Don't use coffee as a stimulant between meals. Instead, eat frequent small meals for energy.

Better than coffee: Green, white and black teas have less caffeine and are high in disease-fighting antioxidants. Try substituting tea for coffee. Then transition to herbal tea or hot water with lemon.

• **Add flaxseed.** Ground flaxseed contains lignans, which seem to modulate fluctuating estrogen and progesterone levels. Aim for two tablespoons a day. Ground flaxseed has a pleasant nutty flavor—sprinkle it on cereal, yogurt and salads.

Bonus: Flaxseed reduces cholesterol, helps prevent certain cancers and relieves constipation (be sure to drink plenty of water).

• **Eat soy foods in moderation.** Some countries with diets high in soy report low rates of menopausal symptoms and breast cancer. But I'm cautious about soy. Preliminary research suggests that while isoflavones in soy appear to protect against some breast cancers, they may stimulate growth of other types of breast cancer.

I'm especially concerned about isolated soy protein, which often is added to protein powder, energy bars and supplements. This puts far more soy isoflavones into the diet than other cultures typically consume—and these high amounts may not be healthful.

If you enjoy soy foods, limit your consumption to two servings a week, and eat them in their whole-food form—as tofu, tempeh, miso and edamame.

• **Be wary of herbal remedies.** I'm cautious about black cohosh, red clover and other plant remedies with estrogenlike properties. Research has not demonstrated clearly that they help, and some can have harmful side effects if not properly monitored. However, some women do report good results from these remedies. Check with your doctor first. If you don't notice a clear change in symptoms after two to three weeks of trying a new remedy, ask your doctor about trying something else.

What men can do: Buy a dual-control electric blanket so that you both will be comfortable. Make her a cup of herbal tea. Join her in eating flaxseed—it is good for your colon and prostate.

INSOMNIA

During menopause, elevated levels of the stress hormone cortisol make it difficult to fall asleep and can trigger intermittent awakening throughout the night. *Natural sleep aids...*

• **Wild yam cream.** This topical cream extracted from yams grown in Mexico is a source of natural progesterone. It's available at most health-food stores and some pharmacies. Applying small amounts of wild yam cream daily may help to balance cortisol levels and enhance sleep. (The cream also helps reduce anxiety and hot flashes.)

Apply one-quarter teaspoon once in the morning and once at night. Gently rub the cream into areas where you see capillaries, such as the wrist, back of the knee and neck—these are the places where skin is thinnest and the cream is easily absorbed. Alternate where you apply the cream on a daily basis.

• **Magnesium.** Levels of magnesium, a natural sleep aid, are depleted when you consume too much coffee, cola, alcohol, sugar or salt. Foods high in magnesium include halibut...whole-wheat bread...leafy green vegetables such as spinach...nuts...and dried beans (soaked and cooked). If your diet is low in magnesium, take 200 milligrams (mg) to 400 mg in supplement form at bedtime.

• **Zinc.** This mineral can help quiet an overactive mind. Foods rich in zinc include poultry, red meat and nuts, but it is hard to get enough zinc from food. Take 25 mg to 45 mg in supplement form before bed.

• **Exercise.** One study found that women over age 50 who walked, biked or did stretching exercises every morning fell asleep more easily. Try to get a half-hour of exercise most mornings. Avoid working out in the evening—you may have trouble winding down. And don't go to extremes. Overexercising (more than two hours of strenuous, nonstop activity every day) can lead to hormonal imbalance.

What men can do: Exercise with her in the morning. Make sure there is a bottle of magnesium tablets by the bedside at home and when traveling.

MOOD SWINGS

Drinking less coffee and eating frequent small meals will go a long way toward balancing your moods by reducing spikes in blood sugar and stress on adrenals. *In addition...*

• **Eat a balanced diet.** The emotional and mental stress of menopause can lead to a vicious cycle in which stress depletes important mineral stores, further taxing the adrenals.

Among the minerals depleted by stress are copper, calcium, magnesium, potassium, sodium and zinc. To restore these minerals, eat an adrenal-supportive diet rich in bright-colored fruits and vegetables, legumes, lean meats and whole grains. Avoid sugar and other refined carbohydrates.

Recommended: Sea vegetables, such as nori, arame, wakame and hijiki. These are especially high in key minerals. Health-food stores sell them in dried form. They can be crumbled into soup and over fish, salad and vegetables.

•**Get the right kind of fat.** Though you should avoid saturated fats (found in pork, beef and high-fat dairy products) and hydrogenated fats (in margarine, shortening and many packaged baked goods), certain fats are necessary for hormonal regulation and proper functioning of the nervous system. Known as essential fatty acids (EFAs), these healthy fats help to stabilize blood sugar.

Strive to consume two tablespoons a day of healthy oil (use it in cooking, salad dressings, etc.). Olive, sesame, almond, macadamia and flaxseed oils are especially high in EFAs. (Flaxseed oil does not cook well.)

•**Take B-complex vitamins.** B vitamins are known as the antistress vitamins because they nourish the adrenals. Good sources of B vitamins include whole grains and dried beans (soaked and cooked). Most diets are too low in these vitamins, so supplements usually are needed to make up the deficit. Take 50 mg to 100 mg of a vitamin-B complex daily.

What men can do: Make it easy for her to avoid sugar and caffeine by cutting back on them yourself—your health will benefit, too. If she seems distant or on edge, don't take it personally. Remind yourself that it is not you—it is her biochemistry that is acting up.

WEIGHT GAIN

One reason why so many women gain weight during menopause is that the ovulation process burns calories—as many as 300 per day during the first 10 days of the menstrual cycle. When ovulation stops, fewer calories are burned and metabolism slows. *Foods to counter the slowdown...*

•**Protein.** Increasing protein intake can raise the body's metabolic rate by as much as 25%. Aim for three to four ounces of lean pro-

tein from fish, poultry, beef or lamb twice a day. Eggs and beans also are good sources.

•**Healthy carbohydrates.** Whole grains, vegetables and fruits metabolize slowly and give you energy throughout the day. Try to consume daily at least two servings of fruits, three servings of vegetables and three servings of whole grains.

What men can do: Don't nag her about her weight. Support her by not buying high-calorie foods, such as potato chips and rich desserts.

REPORT #147
Asian Herb May Fight Urinary Infections

Soman N. Abraham, PhD, professor, Department of Pathology, Duke University Medical Center, Durham, North Carolina.

With their typical symptoms such as burning urination, a frequent urge to urinate and a general feeling of being unwell, *urinary tract infections* (UTIs) are an especially unpleasant problem for women. One in five women develop a UTI at some point during their lifetime and—even worse—many go on to have infection after infection, for UTIs are notoriously stubborn and often difficult to completely eliminate.

While many women rely on cranberry juice to avoid and/or ease their UTIs, there is another herbal remedy that might turn out to be even more effective—the Asian herb *forskolin*, an extract from the Indian coleus plant. The good news for all of those scientifically minded individuals in search of research studies on natural products is that researchers at Duke University in Durham, North Carolina, have found that this herbal extract, which is commonly found in weight loss aids or body-building products, may also help flush harmful bacteria from the bladder lining. Forskolin has a long history of medicinal use in Asia for ailments such as painful urination.

FLUSHING OUT HIDDEN BACTERIA

More than eight out of 10 uncomplicated UTIs are caused by *Escherichia coli*—better known as E. coli—bacteria. Even when you take antibiotics, UTIs often hang on or return, and as many as one in five women experience another infection, with some women getting three or more in one year.

Why? According to Duke University Medical Center professor and study author Soman N. Abraham, PhD, many E. coli and other disease-causing pathogens avoid elimination from antibiotics by "hiding" within the cells of the bladder mucosa.

Dr. Abraham and his colleagues tested the effects of forskolin alone in reducing urinary tract infections in experimental mice. They discovered that the extract appeared to flush out more than 75% of hidden E. coli from their intracellular niches in mice bladders.

Once flushed out of cells, these pathogens can be eliminated in the urine and/or readily killed by antibiotics.

DON'T TRY THIS AT HOME

Although forskolin is a common herbal extract that can be purchased over-the-counter at health-food stores, Dr. Abraham emphasizes that this should only be seen as a treatment that shows promise for the future.

It hasn't been studied for efficacy for UTIs in humans. Research is ongoing at Duke, and only time will tell if forskolin will come to play a role in eradicating UTIs.

Until we know for sure, Dr. Abraham does not advise using it for urinary tract infections. Forskolin has other effects on the body as well—for instance, it is a potent anticoagulant and a reducer of intraocular pressure and blood pressure in some. So, as always, remember "natural" and "safe" aren't necessarily the same thing.

While this finding may turn out to be important news for frequent UTI sufferers, let's wait and see what further research turns up.

REPORT #148
Why Women Get Shorter...And How to Stand Tall

Arthur H. White, MD, retired orthopedic spine surgeon, Walnut Creek, California. He is author of *The Posture Prescription: The Doctor's Rx for Eliminating Back, Muscle, and Joint Pain* (Three Rivers). He has published more than 200 medical journal articles related to spinal health.

The cliché of the hunched-over "little old lady" may seem outdated, yet it's true—we all get shorter as we age. However, a good portion of this shrinkage can be prevented or corrected. The following steps can help you stand tall...plus reduce your risk for back pain and slim your silhouette.

PROTECT YOUR SPINE

Each vertebra (an individual segment of the spine) is separated from adjoining ones by water-filled cushions called discs. In young adults, each disc is about one inch thick.

After about age 40, these discs begin to crack and tear, which causes them to dehydrate and flatten. Over two decades or so, each disc loses about one-twelfth of an inch of thickness—and with 23 discs, that equates to a loss of nearly two inches of height.

Any uncontrolled motion that stresses your back can increase the risk for disc damage. Activities that involve abrupt twisting—racket sports, skating, roughhousing with kids—can tear the discs, hastening dehydration. There is no need to quit these activities, but do try to avoid wrenching twists.

Three other reasons we shrink as we get older are poor posture, loss of abdominal muscle tone and reduced bone density. These problems tend to worsen over time. The humpback seen in many older women is an obvious manifestation of this, but there also are more subtle warning signs that you may be aging yourself prematurely.

PERFECT YOUR POSTURE

Poor attention to posture may be to blame for height loss if you...

•**Slump forward when sitting.**

165

- **Drive, watch TV or work at a computer with your head jutting forward** (instead of centered over your torso).

- **Experience back or neck pain.**

- **Have frequent headaches.**

- **Have pain in your arms or hands (pain radiates from the spine).**

Chronic slouching weakens back and chest muscles, so you eventually may find it difficult to stand up straight even when you try. Large-breasted women are particularly prone to slouching. The extra weight they carry in front places more strain on the back muscles.

Simple steps to stand tall...

- **First, check your posture.** Have someone take your picture while you stand sideways in a doorway. Stand as you normally do—if you don't, you'll only be fooling yourself. The door frame provides a visual guide to what is straight.

- **Second, stay aware.** Whenever you pass a mirror or window, notice the position of your neck, shoulders and back. If your head juts forward, pull it back in line with your shoulders...roll your shoulders back...squeeze your shoulder blades together more...draw in your tummy...and tuck your rear end under. Even if you can't remain that straight for long, these brief moments of awareness will help to realign your spine and strengthen your muscles.

- **Third, stretch and strengthen.** When muscles are not used, they get smaller and weaker. Prevent or reverse problem posture with a few simple exercises. These are generally safe for everyone, though it is best to check with your doctor before beginning any new type of workout.

- **Secret stretch can be done anywhere.** It returns shoulders to their proper position and strengthens muscles between shoulder blades. Clasp your hands behind your back at the level of your buttocks. Push your hands down and roll your shoulders back (don't arch your back). Hold for 30 seconds. Repeat several times daily—while waiting for an elevator, watching TV or anytime you are idle.

Advanced: With hands clasped behind you and arms straight, raise arms up and away from you.

- **Doorway stretch strengthens your shoulders and back and stretches chest muscles.** Stand in a doorway, a few inches behind the threshold, feet shoulder-width apart. Place one hand on each side of the doorjamb, level with your shoulders. Keeping your back straight, lean forward, feeling the stretch across your upper chest as your back muscles work to draw your shoulder blades together. Hold for 30 seconds...repeat five times. Do every other day or whenever you feel upper-back tension.

FABULOUS ABS HELP

When tightened, abdominal muscles act as a muscular corset, supporting the vertebrae and protecting them from injury. Strong abs allow you to stand tall by preventing your rib cage from slumping down toward your pelvis.

Women generally have a more difficult time maintaining abdominal strength than men because pregnancy overstretches the belly muscles. A little effort goes a long way, however, in restoring the strength of the abs. *To try...*

- **Isometric crunch and hold.** Lie with knees bent and feet flat on the floor. Cross arms across your chest. Tuck chin slightly... then raise your head and shoulders (not your entire back) off the floor by tightening your belly muscles. Keep your head in line with your shoulders, and leave enough space to fit a tennis ball between your chin and chest. Hold the position as long as possible, then slowly lower down to the starting position. Repeat, continuing for three to five minutes. At first, you may be able to hold the pose for only a second or two and may need to rest between each crunch. Keep at it daily—soon your abs will get stronger.

BUILD STRONGER BONES

Osteoporosis is a disease in which bones become so fragile that even the jolt of slipping off a curb can fracture the spine. In severe cases, the weight of the person's own body can slowly crush vertebrae, producing a rounded humpback that steals as much as four inches of height.

Because estrogen helps to build bone, women are susceptible to osteoporosis after menopause, when estrogen levels drop. Ask your doctor about taking supplements of calcium and vitamin D. *Also...*

• **Go for a walk.** Every time your foot hits the ground, the impact sends a vibration through your bones. This produces an electrical force (the *piezoelectric effect*) that strengthens bones by encouraging calcium deposits throughout the skeleton.

Alternatives: Running builds even more bone density but may injure joints—so stick to brisk walking unless you're already an accomplished runner. Weight lifting also builds bone through similar forces, but the effect is less because there is no impact or vibration.

REPORT #149
The Strange, Bone-Saving Power of Prunes

From Bottom Line's *Breakthroughs in Drug-Free Healing* by Bill Gottlieb. Bottom Line Books. *www.bottomlinebooks.com.*

Dried plums—known to scientists as *Prunus domestica*, and to the rest of us as prunes—are loaded with powerful natural compounds that fight cell-damaging oxidation and inflammation. Could they protect bones?

In a recent study, postmenopausal women who ate nine to 10 prunes a day for three months had big boosts in two biomarkers that indicate bone growth. A group that ate dried apples didn't have an increase.

In 2005, female rats that had eaten a bone-eroding diet were given diets rich in prunes, and bone mass returned. The animals had incurred a type of bone damage that scientists up to then thought was irreversible—but prunes reversed it, says Bahram H. Arjmandi, PhD, RD, a professor at Florida State University and the lead researcher on all the prune studies.

In 2006, Dr. Arjmandi and his colleagues showed that prunes prevent bone loss in male rats.

In 2007, a study showed that prunes strengthen the structure of bone in male and female laboratory animals.

And recently Dr. Arjmandi launched another study with postmenopausal women, who will eat nine or 10 prunes a day for one year. At the start of the study, the women had their bone density measured; similar measurements will be taken at the end of the study.

Of course, you don't have to wait until the study is concluded to begin snacking on prunes.

Try this: The California Dried Plum Board (which calls prunes dried plums) offers the following ideas for putting more prunes in your diet...

• **Snack on prunes.**

• **Sprinkle prunes on oatmeal or ready-to-eat cereal, or into pancake batter as a complement to sliced bananas.**

• **Add chopped and pitted prunes to apple butter, orange marmalade, peanut butter or low-fat cream cheese.**

• **Add halved and pitted prunes to turkey or chicken salad.**

More Information: You can find dozens of prune recipes at *www.californiadriedplums.org. Address:* California Dried Plum Board, 3840 Rosin Court, Ste. 170, Sacramento, CA 95834, 916-565-6232.

Volume 15
Prostate and Men's Cures

REPORT #150
Breakthrough Treatments for Hair Loss

Why do some men go bald in their 30s while others have a full head of hair until their final days? Why do some women have ever-thinning hair, while others never seem to lose a single strand?

Blame your genes, first of all. If your mom, dad or a grandparent had hair loss, chances are greater that you will, too. Even so, there are ways to slow hair loss and stimulate growth.

THE HORMONE FACTOR

You grow and shed hair all the time. Of the 100,000-plus strands of hair on your head, it is perfectly normal to lose 50 to 100 every day. Once a hair is shed, a new hair grows from the same follicle. Hair grows at a rate of nearly one-half inch per month (faster in warm weather, slower when frost is on the vine).

Baldness results when the rate of shedding exceeds the rate of regrowth.

Hair loss usually accelerates when you're over age 50. One hormone, *dihydrotestosterone* (DHT), seems to be the chief culprit. DHT is a derivative of testosterone (the sex-determining hormone that is more abundant in men than women). In both men and women, DHT increases in the presence of the enzyme *5-alpha reductase*, which is produced in the prostate, adrenal glands and the scalp. 5-alpha reductase is more likely to proliferate after age 50. When DHT is overproduced, hair follicles are damaged. Some follicles die, but most shrink and produce thinner, weaker hairs—and the weak hairs are the ones that fall out.

An oily skin substance called *sebum*—produced by the sebaceous glands—makes mat-

Mark A. Stengler, NMD, licensed naturopathic medical doctor in private practice, La Jolla, California...adjunct associate clinical professor at the National College of Natural Medicine, Portland, Oregon...author of many books, including *The Natural Physician's Healing Therapies* and coauthor of *Prescription for Natural Cures* (both from Bottom Line Books)...and author of the *Bottom Line/Natural Healing* newsletter.

ters worse. Excess sebum clogs follicles and contributes to high 5-alpha reductase activity, which stimulates production of DHT.

STRESS

Among my own patients, stress is a factor for both men and women. I have found that highly stressed women, in particular, have higher-than-normal levels of cortisol, a stress hormone that can contribute to hair loss.

A study published in the *Journal of Clinical Biochemistry* confirms that cortisol is indeed elevated in some women who suffer hair loss—and that when they learn to cope better with stress, hair growth improves.

For stress relief, I recommend daily exercise, such as brisk walking, as well as relaxation techniques, including deep breathing and meditation. B vitamins and ashwagandha (a stress-reducing herb from India) also can help counteract the effects of cortisol.

A regular daily dose of 100 mg of a B-vitamin complex and 250 mg to 500 mg of ashwagandha can help control cortisol levels. Look for Sensoril Ashwagandha, a patented extract formula by Jarrow Formulas, available at many health-food stores or by calling 800-726-0886 or at *www.jarrow.com*.

A PROMISING FORMULA

Taking a daily multivitamin and mineral supplement as well as the herbal remedy saw palmetto also can help slow hair loss. A daily scalp massage with essential oils is beneficial, too.

Saw palmetto helps block the effects of DHT on hair follicles, strengthening hair. In a study in the *Journal of Alternative and Complementary Medicine*, researchers used a product containing saw palmetto and a plant compound called beta-sitosterol that is found in saw palmetto and other plants. The study included 19 men between ages 23 and 64 who had mild-to-moderate hair loss. Men in one group were given a placebo daily...and men in the other group received the saw palmetto/beta-sitosterol combination (none of the participants knew which group they were in). After five months, researchers found that 60% of the men who received the saw palmetto/beta-sitosterol combination showed improvement, while only 11% of the men receiving a placebo had more hair growth.

In my clinical experience, saw palmetto is helpful for both men and women. I recommend 320 mg to 400 mg daily of an 85% liposterolic extract. It is safe to use long term but should not be taken if you are pregnant or nursing.

For a more aggressive approach, you should also take beta-sitosterol. Source Naturals (800-815-2333, *www.sourcenaturals.com*) offers a 113-mg tablet that can be taken daily. It is available at health-food stores and at *www. iherb.com*.

The essential oils of rosemary and lavender have been shown to improve hair growth when applied to the scalp. My own belief is that they improve blood flow to the scalp, ensuring that nutrients get to the sites where they're needed.

You can purchase these essential oils in separate containers. Pour some of your regular shampoo into the lid of the shampoo bottle, then add five to 10 drops of each essential oil. Massage into the scalp and leave on three to five minutes before rinsing thoroughly.

OTHER SUPPLEMENTS

If you have tried these approaches for two to three months and still aren't satisfied with the growth of your locks, here are some other supplements that can help both men and women...

Biotin, a nutrient that is required for hair growth, is particularly good for brittle hair. Food sources of biotin include brewer's yeast, soybeans, eggs, mushrooms and whole wheat. For supplementation, take 3,000 micrograms daily for at least two months or use a biotin-enriched shampoo daily.

A great source of sulfur, *methylsulfonylmethane* (MSM) is an integral component of the amino acids that are the building blocks of hair protein. MSM improves the strength, sheen and health of hair. In one study, 21 adults (16 men and five women) who were assessed by a certified cosmetologist under the direction of a medical doctor were given MSM or a placebo and then were reassessed at the end of six weeks. The participants did not know who was given MSM and who was given a placebo.

Those given MSM showed significant improvement in hair health, while those taking a placebo showed few or no changes.

I recommend a 3,000-mg daily dose of MSM. Look for Opti-MSM or Lignisul MSM, available from many manufacturers and at health-food stores.

Essential fatty acids keep hair from becoming dry and lifeless by decreasing inflammation. Inflammation worsens the quality of hair follicles, and essential fatty acids are needed for the proper development of hair.

Food sources include walnuts, eggs, fish, olive oil, flaxseed and hempseed and flax oils. Or you can take a formula like Udo's Choice Oil Blend, produced by Flora (800-446-2110, *www.florahealth.com*). Follow directions on the label. The formula contains both omega-3 fatty acids (from flax oil or fish oil) and omega-6 fatty acids from evening primrose oil or borage oil.

Don't expect immediate results, however. It can take four to six weeks to see improvement.

REPORT #151
Fight Hair Loss by Getting More Iron

You normally shed about 100 hairs a day, but if hair comes out in clumps, get screened for iron deficiency. Getting more iron (through diet or supplements) may limit shedding and promote regrowth.

Caution: Do not take supplements without consulting a physician—too much iron can lead to heart disease, liver disease and diabetes.

Leonid Trost, MD, resident physician in dermatology at Cleveland Clinic Foundation, Cleveland, and co-author of a research review published in *Journal of the American Academy of Dermatology.*

REPORT #152
The Secret Recipe for Hair Growth

Jane Buckle, RN, PhD, president, RJ Buckle Associates LLC, Hazlet, New Jersey.

When you hear the word "aromatherapy," you probably think of a scented bath or a fragrant candle. But medical practitioners in the United States and around the world are using distilled oils of aromatic plants medicinally. Essential oils activate the parasympathetic nervous system, causing relaxation, which speeds healing.

AROMATHERAPY IN ACTION

Plant oils can be used in a warm bath...in a "carrier oil"—such as almond or sesame oil—for massage...or in a lotion.

The aromas can be sniffed from a bottle...a cotton ball...or a diffuser—a machine that emits the aroma into the air.

Clinical and scientific studies support the use of aromatherapy as an adjunct to medical care for treating...

•**Anxiety.** Essential oils that were inhaled for three minutes relieved anxiety in men and women, according to research published in the *International Journal of Neuroscience.* Use rosemary, Roman chamomile or patchouli.

Typical treatment: Sniff one to three drops when anxious.

Caution: Avoid using rosemary if you have high blood pressure.

•**Bronchitis.** Use spike lavender.

Typical treatment: One drop of spike lavender in a bowl of three cups of boiling water. Drape a towel over your head and inhale the steam. Do this for five minutes, four times a day.

•**Hair loss.** In people with hair loss due to *alopecia areata*, essential oils helped restore hair growth, notes an *Archives of Dermatology* study. A carrier oil contained a mixture of thyme (two drops), rosemary (three drops), lavender (three drops) and cedarwood (two drops).

Typical treatment: Massage the mixture into the scalp for two minutes daily.

- **Headache.** Use peppermint. If pain isn't gone in five minutes, try Roman chamomile or true lavender.

Typical treatment: Five drops in one teaspoon of carrier oil. Apply to temples or sniff.

- **Hot flashes.** Use clary sage, fennel, geranium or rose.

Typical treatment: Ten drops in two cups of water in a spray bottle. Spray on face during hot flash.

- **Insomnia.** Use ylang-ylang, neroli or rose.

Typical treatment: Five drops in a diffuser placed in the bedroom.

- **Low-back pain.** Use lemongrass. If you feel no relief in 20 minutes, try rosemary or spike lavender.

Typical treatment: Five drops in one teaspoon of carrier oil. Apply to the painful area every three hours.

- **Menstrual cramps.** Use geranium.

Typical treatment: Five drops added to one teaspoon of carrier oil. Rub on the lower abdomen and lower back every three hours.

- **Muscle spasms.** Use clary sage, sage or try lavender.

Typical treatment: Five drops added to one teaspoon of carrier oil. Apply to the affected muscles at least every three hours.

- **Osteoarthritis.** Use frankincense, rosemary or true lavender.

Typical treatment: Five drops added to one teaspoon of carrier oil. Apply to the painful area every three hours.

WHAT TO BUY

Aromatherapy is most effective when the essential oils are prepared with no extraneous ingredients. One good brand includes Scents & Scentsibility (*www.scentsibility.com*). Its products are also available in health-food stores.

USING AROMATHERAPY SAFELY

Some essential oils are irritating if applied undiluted. Always dilute with a plain carrier oil (scentless organic vegetable oils such as sunflower or safflower are good choices) before using topically. If skin stings or becomes red, wash with unperfumed soap.

Essential oils are flammable. Store them away from candles, fires, cigarettes and stoves. Don't pour oil on lightbulbs to scent a room.

Caution: Essential oils can be lethal if they are ingested—even in tiny doses. Keep away from children and pets. People with asthma or epilepsy and pregnant women should consult their doctors before using aromatherapy.

REPORT #153
"Natural" Treatment for Prostate Enlargement: Hope or Hype?

Kevin T. McVary, MD, professor of urology, Northwestern University Feinberg School of Medicine, Chicago. He is chairman of the American Urological Association's Benign Prostatic Hyperplasia Guidelines Panel. *www.auanet.org.*

Besides saw palmetto, which has been proven ineffective, there is an array of natural supplements that are reputed to relieve symptoms of *benign prostate enlargement* (BPH). While none of these supplements is believed to be unsafe, that doesn't necessarily mean that they're all effective. *A quick report card on the most popular natural BPH treatments…*

PROMISING

- **Lycopene.** There's evidence that this antioxidant compound—found in red tomatoes and in processed tomato products, such as tomato sauce, tomato paste and ketchup—may lower the risk for prostate cancer. It's currently an area of active investigation as a potential treatment for BPH as well.

- **Omega-3 fatty acids** (taken in food, such as fish or avocados, or in flaxseed or fish oil supplements) have a beneficial impact on the vascular system, which is good for general health—including the health of the prostate gland. Their vascular effects may improve erection quality (which can be impaired by some

BPH medications) and may also hold benefits for certain urinary disorders.

• **Pygeum africanum.** This bark extract is a promising medication based on preliminary data from human and laboratory studies, but at this point, no specific mechanism of action has been identified and no proven impact on BPH has been demonstrated. Further investigation is needed.

NOT PROMISING

• **Rye grass pollen extract.** No sound studies have found convincing evidence of its effectiveness.

• **Stinging nettle.** No sound studies have found convincing evidence of its effectiveness.

• **Zinc** (taken in food, such as pumpkin seeds, or in supplement form). Studies have found that zinc has no impact on BPH.

REPORT #154
Natural Help for Men's Urological Problems

Geovanni Espinosa, ND, MS.A.c, director of clinical trials, clinician and co-investigator at the Center for Holistic Urology at Columbia University Medical Center in New York City (*www.holisticurology.columbia. edu*). He is author of the naturopathic section in *1,000 Cures for 200 Ailments* (HarperCollins).

I f you've ever had an acute infection of the prostate, you may know that antibiotics often clear up the problem in just a few days.

But as the antibiotics eliminate infection-causing bacteria, these powerful drugs also wipe out "healthy" organisms that aid digestion and help fortify the immune system. You may experience diarrhea, upset stomach or a yeast infection while taking the medication.

What's the answer? Holistic medicine uses alternative therapies, such as dietary supplements, nutritional advice and acupuncture, to complement—or replace—conventional medical treatments, including prescription drugs.

For example, probiotic "good" bacteria supplements help replenish the beneficial intestinal bacteria killed by antibiotics. Ask your doctor about taking 10 billion to 20 billion colony forming units (CFUs) of probiotics, such as *lactobacillus* or *acidophilus*, two to three hours after each dose of antibiotics.*

Holistic treatments for other urological problems that affect men...**

IMPOTENCE

For stronger, more reliable erections, conventional medicine offers several medications, such as *sildenafil* (Viagra) and *vardenafil* (Levitra). But these drugs can have side effects, including painful, prolonged erections and sudden vision loss. *Holistic approach...*

• **Maca** is a root vegetable from South America. In supplement form, it has been shown to increase libido in healthy men.

Recommended dosage: 500 mg to 1,000 mg three times daily.

• **Niacin,** a B vitamin, widens blood vessels when taken in high doses (500 mg to 1,000 mg daily) and may help promote erections in some men who do not improve with the impotence remedy described above. A doctor should monitor high-dose courses of Niacin.

CHRONIC PROSTATITIS

Pain and swelling of the prostate (prostatitis) may be caused by inflammation that develops for unknown reasons or by an infection. The prostate enlargement that characterizes BPH, on the other hand, is likely due to hormonal changes that occur as men age. Symptoms of chronic prostatitis, such as pelvic pain and pain when urinating, can linger for months. Conventional medicine has little to offer other than antibiotics. *Holistic approach...*

• **Fish oil and quercetin** (a plant-based supplement) are both anti-inflammatories. The fish oil supplements should contain a daily total of about 1,440 mg of *eicosapentaenoic acid* (EPA) and 960 mg of *docosahexaenoic acid*

*To find a doctor near you who offers holistic therapies, consult the American Holistic Medical Association, 216-292-6644, *www.holisticmedicine.org.* Holistic doctors can help you choose high-quality supplements—these products may contain impurities.

**Because some supplements can interact with prescription drugs, raise blood sugar and cause other adverse effects, check with your doctor before trying any of the therapies mentioned in this article.

(DHA). Take 500 mg of quercetin twice daily. Fish oil and quercetin can be combined.

INCONTINENCE

Because incontinence can be caused by various underlying problems, including an infection, a neurological disorder (such as multiple sclerosis) or an enlarged prostate, any man who suffers from incontinence should first be evaluated by a urologist.

Holistic approach…

•**Buchu,** cleavers and cornsilk are herbal remedies that often help when overactive bladder (marked by a sudden, intense need to urinate) causes incontinence. Some products contain all three herbs. For dosages, follow label instructions.

•**Bromelain,** an enzyme derived from pineapple, acts as an anti-inflammatory to help treat incontinence caused by an inflamed prostate. Take 500 mg to 2,000 mg daily in two divided doses.

•**Pumpkin seed oil extract** may ease incontinence in men when overactive bladder is related to an enlarged prostate. Typical dosage: 160 mg of pumpkin seed oil extract, taken three times daily with meals. Pumpkin seed oil extract can be combined with saw palmetto. Ask your doctor for advice on combining pumpkin seed oil extract with any of the other incontinence remedies described above.

REPORT #155
Beta Sitosterol a Plus

Beta sitosterol is found in wheat germ, rice bran, corn oil, soybeans and other plants. Several human studies have shown that it reduces the urinary symptoms of benign prostate enlargement, including nighttime urination. Beta sitosterol also may help to shrink an enlarged prostate—animal studies show that it inhibits activity of the enzyme that causes the prostate gland to swell. The herb saw palmetto, commonly used by men with enlarged prostate, also contains beta sitosterol. Studies of beta sitosterol have used 60 mg to 130 mg

daily. Take it two hours or more away from any vitamins or medications you take, because it may prevent them from being properly absorbed. Otherwise, side effects are rare.

Mark A. Stengler, NMD, licensed naturopathic medical doctor in private practice, La Jolla, California… adjunct associate clinical professor at the National College of Natural Medicine, Portland, Oregon…author of many books, including *The Natural Physician's Healing Therapies* and coauthor of *Prescription for Natural Cures* (both from Bottom Line Books)…and author of the *Bottom Line/Natural Healing* newsletter.

REPORT #156
Eating Fish Helps Prostate Cancer Survival

Mark A. Stengler, NMD, licensed naturopathic medical doctor in private practice, La Jolla, California…adjunct associate clinical professor at the National College of Natural Medicine, Portland, Oregon…author of many books, including *The Natural Physician's Healing Therapies* and coauthor of *Prescription for Natural Cures* (both from Bottom Line Books)…and author of the *Bottom Line/Natural Healing* newsletter.

A 22-year Harvard School of Public Health study of 20,167 men found that fish intake did not reduce the incidence of prostate cancer but did improve survival rates among men who had prostate cancer. Men with prostate cancer who ate fish five or more times weekly had a 48% lower risk of dying from the disease than those who ate fish less than once a week.

My view: Several animal studies have shown that omega-3 fatty acids found in fish inhibit prostate cancer growth. One component of omega-3 fatty acids, known as *eicosapentaenoic acid* (EPA), and one of its metabolites have been shown to suppress the proliferation of prostate cancer cells. I recommend consuming five weekly servings of fish, especially those with the least mercury and other contaminants, such as sardines, trout and wild Alaskan salmon. Or take a fish oil supplement that supplies a combined daily total of 1,000 mg of EPA and *docosahexaenoic acid* (DHA).

REPORT #157
Natural Ways to Fight Prostate Enlargement

Mark A. Stengler, NMD, licensed naturopathic medical doctor in private practice, La Jolla, California...adjunct associate clinical professor at the National College of Natural Medicine, Portland, Oregon...author of many books, including *The Natural Physician's Healing Therapies* and coauthor of *Prescription for Natural Cures* (both from Bottom Line Books)...and author of the *Bottom Line/Natural Healing* newsletter.

If you're a man approaching age 45, you have a nearly 50% chance of having an enlarged prostate. By age 70, the chances are almost nine in 10 that you'll have it. Called *benign prostatic hyperplasia* (BPH), the condition involves an enlarged prostate that compresses the urethra and partially blocks urine flow. BPH is the most common prostate problem among men. While it's not life-threatening—it is not, for example, related to the development of prostate cancer—symptoms can be troublesome. Fortunately, there are natural ways to prevent and treat it.

THE PROSTATE PRESSURE POINT

The job of the prostate is to produce fluid that nourishes and transports sperm. This walnut-sized gland weighs approximately 20 grams, about as much as two Fig Newtons. Located in front of the rectum and below the bladder, the prostate surrounds the urethra, the passageway that carries urine away from the bladder and into the penis.

A swollen prostate can compress the urethra like a clamp on a garden hose, restricting urine flow. It also may press upward, irritating the outer wall of the bladder. This irritation makes the bladder wall thicker and even more easily irritated. A man with BPH might start having bladder contractions, making him feel the need to urinate frequently even when there's not much urine. Over time, the bladder may lose the ability to completely empty, increasing discomfort.

POSSIBLE CAUSES

There remains a lot to be answered when it comes to the causes of BPH. One thing researchers can agree on is that hormonal factors play the largest role.

Research has focused on the hormone testosterone and a related substance called *dihydrotestosterone* (DHT). Some researchers believe that testosterone, an anabolic (growth-promoting) hormone, is the main culprit. Others disagree because prostate growth tends to be a problem later in a man's life, while the amount of testosterone is at its highest when males are in their late teens or early 20s.

The conversion of testosterone to DHT increases as men get older—and DHT is very potent. It stimulates the proliferation of new prostate cells and slows the death of older ones. But if DHT is a cause, why do some men with prostate enlargement have normal DHT levels? Could another hormone be involved?

Now researchers are looking at the effect of the hormone estrogen (especially the kind called *estradiol*) on prostate growth. Estrogen isn't just a "female" hormone. Men have it as well, and as they age, estrogen levels increase. High estrogen-to-testosterone ratios could increase the effects of DHT on prostate cells.

LOOKING FOR TROUBLE

The most common test to diagnose BPH and other prostate-related problems is a digital rectal exam. Your physician inserts a gloved finger into the rectum and feels the part of the prostate next to the rectum for any enlargement or hardness. All men over age 40 should have this test once a year.

A variety of pharmaceuticals can help relieve BPH symptoms, but each has potential side effects. Many doctors prescribe alpha-blockers, such as *terazosin* (Hytrin) or *doxazosin* (Cardura), which relax the neck of the bladder, making urination easier—but these can cause fatigue, weakness, headaches and dizziness. Another prescription drug, *finasteride* (Proscar), relieves symptoms by shrinking the prostate gland, but it can cause impotence and reduced sexual desire.

For men who have very serious BPH problems that are interfering with their lifestyle, some doctors recommend surgical procedures—but surgery can also lead to impotence or incontinence.

I find that drugs and surgery usually are unnecessary. As long as a man is getting his prostate checked at least once a year and there are no signs of tumor growth or urinary blockage, BPH can be treated with natural therapies. These include improved diet and supplements. Also, 30 minutes of daily exercise has been shown to reduce BPH symptoms quite significantly.

HEALING FOODS

Avocados contain beta sitosterol, a phytonutrient that protects against prostate enlargement by inhibiting growth factors that cause prostate swelling. Avocados also are a good source of oleic acid, a monounsaturated fatty acid that is thought to reduce inflammation, which can contribute to BPH. Have at least two weekly servings (one-fifth of a medium avocado per serving). If you don't like avocados, you can have three half-cup servings a week of peanuts, rice bran or wheat germ.

Fish is a good source of *eicosapentaenoic acid* (EPA), a powerful omega-3 fatty acid that helps reduce swelling and inflammation. Eat at least two three-ounce servings of trout, salmon or sardines each week.

Ground flaxseed has been shown to reduce estrogen levels, and it contains anti-inflammatory omega-3 fatty acids. I advise men to take one or two tablespoons daily along with 10 ounces of water (to prevent constipation). Ground flaxseed has a mild, nutty flavor and can be added to salads, cereals, yogurt, smoothies and protein shakes or just eaten plain.

Pumpkin seeds are natural sources of zinc. This mineral helps keep your prostate healthy by reducing the activity of the enzyme *5-alpha-reductase*, which produces DHT. Sprinkle a tablespoon or two of pumpkin seeds—raw or roasted, with or without the hulls—on salad, yogurt, cereal, etc. four times weekly.

Soy contains a number of phytoestrogens (plant chemicals that balance estrogen), including *genistein*, which can help control prostate enlargement. I prefer fermented soy foods, such as miso, tempeh and fermented soy protein powder, which provide a form of genistein that can be readily absorbed by the body. Have at least one-half cup serving daily.

Tomatoes are rich in the disease-fighting antioxidants known as carotenoids. Preliminary scientific research has suggested that tomatoes and tomato products help prevent prostate cancer. They also may have a beneficial effect on prostate enlargement. Consume two servings of fresh tomatoes and two servings of cooked tomatoes (e.g., tomato paste/sauce) weekly (one serving equals one-half to one cup of tomatoes and/or tomato sauce). If you don't like tomatoes, eat watermelon or cantaloupe.

Foods to avoid: Men with BPH should avoid caffeinated beverages and alcohol—they irritate and inflame the prostate. Also reduce your intake of foods that contain harmful fats, such as hydrogenated or partially hydrogenated oils, that promote inflammation. Stay away from packaged foods that are high in sugar, which also can worsen inflammation.

NATURAL SUPPLEMENTS

The following supplements are listed in order of importance—start with the first and move down the list until you find what works best for you. Many formulas contain a blend of two or three of the ones listed.

Saw palmetto berry extract is a mainstay in the natural treatment of BPH and alleviates most symptoms. It was first used medicinally by Native Americans for prostate and urinary tract problems. Recently, researchers have found that saw palmetto helps the prostate by reducing activity of the DHT-producing enzyme 5-alpha-reductase. A review of 18 randomized, controlled trials involving 2,939 men found saw palmetto to be as effective as the BPH drug *finasteride*.

It can take six to eight weeks before this natural prostate protector begins to fully take effect. I recommend a product that is standardized to contain 80% to 95% fatty acids (check the label) and a total daily dosage of 320 mg, which can be taken all at once. Two brands I recommend are Nature's Way Standardized Saw Palmetto Extract and Enzymatic Therapy Super Saw Palmetto, which are widely available at health-food stores. It is best to take it on an empty stomach. A small percentage of men get stomach upset from saw palmetto. If this occurs, try taking it with meals.

Pygeum africanum, an extract that comes from the bark of the African plum tree, decreases the need to urinate at night and improves urine flow during the day. I prefer a formula that combines pygeum with saw palmetto, such as Ultra Saw Palmetto and Pygeum by Jarrow Formulas (800-726-0886, *www.jarrow.com*). The daily pygeum dosage is 100 mg.

Nettle root can provide modest benefits. The nettle-containing product from Nutrilite, Saw Palmetto with Nettle Root, produced good results in a UCLA study. Over six months, the 44 men in the study showed modest improvements in BPH symptoms. The Nutrilite formula includes saw palmetto, nettle root, beta-carotene, pumpkin seed oil and lemon bioflavonoid concentrate (Nutrilite, 800-253-6500, *www.quixtar.com*). Take one softgel three times daily.

Rye grass pollen extracts seem to relax the muscles of the urethra and improve the ability of the bladder to contract. Take three 63-mg tablets twice daily for a total of 378 mg.

Fish oil can help reduce prostate swelling and inflammation. Take 3,000 mg to 5,000 mg daily in addition to two weekly servings of fish. If you prefer a vegetarian source of omega-3 fatty acids, use one to two tablespoons of flaxseed oil.

Caution: Fish oil should not be used by anyone who takes blood-thinning medications such as *warfarin* (Coumadin).

REPORT #158
Exercise for Better Sex

Men who exercise vigorously at least three hours a week are 30% less likely to suffer from *erectile dysfunction* (ED) than men who are sedentary. A daily walk is also beneficial. It lowers the risk for ED by 15%.

The Medical Post.

REPORT #159
Soy Protection?

Soy seems to protect against localized prostate cancer—but it may fuel more advanced cases.

Recent study: Men who ate the most soy—in miso soup, tofu and other forms—had up to 50% less risk for developing prostate cancer over a 10-year period than men who consumed the least. The effect was especially pronounced among men over age 60.

However: The study also showed that among the men who did develop cancer, those who ate two bowls of miso soup daily had twice the risk for developing advanced prostate cancer as men who ate less than one bowl a day. More research is needed before recommendations can be made about the use of soy supplements.

Shoichiro Tsugane, MD, chief of epidemiology and prevention, National Cancer Center, Tokyo, Japan, and coleader of a study of 43,509 men, published in *Cancer Epidemiology, Biomarkers & Prevention.*

REPORT #160
Good News About Omega-3 Fatty Acids

Omega-3 fatty acids may cut prostate cancer risk in men with a family history of the disease. Omega-3s—found in fish-oil capsules and certain fish—slowed disease progression in mice genetically engineered to develop prostate cancer.

Yong Q. Chen, PhD, researcher, Wake Forest University School of Medicine, Winston-Salem, North Carolina, and leader of a study published in *Journal of Clinical Investigation.*

REPORT #161
Vegetables Protect The Prostate

Recent study: In a 14-year analysis of the diets of 32,000 men, researchers found that men who ate the most vegetables—six one-half cup servings daily—had an 11% lower risk for *benign prostatic hyperplasia* (BPH), or enlarged prostate, than men who ate the least—an average of 1.5 servings daily.

Theory: Antioxidants in vegetables may reduce the negative effect of free radicals on prostate cells.

Sabine Rohrmann, PhD, MPH, researcher, German Cancer Research Center, Heidelberg, Germany.

REPORT #162
Common Symptoms Of BPH

Here is a list of the seven most common symptoms of *benign prostatic hyperplasia* (BPH).

- **A need to urinate frequently**
- **Urination that is hard to start or stop**
- **Weak urination or "dribbling"**
- **Sensation of an incompletely emptied bladder**
- **Increased need to urinate at night**
- **Burning pain accompanying urination**
- **Recurring bladder infections**

REPORT #163
Red Wine Cuts Prostate Cancer Risk

The fermentation process concentrates *resveratrol*, the compound in grapes that is believed to protect against prostate cancer. This natural antibiotic also is a strong anti-oxidant and anti-inflammatory agent. To benefit, men need at least four four-ounce glasses of red wine a week. White wine, grapes and grape juice contain little resveratrol.

Janet Stanford, PhD, director of the prostate cancer research program, Fred Hutchinson Cancer Research Center in Seattle. Her study of prostate cancer patients and healthy men was published in the online edition of *International Journal of Cancer*.

REPORT #164
Sunshine May Protect Against Prostate Cancer

Men with high sun exposure were 49% less likely to have prostate cancer than men with the least exposure. Sun helps the body manufacture vitamin D, which may protect against prostate cancer.

Downside: Frequent exposure still puts people at risk for skin cancer.

Best: Spend 10 minutes a day in the sun without sunscreen.

Esther M. John, PhD, MSPH, epidemiologist at Northern California Cancer Center, Fremont, and principal investigator and lead author of a study of 905 men, published in *Cancer Research*.

Volume 16
Better Sex Breakthroughs

REPORT #165
Maca: The Super Food That Helps with Everything from Memory to Arthritis and Even Sex Drive

Super foods are foods and herbs considered to be especially healthful due to their hefty nutritional content. The list includes familiar favorites, such as blueberries, broccoli and beans. Now a more exotic super food you may never have heard of is generating excitement in the world of natural health—a Peruvian root vegetable called *maca* (*Lepidium meyenii* or *peruvianum*), pronounced MACK-ah.

The root of the maca is shaped like a large radish. It is a cousin to other cruciferous plants, such as cauliflower and brussels sprouts. Peruvians traditionally boil or roast the maca root or grind it into flour for baking.

However, despite maca's popular description as a "super food," you won't see it in food form in this country. Instead, the root is dried and ground into a fine powder. It then is distributed primarily in capsules, although you also can buy the powder to blend into beverages or sprinkle on foods.

I began looking into maca for my patients about seven years ago. In addition to its healthful fiber, complex carbohydrates and protein, maca provides numerous minerals, including calcium, magnesium, phosphorous, potassium, sulfur, iron, zinc, iodine and copper...vitamins B-1, B-2, C and E...nearly 20 amino acids, including linoleic acid, palmitic acid and oleic acid...as well as various plant sterols, which are natural cholesterol-lowering agents. All of

Mark A. Stengler, NMD, licensed naturopathic medical doctor in private practice, La Jolla, California...adjunct associate clinical professor at the National College of Natural Medicine, Portland, Oregon...author of many books, including *The Natural Physician's Healing Therapies* and coauthor of *Prescription for Natural Cures* (both from Bottom Line Books)...and author of the *Bottom Line/Natural Healing* newsletter.

these nutrients have been shown to promote health in a multitude of ways.

Here is what this super food can do for you…

BOOST SEX DRIVE

Legend holds that in the era of the Inca empire, battle leaders provided maca to warriors to enhance their strength—then cut off the supply after the fighting ended to protect women from the warriors' maca-heightened libidos.

Modern research has suggested that maca does indeed increase sex drive in men. One double-blind, randomized study published in the journal *Andrologia* examined the effect of maca on sexual desire in 57 men, ages 21 to 56. Participants took either placebos or 1,500 mg or 3,000 mg of maca daily. After four, eight and 12 weeks, they reported on their sex drive levels. Placebo users experienced no change in libido, while the men taking either quantity of maca reported heightened sexual desire starting at eight weeks and continuing throughout the study.

How it works: Maca's libido-enhancing powers are attributed primarily to its amino acids and sterols, among other properties. Blood tests indicated that maca did not affect the men's levels of the hormones testosterone or *estradiol* (a form of estrogen present in women and men). This is just one of maca's virtues—it does not change hormone regulation in men.

A small study published in the *Asian Journal of Andrology* yielded some interesting results, indicating that maca also improves male fertility. Nine men, ages 24 to 44, received either 1,500 mg or 3,000 mg of maca per day. Compared with tests done at the outset of the study, semen analysis performed at the end of the four-month research period demonstrated that maca increased semen volume, sperm count and sperm motility at both dosage levels. Again, maca achieved these results by unknown mechanisms that were not related to increases in testosterone or other hormones.

SOOTHE MENOPAUSAL SYMPTOMS

For women, maca has a long-standing reputation for soothing menopausal symptoms. A study published in the *International Journal of Biomedical Science* details research at five sites in Poland, focusing on 124 women, ages 49 to 58, in the early stages of menopause.

During the study, the women took varied combinations of either a placebo or 2,000 mg of maca every day.

Results: Compared with placebo users, those taking maca experienced significant reductions—84%, on average—in the frequency and severity of menopausal symptoms, particularly hot flashes and night sweats. The participants also reported that maca reduced nervousness, mood swings, fatigue, stress, headaches and depression, as well as improved sleep patterns and libido.

Bonus: In a substudy of the trial, researchers found that the women taking maca had a notable increase in bone density.

How it works: Blood tests showed that maca reduced follicle-stimulating hormone, which normally increases during menopause and is thought to be one cause of troublesome symptoms, such as hot flashes and night sweats. Study authors speculate that maca stimulates the regulatory mechanism responsible for optimizing ovarian function and estrogen secretion, significantly increasing the level of estradiol in a woman's body.

It appears, then, that maca offers a safe and effective way to reduce menopausal symptoms—and it is unlikely to increase a woman's risk for breast cancer, heart disease and stroke, as can non-bioidentical hormone replacement therapy.

We don't know this for certain, but the fact that breast cancer is not among the leading causes of death in Peruvian women, despite a diet rich in maca, supports the assumption. In addition, increases in estradiol as a result of taking maca supplements may be safer than adding a hormone to a woman's system because maca appears to stimulate the body's natural estrogen production.

Historically, maca also has been used to improve libido in women. The National Institutes of Health (NIH) conducted a study to determine if maca effectively addresses female sexual dysfunction caused by antidepressant drugs.

The result: "It appears maca root may alleviate SSRI-induced sexual dysfunction and there may be a close-related effect. Maca may also have a beneficial effect on libido.

FIGHT STRESS AND DISEASE

Any kind of stress—from work, personal problems, illness, injury, toxins, hormonal imbalances or any other source—can negatively affect how our bodies function. Maca is what holistic doctors call an *adaptogen*, a plant or herb that boosts the body's ability to resist, deal with and recover from emotional and physical stress.

Practitioners of traditional medicine from China and India have known about and made use of adaptogens for centuries, though the term itself was not coined until the middle of the 20th century. Well-known adaptogens include the herbs ashwagandha, ginseng, rhodiola and licorice root, all of which I have prescribed to my patients with much success over the years.

How it works: To be classified as an adaptogen, a natural substance must meet specific criteria. It must be nontoxic…normalize levels of chemicals raised during periods of stress…and produce physical, chemical and/or biological responses that increase the body's resistance to stress.

Although all adaptogenic plants contain antioxidants, researchers do not believe that antioxidants alone account for adaptogens' normalizing powers. Rather, it is thought that a variety of phytochemicals helps balance the dozens of endocrine, digestive and neural hormones that operate throughout the body—including insulin (which regulates blood sugar levels) and dopamine (which enhances and stabilizes mood). Many adaptogens also stimulate immune system components, leading to better immune function.

MORE OF MACA'S SUPER POWERS

In addition to its documented beneficial effects on the human reproductive system, laboratory tests and animal studies suggest that maca may reduce the risk for…

•**Arthritis**—by promoting cartilage growth.

•**Blood toxicity**—by improving the function of the liver.

•**Diabetes**—by allowing for better control over blood sugar levels and body weight.

•**Digestive health**—by combating ulcers.

•**Fatigue**—by increasing energy and by increasing endurance.

•**Heart disease**—by lowering levels of LDL "bad" cholesterol and triglycerides (a type of blood fat).

•**Infertility**—by stimulating production of estrogen and other hormones in women and boosting sperm count in men.

•**Memory and mood**—by enhancing certain brain chemicals.

•**Osteoporosis**—by increasing your bone density.

•**Premenstrual syndrome (PMS)**—by regulating hormone levels.

•**Prostate problems**—by reducing prostate enlargement.

THE SAFEST WAY TO START

Maca generally appears to be safe, given its long history of use by Peruvians…but there are a few guidelines to bear in mind. Women who take estrogen to ease menopausal symptoms should talk to their doctors about using maca. They may be able to wean off hormone therapy or at least lower the estrogen dosage under a doctor's supervision.

Breast cancer patients taking tamoxifen or other estrogen blockers and women who have had breast cancer must not use maca, because it raises estrogen levels. Women in a family with a strong history of breast cancer should discuss maca use with their doctors first. People who take thyroid medication should be monitored by their doctors because maca may increase thyroid activity. Women who are pregnant or breast-feeding should not take maca, as a general precaution.

Since its long-term effects have not been scientifically studied, I recommend taking a break from maca now and then in order to give the body's cell receptors a break from any hormone stimulation. People who want to try maca to see if it is a "super food" for them should take supplements for three months (six months for women with severe menopausal symptoms), then stop using maca for one or two weeks. They may then continue this regimen as needed for symptom relief.

HOW MUCH TO TAKE

Maca is available in supplement and powder form.

The average dose of maca supplements is 1,000 mg to 2,000 mg daily—which you can take with or without food at any time of day.

Or you can get your maca by adding powder to your favorite foods and drinks. It has a slightly nutty flavor, so you may enjoy mixing it with almond milk. *Other ways to incorporate maca into your diet…*

- **Sprinkle on cereal (hot or cold).**
- **Mix into your favorite smoothie or protein shake.**
- **Add to yogurt or applesauce, perhaps with a little cinnamon.**
- **Stir into tea**—especially chai blends, as the flavors complement each other.
- **Use in baking**—substitute maca powder for one-quarter of the flour in any recipe (no more, or it might affect texture or consistency).

Be aware: Maca powder has a high fiber content and may initially cause gassiness. I suggest beginning with one teaspoon a day, then gradually increasing your intake by one teaspoon every five days until you find your comfort zone. The optimum dosage is three to six teaspoons daily.

HOW TO GET YOUR MACA

I recommend organically grown maca products from Natural Health International, or NHI (888-668-3661, *www.naturalhi.com*, available online or through naturopathic doctors). The company sells a blend for women called Femenessence MacaPause (the same blend used in the study of Polish women, who experienced significant improvement in their menopausal symptoms) and another for men, Revolution Macalibrium, formulated to enhance energy and vitality in men as they age.

Cost: $35 to $38 for 120 capsules of 500 mg each. The average dosage of maca supplements is 1,000 mg to 2,000 mg daily, which you can take anytime.

You can also sprinkle maca powder into your favorite foods and drinks. The powder costs about $17/pound and is available online from *www.macaweb.com*.

REPORT #166
Why Men Never Remember and Women Never Forget

Marianne Legato, MD, FACP, physician and professor of clinical medicine at Columbia University, New York City, and founder of Columbia's Partnership for Gender-Specific Medicine. She is author of several books, including *Why Men Never Remember and Women Never Forget* (Rodale).

Neither men nor women can claim that their brains are "better." While men's brains are 10% larger on average, women's brains have more elaborate connections that make them more efficient. Male and female brains unquestionably are different, in terms of both structure and chemistry, and that can cause problems when we try to communicate with one another.

Most of us speak to our spouses just as we would speak to members of our own sex—then wonder why they don't seem to understand us.

Here's how to communicate more effectively with the opposite sex…

NONVERBAL CUES

The female brain is good at decoding nonverbal signals, including facial expressions and tone of voice, perhaps because mothers must understand the needs of children too young to speak. When women send nonverbal signals to men, women are often dismayed to find that these signals are ignored.

Women don't realize that the typical male brain is not skilled at interpreting nonverbal communications. Men are particularly bad at identifying signs of sadness in women—though men are pretty good at spotting signs of anger and aggression.

Women: Tell him verbally when something is bothering you. A sad expression or the silent treatment won't get you anywhere. It's not

181

that he is ignoring your feelings—he is just unaware of them.

If a man asks you what he can do to make you feel better, tell him. If you say "nothing," he'll assume that you mean nothing and he'll do nothing. He isn't trying to hurt you—men's brains just work in a more linear, literal manner. Because men often like to be left alone when they're upset, he might conclude that he is doing you a favor by giving you some space.

Men: Search for clues beyond her words when she seems unusually quiet or terse. She might be sending signals that you're not picking up. If you can't figure out the signals and she won't tell you what she needs, remind her that you really want to help, but it's hard for you to pick up her nonverbal cues.

LISTENING

The female brain seems to be better at listening than the male brain—women have more nerve cells in the areas known to process language and put a larger percentage of their brains to work when they hear someone speak.

The more elaborate wiring of the female brain also makes women better multitaskers than men. Evolution likely made women this way so that mothers could keep an eye on the children and still get other things done. Evolution shaped the male brain to focus on one very difficult task at a time. Tiger hunts were more successful when the hunters could focus all their attention on the tiger.

Add men's inferior listening ability to their superior focus, and the result is a phenomenon most wives know well. Tell a man something important while he's watching a ball game, and he might not remember a word of it. He isn't purposely ignoring you—his brain simply isn't wired to hear what you said.

Women: Put him on alert that what you're about to say is important. If it's particularly vital information, begin with a gentle "I need you to look me in the eyes." If there are too many distractions in your present location, ask him to go with you for a walk or out to a very quiet restaurant.

Men: Don't be insulted if she doesn't stop what she is doing when you want to talk. Chances are that she can pay attention to you even if she's occupied. If you want her undivided attention, ask for it.

PROBLEM SOLVING

The structure of the male brain makes men straight-ahead thinkers—when they see a problem, their instinct is to try to solve it.

Women are more likely to ruminate over decisions. They'll verbalize a problem and talk though all the implications and issues before they proceed. When women try to talk through their problems with men, they're often dismayed and insulted that the men try to tell them what to do. This confuses the men, who thought they were being asked for a solution to the problem.

Women: Tell a man the specific type of response you want before you share a problem. Are you asking the man for a solution, or do you just want to talk through the issue so it's clear in your mind? If you don't specifically tell him that it's the latter, he'll assume it's the former. If he tries to solve your problem anyway, understand that this is just how his brain responds.

As for how to respond to a man's problems, this rarely comes up. Men tend not to share their problems with anyone.

Men: Understand that women like to verbalize their thinking and don't always want you to solve their problems.

Instead, wait for a question before providing an answer. Ask what you can do to help rather than assume you know. And if your wife starts crying, holding her quietly works better than telling her she's being too emotional.

DIFFERENT INTERESTS

Women tend to expect their male partners to be interested in every subject they wish to discuss. That isn't fair. A woman wouldn't expect her female friends to chat about a subject that she knows bores them.

Women: Tailor your conversation to your partner's interests. (Men should do this, too, but because men talk less, it isn't as often an issue.) Find other conversation partners for topics that don't interest him.

Men: Encourage your partner to spend time with female friends so there's another outlet for the conversations that don't interest you.

Don't get upset if she's busy with friends when you want to see her.

BETTER ARGUMENTS

During an argument, women are more likely to bring up past events. Estrogen increases the amount of cortisol, a memory-boosting hormone, released by the adrenal glands during stressful moments. Because the female brain has more estrogen, memories of old fights remain fresher in a woman's mind. The male brain finds it easier to forget emotional situations and move on. Maybe forgetting a close call on a tiger hunt made it easier for men of the past to continue to hunt.

Women: Use simple, declarative sentences, and state what you want in outline form when imparting important information to men. Leave out anecdotes and unnecessary adjectives. Take advantage of your ability to read his emotions to spot the signs of boredom. When you see them, sum up your argument with a closing statement and end the conversation. Try not to rehash old arguments.

Men: Try to keep women focused on the point under discussion. If during an argument she brings up a fight you had five years ago, tell her, "We've discussed that already and it isn't going to help to go over it again. Let's focus on the current problem."

REPORT #167
Gender Bender

Men and women view their fitness levels differently.

Recent study: Men and women who practiced strength training for 12 weeks all felt better about themselves in the end—but men based their new body image on feeling thinner, while women were more focused on their strength and the size of their muscles.

Kathleen A. Martin Ginis, PhD, associate professor of kinesiology, McMaster University, Hamilton, Ontario, and leader of a study of body image changes in 44 men and women in a strength-training program, published in *Body Image.*

REPORT #168
Diseases Strike Men and Women Differently

Women who don't smoke may be more susceptible to lung cancer than male nonsmokers...women are more likely to get autoimmune diseases, such as rheumatoid arthritis and lupus...heart attacks in women often don't involve chest pain, but instead produce vague, flu-like symptoms.

Catherine DeAngelis, MD, MPH, editor in chief, *Journal of the American Medical Association,* 515 N. State St., Chicago 60610.

REPORT #169
Is Your Marriage Making You Sick?

Theodore Robles, PhD, assistant professor of health psychology in the department of psychology at the University of California, Los Angeles. Robles' research focuses on the effects of marital conflict on endocrine and immune functioning in healthy adults. He was lead author of "Positive Behaviors During Marital Conflict: Influences on Stress Hormones," *Journal of Social and Personal Relationships.*

Researchers have long known that marriage can improve one's health. But only recently has scientific evidence emerged indicating that serious health consequences can result from a chronically stressful marriage.

Important new findings...

• **Increased heart disease risk.** Negative marital interactions have been convincingly linked by studies at the University of Utah to increases in heart rate and blood pressure, coronary artery fatty deposits (plaques) and decreased elasticity in the arteries—all of which contribute to heart disease.

• **Weakened immunity.** Married couples who were more hostile or angry during a single interaction were found to have decreased function of infection-fighting natural killer cells in a study at Ohio State University and, in a later study, slower rates of wound healing.

As a health risk, marital stress is on par with social isolation, high cholesterol, poor diet and lack of exercise, according to these and other findings. For unknown reasons, women seem to be particularly hard hit by marital woes—studies consistently show that wives experience stronger cardiovascular, hormonal and immunological reactions to marital stress.

Good news: While virtually all marriages endure some degree of conflict, studies suggest that it's how we deal with disagreements—not just whether we have them—that largely determines the effects on our health. For example, University of Utah researchers have shown that a couple's demeanor during disputes—warm, hostile, controlling, submissive—is as good an indicator of underlying heart disease as cholesterol levels.

To minimize the health impact of marital stress…

•**Break the tension.** Ohio State University researchers recently measured blood levels of the stress hormones *cortisol* and *adrenocorticotropic hormone* (ACTH) in 90 newlywed couples before, during and after a 30-minute discussion about sensitive marital issues. When both partners were consistently negative, the wives' cortisol and ACTH levels escalated.

However, when one or both partners were supportive and constructive—even during heated discussions—the wives' stress hormones declined throughout the discussion. (Men's hormone levels were unaffected by both the negative and supportive behaviors.)

What both spouses can do: Agree with your partner on some points…accept responsibility for your shortcomings…and propose compromises.

Research involving women with high blood pressure suggests that more hostile behaviors during marital discussions are associated with elevated blood pressure during the exchanges, and more supportive behaviors are associated with lower blood pressure during the discussions.

•**Watch your words.** While husbands appear less physiologically affected by their wives' hostility, they do react—with increased heart rate and blood pressure—to perceived challenges to their competency or skills.

What both spouses can do: Avoid controlling statements such as "You're never on time…why don't you wear your watch?" or "Why can't you just do what I ask?"

Replace comments such as: "You're spending us into bankruptcy!" with: "I know you love to shop for the grandkids, but we need to stick to a budget."

Helpful: Because we cannot control everything about our spouses, look for something to value even in those things you may not readily admire. For example, if you resent your spouse's messiness but value his/her easygoing nature, try viewing these qualities as flip sides of the same coin. You may find you have greater tolerance for—and less need to control—the clutter.

•**Trust your spouse.** In a University of Utah study involving 300 middle-aged and older couples, researchers found no correlation between self-reports of anger or antagonism and calcium buildup in their coronary arteries (a risk factor for cardiovascular disease). However, partners whose spouses had rated them high on scales of anger and antagonism were more likely to have significant calcium buildup.

What both spouses can do: Pay attention if your partner says you are being angry, hostile, unreasonable or cold. While you may be unaware of your negativity, your arteries could be paying the price.

•**Speak your mind.** In a University of Michigan study involving 192 older couples, those in which both spouses clammed up to avoid confrontation were much more likely to experience the death of one or both partners over a 17-year period. In fact, among 26 such "dual-suppressor" marriages, 27% suffered the loss of one spouse, and 23% experienced the death of both partners, while among the 166 more communicative couples, a significantly lower 19% experienced one death, and only 6% experienced the death of both partners.

Shocking new finding: In a recent study involving nearly 4,000 married adults from Framingham, Massachusetts, women who reported regularly stifling themselves during marital disagreements were four times more likely than outspoken wives to die during a 10-year period.

The culprit could be stress—when husbands respond with silence to their wives' anger, studies show that wives' cortisol levels go up and stay up for the day. Chronically elevated cortisol has been linked to impaired cognitive and immune functioning, heart disease, diabetes and other ills.

What both spouses can do: Communicate openly.

• **Relax.** Studies have shown that the higher a woman's levels of stress hormones before she and her husband engage in a discussion about their relationship, the more likely she and her husband are to be critical, defensive or hostile to one another during conflict. Unfortunately, these negative behaviors only exacerbate the wife's already elevated ACTH and cortisol levels.

What both spouses can do: Make time daily to relax, whether with exercise, meditation, hobbies or spending time with friends. By lowering stress, women, in particular, may be able to keep hostility—and their stress hormones—from escalating during marital conflict.

REPORT #170
Men, Women and Weight

Men who weigh too much are likely to have poor sperm quality. Overweight women have trouble conceiving naturally—and are less likely to become pregnant even when embryos are fertilized in the lab and implanted.

David Ryley, MD, clinical fellow, reproductive endocrinology and infertility, Beth Israel Deaconess Medical Center, Boston, and leader of a study of more than 5,800 attempts at in vitro fertilization, published in *Fertility and Sterility.*

REPORT #171
To Cut Calories, Dine With a Man

When eating out, whom you are with can influence how much you eat.

Recent study: Women consumed, on average, about 665 calories when eating with one other woman and about 800 calories when eating with three other women—but just 552 calories when eating with a man. Men ate about the same amount regardless of the sex or number of companions.

Theory: Women want to look attractive and in control when with a date or mate.

Lesson: There's no need to skip a night out with the girls—just be mindful of how much you are eating.

Meredith E. Young, PhD, assistant professor of cognitive psychology, Centre for Medical Education, McGill University, Montreal, Canada, and leader of a study of 469 people.

REPORT #172
Libido Boost

In order to wake up your libido, try combining and drinking equal parts of the tincture form of the herbs *damiana* and *Panax ginseng* to stimulate arousal and increase levels of the hormone testosterone. Works for women and men. Consult a health-care professional knowledgeable in herbal medicine to determine if the formula is right for you and what dosage you should use.

If that doesn't work: Ask your doctor to check you for a deficiency in *dehydroepiandrosterone* (DHEA). The steroid hormone is available at health-food stores and is a precursor to such hormones as estrogen and androgen. Ask your doctor if this is right for you.

Jane Guiltinan, ND, director, National Medicine Institute for Women's Health, Bastyr University, Seattle.

REPORT #173
Eastern Practices for Better Sex

Women with low libido who began a regular practice of mindfulness (a meditative focus on the moment) reported improved sexual arousal. Women with a genital pain disorder who received a varying number of acupuncture treatments in areas linked to the liver, spleen and kidneys reported reductions in pain. Both groups reported increased vaginal lubrication and sexual satisfaction.

Lori A. Brotto, PhD, assistant professor, department of obstetrics and gynecology, University of British Columbia, Vancouver, Canada, and co-reviewer of 48 studies.

REPORT #174
Sex Can Ease Migraine Pain

Women who have sex when they feel a migraine coming on experience less head and neck pain, fatigue and moodiness. Nearly one-third of women who had sex at the start of a migraine reported reduced symptoms...and for 12%, sex stopped the migraine completely.

Possible reason: Sex and orgasm boost levels of the pleasure hormone *serotonin*—which is known to be low in migraine sufferers.

James Couch, MD, PhD, professor and chair of neurology, University of Oklahoma Health Sciences Center, Oklahoma City, and leader of a study of 82 women with migraines, published in *Headache: The Journal of Head and Face Pain.*

Volume 17
Weight-Gain Cures

REPORT #175
Your Lucky 13—The Best Secrets for Losing Weight Without Feeling Hungry!

When your stomach is sending out insistent, incessant "feed me!" messages, it makes it almost impossible to stick to a strict diet. That's why the real key to weight-loss success is to shut down hunger and short-circuit food cravings—because then it is easier to cut down on calories. *Here are 13 simple strategies for slimming down without making yourself feel deprived…*

1. Have two servings of protein at breakfast. Proteins are natural appetite suppressants. This means that even if eating more protein ups your usual morning calorie count, you will feel fuller longer—so over the course of the day, you'll wind up eating less.

Breakfast combinations: An egg scrambled with an ounce of shredded cheese…or eight ounces of low-fat yogurt mixed with an ounce of slivered almonds. Do not just have coffee for breakfast—you'll feel ravenous later.

2. At lunch and dinner, consume items in order of least-to-most calories. Start the meal with your salad and vegetables…eat the grains next…and then work your way around the plate to the heavier foods, such as meat. By the time you get there, you're already starting to feel full—so it is easier to control your portions of those calorie-dense items.

Interactive tool: Gauge proper portion sizes based on your weight, height and exercise level at *www.mypyramid.gov* (click on "My Pyramid Plan").

3. Don't think of snacking as cheating. Wisely chosen snacks keep hunger pangs at

Keith-Thomas Ayoob, EdD, RD, nutritionist and associate clinical professor, Department of Pediatrics, at Albert Einstein College of Medicine, Bronx, New York. He is coauthor of *The Uncle Sam Diet: The 4-Week Eating Plan for a Thinner, Healthier America* (St. Martin's).

bay, so you won't overindulge later in the day. Have a midafternoon and an evening snack every day, combining two food groups.

Examples: Pair a vegetable with a whole grain (hummus or salsa with whole-wheat pita or crackers)…or pair fruit with dairy (pineapple with low-fat cottage cheese, a smoothie made with blueberries and low-fat yogurt). Prepare healthful snacks ahead of time so you'll reach for them—not candy or chips—when your stomach grumbles.

4. Choose foods that you can't eat quickly. Labor-intensive foods—pistachios in the shell, edamame in the pod, peel-and-eat shrimp—force you to savor each bite instead of shoveling everything down. This leisurely pace fools your brain into thinking that you're consuming much more than you actually are.

5. Drink water to squelch the munchies. People often mistake thirst for hunger—so downing eight ounces of water may quickly quell food cravings.

Also helpful: Make sure your diet includes high-water–content foods—cucumbers, lettuce, zucchini…oranges, peaches, strawberries, watermelon…low-fat broth and tomato-based soups.

6. Cut down on caffeine. Yes, caffeine gives a short-term energy buzz—but it also contributes to hunger.

Reason: Caffeine stimulates insulin secretion…which reduces blood sugar…which tells your brain that it's time to eat. Limit caffeinated coffee, tea and cola to two cups daily, consumed with meals, to see if this eases food cravings. Cut back further if you have insomnia.

7. Chew sugarless cinnamon gum. Of course, when there's gum in your mouth, you won't be tempted to put food in there, too—but there's more to this strategy. Chewing gum helps improve mental focus, so that you stay engaged in your activity and are less apt to hear the call of the refrigerator. Also, chewing gum helps relieve the stress that can lead to overeating. Why choose cinnamon? It retains its flavor longest.

8. Fill up on fiber. Soluble and insoluble fibers hold water and expand in your stomach, making you feel fuller longer.

Daily goals: Four cups of fruits and vegetables (assuming foods are small, such as berries, or chopped)…one-half cup of beans (which are highly nutritious yet underappreciated) or other legumes…and three servings of whole grains (brown rice, oatmeal, whole-wheat bread).

Party trick: Eat half an oat-bran muffin before you go out. Those 100 calories will save you hundreds more because you'll feel less enticed by the hors d'oeuvres.

9. Indulge in chocolate for dessert. One ounce of dark chocolate with 70% or more cocoa content has only about 150 calories. Savor it with a cup of decaf coffee or herbal tea—its big taste belies its relatively modest calorie count.

Delectable brands: Scharffen Berger (866-972-6879, *www.scharffenberger.com*)…and Valrhona (888-682-5746, *www.valrhona.com*).

10. Fool the hunger hormone. *Ghrelin,* a hormone that stimulates hunger, drops about a half-hour after you eat—so nibble on a half-ounce of nutrient-rich nuts 30 minutes before dinner to make it easier to keep meal portions modest. If you're going out, carry nuts in your purse. (Recycle an Altoids mint tin—it's the perfect size for your portable nut stash.)

11. Shake your booty—or just take a brisk walk. Aerobic exercise lowers hunger-triggering ghrelin…increases levels of the appetite-suppressing hormone *peptide YY*…burns calories…and relieves stress.

Goal: At least 30 minutes of aerobic exercise (such as quick-paced walking) every day.

12. Retrain your palate. When you habitually consume lots of sugar, salt or fat, your taste buds become desensitized. Like addicts, they need a bigger and bigger "fix" to feel satisfied. But when you cut back on those three troublemakers, within a few weeks you regain the ability to detect and enjoy subtler flavors—and sugary, salty and fatty foods lose their appeal.

13. Move up your bedtime. People who sleep less than five hours a night have higher ghrelin levels—causing them to feel near-constant hunger. Sleeping for about eight hours per night helps normalize ghrelin levels. Also, fatigue increases stress and impairs judgment—so by getting more rest, you become better able to make sensible decisions about food.

Bonus: An early bedtime means that you won't be tempted to have a midnight snack, so you're likely to wake up weighing less—and feeling proud.

REPORT #176
Diet Personality— What's Your Secret To Getting Slim and Staying Slim?

Heather K. Jones, RD, nutritionist and journalist in private practice in Seattle. She is coauthor of *What's Your Diet Type?* (Hatherleigh) and a nutrition consultant for *The Best Life Diet* (Simon & Schuster) by Bob Greene, Oprah Winfrey's personal fitness trainer. *www.MyDiet Type.com.*

If you struggle over and over again to lose weight (or at least to avoid gaining more), yet seldom have much success, you probably chide yourself for being weak-willed. Stop that! The problem isn't your flawed character—it's that your dieting strategies are out of sync with your personality.

Just as you are born right- or left-handed, you come into the world with a distinct personality type. Though you continue to evolve physically, emotionally, mentally and spiritually throughout your life, your inborn personality type doesn't change much.

What this means: Rather than trying to force yourself to fit the mold of a preconceived diet plan, you'll have better results if you customize your dieting approach to suit your personality.

Here are the four distinct "Diet Types"... clues that help you determine which type you are...and the corresponding tactics that will help you lose weight and keep it off.

THE DIET PLANNER

Security and stability are of utmost importance for this type of person. *You're a Diet Planner if you...*

•**Have a strong sense of right and wrong**
•**Value your traditions and enjoy your regular routines**
•**Take your various duties and responsibilities very seriously**
•**Are organized, disciplined and hard-working.**

Your trouble spot #1: When life throws you a curveball (for example, your mother breaks her hip), you move your own needs to the bottom of your priority list so that you can get everything else done. Caught up in your duties (doctor appointments, insurance claims), you have no time left to plan your meals and instead eat haphazardly.

Solution: To stay organized, devise a week's worth of menus so you know exactly what to buy at the grocery store. Keep healthful snacks (baby carrots, an apple) in your purse so you needn't resort to the vending machine if you are delayed (for instance, at your mother's physical therapy appointment). Make a backup plan for missed workouts, committing to an evening aerobics class if you miss your usual morning class.

Your trouble spot #2: You're nostalgic—so it's hard to give up that customary buttered popcorn at the movies or ham-and-cheese quiche for Sunday brunch.

Solution: Go ahead and eat your traditional favorite treats—but make small modifications that cut big calories.

Examples: Leave the popcorn unbuttered ...make a veggie quiche for brunch.

THE DIET PLAYER

This personality type is characterized by spontaneity and adaptability. *You're a Diet Player if you...*

•**Focus on today rather than worrying about tomorrow**
•**Seek fun, variety, stimulation and also excitement**
•**Trust your impulses**
•**Dislike rules and regulations.**

Your trouble spot #1: You get bored eating the same diet foods day after day. So when the impulse to eat strikes, instead of having yet another ho-hum salad, you reach for something fun—and fattening—instead.

Solution: Clear your kitchen of all high-calorie, low-nutrition items, then stock up on healthful foods you actually enjoy—exotic fresh fruits, five different flavors of yogurt, a sampler of imported nuts.

Your trouble spot #2: You feel burdened by rules, so you rebel against regimented diet plans.

Solution: Forget about following a by-the-book diet, and simply focus on paring down portions. Make whatever type of sandwich suits your fancy today, but save half of it for tomorrow...try the black squid ink pasta in cream sauce if it intrigues you, but order the appetizer size, not the entrée.

THE DIET FEELER

Relationships and unity are top priorities for this type of person. *You're a Diet Feeler if you...*

• **Value family and friends far more than money or prestige**

• **Are very conscious of your own and other peoples' emotions**

• **Enjoy the role of teacher, counselor or confidant**

• **Are concerned with personal growth and development.**

Your trouble spot #1: You are a classic emotional eater. Because relationships are so important to you, interpersonal conflict often makes you reach for comfort foods—even though the comfort is only temporary and does nothing to resolve underlying issues.

Solution: Keep a food/mood journal, writing down everything you eat and how you feel before and after. Look for patterns. Do you long for macaroni and cheese when you're mad or crave chocolate cake à la mode when you're sad? Make a list of food-free activities to turn to when you need an emotional boost—such as phoning a friend when you're lonely or practicing yoga when you feel worried.

Your trouble spot #2: You love feeling connected to the people around you, so you fall prey to peer pressure to eat.

Example: If your friends all order pie at the restaurant, so do you—even if you're not hungry and don't particularly like pie.

Solution: You can share fun without sharing food. Meet up with friends at a bowling alley instead of a bistro. When the family lingers over dinner, let them pick at what's left on the serving platters while you sip a cup of coffee or tea and focus on what really matters—the conversation.

THE DIET THINKER

This type of personality centers on knowledge and accomplishment. *You're a Diet Thinker if you...*

• **Are a lifelong learner who strives to understand the world**

• **Look for logical answers for everything**

• **Enjoy discovering new and different ways of doing things**

• **Hate to fail and are your own worst critic.**

Your trouble spot #1: You take a scholarly approach to weight loss, researching and contemplating various diet plans and exercise routines—but you're so busy thinking that you don't actually do anything.

Solution: Consider why you are procrastinating. Because you haven't found the "perfect" plan? Because you're afraid you'll fail at losing weight? Give yourself a deadline of two weeks to research your options (for instance, the various online calorie-monitoring plans or the latest high-tech pedometers), then commit to a specific approach.

Your trouble spot #2: Your keen analytical abilities let you rationalize diet-sabotaging behaviors.

Example: You justify eating potato chips because they provide more potassium than a banana.

Solution: Instead of finding excuses for indulgences, do what you do best—seek knowledge from reliable sources. Once you are convinced of the many benefits of weight control, it is easier to make healthful decisions based not on twisted logic but on irrefutable facts.

REPORT #177
Foods that Boost Your Mood...And Help You Lose Weight

Susan M. Kleiner, PhD, RD, Mercer Island, Washington–based nutritionist who has worked with Olympic athletes, professional sports teams and Fortune 500 company executives. She is the author of *The Good Mood Diet: Feel Great While You Lose Weight* (Springboard), *www. goodmooddiet.com*, and *Power Eating* (Human Kinetics).

It's long been known that our eating habits can have a dramatic effect on our overall health.

Now: A growing body of scientific evidence shows that the foods we eat can either improve —or harm—our mood.

Bonus: Mood-boosting foods will help you lose weight if you have some extra pounds to shed. They can give you the mental and physical energy to be active as well as the nutrition that best supports physical activity, muscle growth and fat burning. People of normal weight can adapt these food recommendations to their daily calorie needs.

FEEL-GREAT BUILDING BLOCKS

The basic nutrients in the food we eat each play a role in optimizing our mood and energy levels...

• **Carbohydrates are viewed negatively by most people who are trying to eat healthfully.** But, in fact, these nutrients—when eaten in the proper form—are crucial to maintaining mood.

Here's why: Your mood is largely determined by a proper balance of brain chemicals (neurotransmitters). One key neurotransmitter, *serotonin*, is strongly linked to positive feelings.

Surprising fact: The brain uses the amino acid *tryptophan*, which is contained in most dietary proteins, to manufacture serotonin. But to cross from the bloodstream to the brain, tryptophan must compete against other amino acids. Carbohydrates help displace the other amino acids, thus increasing the amount of tryptophan that gets through—and the amount of serotonin that is produced.

A steady stream of carbohydrates will help your brain reach ample levels of tryptophan.

Best carbohydrate sources: Fruits (such as bananas, blueberries, mangoes, oranges, pomegranates and strawberries) and vegetables (such as broccoli, spinach, yams and carrots). These foods not only supply carbohydrates, but also contain water and fiber that slow the rate at which the carbohydrates are digested and absorbed into the bloodstream.

Helpful: When your favorite fruits and vegetables are out of season, frozen versions (without added sauces) are economical and convenient.

• **Fats, like carbohydrates, have been pegged as "no-nos."** But dietary fats should not be eliminated altogether—they make foods filling and satisfying.

Surprising fact: Fats are essential in keeping brain-cell membranes supple and well-functioning. For example, the omega-3 fatty acids found in certain fish (such as salmon, mackerel and sardines) have been shown to improve mood in people who are depressed.

Best fat sources: In addition to fish, try olives (any type), nuts, seeds, avocados, extra virgin olive oil and cold-pressed canola oil.

• **Proteins can be converted into blood sugar (glucose)**—but slowly, to keep glucose on an even keel. These nutrients also help keep metabolism (the rate at which you burn calories) high.

Surprising fact: Proteins are the raw materials from which neurotransmitters, including serotonin, are manufactured.

Best protein sources: Lean organic meat (beef, pork or lamb) or poultry...fish...low-fat or fat-free dairy products...eggs...and legumes (such as pinto beans or lentils).

GOOD MOOD MEALS

After three hours of not eating, glucose levels fall and so do your spirits and energy levels. To avoid "panic eating," have a meal or substantial snack every two to three hours. *For example...*

Breakfast: ½ cup of shredded wheat cereal...2 tablespoons of raisins...1 cup of fat-free milk...1 egg (cooked without butter or margarine).

Mid-morning snack: 1 cup of fat-free milk…omelet from 4 egg whites or 2 ounces of sliced turkey.

Lunch: 1 cup of bean soup (low-sodium canned soup is okay)…tuna salad (without mayonnaise, but with reduced-fat salad dressing made with olive oil and vinegar)…and mixed greens.

Afternoon snack: Orange…mini-carrots with 1 tablespoon of natural-style peanut butter.

Dinner: 1 cup of whole-wheat pasta tossed with 1¼ tablespoons of pesto (homemade or store-bought)…4 ounces of chicken (grilled, broiled, baked or roasted)…2 cups of sliced cucumber…at least 1 cup total of carrots and cherry tomatoes…and 1¼ cups of fresh strawberries with 1 tablespoon of full-fat dairy whipped topping (it has only a few more calories than a "lite" version).

Evening snack: 1 cup of hot cocoa made with fat-free milk, 1 to 2 rounded teaspoons of unsweetened cocoa powder and Splenda (one packet or to taste) or another sweetener, such as agave nectar (a syrup derived from a desert plant). It is sold in health-food stores.

EXERCISE-MOOD CONNECTION

Exercise not only helps control your body weight, but also has been shown to improve mood and reduce depression (as effectively as medication, in some studies). At a minimum, get 30 minutes of activity (at the level of brisk walking) five to six days a week.

REPORT #178
Yoga May Slow Midlife Weight Gain

People in their 50s who regularly practiced yoga lost about five pounds over 10 years, while those who did not practice yoga gained about 13 pounds. Most yoga exercises do not burn enough calories to account for the weight loss, but some practitioners believe that yoga keeps people aware of their bodies and their eating habits.

Alan Kristal, DrPH, researcher, Fred Hutchinson Cancer Research Center, Seattle, and leader of a study of 15,550 people, published in Alternative Therapies in Health and Medicine.

REPORT #179
A Better Way to Walk— Boost Calorie Burn by Nearly 20%

Timothy S. Church, MD, MPH, PhD, professor of preventive medicine research at Pennington Biomedical Research Center in Baton Rouge, Louisiana. He has coauthored a number of journal articles on pole-walking and the role of exercise in health.

You can turn a walk into a whole-body workout with a pair of Nordic fitness poles—long, handheld poles modeled after cross-country ski poles. Pole walking (or Nordic walking) is a low-impact aerobic activity that strengthens the upper body…improves posture…minimizes back and leg strain…and boosts your calorie burn during a walk by almost 20%.

•**Picking poles.** One-piece poles are safest, especially for seniors and people with balance problems, because they won't collapse the way adjustable-length telescoping or twist-locking poles might.

Test for size: Grasp the pole handle and place the tip on the ground a few inches in front of you, elbow bent and tucked into your side. If your elbow makes a 90-degree angle, the pole is the proper length.

Or: Multiply your height in centimeters by 0.68—the resulting number is your pole size. Choose poles with interchangeable tips— metal for trails, grass, sand or snow…rubber for pavement and mall walking. Poles are sold at sporting-goods stores and online (check 877-754-9255, *www.skiwalking.com*).

Cost: $70 to $160.

•**Correct technique.** To get started, swing your arms normally as you walk—left arm moving forward as the right foot takes a step and vice versa. As the right foot lands, bend your left elbow to 90 degrees and plant the left pole tip across from your right heel...then push the pole against the ground to help propel yourself forward. Keep poles angled rearward—they should never be farther forward than the front foot.

Goal: Walk at a moderate to brisk pace for at least 30 minutes five times a week. Pole-walking is safe for just about everyone—but it's best to check with your doctor before starting any exercise program.

REPORT #180
Money Motivates Weight Loss

Overweight people offered $14 for every 1% decrease in body weight lost more weight than those offered $7 for the same amount of weight loss. People offered no financial incentive lost the least weight.

Eric Finkelstein, PhD, director, Public Health Economics Program, RTI International, a research organization, Research Triangle Park, North Carolina, and author of a weight-loss incentive study, published in *Journal of Occupations and Environmental Medicine.*

REPORT #181
Rice Cakes Can Cause Weight Gain

Even though they are low in calories, they boost blood-sugar and insulin levels, causing the body to store extra sugar as fat.

Other products to avoid for the same reason: Mashed potatoes, instant rice, dried dates, fruit roll-ups and jelly beans.

Men's Health, 33 E. Minor St., Emmaus, Pennsylvania 18098.

REPORT #182
Medical Scams, Cons And Rip-Offs

Chuck Whitlock, journalist whose work exposing scams has been featured on many television programs, including *Inside Edition* and *Extra.* He is author of several books about scams, including *MediScams: Dangerous Medical Practices and Health Care Frauds* (St. Martin's Griffin). *www.chuckwhitlock.com.*

Bogus "miracle cures" and quack physicians probably have been around as long as the health-care profession. Con artists prey upon the unhealthy because sick people may be so desperate to find a cure that they will try any possible treatment, however expensive and farfetched.

These snake oil salesmen have been on the rise in recent years, as our aging population has more medical problems...millions of underinsured and uninsured Americans search for health-care options that they can afford... and the surging popularity of "alternative medicine" makes unscientific treatments seem more mainstream.

Sometimes it's obvious when a claim is fraudulent—but certain scams and unethical practices are difficult to spot...

SCAMS

• **Cheap health insurance.** Many of the more than 45 million Americans who are without health insurance are desperate to find affordable coverage. Disreputable insurance companies offer these people exactly what they want—health insurance at a low price, sometimes as little as $50 per month.

Most buyers are so thrilled to find insurance they can afford that they don't pay attention to the fine print. Many of these policies have huge deductibles, scant benefits and other restrictions that make them virtually worthless.

Most policyholders do not discover the problems until they have a serious health condition and receive the bill.

What to do: Look for a policy that covers doctor visits and protects against a major medical expense. A way to spot-check the quality of a policy is to look at the benefits for hospital stays. A good policy should pay $500 or more per day for the hospital room, with additional coverage for other hospital costs. An inadequate policy might provide only $100 a day.

Wise: Contact your state's insurance commissioner to find out if complaints have been filed against the company. Blue Cross/Blue Shield offers many reputable plans, and Kaiser Permanente has a good reputation for a health maintenance organization (HMO).

•**Natural appetite suppressants.** Unscrupulous marketers claim that there are natural supplements that help you lose weight—but these supplements don't work or have dangerous side effects. The most heavily promoted "appetite suppressants" include *ephedra, garcinia cambogia* and *hoodia.*

•Ephedra is an herbal stimulant, and like other stimulants, it does suppress appetite but at the price of increased heart rate, nervousness and agitation. In large doses, ephedra has killed people, and the FDA has pulled it off the market, though it's still available on the Web.

•Garcinia cambogia (a fruit from Asia) and hoodia (from a succulent African plant) are not stimulants and seem to be safe—but they don't work. No studies have shown them to be effective in suppressing one's appetite.

What to do: The only reliable cures for excess weight are consuming fewer calories and getting more exercise.

•**Organ transplants in developing countries.** America's organ donation program can't keep pace with the demand for transplants. For patients languishing on waiting lists, flying to a developing country where organs can be purchased on the black market might seem viable. Before you board a plane to India, the Philippines, Hungary or Russia and agree to pay $1,000 to $100,000 for an organ, consider that you're putting yourself in the hands of people who are more interested in taking your money than saving your life.

These people might find an organ for you—but you might not receive it until you've been milked for many times the agreed-upon price. Some patients are told at the last minute that someone else will pay more for the organ, which might or might not be true. To get the organ, you have to top this other offer. Even

when patients do get their organs, their transplants often are performed according to medical standards that are not as strict as they are in the US.

What to do: Talk to your doctor about the best options.

UNETHICAL PRACTICES

•**Bonuses from HMOs and PPOs to doctors who skip useful tests.** HMOs and preferred provider organizations (PPOs) often give cash bonuses to doctors who don't perform pricey tests—even when those tests are in the patient's best interest. They are essentially bribing doctors to scam their patients.

Example: Your HMO or PPO doctor tells you that he/she is going to spare you the invasive thallium stress test (where radioactive dye is injected into your bloodstream) and perform a routine treadmill test without thallium, though the thallium test is warranted.

What to do: When your HMO or PPO doctor tells you that you have a particular health condition, research that condition on a reliable Internet Web site, such as *WebMD.com* or *MayoClinic.com.* If the site mentions a test that your doctor has not performed, ask him why it was skipped. If the doctor's response seems evasive, consider getting a second opinion.

•**Unqualified plastic surgeon.** Many doctors have switched to plastic surgery in recent years, drawn by the lucrative nature of the specialty and its lower reliance on insurance payments. (Most plastic surgery procedures are elective and not covered by insurance.) No law or regulation prevents doctors from changing their specialty to plastic surgery—even if they have no background or training in this field. Patients likely have no idea that they are trusting their lives and appearances to what are essentially unqualified, untrained novices.

What to do: If you're considering plastic surgery, ask the surgeon…

•**Are you board-certified in plastic surgery?** He/she should be.

•**At what hospital do you have physician's privileges?** A general hospital is fine, but a university hospital is even better—university hospitals tend to have very high standards.

•**Who will be handling my anesthesia?**
Don't trust a plastic surgeon who says he'll handle it himself. He may be trying to cut corners and putting your health at risk in the process.

REPORT #183
Natural Alternative To Sugar

Mark A. Stengler, NMD, licensed naturopathic medical doctor in private practice, La Jolla, California…adjunct associate clinical professor at the National College of Natural Medicine, Portland, Oregon…author of many books, including *The Natural Physician's Healing Therapies* and coauthor of *Prescription for Natural Cures* (both from Bottom Line Books)…and author of the *Bottom Line/Natural Healing* newsletter.

Artificial sweeteners and the chemical processes used to create them have been making headlines recently. The controversy focuses primarily on the fact that the sugar in Splenda is converted to a sweetener using *chlorine*. Little information has been published about all the truly natural alternatives to sugar.

The result is that most Americans remain unfamiliar with healthy, natural options like *Luo Han Guo*, also referred to as *Lo Han*. A rare fruit found in China, Luo Han yields a powder 250 to 300 times sweeter than sugar.

And that's just the tip of the iceberg when it comes to the benefits of Luo Han.

As a sweetener, Luo Han Guo has no calories, does not elevate blood sugar, and is heat stable—which means it can be added to both hot and cold foods. It also helps prevent cavities and has no after-taste. These attributes make it an ideal, versatile option as a natural sweetener for tea, coffee or other beverages, and for use in making desserts.

ITS ORIGINS

While Westerners may have much to learn about Luo Han, the fruit has been used in a variety of ways, for thousands of years in China. The Lo Han Guo is a round, green perennial vine fruit in the melon family that grows wild throughout the mountainous terrain of Southwest China. Historic Chinese writings describe Song Dynasty monks brewing the fruit for medicinal beverages more than 800 years ago.

Luo Han, which is typically dried and sold in Chinese medicinal herb shops, has long been used in China and other Asian countries as a food and beverage, and also treats colds, coughs, sore throats, stomach distress, heat stroke, constipation and diarrhea.

The dried fruit is sold in a variety of forms, including whole, liquid, powdered or in a tea.

Often, in Chinese households, Luo Han is cooked with pork as a remedy for lung congestion. In fact, the *Encyclopedia of Traditional Chinese Medicine* recommends 10–15 grams—or one fruit—boiled in water per day, to address lung complaints, as Luo Han is a natural expectorant and helps clear the lungs of airborne pollutants.

The move toward using Luo Han as a sweetening agent is a more recent development.

THE VERSATILITY OF LUO HAN

In 1995, Procter & Gamble Company patented a process for making a sweetener from the fruit. Now, many sugar substitutes derived from Luo Han are available for manufacturing and home use.

The Luo Han fruit, which is sold mostly in Chinese grocery stores in the United States, can be simmered into a thick, sweet juice and used during food preparation.

There are many benefits to using the Luo Han extract as a sweetening agent and sugar substitute—chief among them is the fact that the fruit contains sweet compounds called glycosides, specifically *triterpene glycosides*. The body does not break glycosides down like other simple sugars, which means blood glucose or insulin levels do not rise like they do with other sugars—making it ideal for diabetics.

Luo Han also contains high amounts of amino acids, vitamins, minerals and potent antioxidant properties, which benefit immune function and the body's ability to maintain healthy balance.

REPORT #184
Why the French Don't Get Fat

Will Clower, PhD, president and founder of PATH Healthy Eating Curriculum, an educational and consulting program based in Pittsburgh that teaches weight-control strategies in corporate and academic settings and founder of Mediterranean Wellness, LLC, also in Pittsburgh. He is a neurophysiologist and former neuroscience historian at University of Pittsburgh and author of *The Fat Fallacy: The French Diet Secrets to Permanent Weight Loss* (Three Rivers). *www.willclower.com.*

The fad diets that sweep America are almost unheard of in France. The French don't count carbs or fill their pantries with low-fat snacks. They eat foods that make diet-conscious Americans cringe—buttery croissants, rich cheeses, fat-laden pâtés. Few belong to health clubs.

Yet the French don't get fat. In France, the obesity rate is only about 8%—while about 30% of Americans are obese. The French are three times less likely than Americans to get heart disease. And they live longer—men live an average of two years more...women, three years more. Why are the French trimmer and healthier?

Americans focus on what they should not eat. They look at a piece of pie and say to themselves, "I shouldn't eat that—it will make me fat." Eating becomes less about pleasure than avoiding hazards. That's a key reason why many people don't stick with a diet. A Tufts University study showed that 22% of people on low-carb or low-fat diets abandoned them after two months. After a year, the drop-out rate was almost 50%.

The French have a healthier relationship with food. They don't have to diet because they're not overweight. *And they're not overweight because they...*

• **Choose quality over quantity.** A Frenchman would rather have 10 perfect pommes frites than a plateful of soggy French fries or a small dish of creme brûlée rather than a mass of store-bought cookies. Also, the stomach stretches and demands more food if you take big servings on a regular basis.

Helpful: Take a little less than you think you want. Studies show that people typically overestimate the amount of food they need—and once it's on the plate, they tend to eat it even if they have had enough. If you're going out to eat, share an entrée or just have an appetizer as your main course.

• **Savor each bite.** It's common in France to linger for hours over meals. Eating quickly almost guarantees that you'll take in excess calories. It takes 15 to 20 minutes for the stomach and small intestine to signal the brain that you're full.

Helpful...

Make a conscious effort to take small bites. Give yourself time to appreciate the aroma, texture and flavors.

Set down your fork between bites. Don't pick it up until you have chewed and swallowed your food. Americans often fill their forks for the next bite before they have finished the previous one.

Make time for conversation...and only talk when your mouth is empty. This naturally slows the pace of meals and reduces the calories you consume.

• **Plan on seconds.** Knowing that you can have a second helping is psychologically reassuring—you're more likely to take a smaller portion the first time around if you know that you can have more. By the time you're ready for seconds, you may not want them—or you may choose to have a small dessert instead.

• **Don't combine eating with other activities.** This means not nibbling in front of the TV or while driving. The French make eating a special occasion, and they rarely snack.

• **Forgo "faux" foods.** A lot of things we eat are little more than an accumulation of chemicals. If you look at the labels on chips, sodas and other snacks, you'll see *partially hydrogenated oils, sodium stearyl lactylate, polysorbate 60*, etc. Also because these products lack flavor, they're often loaded with corn syrup.

The French rarely eat processed foods or have soft drinks. Most of their diet consists of grains, legumes and fresh fruits and vegetables. They get fewer sugar calories...and the fiber that is in natural foods slows digestion and increases feelings of satiety.

• **Get enough healthy fat.** The French don't worry about fat. About 35% to 45% of their daily calories come from fat. Some comes from the saturated fat in butter, cheese and red meat, though the French eat red meat only about once a month. They mainly eat fish or game meats, such as rabbit or pheasant, which are naturally low in saturated fat. Most of the fat the French consume comes from nuts, fish and olive oil—healthy fats that cause you to feel full without elevating cholesterol or heart disease risk. (The French also drink wine regularly, and wine—in particular, red wine—has been shown to improve cardiovascular health.)

Adequate fat intake increases metabolism—by as much as 15%, compared with diets that are very low in fat and calories. Eating fat causes you to burn more calories...and promotes the absorption of beta-carotene and other fat-soluble nutrients.

• **Exercise daily.** Even though the French don't work out in gyms as often as Americans, they're not sedentary. They ride bikes. They go for long walks.

I usually advise people to try dance classes, yoga or tai chi. These activities burn calories and are more enjoyable for most people than lifting weights or running on a treadmill.

REPORT #185
Too Busy to Go to the Gym? Get Fit in Just a Few Minutes

Joan Price, certified fitness instructor and motivational speaker based in Sebastopol, California, and author of six books, including *The Anytime, Anywhere Exercise Book* (iUniverse). *www.joanprice.com.*

L ack of time is a primary reason people give for failing to get the recommended 30 to 60 minutes of moderate-intensity exercise most days of the week. Admittedly, it can be tough to find such a big chunk of time in your busy schedule.

What helps: Instead of feeling compelled to cram an entire day's worth of exercise into a single block of time, commit to fitting in little bursts of physical activity—two minutes, five minutes, 10 minutes—throughout the day. The more these "fitness minutes" add up, the more you reap the benefits of exercise, including improved health, better weight control, increased energy and a sense of well-being.

IN THE MORNING

• **When your alarm clock rings**—instead of pressing the snooze button, get up and use those extra minutes to do some gentle yoga poses.

• **While brushing your teeth**—do calf raises. Standing, slowly rise onto the balls of your feet...hold for several seconds...return to the starting position. Repeat, continuing for two minutes.

• **In the shower**—give your upper back muscles a workout. Squeeze your shoulder blades together...hold for five to 10 seconds... rest for a moment. Repeat 10 to 15 times.

• **While you style your hair**—squeeze your buttocks muscles as hard as you can for 10 seconds...rest for several seconds...repeat five to 10 times.

• **When going down stairs**—turn around at the bottom of the stairs and go back up, making one or more extra up-and-down trips.

• **As the coffee is brewing**—hop on your right foot 10 times...then hop on the left foot. Repeat twice.

• **When letting the dog out**—go with him for a short walk.

OUT AND ABOUT

• **At the gas station**—walk inside to pay rather than swiping a credit card at the pump. Instead of sitting in your car as the gas flows, clean all your windows, alternating the hand that holds the squeegee.

• **At every red light**—do shoulder shrugs and roll your shoulders...repeatedly tighten and release your thigh muscles...rotate one wrist, then the other wrist.

• **When parking**—instead of finding a spot close to your destination, get one a few blocks away.

•**Upon entering a store**—if all the items you need will fit in a shopping basket, choose a basket instead of a cart.

•**As you shop**—if you need a cart, do 10 bicep curls with weightier items—soup cans, juice jugs—before placing them in your cart. (If you feel silly doing this in public, do your bicep curls at home as you put the items in the pantry.)

•**While waiting in line**—work your abdominal muscles. Suck in your belly and tighten your abs…hold for 10 seconds…relax. Repeat five to 10 times.

•**On a long car trip**—stop every 50 miles or so, and take a walk around a rest stop or scenic area.

•**When traveling by bus, plane or train**—walk up and down the aisle for at least five minutes every hour.

AT YOUR DESK

•**While on the phone**—march in place or pace around your office.

•**As you read e-mail**—lift your right foot several inches off the floor…rotate your ankle clockwise several times, then counterclockwise…lower the foot. Repeat on the left side.

•**If you need to talk with a coworker**—walk over to her office instead of phoning. When you get back to your own desk, before sitting down, hold your arms out to the side and circle them forward 15 times, and then backward.

•**Each time you finish a task**—do "chair dips." With feet flat on the floor, place your hands on the armrests and push your body up (so your rear end hovers above the seat)…hold for several seconds…lower yourself back into the chair. Repeat 10 times. (Skip this if your chair has wheels.)

•**During your lunch break**—take a walk through the office complex.

•**In the restroom**—stand and reach for the sky for 30 seconds…then do 10 jumping jacks.

•**If you drop a pencil (or at least once a day)**—do a variation on toe touches. Stand up, bend down, pick up the pencil, straighten up…drop the pencil again. Repeat 10 times.

IN THE EVENING

•**Before starting dinner**—take a quick ride around the neighborhood on your bicycle.

•**At the dinner table**—do leg lifts. Sit with feet flat on the floor. Straighten your right leg to hold your right foot out in front of you…lift your right thigh a few inches off the chair and hold for several seconds…lower the foot. Repeat 10 times, then switch to the left leg.

•**Doing laundry**—when you grab a basket of clothes, tighten abdominal muscles and, with your back straight, lift the basket from hip height to chest height five times.

•**Listening to the radio or a CD**—dance around the room for one entire song. Repeat several times.

•**While watching TV**—pop an exercise video or DVD in your player. Every time the TV show cuts to a commercial break, turn on the player and follow along with the workout for several minutes.

•**Climbing the stairs**—take the steps two at a time. (Do not do this if you have balance problems.)

•**After washing your face**—tilt your head slowly from side to side, feeling a good stretch along your neck…try to touch your chin to your chest to stretch the back of your neck.

•**Before climbing into bed**—raise your arms overhead…tilt gently to the right, feeling the stretch along the left side of your torso…then tilt to the left. Repeat five times.

•**When you lie down**—do knee hugs. Lie on your back with your knees bent, feet flat on the mattress. Raise one leg, place your hands behind the thigh and draw the leg toward your chest. Hold for 30 seconds…return to starting position. Repeat with the other leg.

•**Closing your eyes**—breathe in and out deeply 10 times, feeling grateful for all that your body was capable of doing during the day.

REPORT #186
A Drink a Day May Keep The Pounds Away

People who drink one alcoholic drink a day, including wine, beer and mixed drinks, are 54% less likely to be obese than those who don't drink at all. Those who have two drinks are 41% less likely to be obese.

But: Don't overdo it—people who drink four or more drinks a day are 46% more likely to be obese than nondrinkers. Binge drinkers, who sometimes have five or more drinks per day, are 80% more likely to be obese.

Ahmed A. Arif, PhD, associate professor, Department of Public Health Sciences, College of Health and Human Services, The University of North Carolina at Charlotte, Charlotte, NC, and leader of a study of the link between obesity and alcohol consumption in 8,236 nonsmokers, published in *BMC Public Health*.

REPORT #187
Dieting? Don't Drop Dairy

Dieters don't have to skip dairy products. Thirty-four overweight men and women drank 20 ounces of skim milk or a fruit drink with breakfast (two slices of toast with jam and margarine), followed by lunch (a sandwich) four hours later.

Result: The skim milk group ate 50 fewer calories, on average, at lunchtime compared with the fruit-drink group, and reported feeling fuller.

Theory: Milk's high protein content, lactose (natural sugar) and/or thickness may contribute to feelings of fullness.

If you are trying to manage your weight: Consider drinking skim milk with your breakfast.

Emma R. Dove, MD, research associate, School of Medicine and Pharmacology, University of Western Australia, Perth.

REPORT #188
Vitamin C Helps You Burn More Fat When You Exercise

People who took 500 milligrams (mg) of vitamin C daily burned 39% more fat while exercising than people who took less. Since it is difficult to get enough vitamin C just from fruits and vegetables, take a vitamin C supplement to be sure you get at least 500 mg per day.

Carol S. Johnston, PhD, RD, professor and chair, in Mesa, Arizona. She has published more than 75 research papers and book chapters on nutrition subjects and received the 2004 Grace A. Goldsmith Award from the American College of Nutrition in recognition of her research.

REPORT #189
Not Enough Sleep Can Contribute to Weight Gain

Lawrence J. Epstein, MD, instructor in medicine at Harvard Medical School in Boston, medical director of Sleep HealthCenters, based in Brighton, Massachusetts and author of *The Harvard Medical School Guide to a Good Night's Sleep* (McGraw-Hill).

If a busy schedule prevents you from getting the full seven-and-a-half to eight hours of sleep per night that the vast majority of adults require, it's no wonder that you often feel drowsy during the day.

But what if you spend plenty of time in bed yet still never feel fully rested? Something in your sleep environment may be keeping you up or creating disturbances that, even without waking you fully, interfere with the normal progression of sleep stages that you need to feel truly rested.

Concern: Chronic sleep deprivation negatively affects virtually every aspect of life—energy, alertness, work performance, mood, sex drive.

New finding: Sleep deprivation also contributes to weight problems. Studies show that losing sleep for just a few nights raises levels of hormones linked with overeating and weight gain and makes a person more likely to reach for fattening comfort foods instead of nutritious fare.

Even worse: Sleep deprivation increases the risk for diabetes and heart disease as well as car crashes and other accidents.

What to do: Speak to your doctor—sleep problems sometimes signal a potentially serious condition, such as sleep apnea (repeated cessations in breathing during sleep) or depression. If you still have trouble sleeping well even after underlying medical problems are ruled out or treated, chances are that your bedroom is not offering an optimal sleep environment.

REPORT #190
Vinegar to Lose Weight (Lower Blood Sugar, Too)

Mark A. Stengler, NMD, licensed naturopathic medical doctor in private practice, La Jolla, California…adjunct associate clinical professor at the National College of Natural Medicine, Portland, Oregon…author of many books, including *The Natural Physician's Healing Therapies* and coauthor of *Prescription for Natural Cures* (both from Bottom Line Books)…and author of the *Bottom Line/Natural Healing* newsletter.

Vinegar has been used as a folk medicine for such things as headaches and indigestion. Now several studies reinforce its benefit for weight management and blood sugar control. Researchers believe that it is the *acetic acid* in any type of vinegar (apple cider, balsamic, white or red wine) that produces this effect, interfering with enzymes involved in the digestion of carbohydrates and those that alter glucose metabolism (so that insulin does not spike).

One recent study found that mice fed a high-fat diet—and given acetic acid—developed up to 10% less body fat than those not given acetic acid. Another study found that having small amounts of vinegar at bedtime seemed to reduce waking blood glucose levels in people.

More studies need to be done on vinegar, but it does seem that people can benefit from sprinkling vinegar on salads…adding a teaspoon to marinades…and adding a few drops to mustard. For blood sugar balance (for those with diabetes or on diabetes medication) or weight loss, dilute one to two tablespoons (some people start with teaspoons) in an equal amount of water—and drink it at the beginning of a meal.

REPORT #191
The Pen and Paper Diet

Jack F. Hollis, PhD, senior investigator, Center for Health Research at Kaiser Permanente Northwest, Portland, Oregon.

Losing weight and keeping it off remains at the top of the list of difficult challenges for most people in America, with about 65% of adults in this country currently overweight or obese. Research shows that between 20% and 40% of Americans are currently trying to lose weight…sadly, without much success. Now a recent study from the Kaiser Permanente Center for Health Research in Portland, Oregon, has identified what weight strategies appear to be most highly associated with successful weight loss. One of the most effective is also one of the easiest to do.

ABOUT THE RESEARCH

Researchers enrolled 1,685 overweight or obese adults in a weight loss program that included 20 group training sessions over six months. During that time, participants were given instructions on how to follow a calorically appropriate diet, low in sodium and high in fruits and vegetables and containing low-fat dairy. According to Jack Hollis, PhD, lead researcher, participants were also instructed to engage in 30 minutes of moderate exercise each day, including a 30-minute brisk walk held during the weekly group meeting. They were also taught how to keep a food diary, in which they were to write down everything they consumed, and were strongly encouraged to do so.

After six months, 69% of the participants had lost at least 8.8 pounds of body weight, an amount considered to be clinically significant. The mean amount lost was 13 pounds after 20 weeks. Researchers then analyzed what behaviors were most correlated with success.

A particularly striking finding was that participants who kept daily records of what they ate lost twice as much weight as those who kept no records. "The act of writing down what you eat makes you more conscious of what you're eating," Dr. Hollis says calling it "a powerful self-management tool." Other behaviors that correlated with weight-loss success were number of minutes per week spent exercising and how many group meetings a member attended.

HOW TO DO IT

Dr. Hollis offered some tips for those interested in getting this good habit going…

• **Measure, as much as possible.** Use tablespoons, measuring cups or a food scale to get an approximation of quantity. In the study, the participants were taught to estimate using common visual reference points—for instance, a serving of mashed potatoes the size of a computer mouse is four ounces, while a three-ounce portion of chicken, fish or steak is about the size of a deck of cards.

• **Estimate how many calories you're eating.** Use a calorie book or look up your food online. This is easier than it sounds, says Dr. Hollis, since most people eat the same foods often.

• **Simple notes are fine.** Keeping a food diary doesn't have to mean lugging around a notebook—you can jot intake down on a Post-it and it will still help you be more attentive to what you're eating.

• **If you miss a day…start again.** Those who kept the most consistent food records lost the most weight in the study, but even those who kept some records regularly lost more than those who kept none.

Volume 18
Hearing/Tinnitus Cures

REPORT #192
Everyday Vitamins May Prevent Common Hearing Loss

How about a "morning after" pill for loud concerts? Researchers recently identified supplements so helpful at preventing and healing noise-induced hearing loss that we may very well see pills and snack foods marketed with that premise in the not-too-distant future. Long viewed as a hazard for people exposed to prolonged high-decibel sound (such as workers around jet engines or jackhammers, battlefield soldiers and rock stars), excess noise contributes to more than one-third of the 28 million Americans suffering from some degree of hearing loss.

RESEARCH RESULTS SOUND PROMISING

We spoke with scientist Colleen Garbe Le Prell, PhD, to find out more about the research her team recently conducted, which showed that a simple blend of common nutrients may help reduce hearing loss. In the study, four groups of guinea pigs were exposed to five hours of 120 decibel sound, which is as loud as a jet engine at takeoff. One hour before exposure, each group received either a nutrient blend or placebo. Thereafter, each group continued receiving the treatment regimen once daily for five days. One group was fed the synergistic blend of vitamins A, C and E with magnesium…a second group received magnesium alone…a third group was given A, C and E without magnesium…and a fourth group received a placebo.

The result: Using electrodes to test the animals' threshold hearing sensitivity before and after noise exposure, the group receiving the blend of vitamins A, C and E with magnesium had significantly less hearing loss than any of the three other groups.

Colleen Garbe Le Prell, PhD, associate professor, department of communicative disorders, and director, The Hearing Research Center, University of Florida, Gainesville.

Why should these extremely common supplements make such a big difference in hearing protection? Loud noise causes the over-stimulation of inner ear sensory cells, which drives the production of free radicals even after noise exposure. The free radicals and a resulting constriction of blood flow ultimately damages the outer hair cells. The blend of vitamins A, C and E with magnesium binds with the free radicals in the inner ear, helping to prevent this damage.

YOU HEARD IT HERE FIRST...

According to Dr. Le Prell, the upper limit for intake of vitamins A, C and E and magnesium has been well defined by the US Institute of Medicine (IOM), and should not be exceeded. As with any dietary supplement, moderation and supervision by a physician trained in natural medicine is important. Clinical trials to confirm safety and efficacy of this micronutrient blend for humans, at levels that adhere to IOM limits are underway and soon, says Dr. Le Prell, we may see products marketed to be taken around the time of noise exposure or daily as a preventive measure. For now though, Dr. Le Prell suggests checking with your physician to maintain (but do not exceed) recommended daily doses of vitamins A, C, E and magnesium—and turning down the volume.

REPORT #193
Quiet the Ringing in Your Ears

Aaron G. Benson, MD, otolaryngologist in private practice at Toledo Ear, Nose and Throat in Maumee, Ohio, he specializes in hearing disorders, *www.toledo ent.com.*

Perhaps you hear a high-pitched ringing...perhaps a buzzing, chirping, whistling or whirring. Nobody else can hear it—but the quieter it gets around you, the worse the noise in your head. This bothersome condition, *tinnitus*, afflicts an estimated 10% to 16% of Americans.

Tinnitus most often develops when a person has hearing loss caused by nerve damage from prolonged or extreme exposure to loud noise. It also can be a side effect of antibiotics, aspirin, diuretics and some cancer drugs. Tinnitus usually appears after age 50 but is increasingly common in younger people due to high-volume use of personal music players (i.e. iPod). It can occur during pregnancy due to increased blood volume—and may or may not go away after delivery.

Tinnitus usually is not a serious health problem, but it should be evaluated—so consult an otolaryngologist.

Referrals: American Tinnitus Association, (800-634-8978, *www.ata.org*).

There is no cure, but various strategies can ease symptoms and help you cope...

• **Cut caffeine and salt.** Caffeine (in coffee, tea, cola and chocolate) constricts blood flow to the ear...and salt can raise blood pressure, aggravating tinnitus.

• **Keep ears clean.** Excessive earwax can muffle outside noises and amplify internal ringing.

Home remedy: Mix hydrogen peroxide with an equal amount of water, and place two drops in each ear weekly. Or see your doctor to have your ears irrigated.

• **Reduce stress.** Muscle relaxation, meditation, biofeedback, exercise and other stress-reducing techniques may alleviate symptoms.

• **Fill the room with white noise.** A constant low-level background sound masks the inner ringing. In a quiet room and at bedtime, turn on a fan or tabletop fountain, or use a white-noise machine (about $30 to $60 at home-products stores).

• **Wear a tinnitus masker.** This miniature white-noise device resembles a hearing aid and fits behind or in the ear.

Cost: About $2,000.

To obtain one, ask your doctor for a referral to an audiologist.

• **Try a hearing aid.** This eases tinnitus for about half of people with significant hearing loss. It amplifies outside sounds, which obscures inner sounds.

•**Retrain your brain.** A new treatment provided by trained audiologists, *tinnitus retraining therapy* (TRT) may help up to 80% of patients. Sometimes improvement is noticed after just a few sessions. Typically, you attend weekly or monthly hour-long sessions during which you wear a special hearing aid programmed with a facsimile of your particular tinnitus sound. You are shown how to train your brain to be less sensitive to the ringing.

Rarely, tinnitus may be caused by a tumor. Call your doctor without delay if your tinnitus sounds like a pulsing or whooshing…is heard on only one side of your head…or is accompanied by dizziness or a sudden decrease in ability to discriminate between similar words, such as cat and hat.

REPORT #194
The Ears Have It!

Rebecca Shannonhouse, editor *Bottom Line/Health,* Boardroom Inc., 281 Tresser Blvd., Stamford, CT 06901. *www.bottomlinesecrets.com.*

About one in 20 adults—and up to one-third of older adults who are cognitively impaired—have impacted earwax (*cerumen*). The symptoms are reversible, but not all doctors are paying enough attention to the problem.

Normally, jaw movements—from chewing, for example—cause excess cerumen to gradually migrate out of the ear canal and fall out unnoticed. If this doesn't occur, a feeling of fullness and hearing loss are among the most common symptoms, but *tinnitus* (ringing in the ears) also may occur, explains Richard Rosenfeld, MD, MPH, a professor and chairman of otolaryngology at SUNY Downstate and chairman of otolaryngology at Long Island College Hospital both in Brooklyn, New York.

It's a bad idea to dig out earwax with cotton swabs or other implements—this often pushes earwax deeper into the ear canal. For the first time, there are now evidence-based guidelines for treating earwax impaction, released by the American Academy of Otolaryngology–Head

and Neck Surgery Foundation. *Most important ones…*

•**Use body-temperature water in an ear syringe to dissolve cerumen buildup.** You do not need expensive wax-dissolving drops.

•**Do not clean your own ears if you have diabetes or your immune system is weakened—this may occur during steroid use, cancer therapy or with certain infections.** Syringing with water can trigger a serious outer-ear infection that may require hospitalization. Instead, a physician can safely remove excess cerumen with a microscope and specialized instruments.

•**If you use a hearing aid, get your ears checked twice a year.** The repeated removal and replacement of hearing aids increases the risk for impaction.

REPORT #195
Do-It-Yourself Tinnitus Treatment

Sujana S. Chandrasekhar, MD, director, New York Otology, associate clinical professor of otolaryngology, Mount Sinai School of Medicine, New York City.

Tinnitus can be like the soundtrack to a scary movie—a constant, high- or low-pitched drone, whistling, clicking, even roaring sound in your ear that never stops. There's no medicine or procedure that can be relied upon to make it go away. Nor is there a single specific cause—tinnitus can be brought on by loud noise or a head injury, it is sometimes a side effect of medication and sometimes can arise seemingly out of nowhere.

It's common, too: According to the Cleveland Clinic, 12 million people in the US suffer from persistent tinnitus that interferes with daily life.

What I'm about to tell you may come as music to your ears, then, if you or someone you know suffers from tinnitus: A new treatment shows great promise—though it is important to note that the initial research was done on a very small group. That said, this is a simple, straightforward technique that can actually be enjoyable (and if you're good with computers, you might even be able to do it on your own). It's called "notched music," and it's a technique that lets you change your favorite music and then use it as treatment for your tinnitus. That's it—no drugs, no complicated procedures.

When you "notch" music, you remove a one-octave frequency range, in this case it would be the range that is centered on the tone of your own tinnitus.

The treatment is very simple: After you have found the tone and removed that frequency range from your favorite music, you just listen to it often. How does it work? Over time, the brain begins to respond differently to frequencies that it is not regularly exposed to—therefore, the loudness of your tinnitus gradually subsides (it typically takes six months or so) though it is unlikely to disappear altogether.

This therapy was tested on 23 patients at the University of Munster in Germany. Researchers found that after one year of listening to notched music for approximately 12 hours per week, patients reported a significant reduction in the loudness of their tinnitus. In comparison, there was no change at all in the two control groups used in the study, one of which listened to randomly notched music, the other to unnotched music.

HOW TO DO IT

To notch music, you'll need a "tone generator" to pinpoint the frequency of your tinnitus and music-editing software to notch your digital music files. Examples I found online are ToneGenerator ($80) and WavePad ($80), both offering free demonstrations at *www.nch.com. au*. From there, it's easy—just listen to the music you love and see how it helps. It's a low-cost, non-invasive solution that sounds to me like a treatment worth trying.

REPORT #196
Cures for Tinnitus

Mark A. Stengler, NMD, licensed naturopathic medical doctor in private practice, La Jolla, California...adjunct associate clinical professor at the National College of Natural Medicine, Portland, Oregon...author of many books, including *The Natural Physician's Healing Therapies* and coauthor of *Prescription for Natural Cures* (both from Bottom Line Books)...and author of the *Bottom Line/Natural Healing* newsletter.

Tinnitus is the medical term for noise or ringing in the ears. While many cases have no known cause, the disorder can result from a loud noise that causes damage to the ear...changes to the bones of the inner ear...or circulation problems within the inner ear. I find that the herb ginkgo biloba, which can improve circulation to the inner ear, helps some patients, although studies have shown mixed results. Take 120 mg daily of a ginkgo biloba extract (it should contain 24% *flavone glycosides* and 6% *terpene lactones*). Since ginkgo biloba is itself a blood thinner, don't take it if you are on blood-thinning medication. One product that contains both homeopathic remedies and Chinese herbs is Clear Tinnitus from Clear Products Inc. (888-257-2532, *www.clearproductsinc.com,* which was shown in a small trial to benefit most people with tinnitus. Follow the instructions on the label.

REPORT #197
Hearing Loss

Barbara McLay, MA, clinical associate professor of communication science and disorders and head of the hearing conservation program, University of Missouri, Columbia.

Whether hearing loss can be reversed depends on where in the ear it occurs and what causes it.

Inner ear: Damage to the inner ear from aging, hereditary factors, disease (such as meningitis) and exposure to a sudden loud sound can be irreversible. Some medications (for example, certain antibiotics and chemotherapy drugs) also can cause irreversible hearing loss.

Middle ear: Upper respiratory infections can lead to fluid buildup and difficulty hearing. Treating the infection will restore hearing.

Abnormal bone growth around the tiny bones in the middle ear also can cause hearing loss and can be corrected with surgery.

Outer ear: The most common reason for outer-ear hearing loss is wax buildup.

Have earwax removed at the doctor's office or try an over-the-counter wax-removal product to help restore hearing.

To prevent hearing loss…

•**Maintain your general health by eating right, not smoking, etc.**

•**Protect ears from loud noises.**

•**Do not put cotton-tipped swabs or other objects in your ears.**

•**See your doctor immediately if you experience sudden hearing loss in one or both ears.**

REPORT #198
Melatonin May Help Symptoms of Tinnitus

Melatonin may improve symptoms of *tinnitus* by allowing sufferers to sleep better. About 15 million Americans have severe tinnitus, the sensation of a ringing, roaring or humming sound. Sleep disturbance is common among tinnitus sufferers.

Recent study: Researchers gave people with tinnitus 3 milligrams (mg) of melatonin every night for one month to help them sleep, then tracked them for a second month when they did not take the supplement. By the end of the study, tinnitus symptoms had been reduced by nearly 30%. Participants slept best while taking melatonin, but the improvement in their sleep and tinnitus symptoms continued through the month when they were not taking it. Patients with the greatest sleep disturbances improved the most.

Jay F. Piccirillo, MD, professor, otolaryngology, head and neck surgery, Washington University School of Medicine, St. Louis, and lead author of a study of tinnitus sufferers, published in *Otolaryngology—Head and Neck Surgery*.

Volume 19
Cataract, Glaucoma and Vision Cures

REPORT #199

8 Simple Steps that Keep Your Eyes Young

If you are holding this article at arm's length or had to reach for your reading glasses to make out the words, you are well aware that aging affects the eyes. But farsightedness is just one of the vision problems brought on by the passage of years.

Diet and lifestyle choices, genetic risk factors, exposure to sunlight and the gradual deterioration of eye tissue all combine to make eyes increasingly vulnerable to various diseases and disorders. *Examples...*

• **Macular degeneration,** a deterioration of the retina (the light-sensing lining at the back of the eye), is the leading cause of blindness in the US.

• **Glaucoma,** the second most common cause of blindness, results from increased fluid pressure inside the eye.

• **Cataract,** a clouding of the eye's normally clear lens, obscures the vision.

Fortunately, there's a lot you can do to protect yourself against these and other types of age-related vision loss. *Starting today...*

1. Get treated for any other health problems. Sleep apnea is a common condition that has been linked to glaucoma. People with apnea periodically stop breathing during sleep, which leads to a buildup of carbon dioxide and a shortage of oxygen circulating to various parts of the body—including to the optic nerve. As a result, fluid pressure could increase and cause nerve cells to die. If you have been told that you snore (a sign of apnea), get evaluated at a sleep center.

Diabetes also can affect eye health. Poorly controlled blood sugar levels contribute to *diabetic retinopathy* (blockage, bleeding or fluid

J. James Thimons, OD, clinical professor of optometry at Pennsylvania College of Optometry in Philadelphia and an optometrist in private practice in Fairfield, Connecticut. He is chairman of the National Glaucoma Society and a member of the national board of directors of Prevent Blindness America.

leakage in the retinal blood vessels) and loss of vision.

Best: Work with your doctor and a nutritionist to stabilize blood sugar levels.

2. Eat foods that protect eye cells. The retina, lens and eye fluid require large amounts of antioxidants to fight cell damage from oxidation. Numerous studies show that the antioxidants *lutein, zeaxanthin,* and vitamins A, C and E promote better overall vision and reduce the risk for macular degeneration, cataracts and possibly glaucoma.

Good food sources of antioxidants: Fortified whole-grain hot and cold cereals…nuts and peanut butter…cantaloupe and citrus fruits… avocado, broccoli, carrots, collard greens, corn, kale, peppers, spinach and turnip greens. Have at least five to seven servings of these foods weekly.

3. Consider supplements to slow macular degeneration. Once an eye disease develops, larger doses of antioxidants are needed than can be obtained just from foods.

Study: A six-year trial of nearly 4,000 people showed that taking a supplement combination of vitamin C (500 mg), vitamin E (400 IU), beta-carotene (15 mg) and zinc (80 mg as zinc oxide) slowed the progression of early macular degeneration by about 25%. In other studies, daily supplementation with both lutein and zeaxanthin also delayed vision loss from macular degeneration.

4. Boost night vision with bilberry extract. Similar to the blueberry, bilberry contains antioxidant *anthocyanosides.* The extract may improve circulation in the eyes and protect against retinal damage, helping you to see better when driving in the dark or reading in low light.

Dosage: Three times per week, take 80 mg to 100 mg of a bilberry extract containing 20% to 25% anthocyanosides.

5. Increase omega-3s to relieve dry eye. Dry eye syndrome (a lack of tears) is more than a nuisance—it can lead to pain, infection and blurred vision. The problem results from age-related eye inflammation and a decrease in oil production. Changes in hormone levels also may play a role.

A study that evaluated the diets of more than 32,000 women found that those who consumed the least fish (and thus got the least omega-3 fatty acids) had the highest risk for dry eye. Consuming omega-3–rich fish (anchovies, mackerel, salmon, tuna) several times a week is smart—but if you already have dry eye, you also need supplements.

Bonus: Fish oil may delay macular degeneration.

Dosage: Each day, take 1,000 mg of fish oil (which reduces eye inflammation)…and 1,000 mg of flaxseed oil (which improves the quality of oil in the eye gland). It takes about a month to notice the effects of omega-3s on dry eye. If discomfort doesn't ease within six to eight weeks, ask your eye doctor about the prescription eyedrop medication *Restasis*, which increases tear production.

6. Wear sunglasses—especially if your eyes are blue or green. Exposure to bright sunlight, particularly during childhood but also accumulated over a lifetime, significantly increases the risk for cataracts and macular degeneration. Compared with dark-eyed people, those with light-colored eyes have less eye pigment—allowing more light to enter the lens—which increases sensitivity to sunlight and glare.

Important: When outdoors, wear high-quality sunglasses that do not cause optical distortion and that block both UVA and UVB rays. Polarized lenses, which have special glare-blocking filters, are best for driving or whenever there is glare from snow, water or pavement. Use wraparound-style sunglasses if your eyes are very sensitive to light or if you've had cataract surgery.

7. Stop smoking. Compared with a non-smoker, a pack-a-day smoker is significantly more likely to go blind from macular degeneration by age 65. Smoking damages blood vessels throughout the body, including in the eyes…depletes antioxidants…and greatly increases cataract risk. It takes about 10 years for the effects of nicotine to clear from the eyes—so quit now rather than later.

8. Have an annual eye exam—even if you see as well as ever. Your eye doctor checks not only for changes in vision, but also for eye problems that may not be evident to you.

Example: Glaucoma causes no symptoms until permanent damage has been done.

Referrals: American Optometric Association, 800-365-2219, *www.aoa.org.*

REPORT #200
What You Don't Know About Arugula and Other Salad Stars

Leo Galland, MD, director, Foundation for Integrated Medicine, New York City. His latest book is *The Fat Resistance Diet* (Broadway). *www.fatresistancediet.com.* Dr. Galland is a recipient of the Linus Pauling award.

Peppery arugula...crisp endive and romaine...crunchy green peppers. Stars of restaurant menus, these vegetables can turn an ordinary salad into an extraordinary treat. They are power-packed with surprising nutritional benefits, according to Leo Galland, MD, author of *The Fat Resistance Diet*, including the ability to help fight the effects of aging, preserve vision and build bone strength.

Dr. Galland notes that salads are an excellent example of the high nutrient density foods he uses in his "fat resistant" diet program. "The vegetables in garden salad have a high ratio of nutrition to calories—I believe eating foods with high nutrient density is the key to healthy weight loss." *Here are some of the best...*

ARUGULA

The taste of arugula is distinctively sharp with an earthy aroma. Arugula is not only an excellent source of bioflavonoids, but it also contains vitamin A, which helps build immunity...potassium, important for muscles... and calcium, with 32 mg of calcium per one cup. Plus the body absorbs calcium in arugula (along with kale and broccoli) more readily than from milk. For those cutting back on milk-based dairy products, this makes arugula a very nice vegan source of calcium.

ENDIVE

Endive is widely used in Northern Europe, especially Belgium, Holland and France. It is a potent source of vitamin K, helping to maintain bone strength, as well as vitamin A. Endive packs a big appetite-satisfying crunch for super-low calories...there are only eight calories in one cup of chopped endive! This amount of Belgium endive also contains 1.6 grams of fiber.

ROMAINE LETTUCE

In spite of its light taste, fresh romaine lettuce is a big source of antioxidants, which are higher after consumption of fresh lettuce than after consumption of packaged lettuce. Romaine is also a good source of vitamin A, folate and vitamin K.

GREEN, RED AND ORANGE PEPPERS

Sliced bell peppers are an appetizing addition to any garden salad and enhance your body's levels of anti-inflammatory carotenoids. With bell peppers, the color is key to the special nutrients found in each. For example, green bell peppers are an excellent source of the carotenoids *lutein* and *zeaxanthin*, which help to preserve vision. Sweet orange peppers are also high in zeaxanthin and reduce the risk of macular degeneration, the leading cause of vision loss in older Americans. Red bell peppers are very high in the carotenoids *beta carotene* and *beta cryptoxanthin*. These antioxidants can help protect the body against free radical damage and fight the effects of aging.

EASY TIPS ON MAKING THE BEST SALAD

When shopping for salad, freshness comes first. Select vegetables that are vibrant, brightly colored, firm and crisp. When buying romaine lettuce and arugula, look for deep green leaves that appear fresh-picked. Skip anything that is wilted or waterlogged. Buy fresh greens, rather than the packaged products and plan to eat as quickly as possible—they taste better and are more nutritious, too. For Belgium endive, look for leaves that are firm, mostly white with green-tinged edges. Don't buy endive that has browned or softened. Same idea for bell peppers—these should be very firm to the touch when you buy them, with no soft areas.

All vegetables should be washed carefully, even fresh-picked organic ones.

Here is another surprising tip: To get the most nutrition from salad, don't use fat-free dressing, Dr. Galland told me. "You have to consume a bit of healthy oil with vegetables to absorb carotenoids, so I recommend eating salad with dressing made with olive oil, for example."

REPORT #201
The Miraculous Power Of Nuts

Joy Bauer, RD, nutrition expert for the *Today* show and Yahoo.com, with offices in New York City and Westchester, New York. She is a weight-loss columnist for *Self* magazine and coauthor, with Carol Svec, of *Joy Bauer's Food Cures* (Rodale). *www.joybauernutrition.com.*

Nuts are among the most healthful foods you can eat. Rich in nutrients, they can help prevent some of the most common—and most serious—diseases.

Example: In a long-running health study conducted by researchers at Loma Linda University, participants were asked what foods they ate most often. Those who ate nuts five or more times a week were about 50% less likely to have a heart attack than those who ate them less than once a week.

FORGET THE FAT

Many Americans avoid nuts because they want to cut back on fat and calories. It's true that a single serving of nuts can have 20 grams (g) or more of fat and 180 to 200 calories, but most of the fats are healthful fats, such as omega-3 fatty acids and monounsaturated fat. Americans need to get more, not less, of these fats. As long as you limit yourself to a small handful of nuts daily—the recommended amount, unless otherwise noted—you don't need to worry about the "extra" calories.

Each type of nut contains a different mix of nutrients, fats and protective antioxidants, which can "neutralize" cell-damaging free radicals. People who eat a variety of nuts will get the widest range of benefits. Raw, toasted or roasted nuts are fine as long as they are unsalted.

Here's what nuts can do...

NUTS FOR THE HEART

All nuts are good for the heart, but the following nuts are especially beneficial...

• **Macadamia nuts.** Of the 21 g of total fat in a serving of macadamias, 17 g are monounsaturated—the kind of fat that lowers a person's levels of harmful LDL cholesterol without lowering levels of beneficial HDL cholesterol. Both the antioxidants and the monounsaturated fat in macadamias have anti-inflammatory effects—important for curtailing arterial damage that can lead to heart disease.

• **Peanuts.** Actually a type of legume, not a true nut, peanuts contain 34 micrograms (mcg) of folate per one-ounce serving, a little less than 10% of the recommended daily amount. Folate is a B vitamin that lowers levels of homocysteine, an amino acid that damages arteries and increases the risk of heart disease.

Peanuts also are high in *L-arginine,* an amino acid that is converted by cells in blood vessels into nitric oxide. Nitric oxide improves circulation and may inhibit fatty buildups in the arteries.

• **Pistachios.** A study conducted by Penn State University found that pistachios lower blood pressure. Men who added 1.5 ounces of shelled pistachios to their daily diets had drops in systolic pressure (the top number in a blood pressure reading) of 4.8 points. The antioxidants and healthy fats in pistachios relax blood vessels and allow blood to circulate with less force.

ALMONDS FOR BONES

Just about everyone needs more calcium, the mineral that strengthens bones and reduces the risk of osteoporosis. The recommended daily amount is 1,000 milligrams (mg). Almonds have more calcium than other nuts, with about 80 mg in 20 to 25 nuts. For people with lactose intolerance, who have trouble digesting dairy, a daily dose of almonds helps raise calcium to bone-protecting levels.

Blood pressure bonus: One serving of almonds has 98 mg of magnesium, about one-fourth the recommended daily amount. Magnesium, along with potassium and calcium, controls the relaxation and contraction of blood vessels and can help control blood pressure.

BRAZIL NUTS FOR PROSTATE

Brazil nuts are a superb source of selenium, with about 155 mcg in just two nuts. The recommended daily amount is 55 mcg. They're also high in vitamin E. One study—the Selenium and Vitamin E Cancer Prevention Trial—found that men getting selenium and vitamin E, alone or in combination, reduced their risk of prostate cancer by up to 60%. Selenium improves the ability of the immune system to recognize and destroy cancer cells in the prostate. Vitamin E is an antioxidant that also has been linked to reduced cancer risk.

Caution: People who get too much selenium may have decreased immunity. Because Brazil nuts are so high in selenium and calories (50 calories in two nuts), don't have more than two nuts daily. If you take a multivitamin that has more than 50% of the daily value of selenium, opt for one nut.

PECANS FOR THE EYES

The most serious eye diseases, including cataracts and macular degeneration, are caused, in part, by free radicals. The antioxidants in nuts and other plant foods fight free radicals to keep the eyes healthy.

A study conducted by the US Department of Agriculture (USDA) found that pecans are particularly rich in antioxidants. The National Eye Institute's Age-Related Eye Diseases Study reported that patients with macular degeneration who had adequate intakes of antioxidants were 29% less likely to experience disease progression than those who got lower levels.

Bonus for heart health: The vitamin E in pecans reduces the tendency of LDL cholesterol to oxidize and stick to artery walls. Pecans also are high in phytosterols—plant compounds that are similar to the active ingredients in cholesterol-lowering margarines, such as Benecol.

WALNUTS FOR MOOD

A part from fish and flaxseed, walnuts are one of the best sources of omega-3 fatty acids. They're the only nut that contains *alpha lino-*lenic acid* (ALA), a polyunsaturated fat that is converted to omega-3s in the body.

The omega-3s appear to help maintain healthy brain levels of serotonin, a neurochemical involved in mood. People who eat walnuts and/or two to three fish meals a week may experience a reduction in symptoms of depression.

Bonus for heart health: Omega-3s lower LDL cholesterol and triglycerides, another type of blood fat...increase HDL good cholesterol...inhibit blood clots in the arteries...and reduce arterial inflammation.

REPORT #202
The "Clothing Cure" for Glaucoma

Robert Ritch, MD, professor of clinical ophthalmology, New York Medical College, Valhalla, and chief, Glaucoma Services, The New York Eye and Ear Infirmary, New York City.
British Journal of Ophthalmology.

Ties that bind the neck may raise the risk of the eye disease glaucoma. So says a controversial study that found snug neckwear can increase intraocular pressure (IOP) in the eyes, possibly leading to glaucoma.

"If men wear tight neckties when their IOP is measured, it can raise their IOP," says Robert Ritch, MD, lead author of the study and a professor of clinical ophthalmology at New York Medical College.

DOUBLE TROUBLE

That double Windsor knot may be double trouble. If a person has moderate or severe glaucoma damage, the increase in IOP caused by a tight tie may make it worse. What's more, patients without glaucoma whose tight tie falsely increases IOP might end up being treated for glaucoma when they don't need to be. Although there are no reported cases of glaucoma being caused by a tight necktie, Dr. Ritch says it's theoretically possible.

Dr. Ritch became aware of the issue during his regular practice. "I noticed that some patients had tight neckties. When I loosened the neckties, their IOP would go down several points," he says.

To quantify his observation, Dr. Ritch and his colleagues looked at 20 healthy men and 20 men with open angle glaucoma, the most common form of the disease.

The researchers measured IOP first while the men weren't wearing neckties, then three minutes after they put on a tight necktie, and once again three minutes after the tie was loosened.

Dr. Ritch's team found that in 70% of the healthy men, a tight necktie increased mean IOP, as it did in 60% of those with glaucoma.

Increases in IOP while wearing a tight necktie ranged from more than 2 mmHg to more than 4 mmHg (millimeters of mercury, a measure of pressure), compared with IOP readings when no ties were worn and after ties were loosened. This is a clinically important increase.

Dr. Ritch speculates that when a necktie exerts too much pressure on the jugular vein located in the neck, pressure is increased in the entire venous system, including in the eyes.

To learn more about glaucoma, visit the Glaucoma Research Foundation at *www.glaucoma.org*.

REPORT #203
Surgery Isn't the Only Answer

Marc Grossman, OD, LAc, optometrist in private practice in Rye and New Paltz, New York.

More than 50% of Americans over 65 and 70% over 75 have a vision-blurring (and sometimes vision-dimming, vision-clouding and vision-yellowing) cataract. That's why cataract surgery is the most frequently performed operation among seniors, with about 400,000 procedures a year.

And cataract surgery works very well, says Marc Grossman, OD, LAc, an optometrist in private practice in Rye and New Paltz, New York, and medical director of the Web site, *www.naturaleyecare.com*.

In about 15 minutes, the surgeon removes the damaged lens and inserts a clear artificial replacement. You recover in about a day, with your eye adjusting to the new lens over the next few weeks. Piece of cake!

However: If you have a cataract, it's a myth that cataract surgery is always a must, says Dr. Grossman. You can reverse a cataract without surgery. *And it might not take any longer than squeezing an eye drop or two out of a bottle...*

• **NAC**—the super-antioxidant that can prevent, stop or reverse cataracts. Cataracts are caused by the same process that scientists now understand contributes to and causes a range of age-related diseases, such as heart disease and Alzheimer's—oxidation, a kind of biochemical rust. Oxidation is carried out by molecular bad guys called free radicals, hyperactive compounds that damage the delicate outer lining (membranes) of cells and the DNA inside them, leading to cell mutation and death. Free radicals are generated by many factors, including sunlight (think age spots, wrinkles and skin cancer), smoking (think lung cancer) and diets high in fat and sugar (think heart disease and diabetes).

Fortunately, there are antiaging antioxidants such as vitamin C and vitamin E that can neutralize free radicals. And a particularly powerful antioxidant is *carnosine*, a combination of two amino acids, the building blocks of protein.

Now, scientists have found that a form of carnosine—*N-acetyl-carnosine*—is uniquely effective at stopping the aging process in the eyes.

"Research shows that N-acetyl-carnosine eyedrops can help improve cataracts—and possibly enable the patient to keep their natural lens, avoiding the need for cataract surgery," says Dr. Grossman.

Study: Researchers in Russia studied 49 people (average age 65) with "minimal to advanced" cataracts, dividing them into three groups. One received twice-daily eye drops with N-acetyl-carnosine, one group received placebo drops, and one group didn't receive any treatment.

After six months, 90% of the group receiving the drops had an improvement in glare sensitivity (a common symptom of cataracts), 42% had an improvement in the light transmission through the lens and 90% had an improvement in "visual acuity" (they could see better). Those not using the drops had negative changes in all those parameters.

"As shown by this study, the N-acetyl-carnosine drops can help the aging eye to recover from cataract, by improving its clarity, glare sensitivity, color perception and overall vision," says Dr. Grossman.

"I recommend a minimum six-month period of use to evaluate the benefits."

Product: Can-C Eyedrops, available at *www.naturaleyecare.com*, or call 845-255-8222. Address: Natural Eye Care, 3 Paradies Lane, New Paltz, NY 12561.

How to use: "You can also use the drops to prevent cataract," says Dr. Grossman.

For prevention, he suggests one to two drops in each eye, one to two times per day. For treatment, he suggests two drops in the affected eye, two times per day.

"To apply the drop, lean your head back and look up. Put one drop into your eye, blink a couple of times and then gently close the eye. Do not blink again or reopen for sixty seconds. If you use a second drop, repeat this procedure. This allows each drop to be absorbed into the eye tissue."

As with all natural remedies, use these eyedrops only with the approval and supervision of a qualified health professional, such as an optometrist or ophthalmologist.

• **Eat "The Vision Diet."** "If you're thinking about cataract surgery, try following these dietary recommendations for several months first," says Dr. Grossman. "You may find that your vision has improved enough to skip the surgery."

• **Cut back or eliminate sugar.** "High levels of sugar in the blood contribute to cataract formation," says Dr. Grossman. "People with diabetes, for example, are at three to four times the risk of cataracts. That's because blood sugar interferes with the lens' ability to pump out excess sugar from the eye and maintain its clarity."

• **Drink lots of water.** Dr. Grossman recommends eight to ten, 8-ounce glasses a day. "This maintains the flow of nutrients to the lens and the release of waste and toxins from the tissues."

• **Eat foods high in beta-carotene, vitamins C and E, and sulfur-bearing amino acids.** "These are antioxidants that combat free radicals," says Dr. Grossman.

Foods rich in these factors include garlic, onions, beans, yellow and orange vegetables, spinach and other green, leafy vegetables, celery, seaweed, apples, carrots, tomatoes, turnips and oranges.

• **Watch out for "congesting" foods.** "For many people, dairy, wheat and soy foods create sinus congestion, which impairs lymph and blood drainage from the area around the eyes—speeding the development of cataracts," says Dr. Grossman. "Try avoiding these foods for a month to see whether you are less congested," he says. "Then reintroduce them one at a time to help you identify your specific problem foods."

• **Wear (the right) sunglasses.** Maybe you routinely wear sunscreen to protect yourself from skin-damaging UV radiation. But UV radiation can also damage your eyes.

Fact: Eighty percent of Americans know that UV exposure from the sun can cause skin cancer, but only 5% know it can harm the eyes, causing cataracts.

"Whenever you're outdoors, you should wear sunglasses with UV coating," says Larry Jebrock, OD, a behavioral optometrist in Novato, California.

What most people don't realize: The degree of UV protection has nothing to do with the darkness of the lens of the sunglasses, says Dr. Jebrock.

Look for a pair with at least UV 400, which you should find listed on the product label or a sticker on a lens.

REPORT #204
Miracles Do Happen

Joan Borysenko, PhD, cofounder and former director of the mind-body clinical programs at two Harvard Medical School hospitals, now merged as Boston's Beth Israel Deaconess Medical Center. Based in Boulder, Colorado, she runs workshops and conducts lectures on mind-body healing. *Minding the Body, Mending the Mind* (Da Capo). *www.joanborysenko.com.*

O n occasion, a health problem that was expected to be permanent or fatal instead disappears without medical intervention. The limited research that has been done suggests that the reason why one person recovers when most others do not might have as much to do with the mind as the body.

We interviewed Joan Borysenko, PhD, a former Harvard medical scientist who is a renowned expert in the field of mind/body healing. *She relayed this true story of spontaneous healing…*

A VISION IN LOURDES

Nearly 150 years ago, a teenage girl in Lourdes, France, reported seeing a vision of the Virgin Mary. Ever since, the waters in that area have been credited with healing powers. Most of these incidents involve cancer, multiple sclerosis and other diseases that occasionally go into remission, even without a visit to Lourdes.

The 1908 case of Marie Bire is more interesting. The 41-year-old French woman was blind as a result of optic atrophy—the degeneration of her optic nerve. According to medical science, it should not have been possible for optic nerves to recover from such a condition.

At Lourdes, the blind Bire attended Mass and received Holy Communion. Then, as the Blessed Sacrament in procession was passing the place where she sat, she suddenly regained her sight. Ten doctors examined Bire. They all found that her optic nerves were still withered but that she could see.

What may have happened. We do not have to believe in divine miracles to believe that Bire's faith might have played a role in her recovery. Studies have found that depending upon the medical condition, between 30% and 50%

of people respond to placebos. If you tell these people that you have given them painkillers, their brain activity will show that they actually feel less pain.

REPORT #205
Does MSG Cause Glaucoma?

Marc Grossman, OD, LAc, optometrist in private practice in Rye and New Paltz, New York.
Marc Rose, MD and Michael Rose, MD ophthalmologists at the New Institute for Visual Wellness in Costa Mesa, California, and author of *Save Your Sight!* (Grand Central Publishing).

I f you have glaucoma, you should avoid the food additive *monosodium glutamate*, popularly known as MSG, says Marc Grossman OD, LAc, an optometrist in private practice in Rye and New Paltz, New York. Why?

The amino acid glutamate in MSG targets receptor sites on nerve cells, creating *excitotoxicity*—overstimulation and destruction of the cells. Including the cells in the optic nerve. That fact led an international team of ophthalmologists to conclude, in the journal *Experimental Eye Research* that "a diet with excess [MSG] over a period of several years…may cause retinal cell destruction."

But MSG isn't always called MSG on food labels, say Marc Rose, MD, and Michael Rose, MD, ophthalmologists at the New Institute for Visual Wellness in Costa Mesa, California, and authors of *Save Your Sight!* (Grand Central Publishing).

Watch out for foods with the following ingredient or ingredients listed on the label, which may indicate the presence of MSG: hydrolyzed vegetable protein, hydrolyzed protein, hydrolyzed plant protein, plant protein extract, textured protein, sodium caseinate, calcium caseinate, yeast extract, autolyzed yeast, hydrolyzed oat flour, malt extract, malt flavoring, bouillon, broth stock, flavoring, natural flavoring, natural beef or chicken flavoring, seasoning or spices.

REPORT #206
Thyroid Disorders May Increase Glaucoma Risk

When researchers reviewed health data for 12,376 adults, they found that those diagnosed with glaucoma were 38% more likely to have had a thyroid disorder, such as *hypothyroidism* (underactive thyroid) or *hyperthyroidism* (overactive thyroid).

Theory: Thyroid disease causes chemical deposits to develop in the blood vessels that circulate blood to the eye, causing increased pressure within the eyeball (a hallmark of glaucoma).

If you are diagnosed with a thyroid condition: See an ophthalmologist to be screened for glaucoma, which can be treated if detected at an early stage.

Gerald McGwin, Jr., PhD, professor, department of epidemiology, surgery and ophthalmology, University of Alabama at Birmingham.

REPORT #207
Lower Blindness Risk

In a study of 4,170 people, those who ate the most foods rich in beta-carotene, vitamins C and E and zinc were 35% less likely to develop age-related macular degeneration (the leading cause of blindness in people over age 65) than those who ate less of these nutrients.

Theory: The antioxidants in these foods help protect against free radical damage to the retina.

Self-defense: Eat generous amounts of foods that contain the above nutrients, such as whole-grain cereal, eggs, poultry and olive oil.

Redmer van Leeuwen, MD, PhD, resident in ophthalmology, Erasmus Medical Centre, Rotterdam.

REPORT #208
B Vitamins for Vision Protection

For about seven years, study participants took a daily supplement that included 50 mg of vitamin B-6, 1 mg of vitamin B-12 and 2.5 mg of folic acid (another B vitamin). Compared with women who took a placebo, supplement users were 34% less likely to develop age-related macular degeneration, the most common cause of vision loss among seniors.

Best: Ask your doctor if B-vitamin supplements are right for you.

William G. Christen, ScD, associate professor, division of preventive medicine, Harvard Medical School, Boston, and leader of a study of 5,205 women.

Volume 20
Anti-Aging Discoveries

REPORT #209
Why Vitamin C Gets A's from the Experts

Practically everyone "knows" vitamin C is good for you...but not many people really understand how good. Identification of its import dates back to early explorers crossing the ocean by ship who suffered from something called *scurvy*—caused by a deficiency of vitamin C.

For a long time now, the recommended daily allowance of vitamin C has been at levels that prevent such a deficiency—but decades ago, some scientists, including Nobel Prize-winner Linus Pauling, began to argue that much higher doses of vitamin C are needed for optimal health. There is now a continual stream of research on vitamin C and its related health benefits—which include antioxidant, anti-inflammatory and anti-aging properties, along with the fact that it has been shown to be a heart-health booster. We spoke with naturopathic medical doctor Mark Stengler, NMD, author of *Bottom Line/Natural Healing* newsletter for the latest thinking on the many positive attributes of vitamin C, along with guidelines on how much we need to reap its benefits.

HEART HEALTH

Much of the new buzz on vitamin C relates to its value in reducing risk for cardiovascular disease, Dr. Stengler told me, citing numerous research studies showing its protective role in heart health. Among these is research based on the Nurses' Health Study which followed more than 85,000 women for up to 16 years, and that demonstrated that a higher intake (in this case, more than 359 mg/day from dietary sources and supplements) reduced cardiovascular risk by 27%...and an analysis of

---

Mark A. Stengler, NMD, licensed naturopathic medical doctor in private practice, La Jolla, California... adjunct associate clinical professor at the National College of Natural Medicine, Portland, Oregon...author of many books, including *The Natural Physician's Healing Therapies* and coauthor of *Prescription for Natural Cures* (both from Bottom Line Books)...and author of the *Bottom Line/Natural Healing* newsletter.

nine other studies tracking more than 290,000 adults that showed a 25% reduction in risk in those who took more than 700 mg of supplemental vitamin C, compared with those who took none.

In addition, a Finnish study examining the health of middle-aged men who had no evidence of pre-existing heart disease found that those who were deficient in vitamin C were 3.5 times more likely to suffer heart attack.

Not only has vitamin C been shown to decrease risk for heart attacks, it also seems to reduce damage following one. In a study called the *Myocardial Infarction and Vitamins* (MIVIT) trial, researchers found that patients who suffered an acute heart attack and then supplemented for one month with 1,200 mg of vitamin C (along with 600 mg of vitamin E) after an initial IV infusion of vitamin C had a reduced rate of complications from the heart attack. The supplemented group also had fewer additional heart attacks and deaths, reducing by nearly 20% the combined rate of death, new heart attack and other severe complications. "This doesn't surprise me," Dr. Stengler said, "since vitamin C has so many protective functions, including increasing blood vessel flexibility (so they do not rupture as easily) and preventing the oxidation of LDL cholesterol." Cholesterol becomes problematic when it oxidizes—and vitamin C helps prevent that, he said.

IMMUNE BOOSTING

In addition to acting as a powerful antioxidant and helping protect the body from free radical damage, vitamin C also supports immune function. It enhances the activity of white blood cells, the body's first defense against pathogens. And it improves immune response partly by activating an antiviral chemical produced by the body called *interferon*.

Additionally, vitamin C helps to regenerate other antioxidants, including vitamin E, by acting as a "recycling service" for antioxidants in the body, causing them to re-circulate in the bloodstream and thus delivering "double duty" protective action.

Inflammation is a component of major degenerative diseases and other conditions including diabetes, Alzheimer's, obesity and heart disease—and C-reactive protein is one effective measure of inflammation levels. "Vitamin C as a supplement has been shown in studies to reduce C-reactive protein," Dr. Stengler said.

AND YET MORE HEALTH BENEFITS

"Vitamin C has powerful healing effects on many other systems in the body as well," Dr. Stengler added. "I'd say it's one of the most versatile, multi-factorial nutrients for our bodies."

In particular, vitamin C is…

• **A collagen builder.** Collagen is an important structural component of bones and tissues—and Dr. Stengler notes that vitamin C plays a critical role in the human body's synthesis of collagen, helping replace what is degraded by normal wear and tear.

• **A detoxifier.** "Vitamin C is involved in the production of bile acids, which carry toxins out of the liver," Dr. Stengler explained.

• **An agent for longevity.** Two major studies have associated vitamin C status with longevity. In a study of more than 19,000 adults, those with the highest blood levels of vitamin C had about half the risk for mortality compared with those with the lowest levels of vitamin C in their blood. Also, a decade-long study from UCLA of more than 11,000 adults showed that men with high vitamin C intake (at least 50 mg daily from their diet and regular vitamin C supplement) had a total death rate that was 41% lower than the rate among the men with low intake (less than 50 mg daily).

WHAT YOU NEED TO KNOW ABOUT VITAMIN C SUPPLEMENTATION

Recently, there's been reason to worry about the safety of food and other products imported from China, and it is distressing to hear that about 80% of the ascorbic acid—vitamin C—made in the world originates in that country. We asked Dr. Stengler if we should be concerned. He noted that there is little reason to fear toxicity. "American companies import the raw ingredients but the reliable manufacturers verify quality," he said. "They're doing their own tests before putting their labels on the products. If you stick with the big name brands when buying vitamin C, you have very little to worry about."

Though the current recommended dietary allowance (RDA) for vitamin C is only 90 mg for men and 75 mg for women (add an extra 35 mg for smokers), Dr. Stengler believes a far higher intake is beneficial. "For general prevention and overall health, studies suggest 400 to 500 mg daily," he said. For those with heart disease he recommends 500 mg to 1,500 mg daily. "For my patients with existing disease, such as cancer, I prescribe oral (or sometimes intravenous) doses that are much higher. These should be taken only under supervision—especially when undergoing chemotherapy or radiation."

REPORT #210
Slow Down the Aging Process!

Mark A. Stengler, NMD, licensed naturopathic medical doctor in private practice, La Jolla, California... adjunct associate clinical professor at the National College of Natural Medicine, Portland, Oregon...author of many books, including *The Natural Physician's Healing Therapies* and coauthor of *Prescription for Natural Cures* (both from Bottom Line Books)...and author of the *Bottom Line/Natural Healing* newsletter.

The myth about longevity is that we have no control over how long we live. We do have some control—even though we all know some people who lived healthfully but died suddenly...and others who didn't take care of themselves and lived on and on.

It is easy to fall back on the idea that we can't escape our heredity, but our parentage isn't as important as you might think. Having long-lived ancestors and siblings does increase your odds of living to old age, but it doesn't guarantee longevity.

Reason: Your genes, the biological programs that govern the activity of your body's 70 trillion cells, may influence only half of the factors involved in aging, according to the Okinawa Centenarian Study. That means we can have a direct effect on our aging process by focusing on the other factors.

Proof: Americans are living longer than ever, although not as long as people in other countries. The number of centenarians (people who are 100 years old or older) in the US is at an all-time high of about 50,000!

Surprise: Centenarians often are in better health than younger seniors. About 20% of centenarians are "escapers," people who have entirely avoided serious diseases, and 40% were escapers until at least age 85, according to a *Journal of the American Medical Association* (*JAMA*) article.

While there is no one secret to longevity, we can adopt aspects of healthful aging into our lives and improve our chances of reaching the century mark. I have seen many patients improve their health and add years to their lives. You can do the same by following these recommendations. You'll feel better and have greater vitality right away.

ADD YEARS
TO YOUR LIFE BY...

• **Protecting your genes.** A strong nutritional foundation safeguards our genes. Crucial to this protection is vitamin B, which can help repair genes and slow gene damage.

Advice: I recommend that most adults take a high-potency multivitamin each day that contains at least 50 milligrams (mg) each of vitamins B-1 and B-2, 400 micrograms (mcg) of folic acid and 50 mcg to 100 mcg of vitamin B-12. If your multivitamin is low in B vitamins, take an additional B-complex supplement so that you get the amounts listed above. These amounts are safe for everyone except those taking *methotrexate* for rheumatoid arthritis and for certain types of chemotherapy patients because high amounts of B supplements can interfere with these treatments.

• **Eating healthfully.** Nutrients serve as the building blocks of our biochemistry. Vitamin and mineral deficiencies can impair our normal biochemistry and increase the formation of age-promoting free radical molecules.

A study in *Journal of the American Geriatrics Society* found that centenarians consume, on average, about two-and-a-half times more antioxidant-packed vegetables than seniors ages 70 to 99. Incredibly, the centenarians ate five times more veggies than typical 40-year-olds.

All those antioxidants help protect against the types of cell damage involved in aging. Similarly, studies of Seventh Day Adventists in California—who do not smoke or drink but do eat lots of vegetables—have found that they have higher levels of antioxidants and tend to live longer.

Bottom line: Eat your veggies every day—lots of them.

•**Taking supplements.** It's difficult to study the specific effects of supplements over 80 to 100 years when so many other variables affect longevity. But both animal and human studies demonstrate the many health benefits of supplements.

Recommendation: In addition to taking a multivitamin, there's convincing evidence that a combination of the antioxidant alpha-lipoic acid (300 mg to 400 mg daily) and the amino acid acetyl-L-carnitine (800 mg to 1,200 mg daily) has a rejuvenating effect, making people feel more energetic. These two nutrients are involved in the body's production of energy, which powers every cell in the body. They are safe for everyone, although people with diabetes or seizure disorders should take them under a doctor's supervision. A recent study published in *American Journal of Clinical Nutrition* found that a related supplement, L-carnitine (2 grams daily), which helps transport fatty acids into the mitochondria (cell structures that convert nutrients into energy to power the cells), reduced mental and physical fatigue in centenarians. This supplement is safe for everyone. Magnesium (400 mg daily) helps maintain the length of telomeres, the protective tips of chromosomes. Resveratrol (100 mg twice daily) activates the SIRT1 gene, which is involved in longevity. And vitamin C (1,000 mg daily) enhances immunity and reduces inflammation, both of which can contribute to longevity. It is safe to take all of these supplements.

•**Eating less.** Animal studies dating back to the 1930s have shown that nutritionally complete but calorie-restricted diets (generally with 30% fewer calories than national recommendations) often increase life expectancy by up to 30%. In human terms, that's roughly an extra 22 years, which can bring people very close to the century mark. Studies of people growing up in Okinawa, Japan, during the 1940s and 1950s found that they consumed about 11% fewer calories than their estimated calorie requirements (about 2,000 calories daily for men and 1,600 for women) until middle age, which contributed to greater longevity.

Guaranteed benefit: Eating less will help you maintain a normal weight and lower the odds of developing diabetes and heart disease.

Important: Only 30% of centenarians are overweight.

It takes great willpower to maintain a diet with 30% fewer calories than what feels "normal," but eating less than you do can be an important first step. Assuming that you aren't underweight, I recommend a calorie-reducing compromise—at each meal, eat until you feel 80% full. You may feel hungry initially, but you'll soon adjust to consuming less food.

•**Continuing to learn.** Even more than physical health, mental sharpness (such as memory and the ability to make decisions) is the most likely predictor of independence among people in their 90s and over 100 years of age, according to a *Journal of the American Medical Association* article. Researchers say that some deterioration in cognitive function is inevitable as we age but that building a brain "reserve," or extra brain power, can offset part of this decline.

Mental activity builds your brain's reserve. Be a lifelong learner by taking challenging classes…reading and discussing difficult material…and exposing yourself to new and provocative ideas. All of these activities increase connections among brain cells.

•**Exercising.** The more exercise you do, the better. A study conducted at King's College London in England found that physically active people have healthier cells than those who don't exercise. Researchers found that exercise lengthened telomeres, the tips of chromosomes, which, as I explained earlier, usually shorten with aging.

Recommendation: If you are not physically active, start by walking for 10 minutes daily. Gradually build up speed, time and distance over a few weeks or months.

• **Getting enough—but not too much— sleep.** Seven hours of sleep nightly is the amount most strongly associated with longevity. Getting less sleep—or more—is associated with shorter life spans. People who sleep less than five hours don't give their bodies enough time for physiological recovery, and that may lead to metabolic dysfunction. Metabolic dysfunction also can result from habitually sleeping for more than eight hours.

• **Maintaining a spiritual foundation.** Having a spiritual foundation is associated with longer life. I find that my own spiritual foundation relieves stress. You can develop your inner life through prayer and/or meditation.

• **Being optimistic.** Centenarians tend to be optimists who feel that they have control over major decisions in their lives.

• **Connecting with others.** Strong ties to family and friends play a big role in longevity. Studies show that married men tend to live longer than bachelors. Research also has shown that having friends is even more important than having family in terms of living longer.

My prescription: Take time to thoroughly enjoy the company of family and friends!

REPORT #211
The Ultimate Stay-Young Workout

Joel Harper, New York City–based certified personal trainer who designs equipment-free workouts for Olympic athletes and business executives. His exercise DVDs are *YOU: Staying Young Workout, YOU: On a Diet Workout, FitPack Workout, FitPack Chair Workout* and *Dorm Room Diet.* The exercises described in this article are adapted from the program he created for *YOU: Staying Young* by Mehmet Oz, MD, and Michael Roizen, MD (Free Press).

If you would love to have strong, limber muscles but hate the idea of trudging off to the gym to lift weights or use exercise machines, there's a new no-equipment workout that uses your body to create strength-building resistance.

Muscle strength is key to staying robust as you age. In fact, research shows that building strong muscles is one of the best ways to stay out of a nursing home.

The following exercise plan should be performed three times a week, with at least one day of rest between workouts. The exercises, which take about 10 minutes to complete, are generally appropriate for people of any age or fitness level. Just be sure to check with your doctor before starting the program—especially if you have a chronic health problem. If the basic exercises seem too easy, try the advanced versions.

Important: If you catch yourself holding your breath during the workout, immediately start counting your repetitions out loud. This is a simple way to force yourself to breathe properly. Always count backward rather than forward—it tricks your mind into thinking that you're headed toward a finish line.

My stay-young workout...

TITANIC

Purpose: Stretches your chest, shoulders and arms.

Helps with: Maintaining good posture—especially for people who work at computers.

What to do: While standing with your feet slightly apart, hold your arms out to your sides, palms facing forward, two inches below your shoulders. Keeping your torso upright, stretch your hands back as far as you can reach. Hold for 20 seconds, while breathing deeply into your chest. This will expand your diaphragm, the large muscle that separates the chest and abdominal cavities.

Advanced version: Bend your wrists back and reach the backs of your hands toward each other.

DREAM OF JEANNIE

Purpose: Strengthens your quadricep muscles (in the fronts of the thighs), abdominals and shoulders.

Helps with: Walking up stairs.

What to do: While kneeling, cross your arms and hold them in front of your body like a genie, maintaining a straight line from the top of your head to your knees. Keeping this straight line, lean back slightly, pulling your navel in and squeezing your buttocks together. Hold for 30 seconds, while breathing deeply. If necessary, cushion your knees with a folded towel.

Advanced version: Lean back as far as possible while continuing to maintain the straight line from your head to your knees.

SUPERMAN TOE TAPS

Purpose: Strengthens your lower back and buttocks.

Helps with: Gardening, making the bed or carrying luggage.

What to do: Lie on your stomach with your head turned to the side and resting on your interlaced fingers. Keeping your legs straight, lift them off the ground and raise your knees as high as you can. Tap your toes together 40 times.

Advanced version: Reach your arms (palm side down) as far as you can in front of you. While looking down, lift your elbows as far above the ground as possible, then press your thumbs together and apart 40 times, while tapping your toes together.

HAMMOCK STRETCH

Purpose: Stretches your hips and hamstring muscles (in the backs of the thighs).

Helps with: Easing low-back tension—especially when caused by sitting for long periods, such as during an airplane flight.

What to do: Sit on the floor with your hands behind you and your palms on the floor. Keep your fingers pointing backward and your elbows slightly bent. Bend your knees and draw your heels in until they are two feet from your tailbone. Keeping the sole of your left foot flat on the ground, place your right ankle on top of your left knee and sit up as straight as possible. Focus on pressing your lower back forward toward your right calf. Resist raising your shoulders toward your ears. Hold for 15 seconds, then switch legs and repeat.

Advanced version: For a deeper stretch, gently press the knee of your crossed leg away from you while doing this exercise.

ABDOMINAL BUTTERFLY

Purpose: Strengthens your abdominals.

Helps with: Building strength in the core muscles of the trunk, which, in turn, supports the back.

What to do: Lie on your back and bring your legs into the "butterfly position"—knees pointing out to the sides and the soles of your feet touching. Relax your legs and lace your hands behind your head, resting your thumbs on your neck to ensure that it stays relaxed. Using only your abdominals, lift your upper body two inches off the ground then lower it back down, pressing your belly button toward your lower back. Repeat 25 times. Next, hold your upper body off the ground and lift your legs two inches, then tap the sides of your feet on the ground 25 times.

Advanced version: Lift your legs as high as you can off the ground and simultaneously raise your upper body into a "crunch" 25 times, while tapping the sides of your feet on the ground after each crunch.

CROSS-LEGGED TWIST

Purpose: Stretches your back, abdominals and hips.

Helps with: Releasing low-back tension and opening up the hips—good for those who sit at a desk all day and for activities such as tennis and skiing.

What to do: Sit on the floor with your legs crossed. Keeping your torso upright and the top of your head directly above your tailbone, place your left hand on your right knee and your right hand on the ground behind you. Slowly twist to the right. Take two deep breaths while holding the stretch. Switch sides and repeat, then do once more on each side.

Advanced version: Do this in the lotus position (legs crossed with ankles on top of your crossed legs).

REPORT #212
The Power of Homeopathy

Mark A. Stengler, NMD, licensed naturopathic medical doctor in private practice, La Jolla, California... adjunct associate clinical professor at the National College of Natural Medicine, Portland, Oregon...author of many books, including *The Natural Physician's Healing Therapies* and coauthor of *Prescription for Natural Cures* (both from Bottom Line Books)...and author of the *Bottom Line/Natural Healing* newsletter.

In this country, homeopathy is a source of controversy for medical practitioners and confusion for health-care consumers. That's why I am providing readers with this guide to homeopathic medicine, a therapy that aims to stimulate the body's own healing responses by using extremely small amounts of specific substances.

In my professional practice, I use homeopathy for one reason—it works. Before I get into the science, however, I want to share a personal story about the power of this healing therapy.

My first child was born prematurely, more than three months before he was due. His underdeveloped lungs were not ready for life outside the womb, and he contracted life-threatening viral pneumonia. It was heartbreaking to see my baby boy with tubes down his tiny throat, as four pediatricians worked around the clock to save him. Though antibiotics do not work against viruses, the doctors administered intravenous antibiotics in case there also was a secondary bacterial infection. When my son's condition did not improve, the doctors seemed at a loss for what to do next.

At this point, I took matters into my own hands. I treated my son with homeopathic *Antimonium tartaricum*, a liquid solution derived from antimony (a metal) and potassium salts, which I rubbed onto his chest. Within one day, he had improved visibly. By the following day, my son was off the respirator and on his way to complete recovery.

THE HOMEOPATHY PRINCIPLE

Homeopathy was founded two centuries ago by the German physician Samuel Hahnemann, MD. It is based on the law of similars—the idea that "like cures like."

Underlying principle: The symptoms the body produces in response to illness, injury or stress are not extensions of the condition, but instead reflect the body's attempt to heal itself.

Homeopathy promotes healing by utilizing substances that mobilize the body's natural self-defense processes. For example, the same plant that causes an itchy rash also can cure that rash when given in very minute quantities. In conventional medicine, this principle underlies vaccination and allergy injections—which administer tiny amounts of a disease-causing or an allergy-provoking agent to stimulate the immune system to produce antibodies that protect against this same agent.

For uncomplicated health problems, such as occasional digestive upset or a cold, patients can be helped with simple, common homeopathic remedies sold in health-food stores. For more complex problems, practitioners depend on a deep understanding of the individual patient's health status, an array of potent remedies and careful monitoring of the patient's progress.

We spoke with Iris Bell, PhD, professor of family and community medicine at the University of Arizona School of Medicine in Tucson, whose research on the psychophysiological effectiveness of homeopathy has been granted funding from the National Institutes of Health. Dr. Bell explained, "The human body is a network. Changes to any one system can affect the entire network. Disease is a process that can activate any number of other problems that an individual person may be genetically prone to. That's why homeopathic practitioners look at the larger picture and treat the whole patient."

THE PREPARATIONS

Homeopathy uses thousands of substances derived from plant, mineral or animal sources. Over many years, homeopaths have catalogued the physical and mental symptoms these substances can cause and, from this information, have created substances that can cure these conditions.

Homeopathic remedies generally are safe for everyone, have no side effects when used properly, and are manufactured in accordance with standards set by the FDA.

The process: The particular substance is dissolved in a "mother tincture" of alcohol or alcohol plus water. It is vigorously shaken, then further diluted with alcohol and/or water and shaken again. This process is repeated multiple times, further diluting the substance each time. When the appropriate potency is achieved, the substance is converted into a form appropriate for use—powder, liquid, ointment or tiny tablets (called pellets) to dissolve in the mouth.

A remedy's potency depends on the degree of dilution it undergoes. Classifications include X (for 10, meaning a potency based on a ratio of one part substance to 10 parts dilution), C (100) and M (1,000). Products are formulated by multiples of these ratios. For example, a 6X remedy contains one part active substance to 106—which is 10 x 10 x 10 x 10 x 10 x 10, or one million—parts carrier substances.

Now, here's the seeming paradox of homeopathy—the more diluted the substance is, the more potent it becomes. No one knows why for sure, but experience shows this does happen. Products used for minor conditions, such as colds and headaches, are sold over the counter in health-food stores. A prescription from a licensed health-care practitioner is required for homeopathic drugs that treat more serious problems, such as severe strep infections, as well as for all M-potency products. These can be filled at compounding pharmacies.

Recently, a medical doctor expressed his skepticism regarding the dilution of homeopathic substances. I asked if he would treat a life-threatening allergic reaction by injecting *epinephrine* (adrenaline)—the standard medical treatment—and he said of course he would, because it works. I then pointed out that the epinephrine used for injection is far more diluted than many homeopathic remedies.

SCIENTIFIC EVIDENCE

Researchers have been studying homeopathy for decades. Overall, studies show mixed results. This does not mean that treatments are ineffective, but rather that they are used in a holistic way not easily measured in conventional studies.

Reason: Drugs and nutritional supplements can be matched to specific problems and studied accordingly. For example, the drug (Celebrex) and the natural supplement glucosamine (an amino sugar) both are used to treat osteoarthritis, so studies focus on their effectiveness against that particular disease. However, homeopathic treatment is highly individualized according to a patient's overall profile. If a patient has migraines, I select from among several dozen homeopathic remedies, taking into account the type and location of his/her migraines, how the weather affects him, his diet and exercise habits, etc. With so many variables influencing the choice of homeopathic remedy and the patient's response to it, I'm not surprised that study results sometimes are inconclusive.

Even so, more than 100 clinical trials have demonstrated homeopathy's benefits. For example, a study conducted at the University of Vienna involved 50 patients with chronic bronchitis and/or emphysema and a history of smoking. Compared with participants who received placebos, those who took homeopathic remedies had significantly reduced levels of the mucus secretions that impair breathing…and their average hospital stay was just 4.2 days, compared with 7.4 days for the placebo group. Researchers at the University of Glasgow analyzed data from four studies involving about 250 patients with allergic respiratory symptoms, such as asthma and rhinitis.

Findings: Participants who received a 30C potency homeopathic remedy for hay fever reported a 28% improvement in symptoms, compared with 3% in the placebo group.

Equally convincing, in my opinion, are the many reports I have received from patients who have been helped by homeopathic remedies—often after other treatments failed.

FINDING A HOMEOPATHIC PRACTITIONER

Homeopathy does not work for everyone. For best effect, try to be articulate and open in detailing your symptoms, as this will help practitioners to identify the most appropriate remedies. Also, some practitioners work with a limited number of substances that they have found especially effective—so if you do not get relief with a particular practitioner, try someone else.

In the US, homeopathy is practiced by many naturopathic physicians, chiropractors, nurses, dentists and some medical doctors. In most states, homeopaths are not licensed as such, and there are no national standards for training. However, the following organizations have stringent training requirements for members and offer online directories for finding practitioners in various areas.

•**American Institute of Homeopathy awards a diplomate of homeopathy (DHt) certification.** A practitioner must hold an MD or a DO license, accrue 150 hours of education credits in homeopathy, and pass various exams (888-445-9988, *www.homeopathyusa.org*).

•**All naturopathic physicians are educated in homeopathy.** Those with the most extensive training are eligible to join the Homeopathic Academy of Naturopathic Physicians.

Referrals: American Association of Naturopathic Physicians (866-538-2267, *www.naturo pathic.org*).

For more information on homeopathy, contact the National Center for Homeopathy (703-548-7790, *www.nationalcenterforhomeopathy. org*).

LOOKING AHEAD

You may be surprised to learn that high-potency homeopathic remedies are diluted to the point where they do not contain any of the original substance—yet they continue to have powerful healing properties. This is an aspect of the emerging field of energetic medicine. Energetic medicine heals by affecting the electrical and electromagnetic activity of the body—the means by which cells communicate with one another. Magnet therapy and light therapy also are examples of energetic medicine.

In homeopathy, researchers now believe that the original electromagnetic frequency of the source materials imprints itself on the fluid used to produce the remedy. Because the human body is 70% to 80% water, a fluid medium is an effective way to transmit information throughout the body.

Does this sound far-fetched? Remember that practitioners of Western medicine used to claim that acupuncture and chiropractic were nonsense—yet now these alternative therapies generally are accepted as legitimate. Researchers at a number of major universities are now studying homeopathy's applications in energetic medicine. I believe we will be hearing much more about this therapy in the years to come.

REPORT #213
Homeopathic Remedies

Mark A. Stengler, NMD, licensed naturopathic medical doctor in private practice, La Jolla, California… adjunct associate clinical professor at the National College of Natural Medicine, Portland, Oregon…author of many books, including *The Natural Physician's Healing Therapies* and coauthor of *Prescription for Natural Cures* (both from Bottom Line Books)…and author of the *Bottom Line/Natural Healing* newsletter.

Low-potency homeopathic remedies that are sold in health-food stores generally are safe for everyone. They can be used in combination with other homeopathic remedies. Follow instructions on labels. Consult a doctor trained in homeopathy before using remedies if you have a serious illness…take medication…are pregnant or nursing…or if symptoms do not improve after 48 hours of use.

For this condition…	The remedy is…
Allergies, hay fever	*Allium cepa*
Arthritis pain	*Rhus toxicodendron*
Back pain	*Rhus toxicodendron*
Bee stings, insect bites	*Apis*
Bruising, swelling, sprains	*Arnica*
Cold sores	*Rhus toxicodendron*
Coughs, colds	*Phosphorous*
Earache	*Chamomilla*
Emotional distress, anxiety	*Ignatia*
Fever	*Belladonna*
Flu	*Gelsemium*

Hangover, heartburn	*Nux vomica*
Migraine	*Belladonna*
Muscle cramps, muscle spasms	*Magnesia phosphorica*
Nerve injury	*Hypericum*
Poison ivy	*Rhus toxicodendron*
Sore throat	*Phosphorous*
Skin rash, eczema	*Sulphur*
Stomach cramps, nausea	*Nux vomica*
Toothache, teething pain	*Chamomilla*
Urinary tract infection	*Cantharis*

REPORT #214
Your Genes Are Not Your Destiny

Mark A. Stengler, NMD, licensed naturopathic medical doctor in private practice, La Jolla, California... adjunct associate clinical professor at the National College of Natural Medicine, Portland, Oregon...author of many books, including *The Natural Physician's Healing Therapies* and coauthor of *Prescription for Natural Cures* (both from Bottom Line Books)...and author of the *Bottom Line/Natural Healing* newsletter.

Family history. It's something doctors always ask about, and for many of us, it's a source of worry. After all, our genes are our destiny, right? Heart disease runs in my family, you may say, or cancer, or diabetes. Adding to the concern are all those reports about scientists discovering a gene that may influence our risk for contracting a certain condition. So far, their discoveries include genes that make us more susceptible to heart disease, Alzheimer's disease, breast cancer, prostate cancer, arthritis, diabetes, obesity, depression, osteoporosis and more.

Some of the news stories also mention the good news on the flip side of the coin—that genetic research eventually may lay the groundwork for new medical treatments. But the big advances are, at best, many years away.

There is more good news that we can use right now—eating certain foods can help us fight disease-causing genes, thanks to something called *nutrigenomics*. Just like it sounds, this new field of science merges research on genes with nutrition. One of the most exciting concepts to come out of the labs is the recognition that our genes have a great amount of flexibility, good and bad. We may always have the genes that we were born with, but what we eat—or don't eat—affects how they behave. We can use nutrients as a form of safe, natural gene therapy that aims to help our genes work better and keep us in good health.

I'll give you an example. An acquaintance, Jim, underwent nutrigenomic testing and learned that he had a gene variation that greatly reduced his body's ability to use folic acid, a B vitamin. As a consequence, he had elevated levels of homocysteine, an amino acid that aids in cellular metabolism and, when present in high levels, becomes a risk factor for heart attack, stroke and Alzheimer's disease. Jim can't change the gene—it's hardwired—but he did start taking folic acid supplements, which normalized his homocysteine levels and helped offset his genetic risk.

WHY GENES MATTER

Here's a quick refresher on basic biology. Genes are microscopic biological programs that regulate how each of our trillions of cells functions. They work like computer software, programming the tens of thousands of biochemicals in our bodies. Most cells contain two sets of genes, one from each parent. We also inherit many mutations, or variations, that can alter gene activity. When genes don't function at their best, they can increase our risk for disease.

Nutrition affects our genes in three basic ways...

• **First, we need nutrients to make and repair genes.** We make new genes each time we need a new cell for growth, to heal injuries or to replace dead cells. By eating right and taking nutritional supplements, we help our bodies make healthy new genes and do a better job of repairing those that get damaged.

• **Second, some nutrients, such as folic acid and *genistein* (an isoflavone found in soy), regulate gene activity.** For example, they help turn off cancer-promoting genes, so one of the benefits of these nutrients is a potential decrease in cancer risk.

• **Third, extra amounts of some nutrients can offset genetic weaknesses.** This was Jim's experience, and it is a major focus of nutrigenomic research.

Upping your intake of a few key nutrients can have big benefits when it comes to preventing disease and even slowing down the aging process. Here are the three powerhouse nutrients that you'll want to incorporate into your diet right away.

B VITAMINS
SLOW THE CLOCK

Every living creature ages. On a microscropic level, aging occurs in large part due to the deterioration of our genes and their ability to provide accurate instructions to cells. This is like having genetic instructions increasingly filled with typos. A solid nutritional foundation protects our genes and slows this deterioration… and the accumulation of genetic typos.

For example, studies show that low levels of B vitamins, such as folic acid and B-12, actually increase gene damage…and that damage is reduced when people consume more of these vitamins. Bruce Ames, PhD, of the Children's Hospital Oakland Research Institute in Oakland, California, found that low intake of folic acid and magnesium interferes with gene-repair mechanisms, resulting in more mutations. More mutations translate into faster aging and greater risk for disease.

Dr. Ames has amassed a wealth of data showing that 50 inherited diseases can be improved by taking B vitamins and other supplements, such as vitamin C, magnesium, *indole-3-carbinol* (found in cruciferous vegetables, such as cauliflower) and *chlorophyllin* (a natural derivative of *chlorophyll*, the ingredient that makes plant leaves green). These diseases include cancer, cardiomyopathy (deterioration of the heart muscle), autism, Alzheimer's disease and coronary artery disease. I suspect that these are just a fraction of the conditions that can be modified through nutritional therapies.

Smart strategy: Because B-complex vitamins are so important for gene function and overall health, I recommend that nearly every adult take a daily high-potency multivitamin or B-complex supplement with 800 micrograms (mcg) of folic acid and 50 mcg to 100 mcg of vitamin B-12. Exceptions include anyone who is taking *methotrexate* for rheumatoid arthritis and some chemotherapy patients, because high-dose B supplements may interfere with these treatments.

D IS FOR DEFENSE

Researchers and physicians are increasingly focusing on the health benefits of vitamin D in maintaining healthy bones and muscle as we age…preventing cancer…fighting infections… and lowering the risk for heart disease. Considerable evidence suggests that getting enough vitamin D—at least 1,000 international units (IU) daily—could substantially decrease the risk for breast, colon, lung and other cancers.

Genetics enter the equation when it comes to the amount of sun people need to make their own vitamin D. Those with fair skin can get enough by spending 10 to 15 minutes outdoors daily in the summer sun, while people with darker complexions usually need 30 to 40 minutes in the sun. Unfortunately, most people don't get nearly enough exposure to sunlight. Also, according to a study in the journal *Metabolism,* 35% of Americans have a genetic variation (known as *VDR bb*) that reduces their ability to benefit from vitamin D.

Low levels of vitamin D occur not just in northern states that are sun-starved during the winter. A new study found that one-quarter of adults in sunny southern Arizona were deficient in D. The deficit was higher in some people—38% of Hispanics and 55% of blacks.

Best dosages: Take a minimum of 1,000 IU of vitamin D3 (the form the body makes from sunlight) daily if you are fair-skinned… or 2,000 IU if you have a dark complexion. I would add that some fair-skinned people need 2,000 IU to 4,000 IU to achieve normal blood levels. There are no great natural food sources of vitamin D, and you won't find this much in most multivitamins, so you'll have to take an additional supplement.

SELENIUM STAVES OFF
BREAST CANCER

Selenium, an essential dietary mineral, also helps maintain normal gene activity, and research indicates that it may protect against breast cancer. It is a component of *glutathione peroxidase*, a powerful antioxidant made by the body that works as a natural detoxifying agent.

Mutations in the BRCA1 genes are an established risk factor for breast cancer. Women of Jewish European heritage are at high risk for inheriting this gene, and it also is common in women of Hispanic descent. Men with BRCA1 mutations also have a higher-than-average risk for breast cancer (1,600 men are diagnosed with the disease annually in the US, compared with 200,000 women). But once again, your genes don't have to be your fate.

The BRCA family of genes is involved in repairing damaged genes. As we know, mutations can keep genes from functioning properly. If genes can't do a good job at repair, cell damage accumulates, increasing the risk for breast cancer.

Try this: Selenium is found in most multivitamin/multimineral supplements. If you are in generally good health, strive for 200 mcg to 300 mcg of selenium daily (most multis contain 200 mcg). Don't take more unless your physician recommends it, though, because high doses of this mineral are potentially toxic. Or you could eat a handful of Brazil nuts (about six) each day—they're the richest natural food source of selenium.

GENETIC TESTING
FOR YOU

The best way to evaluate your genetic risk is to consult with a genetic counselor. To find a counselor in your area, visit the National Society of Genetic Counselors at their Web Site *www.nsgc.org*. Click the link "Find a Counselor." Genetic testing may be covered by your insurance (especially if you are in a high-risk group).

THE CARE AND FEEDING
OF YOUR GENES

So how can you start putting some of this knowledge to use? I'll relate the experience of one of my associates who underwent nutrigenomic testing. The tests revealed that Joseph didn't have any single gene that could make or break his health—but he did have a cluster of gene variations that together might increase his risk for diabetes. In fact, he already had been diagnosed with prediabetes.

Through better eating habits, exercise and supplements (chromium, biotin, alpha-lipoic acid and others), Joseph normalized his blood sugar, cholesterol and triglycerides—and lost 20 pounds. He now is in better health than he had been for years. Knowing that he has a genetic risk for developing diabetes has motivated him to stick with a healthier lifestyle to improve his genes.

Is nutrigenomic testing right for you? If there is a strong pattern of illness in your family, it might be worthwhile to evaluate your genetic risk. And for anyone, test results can be a powerful motivator to make healthy dietary and lifestyle choices.

REPORT #215
What Is Aging?

Over the course of a lifetime, our bodies face inevitable decline. Aging is characterized by an accumulation of cell damage. Some of this damage comes from destructive molecules called free radicals.

Another problem: Wear and tear erodes mitochondria, microscopic cell structures that provide us with energy and stamina. In addition, telomeres, the tips of chromosomes, shorten with age, which may accelerate the aging process.

Mark A. Stengler, NMD, licensed naturopathic medical doctor in private practice, La Jolla, California... adjunct associate clinical professor at the National College of Natural Medicine, Portland, Oregon...author of many books, including *The Natural Physician's Healing Therapies* and coauthor of *Prescription for Natural Cures* (both from Bottom Line Books)...and author of the *Bottom Line/Natural Healing* newsletter.

REPORT #216
Drink Coffee...Eat Chocolate...and Other Surprising Ways to Live Longer

Michael F. Roizen, MD, chief wellness officer and chair of the Wellness Institute, Cleveland Clinic in Cleveland, Ohio. He is coauthor, with Mehmet C. Oz, MD, of several books, including *You: Staying Young* (Free Press).

Many of the proven strategies for living longer—such as restricting calories and exercising on a regular basis—can feel like punishment for some people. Fortunately, there are many enjoyable ways to stay healthy—but doctors don't recommend these strategies as often as they should. Research has shown that activities nearly everyone enjoys can literally add years to a person's life.

Fun-filled ways to live longer...

1. Get the Right Kind of Sleep.

Studies have found that people who get deep, restorative sleep typically live three years longer than those who don't. During deep sleep, the body normally produces higher levels of melatonin, a hormone that improves immunity and reduces the risk for infections as well as cancer. Deep sleep also increases levels of growth hormone, which improves energy and helps promote a healthy weight.

Good news: You don't have to sleep uninterrupted through the night to get the benefits of deep sleep, as long as you complete a series of at least 90-minute sleep cycles—each one beginning with light sleep (stages 1 and 2)...progressing through deeper sleep (stages 3 and 4)...and then into the deepest stage, known as rapid eye movement (REM) sleep. As long as you complete this 90-minute cycle several times a night, it doesn't matter if you wake up a time or two.

2. Enjoy Your Coffee.

Many people assume that coffee—unlike green tea, for example—isn't a healthful beverage. But that's not true. Studies have found that caffeinated and decaffeinated coffee are a main source of antioxidants in the average American's diet.

Research has shown that caffeinated coffee decreases the risk for Parkinson's and Alzheimer's diseases by 30% to 40%—health benefits that are largely attributed to the beverage's caffeine. (Decaffeinated coffee does not offer these same benefits.) The caffeine in coffee also is good for cognitive health.

Important: Caffeinated coffee may cause several side effects, such as blood pressure spikes, abnormal heartbeat, anxiety and gastric upset.

My recommendation: If you do not experience any of these side effects, and you enjoy drinking coffee, have as many cups of caffeinated coffee as you like. If you do experience side effects, you may prefer to drink decaffeinated coffee. Even though it does not have the health benefits previously described, studies show that decaffeinated coffee may help fight off type 2 diabetes.

3. Go Dancing.

Men and women who get optimal amounts of physical activity—about 30 minutes a day, seven days a week—can make their "RealAges" (the "biological ages" of their bodies, based on lifestyle and behaviors) 6.4 years younger.

Many types of dancing give a superb physical workout. Ballroom and square dancing are particularly good for cognitive health. They involve both physical and mental stimulation (in order to execute the appropriate dance steps) and may help reduce the risk for dementia. Aim to dance at least 30 minutes a day.

4. Do Some Singing.

Whether you lend your voice to a choir or merely sing for pleasure in the shower, singing improves immunity and elevates levels of hormones known as endorphins and dopamine—both of which reduce stress and activate the brain's pleasure centers. Studies have shown that singing helps people with asthma...reduces stress hormones...and may temporarily help improve memory in patients with Alzheimer's disease.

5. Continue Learning.

People who take pleasure in expanding their minds—for example, by learning to paint, attending lectures or doing puzzles—

can make their RealAges about 2.5 years younger.

Studies have shown that people with higher levels of education, and those who continue learning throughout life, form more connections between brain cells, making them less likely to experience later-life memory loss.

6. Eat Some Chocolate.

The powerful antioxidants known as flavonoids in dark chocolate increase levels of the body's nitric oxide (NO), a gas that dilates arteries (to help prevent blockages) and can help reduce blood pressure in people with hypertension. This is particularly helpful for people over age 50, because age-related buildup of fatty deposits in the arteries (atherosclerosis) reduces natural levels of NO.

My recommendation: Eat one-half ounce of dark chocolate (at least 70% cocoa) twice daily. Don't overindulge in chocolate—it is high in calories. Other good flavonoid sources include brewed black or green tea…red wine…dark grape juice…strawberries, cranberries and apples…and brussels sprouts and onions.

7. Find Opportunities to Laugh.

People who laugh—and who make others laugh—tend to have better immunity than people who are humor-impaired. Telling a joke is also a good way to improve your memory. It requires the teller—as well as the listener—to pay attention, and we laugh when we expect one outcome but are surprised by a different one. Psychologists call this "conceptual blending." In addition, laughter is a well-known stress reducer. People who are calmer and more relaxed have lower levels of heart disease and cancer.

8. Have More Sex.

Men and women who have sex (that results in orgasm) an average of twice a week have arteries with greater elasticity (which helps prevent hardening of the arteries). Men and women who have sex daily, on average, are biologically eight years younger than those who have it once a week.

9. Rest More Often.

Everyone enjoys taking a break from life's stresses. Research shows that people who give themselves time to relax (thus minimizing the effects of stress) can live for up to eight years longer.

Stress reducers—such as meditating, taking long walks, watching the sunset—can add years to your life. Yoga is particularly good. It lowers blood pressure, heart rate and stress hormones, and increases levels of dopamine and the "feel good" hormone serotonin. Aim for about 10 minutes daily of a stress-reduction activity.

10. Get a Pet.

People who own pets can make themselves an average of one year younger. Studies show that taking care of and bonding with a pet reduces depression and blood pressure.

After a heart attack, people with pets have a one-year survival rate of 94%, compared with 72% for people who don't have pets. Studies show that dog owners, who live about three years longer, tend to be a little healthier than those with other pets—in part because they get regular exercise when they walk their dogs.

REPORT #217
Drugs or Supplements?

Alan H. Pressman, DC, PhD, CCN, host of the daily radio show *Healthline with Dr. Pressman* on WWRL 1600 in New York City and syndicated nationally on Air America, *www.drpressman.com.* He is author of numerous books on nutrition and health, including, with coauthor Sheila Buff, *The Complete Idiot's Guide to Vitamins and Minerals* (Alpha).

For many conditions, dietary supplements, along with lifestyle changes, can be safe and effective alternatives to more powerful—and often more risky—drugs. Talk to your doctor before treating a medical condition with supplements instead of drugs.

Caution: When starting a new supplement, begin with the smallest dose and take it for several days to be sure that you don't have a bad reaction. Slowly increase the dose to a level that helps. With some supplements, such as glucosamine (for joint problems) and saw palmetto, you may have to take the pills for several weeks before you notice an improvement. Never go beyond the maximum indicated on the container or recommended by your doctor. Stop taking the supplement if at any time you notice any bad side effects.

Quality caution: Sometimes a supplement doesn't help because the quality is poor. Consider trying a different brand before you give up on it.

Note: Always keep a complete list of all the supplements and drugs you take and review it with your doctor at every visit.

REPORT #218
Surprising Stress Protector

The live bacteria in probiotic supplements (and fermented foods such as yogurt) help reduce intestinal damage caused by chronic stress. Probiotics inhibit the ability of bacteria to penetrate the intestinal wall and to initiate tissue-damaging inflammation.

MedPage Today.

REPORT #219
Can This Patient Be Cured? Multiple Sclerosis

Mark A. Stengler, NMD, licensed naturopathic medical doctor in private practice, La Jolla, California... adjunct associate clinical professor at the National College of Natural Medicine, Portland, Oregon...author of many books, including *The Natural Physician's Healing Therapies* and coauthor of *Prescription for Natural Cures* (both from Bottom Line Books)...and author of the *Bottom Line/Natural Healing* newsletter.

Donna, 70, dragged herself into my office three years ago. Her complaints—muscle weakness and stiffness, fatigue, irritability and sensitivity to noise—were all due to *multiple sclerosis* (MS), a disease she had battled since age 21.

MS is a degenerative autoimmune disease in which immune cells attack the *myelin sheath* (fatty tissue that surrounds and protects nerve fibers), disrupting the flow of electrical impulses between the brain and the nerves. Symptoms may flare up when a patient is stressed or has a viral infection, such as a cold or the flu. Conventional treatment includes the immune-regulating drug *interferon* (Betaseron) or *glatiramer* (Copaxone), which suppresses immune activity against the myelin sheath...and steroids or chemotherapy to reduce inflammation. These therapies can have serious side effects, including depression and flulike symptoms.

Research suggests that a deficiency of vitamin B-12 may be associated with the development of MS. B-12 aids in repairing the myelin sheath, so B-12 injections may help to prevent and treat MS flare-ups. To relieve Donna's symptoms, I prescribed B-12 injections twice weekly, plus a daily sublingual (under the tongue) B-12 supplement. After a month, she had more energy, strength and flexibility... was less irritable...and was less bothered by noise.

I urged Donna to increase her intake of essential fatty acids (EFAs), found in fish, walnuts, almonds and pistachios. I also recommended a high-potency fish oil supplement and a *gamma linoleic acid* (GLA) supplement in the form of evening primrose oil. To encourage her, I showed Donna studies by Roy Swank, MD, a professor of neurology at the University of Oregon, which found that a diet limited in saturated fat (from meat and dairy foods) and hydrogenated oils (from margarines and baked goods made with vegetable oils) and rich in polyunsaturated fatty acids (from fish oil and vegetables) helps to halt the progression of MS.

I also tested Donna's blood level of vitamin D and found that it was low. Vitamin D is a critical nutrient for proper immune function, including prevention of auto-immune disorders. MS is more common in higher latitudes where sunlight—a key source of vitamin D—is limited. A study published in *The Journal of the American Medical Association* reported that higher levels of vitamin D in the body may reduce the risk of developing MS by up to 62%. For Donna, I prescribed 1,000 international units (IU) of vitamin D daily, taken in addition to the multivitamin/mineral formula she was already using.

Since she began this treatment three years ago, Donna has had only occasional minor flare-ups, for which she receives twice-weekly B-12 injections. In general, her condition is well controlled with just one monthly B-12 injection, plus the sublingual B-12 and the vitamin D supplements. She no longer requires steroid medication—and she says that despite having had MS for almost 50 years, she's now in better health overall than her septuagenarian friends.

Volume 21
'Kitchen' Cures

REPORT #220
Cures from Your Kitchen

You don't need to go to the pharmacy to find powerful cures for everyday ailments. The answers could be in your kitchen. Joan and Lydia Wilen have been collecting, researching and testing folk remedies for more than two decades—and all their remedies have been reviewed for safety by medical doctors, naturopathic doctors and other experts.

Bonus: You might even save a few pennies in the process—having to turn no further than your own kitchen. If you have an existing health condition, check with your physician before trying any of these remedies.

BAD BREATH, GUM DISEASE AND TOOTHACHE

• **Coconut oil, baking soda.**

Coconut oil can soothe ailments of the mouth, such as bad breath, gum disease and toothache.

For help with any of these conditions, brush your teeth with a mixture of one-eighth teaspoon of baking soda and one-half teaspoon of organic extra-virgin coconut oil (which you can find at a health-food store). Sore gums also are helped when you rub them with coconut oil.

BUMPS AND BRUISES

• **Lemon.**

Most bruises that turn black and blue go away on their own, but you can speed the healing process—and reduce both the swelling and the bruising—with this Mayan remedy. Cut a lemon in half, and rub the pulpy side over the bruise once an hour for several hours. Avoid any cuts or breaks in the skin.

Mark A. Stengler, NMD, licensed naturopathic medical doctor in private practice, La Jolla, California...adjunct associate clinical professor at the National College of Natural Medicine, Portland, Oregon...author of many books, including *The Natural Physician's Healing Therapies* and coauthor of *Prescription for Natural Cures* (both from Bottom Line Books)...and author of the *Bottom Line/Natural Healing* newsletter.

CONSTIPATION

• **Lemon, honey, prune juice, prunes, papaya, apples, dried figs.**

Drinking water on an empty stomach can stimulate bowel movements. Before breakfast, drink the juice of one-half a lemon in one cup of warm water. If it is too tart, sweeten it with honey. If that doesn't help move your bowels, try one of the following—prune juice (at room temperature, not chilled) or stewed prunes, papaya, two peeled apples or six to eight dried figs. (Soak the figs overnight in water. In the morning, drink the water, then eat the figs.)

DANDRUFF

• **Thyme.**

We all have dead cells that fall from our scalp as new cells come in. But some people have a greater number of cells falling that are bigger and easier to see. Dried thyme can help get rid of dandruff. Boil one cup of water, and add two heaping tablespoons of dried thyme to the cup. Let it simmer for seven to 10 minutes. Use a strainer to collect the thyme, and get rid of it. Let the tea cool. Wash your hair with a regular shampoo. While your hair is still damp, gently massage the cooled tea into your scalp. Do not rinse.

DIARRHEA

• **Milk, allspice, cinnamon and powdered cloves.**

There are several remedies from other countries that use milk. A West Indian remedy is one cup of milk (or warm water) with a pinch of allspice. The Pennsylvania Dutch recommend one cup of warm milk with two pinches of cinnamon. A Brazilian remedy includes two pinches of cinnamon and one pinch of powdered cloves in one cup of warm milk. (Do not drink milk if you are lactose intolerant. It may cause diarrhea.)

HEADACHE

• **Green tea, mint.**

Fatigue, anxiety and stress can trigger headaches. For fast relief, brew one cup of green tea and add sprigs of fresh mint. You can use either spearmint or peppermint. If you don't have fresh mint available, use a peppermint or spearmint tea bag. Combine a bag each of green tea and mint tea to make a powerful brew that will diminish your headache in about 15 minutes.

INDIGESTION

• **Grapefruit, potato.**

If you are prone to any of the unpleasant symptoms of indigestion, including stomachache or nausea, you can prepare this remedy in advance to have at the ready. Grate the peel of a grapefruit, and spread the pieces out on a paper towel to dry overnight. Store the dried peel in a lidded jar. When you feel the first signs of indigestion, eat one-half to one teaspoon of the grated peel. Chew thoroughly before swallowing.

Another remedy: Raw potato juice can neutralize stomach acid. Grate a potato, and squeeze the gratings through a piece of cheesecloth or a fine strainer to get the juice. Take one tablespoon of potato juice diluted with one-half cup of warm water. Drink slowly.

INSOMNIA

• **Whole nutmeg, grapefruit juice, yellow onion.**

Nutmeg can work as a sedative. Crush a whole nutmeg, and steep it in hot water for 10 minutes. Drink it 30 minutes before bedtime. Or drink a glass of pure, warmed grapefruit juice. If you prefer it sweetened, use a little bit of raw honey. Or cut a yellow onion and put it in a glass jar. Keep it near your bed. When you can't sleep, or if you wake up and can't fall back to sleep, open the jar and inhale deeply. Close the jar. Close your eyes, think lovely thoughts and you'll fall back to sleep.

MEMORY PROBLEMS

• **Carrot juice, milk, fresh ginger, sage tea, cloves.**

For mild memory problems, try this memory-improving drink. Mix one-half glass of carrot juice with one-half glass of milk—and drink daily. Or use daily doses of fresh ginger in cooking or in tea. Ginger is known to improve memory. Or brew one cup of sage tea, and add four cloves. Drink daily. Sage and cloves are believed to strengthen memory.

POISON IVY/OAK/SUMAC

• **Banana skin, lemon, garlic, tofu.**

These remedies can help ease the itching and redness of poison ivy. Rub the inside of a banana skin directly on the affected skin. Use a fresh banana skin every hour for a day. (Freeze the leftover banana pieces to use in smoothies or to eat on hot days.)

Or slice one or two lemons, and rub them on the area. This helps to stop the itching and clears the skin. Or chop up four cloves of garlic, and boil them in one cup of water. When the mixture is cool, apply it with a clean cloth to the area.

Another remedy: Mash up pieces of tofu directly on the itchy area—and hold them in place with a cloth or bandage. This should cool off the area and help any poison ivy flare-up.

SINUS PROBLEMS

• **Tomato juice, garlic, cayenne pepper, lemon juice.**

When your sinuses feel clogged and uncomfortable, this bracing drink can help. Combine one cup of tomato juice, one teaspoon of freshly chopped garlic, one-quarter to one-half teaspoon of cayenne pepper (according to your tolerance for spicy food) and one teaspoon of lemon juice. Heat the mixture until it is warm but not too hot to drink. Drink it slowly, and it should help clear up sinuses quickly.

REPORT #221
Kitchen Spices Fight Deadly E. Coli

The food-borne bacterium *Escherichia coli O157* causes severe cramps, bloody diarrhea and kidney failure. Researchers studied the effects of extracts of 20 spices on the bacterium.

Results: Allspice significantly reduced E. coli O157 toxin growth…to a lesser degree, so did cloves.

Worth a try: Add ground allspice and/or cloves to burgers, vegetables and salads.

Kumio Yokoigawa, PhD, professor of food microbiology, University of Tokushima, Japan, and leader of a lab study.

REPORT #222
Migraine Relief

Eliminate migraine pain with pepper. Capsaicin, an ingredient in cayenne pepper, cuts off neurotransmitters in the brain that cause headache pain.

Best: Dissolve one-quarter teaspoon of cayenne powder in four ounces of warm water. Dip a cotton swab into the solution, and apply the liquid inside your nostrils. It will burn—and by the time the burning stops, the headache pain will be reduced and sometimes gone altogether.

Eric Yarnell, ND, assistant professor, department of botanical medicine, Bastyr University, Kenmore, Washington.

REPORT #223
Natural Remedies For Nausea

Suzy Cohen, RPh, registered practicing pharmacist for nearly 20 years and author of *The 24-Hour Pharmacist* (Harper Paperbacks). Her syndicated newspaper column, "Dear Pharmacist," reaches more than 24 million readers. Based in Florida, she is a member of the Association of Natural Medicine Pharmacists and the American Holistic Health Association.

As a pharmacist for almost two decades, Suzy Cohen knows the importance of medication—but she also has learned to "think outside the pill" and recommend natural options that often are just as good or better at promoting health without the risk of dangerous side effects.

Here is the remedy she recommends most often for nausea.

GINGER FOR NAUSEA

Studies have shown that ginger can relieve nausea—due to pregnancy, seasickness, etc.—as well as or better than over-the-counter drugs.

How it works: Ginger increases the pH of stomach acid, reducing its acidity. In one study, published in *The Lancet,* volunteers were given either ginger or Dramamine (a nausea-preventing drug), then were seated in a chair designed to trigger motion sickness. Those given ginger were able to withstand the motion 57% longer than those given the drug.

How to use: Put one teaspoon of peeled, grated fresh gingerroot in a cup of boiling water. Let it steep for 10 minutes, then drink (you can filter out the ginger if you want). Or chew and swallow a piece of crystallized ginger, sold in health-food stores.

Caution: Ginger can increase the risk of bleeding when taken with blood-thinning drugs, such as *warfarin* (Coumadin).

REPORT #224
Kitchen Cures...
Shopping List

Mark A. Stengler, NMD, licensed naturopathic medical doctor in private practice, La Jolla, California... adjunct associate clinical professor at the National College of Natural Medicine, Portland, Oregon...author of many books, including *The Natural Physician's Healing Therapies* and coauthor of *Prescription for Natural Cures* (both from Bottom Line Books)...and author of the *Bottom Line/Natural Healing* newsletter.

Keep your kitchen stocked with these ingredients—and you'll have homemade remedies and cures at the ready!

- **Allspice**
- **Apples**
- **Baking soda**
- **Banana (skin)**
- **Carrot juice**
- **Cayenne pepper**
- **Cinnamon**
- **Cloves (whole)**
- **Cloves (powdered)**
- **Coconut oil**
- **Figs (dried)**
- **Garlic**
- **Ginger**
- **Grapefruit**
- **Grapefruit juice**
- **Green tea**
- **Honey**
- **Lemon**
- **Lemon juice**
- **Milk**
- **Nutmeg (whole)**
- **Onion (yellow)**
- **Papaya**
- **Potato**
- **Prune juice**
- **Prunes (stewed)**
- **Sage tea**
- **Spearmint or peppermint**
- **Thyme**
- **Tofu**
- **Tomato juice**

REPORT #225
5-Cent Cure for
Kidney Disease

Magdi Yaqoob, MD, professor of renal medicine, The Royal London Hospital, London, England.

Finally—some great news for the 26 million people with chronic kidney disease! Because the problem is progressive and incurable, it can seem hopeless, but new research shows that a natural remedy that is safe, effective and costs just a few pennies a day can dramatically slow down kidney decline. What is it? Baking soda, believe it or not—or, if you want to be technical, *sodium bicarbonate.*

Though it may well be the most medically important, this is hardly the first unconventional health-related use for this simple and inexpensive kitchen ingredient—some swear by it as a remedy for acid indigestion, while others use baking soda to brush their teeth or in lieu of antiperspirant or to soothe rashes and skin eruptions. For people with *chronic kidney disease* (CKD), however, it is important

235

to take this only under your doctor's close supervision—read on to learn why.

RATE OF DECLINE
SLOWED BY TWO-THIRDS

CKD affects one in nine adults. It runs the gamut from poor function and minor discomfort to end-stage renal disease that requires dialysis (getting hooked up to a machine to filter blood when your kidneys can no longer do so). The body naturally creates bicarbonate to help maintain the correct acid-alkaline balance (or pH), and insufficient levels can cause problems ranging from minor all the way to death. A low bicarbonate level (the condition is called *metabolic acidosis*) affects 30% to 50% of advanced CKD patients, and doctors have long speculated that baking soda might help boost kidney function by bringing up the level.

In a study of 134 people with advanced CKD and low bicarbonate levels, Magdi Yaqoob, MD, a professor of renal medicine at The Royal London Hospital in England and his colleagues put this theory to the test. They gave half the participants a small daily dose of sodium bicarbonate in tablet form at mealtime while also continuing their regular medical care.

Over a two-year period, investigators discovered that people who took the sodium bicarbonate experienced...

• **A two-thirds drop in kidney decline.** They lost kidney function at the rate of just 1% per year, compared with 3% in those who didn't take sodium bicarbonate. Though these percentages sound tiny, they are quite significant for people losing kidney function.

• **A dramatic decrease in the need for dialysis.** Only 6.5% in the bicarbonate group required dialysis, compared with 33% in the untreated group.

• **Better nutrient absorption.** Nutritional parameters, including the ability to metabolize protein effectively, improved in those who took bicarbonate tablets. While sodium levels rose, blood pressure did not.

Sodium bicarbonate seems to help people with CKD by suppressing production of ammonia and *endothelin* (proteins that constrict blood vessels and raise blood pressure), which in turn discourages scarring and dysfunction in the kidneys, Dr. Yaqoob explains. These findings were published in the *Journal of the American Society of Nephrology* (JASN). They require further validation in a larger, multi-center study but are very significant and encouraging, Dr. Yaqoob said.

ASK YOUR DOCTOR

If you have CKD, Dr. Yaqoob recommends asking your doctor about incorporating sodium bicarbonate into your medical care—but stresses this should not be attempted on your own. Though easily available and very helpful for particular people, sodium bicarbonate is not an innocuous substance. Dosage must be carefully calibrated to keep blood levels within normal limits. Excess can lead to milk alkali syndrome (calcium deposits in kidneys and other tissue), especially for kidney patients—but also in otherwise healthy people who consume excessive amounts.

That said, sodium bicarbonate may be a simple and inexpensive treatment to add to our medical arsenal against CKD. Talk to your doctor about it.

REPORT #226
Mother Nature's Cures For Outdoor Injuries

Mark Blumenthal, founder and executive director, American Botanical Council, Austin, Texas.

Ahh, summer—the delicious season when you can spend many pleasurable hours out of doors...and get bug bites, sunburn, blisters, rashes and, if you love picnics, maybe even food poisoning! Fortunately, for every minor hazard that nature brings, Mother Nature also provides safe, natural treatments that soothe and heal. You can put together an herbal arsenal that will serve you throughout the warm months. To find out what substances we should all have on hand, we called Mark Blumenthal, founder and executive director of the American Botanical Council in Austin, Texas. *His natural first-aid kit...*

OLBAS OIL

Blumenthal's first pick happens to be a product I use all the time—Swiss-made Olbas Oil, an extract of the essential oils of six medicinal herbs (among them eucalyptus, peppermint and wintergreen plus menthol). It is immensely popular in Europe and useful for so many things that Blumenthal, who always carries it with him when he travels and in his backpack for outdoor activities, jokingly refers to it as "20-in-one oil." Olbas Oil squelches a mosquito bite itch in three to five minutes and reduces the pain and swelling of bee stings almost as fast. When applied to a bruise, it minimizes both its size and discoloration (especially if applied soon after the bruising injury), and it soothes and helps heal blisters. Olbas can be delightful as a massage oil (added to a more neutral oil, such as almond oil) to limber up muscles before sports and afterward to relieve stiff and sore muscles. And that's not all...Blumenthal says you can put one drop (but no more) of Olbas into a glass of water and drink to ease an upset stomach...or place a drop or two on a tissue tucked in your pillow case to open stuffy nasal passages for a better sleep. This refreshing remedy is available in many health-food stores and online (*www.olbas.com*).

ACTIVATED CHARCOAL

Though food poisoning can strike at any time of year, there are some particular hazards during the warmer months when we eat so many salads and fresh produce (which has become the most common source of food-borne illness) and when higher temperatures bring on spoilage more quickly. Blumenthal said that a helpful treatment for nausea and minor vomiting from suspected food poisoning is pharmaceutical-grade activated charcoal. It neutralizes the toxins in your system by absorbing them so that they're able to pass through without causing further discomfort. Seek immediate medical attention if symptoms persist for more than several hours, worsen or you have frequent vomiting or diarrhea, or if you experience dizziness, fainting or violent cramping. Activated charcoal is sold in tablet or capsule form at health-food stores—there's also a cherry-flavored liquid version that can be a wise medicine cabinet staple for homes with small children. Follow dosing directions on the manufacturer's label.

GINGER CAPSULES

For milder stomach symptoms, try ginger capsules. These may be especially helpful for quelling nausea from motion sickness—whether from riding in a car, on a boat or even on a roller coaster. To keep nausea at bay, take two ginger capsules (500 mg each) 30 minutes before you start your journey, and they might even help if motion sickness has already started. Unlike with the drugs *dimenhydrinate* (Dramamine) or *meclizine hydrochloride* (Bonine, Antivert), which are antihistamines and induce sleepiness, you will remain alert with ginger.

WITCH HAZEL

Poison ivy, a common summer problem, has been the subject of considerable research to establish which botanicals might successfully treat its itch, pain and blisters. One remedy from way back when is worth a try—witch hazel, a clear liquid made from the flowering tree of the same name. It can be dabbed on with a cotton pad to help dry and heal the blisters and reduce itch and redness. Blumenthal notes that many American commercial witch hazel preparations contain a small amount of alcohol, which may also help healing.

HIBISCUS TEA

Heat can leave you feeling drained and uncomfortable, and in the tropics, says Blumenthal, people often drink chilled hibiscus tea to help themselves feel better. People have long believed that the tea lowers blood pressure, and modern medicine has verified this with several successful clinical studies, the most recent from Tufts University. Many believe that the tea also reduces body temperature, although Blumenthal says this has not been scientifically substantiated—but given how pleasant it is to enjoy a tall, cold glass of iced hibiscus tea on a hot day, it's certainly worth a try. You can find hibiscus tea in health-food and gourmet stores.

MULLEIN FLOWER OIL

Known for its antimicrobial and anti-inflammatory properties, mullein flower oil is a traditional treatment for swimmer's ear (*otitis externa*), a painful bacterial infection of the outer ear canal, Blumenthal says. Just drip a few drops into each ear and cover with a cotton ball inserted into the outer ear.

Caution: Do not do this if there is any possibility you have a perforated eardrum, symptoms of which include discharge (clear, bloody or pus), ear noise or buzzing, increasing pain or a sudden decrease in pain followed by discharge or hearing loss. In fact, it's best to check with a doctor before you use this oil or any other substance in the ear to determine if it is safe and will be effective for you.

ALOE VERA

Blumenthal recommends one more all-purpose natural remedy—aloe vera, the succulent houseplant that has long been valued for its medicinal properties. You may be surprised at how much scientific evidence backs up its use, in particular for soothing and healing skin problems such as sunburn and minor kitchen burns. While the gel inside the leaves of the aloe plant (just cut one across the middle and squeeze) is 95% water, it contains trace amounts of vitamins (A, C, E and B), enzymes and minerals. These make aloe a moisturizer, an anti-inflammatory, an antimicrobial and an analgesic (pain killer) to boot. That's a lot of bang for your buck—and speaking of that, you don't need to purchase any of the many drugstore products that contain aloe vera unless you'll be traveling. Keep a plant in a sunny spot in your house (plant in sandy, well-drained soil and water only when very dry) and pick the mature leaves on the bottom of the plant for instant first-aid gel.

Generally speaking, these natural soothers are safe for almost everyone—but, as always, it is smart to check with your doctor before adding these and other remedies, natural and otherwise, to your personal first-aid kit. This precaution is even more important for people with any type of chronic medical condition.

REPORT #227
Healing Spices: Surprising New Discoveries

David Winston, RH, Washington, New Jersey–based registered herbalist and professional member of the American Herbalist Guild. He is author of several books, including *Adaptogens: Herbs for Strength, Stamina and Stress Relief* (Healing Arts).

Researchers have now identified new health benefits for several popular spices. You may recognize the names of these spices, but the latest studies suggest uses that are not widely known. *Intriguing research…*

CAYENNE PEPPER

• **Cholesterol.** Artery-clogging fatty build-ups are created or worsened when cholesterol oxidizes, a biochemical process similar to metal rusting. Cayenne pepper (also known as chili pepper) contains a plaque-fighting antioxidant (capsaicin), which is also available in supplement form.

Recent research: When researchers asked 27 people to eat a diet that included cayenne-spiced chili or the same diet with no chili for one month, the spicy-chili group had much lower harmful cholesterol than those who did not eat chili. In addition to protecting cholesterol from oxidation, cayenne pepper also stimulates digestion and improves circulation—an important benefit for people with chronically cold hands and feet.

Recommendation: Use a cayenne-based hot sauce, to taste. Add it to a variety of foods, including chicken dishes and sandwiches.

Caution: In some people, cayenne causes digestive problems. If you experience stomach upset or anal irritation, use a milder hot sauce, cut back the amount or stop using it.

SAGE

• **Alzheimer's disease.** Herbalists and many doctors report that sage may help patients with mild to moderate Alzheimer's disease.

Recent research: Neurons of lab animals exposed to *amyloid beta* (the main constituent of harmful plaques in Alzheimer's) and sage leaves or *rosmarinic acid* (an active ingredient in sage) were less damaged than when the cells were exposed to amyloid beta alone. However, you cannot achieve this potential health benefit from the amount of sage used in cooking.

Recommendation: Drink sage tea.

What to do: Pour eight ounces of boiling water over a tea strainer or tea ball that contains one-half teaspoon of ground sage. Let sit for 15 to 20 minutes. Drink four ounces twice a day. (Refrigerate any unused portion and gently reheat before drinking.)

Alternative: Use sage tea bags. Or add 20 to 30 drops of sage tincture to one ounce of water—drink this amount three times daily.

ROSEMARY

• **Cancer.** Laboratory studies of human cells show that rosemary may help prevent certain types of cancer.

Recent research: The rate at which human leukemia and breast cancer cells multiplied in a laboratory study was reduced when researchers exposed the cells to rosemary extract. More research is needed to confirm these benefits in human study subjects, but rosemary extract is safe to use in the meantime. Cooking with rosemary does not provide this potential health benefit.

Recommendation: Drink rosemary tea.

What to do: Pour 12 ounces of boiling water over a tea strainer or tea ball that contains one-half teaspoon of rosemary. Let sit for 15 to 20 minutes. Drink four ounces, three times a day. (Refrigerate unused tea.)

Alternative: Use rosemary tea bags. Or add 40 to 60 drops of rosemary tincture to one ounce of water—drink this amount three times daily.

HOW TO USE SPICES

The active ingredients in spices can eventually deteriorate after processing. For example, the levels of antioxidants, known as carotenoids, in paprika drop by 75% after three months of storage.

Recommendation: Buy no more than a one-year supply of any spice you plan to use—and replace it annually. Keep your spices away from light, moisture and heat—for example, not near the oven. Consider buying whole rather than powdered spices, and grind them right before using, with a mortar and pestle or spice grinder. To tell whether a spice is rich in health-promoting compounds, smell and/or taste it—the richer the odor and flavor, the better the spice.

REPORT #228
My Favorite Natural Treatments for Itching

Jamison Starbuck, ND, naturopathic physician in family practice and a lecturer at the University of Montana, both in Missoula, Montana. She is past president of the American Association of Naturopathic Physicians and a contributing editor to *The Alternative Advisor: The Complete Guide to Natural Therapies and Alternative Treatments* (Time-Life).

The causes of itching are so varied that there is at least one associated with nearly every letter of the alphabet—starting with allergies, bug bites, contact dermatitis (from such things as soap or chlorine), drug reactions (antibiotics and painkillers are common culprits), eczema, fungus, gallbladder disease and hives. Exposure to poison ivy, oak or sumac is another common cause. Unfortunately, the instinctive desire to scratch an itch can exacerbate the underlying problem. Many people scratch their skin raw in an effort to get relief. *Natural medicines that gently—yet effectively—treat the most common causes of itching are much better options…*

• **Chamomile tea.** For itching due to insect bites, eczema, hives or poison ivy, oak or sumac, use two tea bags per 12 ounces of water and let it steep for six minutes. Soak sterile gauze or clean cotton cloth in the tea, and apply compresses for 15 minutes to the itchy area several times per day.

*Pregnant or lactating women should consult their physicians before trying herb-based products.

• **Calendula and comfrey salve.** These plants are common ingredients in topical salves that often include vitamins A and E in an olive oil base. This salve works best for dry, scaly rashes that result from contact dermatitis, fungus or eczema. For a moist, itchy rash with oozing clear or yellow fluid (such as that caused by insect bites or poison ivy, oak or sumac), use a tea or tincture preparation of calendula only. Apply the tea in a compress or pour or spray it on the area.

• **Oatmeal.** It is best for itching caused by hives or insect bites.

What to do: Fill a muslin or cotton bag with one cup of raw, rolled oats. Attach the bag to the spout of your bathtub and let the water flow through the bag as you fill a tub with warm (not hot) water. Lie in the oatmeal water for 20 to 30 minutes several times a day until the itch is gone. An oatmeal bath product, such as Aveeno, also can be used. For poison ivy, oak or sumac, use a compress of the oatmeal water.

• *Grindelia ssp* (**gumweed**). This is my favorite remedy for itching caused by poison ivy, oak or sumac. Wash the plant oil from the skin with soap and water, then apply a lotion or tincture of grindelia three times daily for several days.

• **White vinegar.** Itching caused by sunburn, bug bites or yeast responds well to white vinegar. Dilute vinegar with an equal amount of water and test a small area first to make sure the vinegar solution does not sting. Dab it on the skin or apply it with a compress. If tolerated, the diluted vinegar can be applied to itchy areas several times a day.

• **Water.** It's surprising how often simply drinking one-half ounce of water per pound of body weight daily can heal troublesome dry, itchy skin, which can result from inadequate hydration.

If itching is accompanied by a fever or if you notice skin discoloration or red or purple streaking near a bite, or if you have confused your medications, are urinating frequently, are having shortness of breath or are in significant pain, see your doctor. These could be signs of an infection, a reaction to medication or a medication overdose

REPORT #229
Home Remedy For Insomnia

The Wilen sisters have been using home remedies all their lives, and for the last quarter of a century, they've been researching and writing about them as well.

The Wilens share their remedy for insomnia.

INSOMNIA

Our new best friends are nuts—in this case, walnuts. They're rich in serotonin, the brain chemical that calms anxiety and allows us to turn off the pressures of the day to get a good night's sleep. Eat a palmful (one ounce) of raw walnuts before going to bed. It's important to chew each mouthful thoroughly, until the nut pieces are ground down.

Lydia Wilen and Joan Wilen, folk-remedy experts based in New York City. The sisters are coauthors of many books, including Bottom Line's Healing Remedies: Over 1,000 Astounding Ways to Heal Arthritis, Asthma, High Blood Pressure, Varicose Veins, Warts and More! *(Bottom Line Books).* www.bottomlinesecrets.com.

REPORT #230
Nature's Remedies for Sunburn and Bug Bites

Jamison Starbuck, ND, naturopathic physician in family practice and a lecturer at the University of Montana, both in Missoula, Montana. She is past president of the American Association of Naturopathic Physicians and a contributing editor to The Alternative Advisor: The Complete Guide to Natural Therapies and Alternative Treatments *(Time-Life).*

If you're tired of using the same old products to prevent or treat sunburn, bug bites and other summertime skin problems, there are a number of natural remedies that I've found to be effective in my clinical practice.

My favorite natural remedies for...

• **Sunburn protection.** Beta-carotene is a naturally occurring pigmented compound that helps guard against sunburn—perhaps due to its powerful antioxidant properties. To prevent sunburn, supplement your sunscreen use by loading up on beta-carotene–rich foods. (This nutrient also improves general immunity, so it makes sense to eat these foods year-round.)

Best food sources of beta-carotene: Most orange-colored vegetables and fruits (such as carrots, sweet potatoes, mangos, cantaloupe and apricots)…and green veggies (such as broccoli, spinach and kale). Adults with fair, sun-sensitive skin may also reduce sunburn risk by taking a beta-carotene supplement (50,000 international units daily) June through September in North America.

Note: Some research has suggested that this dose of beta-carotene may be harmful to smokers. If you smoke, consult your doctor before taking beta-carotene. Even though beta-carotene helps protect against sunburn, you still need to wear sunscreen (check a natural-foods grocery store for a chemical-free product). The combination provides even more protection than when either is used alone.

•**Sunburn relief.** If you do get a sunburn, calendula is an herb that may help soothe burned skin, reduce pain and speed healing. Calendula flowers (used to make a soothing tea) and calendula tincture and lotion are readily available wherever botanical medicines are sold. The flowers also can be easily grown in home gardens (most nurseries stock both plant starts and seeds). Use one tablespoon of fresh flowers or two teaspoons of dried flowers per cup of water for tea. Put calendula tea, tincture or lotion directly on sunburned skin three times daily until symptoms improve. You can splash the tea or tincture on your skin or dab it on with cotton balls.

Caution: Do not use calendula if you are allergic to plants in the daisy family.

•**Bee stings.** A homeopathic remedy made from the honeybee, Apis 30C reduces swelling and pain. Take two pellets (under the tongue) twice daily for one to three days.

Caution: Do not take Apis if you are allergic to bees. You can also use calendula tea, tincture or ointment topically for relief.

•**Insect bites.** Homeopathic Lachesis 30C relieves the pain of swollen, tender insect bites, such as those caused by green bottle flies and house flies. The typical dose is two pellets (under the tongue) twice daily for one to three days. Echinacea (a well-known cold and flu preventive) in tincture form can be applied directly on any insect bite, including one caused by a mosquito, to reduce inflammation and soothe irritation. Apply as needed.

Caution: Do not use echinacea if you are allergic to plants in the daisy family.

REPORT #231
Anti-Wrinkle Foods

When dietary data for 4,025 women was analyzed in a recent study, those with high intakes of vitamin C and the essential fatty acid *linoleic acid* had fewer wrinkles than women with lower intakes.

Theory: Vitamin C is an important component in collagen synthesis (which keeps skin supple), and *linoleic acid* promotes normal skin structure.

For younger-looking skin: Eat vitamin C–rich fruits and vegetables, such as oranges and broccoli, and foods high in linoleic acid, such as soybeans and sunflower oil.

Maeve C. Cosgrove, PhD, research scientist, Corporate Research, Unilever Colworth Science Park, Bedford, UK.

REPORT #232
Spice Up Your Health With Everyday Seasonings

Jonny Bowden, certified nutrition specialist, he is author of *The 150 Healthiest Foods on Earth* (Fair Winds) and *The Most Effective Natural Cures in the World* (Fair Winds). His free audio course on 7 Super Foods is available at *www.jonnybowden.com*.

Cinnamon is so good for you it can almost be considered a health food—simple, ordinary, pumpkin-pie flavoring cinnamon, the same stuff they now have in shakers at Starbucks. Its exciting to see the increasing focus of research on the health benefits of everyday spices like this—capsaicin for prostate cancer...turmeric to reduce inflammation...ginger for nausea, to name just a few. A recent *Wall Street Journal* article reported how several plants abundant in China are being studied as a potential source of medicines by drug company Novartis AG. Its no surprise. Herbs and spices, derived from various plants, have a long history of medicinal use in Chinese medicine. So what else is there in the spice rack that we can use to healthify our meals in a delicious way?

Everyday spices are an amazing source of phytochemicals, which are plant compounds with extraordinary healing properties, explained Jonny Bowden, author of *The 150 Healthiest Foods on Earth* (Fair Winds). Many of these spices have been used in traditional medicine for hundreds of years, and Western medicine is just beginning to realize their potential. *Here are a few of Bowden's top picks for powering up your foods...*

CINNAMON

Lets take another look at cinnamon, for example. There are anti-inflammatory compounds in cinnamon that can be helpful in alleviating pain, stiffness and even menstrual discomfort, said Bowden. Additionally, compounds in cinnamon increase the ability of the cells to take in sugar, which is how it effectively lowers blood sugar and reduces the need for higher levels of insulin. A study published in *Diabetes Care* showed that cinnamon lowered not only blood sugar, but also triglycerides, total cholesterol and LDL (bad) cholesterol in people with type 2 diabetes. Though its not always the case with our other plant-based remedies, with cinnamon the inexpensive supermarket variety is basically as good as any of the pricier oils and extracts sold in specialty stores.

GINGER

Then there is ginger, known as the "universal medicine" in Ayurvedic medicine. Ginger can be used to soothe an upset stomach and quell nausea. In fact, in one study on ginger root, it was shown to be as effective as Dramamine in holding seasickness at bay. Ginger also packs plenty of powerful antioxidants, Bowden told me. "And animal studies show that ginger has antimicrobial effects and helps boost the immune system as well."

TURMERIC

Turmeric—the spice Bowden was most enthusiastic about—is a member of the ginger family, and also a heavy hitter in health benefits. "It's as close to a magical substance as you're likely to find in the kitchen cupboard," he told me. He attributes this spice's anti-inflammatory properties to "curcumin," which is also responsible for making Indian food and curry dishes yellow. In India, turmeric is used to treat arthritis precisely because of its ability to lower inflammation, Bowden said, noting that research indicates that curcumin also may have an anti-tumor effect. If you're not an Indian food eater, you can try it in rice dishes or even on eggs. Do not use medicinal amounts of turmeric during pregnancy, though, because it stimulates contraction of the uterus.

OREGANO

Another spice touted for its health properties is oregano, which Bowden tells me "has been shown by research to have 42 times more antioxidant activity than apples and 12 times more than oranges." Oregano contains a powerful cancer-fighting compound called *rosmarinic acid* as well, and its anti-inflammatory properties make it useful in supporting joint function. Oregano is also a source of calcium, magnesium, zinc, iron and potassium.

GARLIC

Of course garlic is not always used as a spice, but it does have a well-deserved reputation for adding flavor and boosting health. One of the oldest medicinal foods we know of, it is recognized even by conservative mainstream medical professionals as being helpful in reducing cholesterol. Bowden cited a study that found garlic reduces triglycerides by up to 17%. It has a small but notably positive effect on blood pressure. "In places where the consumption of garlic is high, theres a decreased risk of stomach and colon cancer," Bowden added.

Some other spices that have health-promoting properties include...

- **Cardamom.** Another member of the ginger family, cardamom is in spiced chai tea and used to flavor Turkish coffee, and is added to baked goods in Scandinavia. It stimulates digestion and flow of bile.

- **Mustard seeds.** These are a source of magnesium and selenium, and can be taken orally to stimulate appetite and circulation, and to help neutralize inflammatory materials in the GI tract.

- **Parsley.** A good source of vitamin K and potassium, and also helpful for detoxification.

- **Rosemary.** Contains lots of antioxidants and anti-inflammatory compounds, plus substances that help prevent the premature breakdown of *acetylcholine*, a neurotransmitter thats vital for memory and healthy brain function.

- **Sage.** Contains rosmarinic acid (like oregano), which is both an antioxidant and an anti-inflammatory, along with *thujone*, which can be protective against salmonella and candida.

- **Thyme.** Helps relieve chest and respiratory problems, including coughs and bronchitis.

MORE THAN A PINCH?

Since many of the research studies on these items used high doses of them, we asked Bowden how much of each is needed to make a difference. The answer varies, he said, but usually more than is typically used for seasoning is required to achieve a notable benefit—though it seems logical that adding a variety of spices, more often and in plentiful amounts, would have a cumulative positive effect. Though some of the dried spices retain their healthful properties, usually fresh herbs are nutritionally superior—not to mention delicious, and fun and easy to grow.

One thing that is especially nice about Bowden's recommendations is the fact that all of these spices are common flavors you can add to all sorts of foods—they're easy to find and don't require a refined palate to enjoy. So go ahead and spice up your menu—your food will taste more interesting and you'll feel better, too.

Volume 22
'Slightly Crazy' Cures

REPORT #233
Chewing Gum Makes You Smarter

We all know to eat a healthy diet, but some brain-boosting foods may very well surprise you...

BRAIN BOOSTERS

• **Chewing gum.** OK, it's not exactly a food, but it's more than just something to keep your mouth occupied. Researchers at Northwestern University found that people who chew gum have increased blood flow to the brain—and a corresponding increase in cognitive performance. People who chew gum also report a reduction in stress, which protects brain cells from stress-related hormones.

Recommended: Chew gum when you are stressed or have challenging mental work to do. Opt for sugarless.

• **Frozen berries.** Raspberries, blueberries and strawberries are among the best sources of brain-protecting antioxidants. Researchers at the USDA Jean Mayer Human Nutrition Research Center on Aging at Tufts University found that animals given blueberries showed virtually no evidence in the brain of the cell-damaging effects of free radicals—and they did better on cognitive tests.

Frozen berries typically contain more antioxidants than fresh berries because they're picked and processed at the peak of ripeness.

Recommended: One-and-a-half cups of frozen or fresh berries at least two to three times a week. Darker berries contain the most antioxidants.

• **Turmeric.** It's one of the most potent anti-inflammatory spices. People who eat turmeric several times a week can have significant drops in C-reactive protein, a substance that

David Grotto, RD, LDN, registered dietitian and founder and president of Nutrition Housecall, LLC, a consulting firm that provides nutrition communications, lecturing and consulting services along with personalized, at-home dietary services, Chicago. He is advisory board chair for the Produce for Kids and PBS Kids health initiatives and author of *101 Optimal Life Foods* (Bantam).

indicates inflammation in the brain and other tissues.

A study that looked at more than 1,000 participants (average age 68.9) found that those who often or occasionally ate turmeric performed better on mental-status evaluations than those who rarely or never ate it.

Recommended: Add at least one-quarter teaspoon of turmeric to recipes several times a week. (Turmeric is one of the spices in curry.)

• **Hazelnuts.** These contain the highest concentration of folate of all the tree nuts (including walnuts, almonds and pecans). Low levels of folate have been associated with poor cognition and depression. Other foods rich in folate include spinach, beans, oranges, avocados and wheat germ.

Recommended: A handful of hazelnuts several times a week.

• **Cilantro.** This herb, also known as coriander and Chinese parsley, has long been used in Iranian folk medicine for stress relief. Stress has been linked to a speeding up of the aging process of the brain. Modern research also has revealed the benefits of cilantro—an animal study demonstrated that cilantro eased stress.

Recommended: One tablespoon of fresh cilantro several times a week. It's often used in salsa and guacamole and to top tacos, chili, stews and soups.

THREE "GOOD" VICES

You may have heard that certain "bad foods," such as coffee, red wine and chocolate, are good for the heart. *They also are good for the brain...*

• **Coffee.** A Finnish study of more than 1,400 participants found that regular coffee drinkers were less likely to develop dementia than those who didn't drink coffee. Those who drank moderate amounts of coffee in midlife (three to five cups daily) had the lowest risk, probably because the antioxidants in coffee inhibit age-related brain damage.

The caffeine in coffee—a five-ounce serving of coffee typically contains 30 milligrams (mg) to 150 mg, depending on how it is prepared—also improves mental abilities. Studies of university students have shown that when students drink coffee before a test, they score higher than when they abstain.

Recommended: One to three cups daily. If coffee gives you the jitters, try green tea, which also is good for the brain but has slightly less caffeine.

• **Red wine.** Red wine contains resveratrol, a polyphenol, that helps prevent inflammation and oxidation of brain tissue. People who drink moderate amounts of red wine have lower risks for stroke and dementia. Laboratory studies indicate that red wine can reduce the accumulation of *beta-amyloid*, the substance found in the brains of Alzheimer's patients. (In a healthy brain, beta-amyloid is broken down and eliminated.) White wine also contains polyphenols but in lower concentrations than reds.

Recommended: Up to two glasses of wine daily for men and one glass daily for women. Moderation is important because too much alcohol has been linked to increased risk for dementia.

Alcohol-free option: Concord grape juice. Some studies suggest that it may be just as healthy as red wine when it comes to improvement in cognitive skills. Aim for one cup a day.

• **Chocolate.** The cocoa flavonols in chocolate inhibit free radicals. Flavonols also relax the linings of blood vessels. This helps reduce high blood pressure, a leading cause of dementia.

One study, conducted at Brigham and Women's Hospital in Boston, found that participants who drank one cup of high-flavonol cocoa daily had, after two weeks, an average increase in brain circulation of about one-third.

Chocolates with a high percentage of cocoa don't necessarily have a high concentration of flavonols—processing techniques can destroy the protective compounds.

Recommended: Look for products that advertise a high flavonol content on the label (60% to 85%). One ounce is enough to get the benefits without unnecessary sugar and calories.

DON'T FORGET FISH

You probably have heard that fish is "brain food," but we couldn't do a brain-boosting article without mentioning it. A study of 3,660 adults age 65 and older found that those who ate omega-3–rich fish three times a week or more were 25% less likely to have silent *infarcts*, blockages in blood vessels that can cause dementia.

REPORT #234
Ancient Healing Secrets From Tibet

Phuntsog Wangmo, TMD, director of the Shang Shung Institute's Traditional Tibetan Medicine Program, Conway, Massachusetts.

I enjoy reading and writing about global medical traditions because they offer different perspectives for understanding health —such as the importance of the seasonal cycle in Ayurvedic Medicine from India or the Traditional Chinese Medicine emphasis on balance. An ancient healing tradition that is not as widely known as those is Tibetan Medicine, which is very "of the moment" with its connection to the five elements—earth, water, fire, wind and space.

To find out more about this ancient form of healing, we called Phuntsog Wangmo, TMD, president of the American Tibetan Medical Association and director of the Shang Shung Institute's Traditional Tibetan Medicine Program in Conway, Massachusetts. She explains that at the core of Tibetan Medicine is the concept that the body, spirit and mind are interconnected and that illness results from an imbalance among them. Also relevant is their interaction with the external environment.

ELEMENTS & HUMORS

The central concept is that there are five elements that exist in the world and our bodies, which directly affect health—earth, water, fire, wind and space. Each corresponds to a body system, for instance, water relates to the body's fluids…fire is expressed in its metabolic functions…wind is involved in all types of circulation…earth corresponds to the stable body parts, including bones and muscle…while space has to do with the body's cavities.

Additionally, there are three systems, called *humors* that control body processes:

- **Wind**—circulation and nervous system impulses. Balance is characterized by mental focus, ease of movement and efficient elimination of impurities. An imbalance can cause symptoms such as anxiety, insomnia and mental instability.
- **Bile**—energy and digestion. In balance, bile brings determination and proper digestion as evidenced by a glowing complexion. Fevers, sharp pain and headaches can indicate an imbalance of bile, which ultimately may lead to anger, aggression and hatred.
- **Phlegm**—or the body's fluids, bring good judgment and a sense of calm. Symptoms of imbalance can include loss of appetite, nausea, depression and laziness.

No single element or humor is more important than another, notes Wangmo, emphasizing that it is the totality of the elements and humors, how they come together and how they are balanced or imbalanced in an individual that is the essence of understanding Tibetan Medicine. Imbalance is usually caused by disruptions, internally and externally.

WHAT HAPPENS AT A VISIT?

The initial visit always begins with an in-depth interview to help the practitioner find what your imbalances and disturbances may be. Usually these are rooted in incorrect diet, unsuitable behavior and/or general unhealthy lifestyle. Next, a Tibetan medical practitioner looks at the interplay between environmental factors, your body and mind, and where illness and mental distress may result. If you have headaches, for example, the practitioner may ask you to describe the nature of your pain…then will ask about a host of possible contributing factors such as time of onset… when, what and how much you ate before it, and also how your body responded to the meal…your mood…and the emotional tenor of the day. Gathering these details helps in understanding and treating the unique "whole" of you, Wangmo explained.

Next comes a simple in-office urinalysis, with the practitioner observing the color, odor and, after vigorously shaking the sample, the sediments and number, size and persistence of bubbles in the urine. He or she then evaluates the 12 organ positions of the pulse. The purpose is to measure pulse strength, speed and quality, all of which helps define and locate the illness. The exam concludes with a check of the color and coating on your tongue and eyes.

TREATING THE ILLS

The first step in treatment is addressing diet and behavior factors. Due to our overscheduled lives, Wangmo says that many Westerners have imbalances in the wind (often resulting in mental imbalance) and fire (leading to lots of digestive issues). To help correct mind issues, she might suggest adding ginger, garlic, leafy greens and pomegranate to the diet, as well as warm, heavier foods such as lamb. For digestive problems, her suggestions would tend toward light foods. She tempers her dietary advice according to the season, the patient's personality and age and where the patient lives —people in cold climates might be advised to use warming spices, for example.

With regard to lifestyle, she observes that our Western tendency to worry and overcommit causes yet more imbalances in, once again, the wind humor. And so in addition to dietary changes, Wangmo teaches relaxation methods—for instance, a variety of breathing techniques. To balance the elements, she guides patients with specific suggestions about breathing such as to picture certain colors while inhaling and others while exhaling. Other techniques include meditations geared to the specific nature of problems, counseling, and working with patients to restructure daily habits, including exercise, sleeping schedules, food selection and timing of meals.

Often the combination of changing diet and lifestyle is sufficient to resolve patients' problems. When it is not, though, practitioners of Tibetan Medicine next turn to some of the huge number of herbs, minerals and animal substances available to them, and again individualize a combination to your needs. They may also add a variety of physical techniques as well—acupuncture, massage, cupping (applying a container with heat inside to create a vacuum effect to draw out harmful fluids) and moxibustion (applying a heated herb to certain points in the body).

HOW TO FIND A TIBETAN MEDICAL PRACTITIONER

At this time there are only a few people practicing Tibetan Medicine in this country—Wangmo estimates around 50. However the Institute that she heads has a four-year medical school and is graduating its first class—of seven mostly American students—in 2009. The only other major schools are in India and Tibet. No licensing yet exists, but the American Tibetan Medical Association (ATMA) is working toward that goal. In the meantime, if you want to consult with a practitioner trained in Tibetan Medicine, visit the Shang Shung Institute

Web site: www.shangshung.org/home/school.html. There are a number of other Web sites that also list practitioners in the US, including that of the ATMA.

Treatment under Tibetan Medicine may be highly individualized, but the practice has a message for everyone. Balancing our bodies, our minds and our spirits with the environment helps to maintain excellent emotional, mental and physical health.

REPORT #235
Chuckle for Cardio

Laughter yoga combines traditional yoga stretches and poses with exercise designed to make people laugh. In terms of cardiovascular benefits, one minute of laughter (about 100 giggles) is the equivalent of six to 10 minutes on a rowing machine. Laughter has aerobic benefits and can help lower blood pressure, lift mood and boost immunity. To find a class near you, call 212-956-5920 or go to *www.laughteryoga.org.*

Alex M. Eingorn, DC, laughter-yoga instructor and director, Better Health Chiropractic, New York City.

REPORT #236
10 Surprising Ways to Stay Healthy and Control Your Weight

Mehmet C. Oz, MD, medical director of the Integrated Medical Center and director of the Cardiovascular Institute at New York–Presbyterian Medical Center and professor and vice chairman of surgery at Columbia University, both in New York City. He is coauthor, with Michael F. Roizen, MD, of *You on a Diet: The Owner's Manual for Waist Management* (Free Press).

Whether you're trying to lose weight or simply find a healthful eating plan you can stick with, you're bound to fail if you try to stay on a diet. Invariably, people on diets end up depriving themselves of certain foods and/or scrupulously counting calories.

Problem: Virtually no one can maintain long-term deprivation because our bodies are programmed to avoid this type of ongoing discomfort. And calorie restriction causes your metabolism to slow down in order to preserve energy, often resulting in more stored fat.

The secret is to work with your body's chemistry rather than against it, so healthful eating becomes automatic, not forced.

Recent development: Body weight used to be considered one of the best indicators of overall health.

Now: Research has shown that your waist measurement (at or just below your navel) may be more reliable. That's because abdominal fat is especially harmful due to its proximity to your vital organs, where it can lead to harmful increases in cholesterol and triglyceride levels. Fat in this area has been linked to heart disease, cancer and diabetes. Studies have found that men should strive for a waist measurement of 35 inches or less, while women should aim for 32½ inches or less. When these measurements are exceeded, health risks increase. For example, risk for metabolic syndrome (a group of conditions, including hypertension and abdominal obesity, that raises diabetes and cardiovascular disease risk) increases by 40% at 40 inches for men and 37 inches for women.

Important: Even if your weight is ideal, you still can benefit from some of the strategies described below because they promote healthy cholesterol and blood pressure levels. *My recommendations…*

1. Spice up your morning eggs. Cayenne and other forms of red pepper contain capsaicin, a substance that suppresses appetite signals, increases metabolism and decreases the desire for food later in the day. In addition, eggs are high in protein, which tends to induce feelings of fullness.

2. Consume fiber early in the day. Fiber increases levels of appetite-suppressing signals in the small intestine. Eating fiber early in the day makes people less hungry in the afternoon—the time when most of us tend to eat snacks and other calorie-dense foods. Consume about 30 g of fiber daily in the form of high-fiber cereals, fruits and vegetables, and 100% whole grains.

3. Eat nuts. The monounsaturated fat in nuts stimulates the production of *cholecystokinin* (CCK), a chemical messenger that slows the rate at which the stomach empties and reduces appetite without putting your body into starvation mode—that is, the point at which it starts conserving calories, rather than burning them. Before lunch and/or dinner, have about six walnuts, 12 almonds or 12 hazelnuts.

4. Drink coffee instead of soft drinks. Coffee (caffeinated and decaffeinated) is a rich source of antioxidants, and Americans consume more of it than any other antioxidant-rich food. Coffee is much lower in calories (if you don't add a lot of sugar and/or creamer) than sugary soft drinks.

Bonus: Caffeine stimulates the release of *norepinephrine*, a hormone that suppresses appetite and promotes calorie burning by increasing heart rate and metabolism. Green tea also is a rich source of antioxidants as well as caffeine.

5. Supplement with *5-hydroxytryptophan* (5-HTP). Related to the amino acid tryptophan and sold as a weight-loss supplement, 5-HTP increases brain levels of serotonin, a neurotransmitter that controls appetite. In one study, people taking 5-HTP for six weeks lost an average of 12 pounds, compared with only four pounds in a control group. Recommended dose: 300 mg daily. Bonus: 5-HTP has mood-enhancing benefits.

6. Turn up the thermostat. One reason that people tend to eat more during the cold months is that cold temperatures stimulate appetite. Also, people with naturally low body temperatures tend to have a slower metabolism and are more prone to weight gain. Staying warm may be a natural form of appetite control, particularly if you increase body temperature with exercise. Every one degree increase in body temperature increases metabolism by 14%.

7. Ask your doctor about Tagamet. The active ingredient (*cimetidine*) in this heartburn drug is thought to activate appetite-suppressing CCK. One 12-week study found that people taking a prescription form of Tagamet (400 mg, three times daily) had about a 5% decrease in waist size.

Important: Tagamet is unlikely to cause significant side effects, but should be taken to aid weight loss only if you have heartburn symptoms.

8. Consider using nicotine. It's common for people who quit smoking to gain weight, probably because the nicotine in tobacco suppresses appetite, increases metabolism and damages taste buds, which makes food less appealing. Studies have shown that nicotine—in the form of patches and gum, not from cigarettes—when combined with small amounts of caffeine, can help some people lose weight.

If you've hit a weight plateau: Talk to your doctor about combining a nicotine patch with two cups of coffee daily. Even for non-smokers, this approach can be used temporarily (to avoid possible addiction risk) to jump-start weight-loss efforts.

9. Smell grapefruit. Grapefruit oil, available from aromatherapy shops, emits an aroma that is thought to affect liver enzymes and help promote weight loss. In preliminary research, animals exposed to grapefruit scent for 15 minutes, three times weekly, had a reduction in appetite and body weight.

10. Control emotional stress. People who live with chronic stress (due to family pressures, a fast-paced job, etc.) produce high levels of *cortisol*, a stress hormone that increases the propensity for the omentum—a structure located near the stomach—to store fat. Excessive fat in the omentum can significantly increase waist size.

Important: Exercise is among the best ways to lower stress—and curb accumulations of omentum fat.

Recommended: A 30-minute walk and five minutes' worth of stretching daily...and three weekly sessions that include basic exercises, such as push-ups, shoulder shrugs, abdominal crunches, etc.

REPORT #237
Surprising Ways to Live Longer

Michael F. Roizen, MD, chair of the division of anesthesiology, critical care medicine and pain management and chairman of the Wellness Institute, both at Cleveland Clinic in Cleveland, Ohio. He is coauthor, with Mehmet C. Oz, MD, of several books, including *You: Staying Young* (Free Press).

Many of the proven strategies for living longer—such as restricting calories and exercising on a regular basis—can feel like punishment for some people. Fortunately, there are many enjoyable ways to stay healthy—but doctors don't recommend these strategies as often as they should. Research has shown that activities nearly everyone enjoys can literally add years to a person's life.

FUN-FILLED WAYS TO LIVE LONGER

1. Enjoy Your Coffee. Many people assume that coffee—unlike green tea, for example—isn't a healthful beverage. But that's not true. Studies have found that caffeinated and decaffeinated coffee are a main source of antioxidants in the average American's diet.

Research has shown that caffeinated coffee decreases the risk for Parkinson's and Alzheimer's diseases by 30% to 40%—health benefits that are largely attributed to the beverage's caffeine. (Decaffeinated coffee does not offer these same benefits.) The caffeine in coffee also is good for cognitive health.

Important: Caffeinated coffee may cause several side effects, such as blood pressure spikes, abnormal heartbeat, anxiety and gastric upset.

My recommendation: If you do not experience any of these side effects, and you enjoy drinking coffee, have as many cups of caffeinated coffee as you like. If you do experience side effects, you may prefer to drink decaffeinated coffee. Even though it does not have the health benefits previously described, studies show that decaffeinated coffee may help fight off type 2 diabetes.

2. Go Dancing. Men and women who get optimal amounts of physical activity—about 30 minutes a day, seven days a week—can make their "RealAges" (the "biological ages" of their bodies, based on lifestyle and behaviors) 6.4 years younger.

Many types of dancing give a superb physical workout. Ballroom and square dancing are particularly good for cognitive health. They involve both physical and mental stimulation (in order to execute the appropriate dance steps) and may help reduce the risk for dementia. Aim to dance at least 30 minutes a day.

REPORT #238
Photos for Pain Relief?

Naomi Eisenberger, PhD, assistant professor of psychology, director of the Social and Affective Neuroscience Laboratory, as well as co-director of the Social Cognitive Neuroscience Laboratory, University of California at Los Angeles.

We all take comfort from the presence of a loved one during tough times—and here is a way to tap into those feelings even if that person isn't able to be physically present. Researchers have found that bringing a picture of a loved one to a medical procedure can help make it less painful—literally.

Naomi Eisenberger, PhD, assistant professor of psychology, director of the Social and Affective Neuroscience Laboratory, at University of California, Los Angeles, led a team exploring how social support can help people cope with physical pain. Twenty-five female undergraduate students were recruited to participate in a study that they were told would "explore how people respond to comforting and uncomfortable stimuli." The study required participants to bring a loved one to the one-hour session.

To produce the "uncomfortable stimuli," researchers placed a probe onto each participant's forearm. It could be heated to a temperature high enough to cause pain but not high enough to create a burn. As the probe heated up, each subject was asked to rate the level of pain on a scale of 0 to 20. There were six different scenarios tested for each participant: holding the hand of her loved one...holding a stranger's hand...holding a "stress ball" to squeeze to release tension...gazing at a computer screen on which was displayed a photo of the loved one...a photo of a stranger...or a photo of a chair.

Predictably enough, participants felt less pain while holding the hands of their loved ones compared with when they held either a stranger's hand or the stress ball. But it also turned out that simply looking at a loved one's photo greatly reduced pain—in fact, more effectively even than holding the loved one's hand.

So this is easy advice you can put to use right away—carry a photo of your partner, family or a friend (or all of them!) with you to look at when something hurts. You can do this for others, too—if you can't be with someone you love who is sick or having a medical procedure, send a photo and explain why you think it will help—chances are, it will.

REPORT #239
Intestinal Worms May Help Your Health

Joel V. Weinstock, MD, professor, immunology, Tufts University School of Medicine, and chief, division of Gastroenterology/Hepatology at Tufts New England Medical Center, Boston, Massachusetts.

Are we too clean for our health? That's the theory behind a surprising (and growing) area of research. Doctors and scientists are exploring the use of *helminths*—more typically known as parasitic intestinal worms—to treat a range of ailments, from inflammatory bowel diseases like Crohn's disease and ulcerative colitis to severe seasonal allergies and asthma to neurological disorders, including multiple sclerosis and even autism.

The thinking is this: Throughout history and in the normal course of our lives, humans have had lots of contact with creepy critters like helminths—in fact, to the point that some helminths are exclusive to humans, meaning that they grow and reproduce only in our systems. However, we've gotten much cleaner these days—with our indoor plumbing, antimicrobial cleansers, frequent laundering and bathing and, in many areas, less exposure to farm animals. This means we now share our homes (and bodies) with far fewer of these tiny, unseen creatures. Meanwhile the same time line has brought an increase in the incidence of inflammatory bowel diseases, asthma, seasonal allergies and the like—problems related to an overreactive immune system. Interestingly, these diseases are still uncommon in countries that don't have hygiene standards similar to ours.

THE HIDDEN CONNECTION

Could there be a connection? Scientists are exploring the possibility that helminths play a role in the healthy human immune system—and it appears that there may be some merit to this odd (and frankly unpalatable) theory.

We asked Joel Weinstock, MD, a professor of immunology at Tufts University School of Medicine in Boston and a leading expert on this topic, to tell us about the latest research. He told us that we should all be aware that there are two major functions of the immune system, noting that most people are familiar with just one—the "fight and kill" response. "But what would happen if you got an infection in your arm and your immune system didn't know when to turn off? That generally doesn't happen because the immune system's regulatory aspect kicks in," he explained. According to Dr. Weinstock, this self-regulating aspect is what gets out of whack in people with conditions like inflammatory bowel disease, in which the mucosal immune system perceives organisms in the gut as much more dangerous than they are—and then attacks them. This same premise also applies to other immune system-related problems, such as asthma, allergies and the like.

Where do the worms come in? Helminths can help regulate an overreactive immune system, Dr. Weinstock explained. Some of his group's early research appears to support this theory, at least in the case of inflammatory bowel diseases: A randomized controlled trial using *Trichuris suis* (pig whipworm) therapy for ulcerative colitis found an improvement in symptoms in 43.3% of those receiving the whipworm treatment, as opposed to 16.7% given the placebo. A similar study for the treatment of Crohn's disease showed similar results. In fact, Dr. Weinstock told us that those studies showed so much promise that helminth therapy is now being studied for other conditions—including a clinical trial that's going to explore using helminths in patients with multiple sclerosis. (Meanwhile, another recently completed trial found that whipworm was ineffective as a treatment for pollen-induced allergic rhinitis, so don't be surmising that this particular organism works for everything!)

WHAT'S NOT SO GREAT

Apart from the "ick factor," there are valid concerns about the growing interest in helminth therapy—most particularly that some unscrupulous human opportunists are worming their way onto the market to peddle parasites that could, in fact, turn out to be quite dangerous. Though he is optimistic about the potential of helminth therapy, Dr. Weinstock points out that an FDA-approved helminth-based treatment is still years away at best... but, because these parasites occur naturally in the wild, some enterprising individuals are already selling them to the public. This could bring more harm to patients who are already vulnerable and suffering, not to mention to the reputation of this promising therapy.

"These products are not monitored or approved by the FDA," Dr. Weinstock says. Many parasites look enough like each other that only a scientist can distinguish among different strains and species, so there is no way for a consumer looking at a Web site hawking parasites to know what is actually delivered. "It could be salt or sugar—or worse, you could end up with a treatment that is worse than the disease—because some parasites (unlike pig whipworm, which is relatively harmless) can be very harmful," he points out. With no oversight and no certification or standards, there is no way to know that what you're buying is safe, let alone effective against a particular complaint.

If you are a person who does happen to have inflammatory bowel disease or another of the immune-related diseases for which this therapy might be helpful, is there any safe, reliable way to try parasite therapy? *Dr. Weinstock offered these important cautions...*

•**Don't go it alone.** "This applies to any alternative approach," he says. "You want to have an expert in the disease work with you to make sure that you don't do any harm." This is a situation where it is a good idea to enlist a physician who specializes in your disease and can help guide the therapy.

Try established, proven therapies first. Before trying helminths, make sure that you and your physician have considered all the conventional therapies, since these less controversial treatments have been proven beneficial for many and are far more straightforward, at least at this point in time.

•**Look for clinical trials.** If you are interested in going forward, the best place to find opportunities to do so safely is to explore clinical trials and studies, most of which are announced through the nonprofit societies that support disease research, such as the National Multiple Sclerosis Society. You can also find them at *www.clinicaltrials.gov*. Another resource for information and research is the site of the manufacturer of the whipworm used in the earlier studies, *www.ovamed.org*.

This ancient "medicine" may someday become conventional again, but it's not to be undertaken casually—stick with resources you know to be clean and safe, "above ground" in every sense of the term.

REPORT #240
3-Second Energy Boost

Patt Lind-Kyle, MA, PhD, psychotherapist and executive coach based in Nevada City, California, and author of *Heal Your Mind, Rewire Your Brain* (Energy Psychology Press).

Yawning is something we mostly stifle—after all, it's embarrassing to yawn in the face of another as if to announce that you didn't get enough sleep or, worse, that you're bored. That's a shame—because researchers have discovered that the humble yawn is a major contributor to mental alertness...keeps our brains properly cooled (literally)...and helps us to shift from one activity to another, even to adjust from one time zone to another. They recommend using yawning consciously as a tool to make life better. For example, yawn soon after awakening to rev up your brain for the day or at night to help calm yourself and promote sleep.

THE SCIENCE OF THE YAWN

Most people believe that we yawn to bring oxygen from the air into the body, but that's wrong, says psychotherapist Patt Lind-Kyle, MA, the author of *Heal Your Mind, Rewire Your Brain*. She calls yawning an "exercise for the brain" based on the growing number of studies that have found that it facilitates mental efficiency. Yawning does its magic by literally forcing extra blood directly to the brain. When you yawn, your facial muscles broadly contract and then relax, and this action pushes oxygen-rich blood into the brain's prefrontal cortex, the location of the "executive function" that covers planning, organization, decision-making, personality expression and many other crucial activities.

The yawn also sends blood to stimulate an area called the *precuneus*, which is involved in consciousness along with memory and motor coordination. As far as serving to cool the brain, a study at State University of New York-Albany found that performing difficult mental tasks, such as processing lots of information, actually increases brain temperature. Though we're all familiar with the way ongoing mental labor can trigger yawning, it's not because it is tiring. Again, the yawn sends blood to the brain to curtail its rising temperature, which is how it helps to maintain mental efficiency. Interestingly, both yawning and body thermo-regulation seem to be controlled by the same area of the brain, the hypothalamus.

PUTTING YOUR YAWNS TO WORK

Okay, so now we know that yawning can increase our efficiency in a number of areas... how can we take better advantage of this? Just decide to yawn and then do it—and I mean do a real face-stretcher! *I'll tell you how in a moment, but first here are some situations in which Lind-Kyle suggests adding a yawn...*

• **To stimulate better thinking.** When you are preparing for an exam, a presentation or an important conversation, you can enhance your performance by yawning several times first. During an exam, don't be shy about yawning when you find yourself losing focus or starting to stumble in your thoughts—it will help.

• **To reduce jet lag and reset energy levels.** At 20 weeks gestation, fetuses start to develop a wake/sleep pattern and as part of the process, they yawn...a lot. Lind-Kyle says that we can consciously use yawning to help reset our wake/sleep patterns, including when suffering jet lag. To start, yawn five times or so as soon as you get off the airplane. When you've experienced how well this refreshes you, Lind-Kyle says you may soon begin to do it intuitively—you'll find yourself yawning whenever you feel yourself starting to drag. She says that yawn-ing can be used in this manner to help you acclimate to high altitudes and to reset your energy level as you switch from one activity to another, such as from sleep to wakefulness.

• **To improve your mood...and, possibly even your relationships.** Yawning is associated with increased levels of *dopamine*, the neurotransmitter released from the hypothalamus that is associated with pleasure, motivation and sociability. Lind-Kyle says that when two people yawn together, it can help diminish tension in the relationship...and fortunately, yawning is highly contagious, so it's easy for both of you to get in on the act. If nothing else, a shared yawning session should make for a few ice-breaking laughs.

• **For relaxation.** Curiously, although yawning serves to stimulate the brain, a deep yawn and wide stretch also relax the body. Lind-Kyle, who leads meditation classes, always starts with a healthy yawn, which she says gets people relaxed quickly. She said that bringing on a few deep yawns at bedtime may help you get to sleep.

HOW TO BRING ON A YAWN

We think of yawns as automatic, but it's surprisingly easy to make yourself yawn...

• **Focus thoughts on yawning.** Yawns are not only contagious from person to person—even thinking about a yawn can help trigger one, says Lind-Kyle. Close your eyes and picture a yawn, or say the word "yawn" repeatedly to encourage one.

• **Fake a yawn...** or two...or three until a real one sets in. Lind-Kyle says she generally gets a real yawn after one or two fakes, but however long it takes, stick with it—it will happen.

• **Consciously slow your breathing.** The decreased oxygen may help trigger a yawn—flaring your nostrils as you breathe in may make this happen faster.

And finally, the best yawn is one you fully experience, Lind-Kyle says. So go all the way—open your mouth wide, scrunch your face fully, and take a deep, full breath. Just be ready to explain yourself if you're in company!

Volume 23

Common and Dangerous Medical Errors

REPORT #241
Preventing Medical Errors

Misdiagnoses...prescription mistakes...hospital-acquired infections...and botched surgeries are among the most common causes of preventable deaths due to medical errors.

What can you do to protect yourself? To find out, we spoke with Peter J. Pronovost, MD, PhD, a patient-safety researcher at Johns Hopkins University.

Dr. Pronovost's commitment to patient safety began more than 20 years ago when his father was mistakenly diagnosed, at age 50, with leukemia instead of lymphoma—an error that prevented him from receiving potentially lifesaving treatment. Determined to make medicine safer, Dr. Pronovost has been involved in various patient-safety initiatives.

His biggest breakthrough: A checklist to eliminate deadly hospital-acquired infections. The checklist reminds health-care providers

of five simple steps proven to reduce infection due to a central line catheter (placed in a vein in the neck, groin or chest to administer medication or fluids). In Michigan, where the checklist has been adopted, catheter-caused bloodstream infections have dropped by 66%. The checklist is being adopted in all 50 states and 3 countries.

For his efforts, Dr. Pronovost was recently awarded a prestigious MacArthur Foundation Fellowship "Genius Grant."

Your father's misdiagnosis was tragic. How common are diagnostic errors? Misdiagnosis is an enormous problem. Most of the evidence we have comes from autopsies, which show that up to 40% to 50% of the time the diagnosis

Peter J. Pronovost, MD, PhD, professor in the departments of anesthesiology and critical care medicine and surgery at Johns Hopkins University School of Medicine and medical director for the Center for Innovation in Quality Patient Care, which promotes patient safety at the Johns Hopkins Hospital, both in Baltimore. In 2003, he founded the Quality & Safety Research Group at Johns Hopkins University to advance the science and safety of health-care delivery (*www.safetyresearch. jhu.edu/index.htm*).

was wrong. It could be that misdiagnoses are disproportionately high among patients who are autopsied. We just don't know, because we still don't have a good way of measuring misdiagnoses in patients before it's too late.

What can patients do to help ensure a correct diagnosis? Take the time to articulate not only your symptoms, but also your perception of what may be wrong. Patients have wisdom. You're living with the disease. When you are diagnosed, ask your doctor: "How confident are you in this diagnosis?" If there's any uncertainty—and especially if there are treatments with varying degrees of risk—get a second opinion. If your doctor's prescribed treatment is not working, ask him/her to re-evaluate the therapy.

Your checklist to prevent catheter infections is said to be saving more lives than perhaps any laboratory advance of the last decade. What explains the checklist's huge impact? The information—from the Centers for Disease Control and Prevention (CDC)—was out there, but it was inefficiently packaged. No one is going to use 200 pages of guidelines. We simplified it into the five most important actions that health-care providers can take to prevent infections.

If we create similar checklists for diagnosing common medical conditions, it's going to make it easier for patients to communicate with their doctors so that they always get the care they're supposed to.

Is there evidence that patients aren't always getting the care they should be receiving? A large study published in *The New England Journal of Medicine* showed that, on average, for a wide variety of conditions at most hospitals in this country, patients get only half of the available interventions or therapies that might benefit them.

What can patients do about it? If you know your diagnosis, you can look up evidence-based clinical practice guidelines through the National Guideline Clearinghouse (*www. guideline.gov*), sponsored by the US Department of Health and Human Services' Agency for Healthcare Research and Quality. I also hope to have checklists for many common

diseases and conditions available to the public within a few years.

What can patients do in an emergency to make sure they are offered the best medicine? ***Help the doctor create his own checklist by asking:*** "What are the three most important things you can do to help me, and are you doing them?" If you are too ill to ask, a family member should do so. It will force the doctor to prioritize.

What other questions should patients ask? When your doctor recommends a therapy, ask about the risks, benefits and alternatives so you can make an informed decision based on your values. For example, if you're taking a blood thinner and need any type of operation, the blood thinner should be stopped prior to the surgery to prevent excessive bleeding. However, discontinuing this medication raises your risk for a blood clot that could lead to a stroke. (Certain patients, such as those with a history of blood clots or a stent—a wire mesh tube used to prop open an artery—should ask their doctors whether their blood thinner should not be stopped.)

In deciding when to resume the blood thinner, we're trading off your risk for stroke against your risk for bleeding. Most of the time, we don't even mention those risks, but you need to know what they are because you may weigh them differently than your physician.

Are there other factors that can affect patient safety? Staffing—especially in the intensive care unit (ICU)—is crucial. Studies show that your risk of dying is 30% higher in the ICU if you don't have an intensive care physician (who has received specialized training in treating ICU patients) looking after you. Even so, 80% of ICU patients do not have intensive care specialists.

My advice: If you or a loved one is in an ICU for more than a day without an intensive care specialist, transfer to a hospital that will provide one.

INFECTION-FIGHTING CHECKLIST

Before a patient receives a central line catheter (to administer fluids or medication), health-care providers should…

•**Assess whether the catheter is necessary.** If yes…

- **Wash their hands with soap.**
- **Clean the patient's skin with** *chlorhexidine* **(an antiseptic).**
- **Place sterile drapes over the entire patient and wear a sterile mask, hat, gown and gloves.**
- **Avoid the femoral (thigh area) site (because of higher infection risk).**

REPORT #242
Are You Getting Too Much Medical Care?

Dennis Gottfried, MD, Torrington, Connecticut–based general internist and associate professor of medicine at the University of Connecticut School of Medicine in Farmington. He is the author of *Too Much Medicine: A Doctor's Prescription for Better and More Affordable Health Care* (Paragon House).

With all the high-tech—and expensive—medical care available in the US, you may assume that Americans are among the healthiest people in the world. But that's not true.

Troubling fact: The US spends more than any other country (about 17% of its gross domestic product) on health care but ranks 12th (among 13 industrialized nations) in measures of overall health, such as life expectancy.

For an insider's perspective on what's wrong with our medical system—and advice on how we can protect ourselves—we spoke with Dennis Gottfried, MD, who has extensively researched this subject and worked as a general practice physician for more than 25 years.

Why is the US health-care system in such bad shape? Medical practices and hospitals are designed to care for patients, but they're also businesses. Doctors are reimbursed by insurers for such services as medical procedures and surgeries that the doctors themselves recommend and order. As a result, many doctors order too many tests, perform too many procedures and prescribe too many medications. Some doctors also provide excessive medical care to protect themselves against malpractice lawsuits. Much of this is not in the best interests of the patient.

What role do patients play? Often, patients go to their doctors asking for specific treatments they've heard about from friends, read about on the Internet or seen in a drug company or advocacy group ad on TV or in a magazine. Doctors want happy customers, so after a while it's easier to acquiesce than to argue. Americans are conditioned to believe that more is better, but that's not always the case. Sometimes it's worse.

How so? All medical procedures and even some tests carry risks for side effects or complications. For example, angioplasty, which uses a catheter and balloon to open a narrowed artery—and is sometimes followed by the placement of a stent (a tube to keep it open)—carries risks for heart attack, blood clots, kidney problems or stroke.

Similarly, some degree of brain damage (loss of cognitive functions, such as memory or judgment, that can last up to 12 months) can occur with coronary bypass surgery.

Yet many of these patients' symptoms, especially those with stable angina (chest pain), could have been treated with medication that has far less risk for side effects. In many cases, patients do not really need the stent and they really don't need the surgery.

Then why were these procedures performed? To a large degree, doctors create their own demand. For example, Miami has a lot more cardiologists than the Minneapolis area. And recent research found that annual Medicare spending on health care for Miami seniors was nearly two-and-a-half times higher than it was for statistically matched older adults in Minneapolis. The Miami health-care costs included six-and-a-half times more visits to specialists, compared with Minneapolis health-care expenditures.

Do doctors create their own demand in other areas of medicine? In general, more specialists mean more expensive health care—and poorer health.

We need specialists to have a good health-care system. But based on several studies, including research by investigators at Dartmouth Medical School, regions in the US that have a greater proportion of primary care physicians (such as family physicians and general internists) than specialists provide better care at lower costs.

However, in the US, medical students want to be specialists because they make more money and usually can arrange less demanding schedules than generalists. And there's more prestige—brain surgeons are referred to often for their intellectual abilities, but you never hear that about pediatricians, for example.

But don't specialists provide better care when treating serious conditions? Not necessarily. Studies by Dartmouth Medical School researchers and others show that as you increase the number of specialists, health care improves—up to a point. Increasing the availability of primary care doctors is associated with lower costs and better health-care quality.

This occurs perhaps because the extra procedures specialists perform increase the odds that something will go wrong. Primary care doctors more often follow a "watchful waiting" philosophy. They put more emphasis on preventive medicine and may know the patient well enough to recognize when stress or other medical conditions are worsening symptoms.

Should we avoid consulting specialists? Certainly not. Just don't see them unless you have to. Go to your primary care doctor first and rely on his/her judgment as to whether specialist care is needed.

When you do go to a specialist, choose a busy one. Because they typically have enough medically indicated work to do, they are less likely to recommend marginal or unnecessary procedures.

And whenever any doctor—generalist or specialist—recommends a procedure, don't be shy about asking, "Is it really necessary?"

This query is particularly important when elective procedures that may carry risks, such as most orthopedic surgery or elective cardiac surgery, are recommended. If you're not convinced, get another opinion.

Does the same advice apply to medication? Yes. Medication can be effective and even life-saving. For example, drugs for elevated cholesterol and high blood pressure have played a substantial role in preventing heart disease and stroke. If you need them, take them.

But just make sure you really need them. In general, weight loss, salt reduction and exercise should be given a chance before using drugs to reduce blood pressure. Type 2 diabetes is often treatable with diet and exercise alone, but doctors frequently skip this step.

Even if you take medication for a chronic illness, such as high blood pressure, heart disease or diabetes, you need to maintain a healthy lifestyle. Patients have responsibility for their own health. However, when doctors prescribe a medication, they don't always choose wisely among available drugs.

What do you mean? Because drug companies market new drugs heavily to patients and doctors, many physicians opt for these expensive medications when older, cheaper generic alternatives would do just as well—if not better.

Only 10% of new drugs are really new—the rest are molecular variations on existing ones, which are more profitable for the manufacturers but no more effective.

One of my patients with *gastroesophageal reflux disease* (GERD) recently came in and asked for "the little purple pill" she saw advertised on TV. I explained that the generic heartburn drug I had prescribed was nearly identical, but she insisted. She was sufficiently impressed by the flashy graphics on the TV ad to pay substantially—out of pocket—for the medication.

Shouldn't patients have access to newer drugs if that's what they want? Yes, but they need to understand that when a drug is approved, it has generally been tested on several thousand people. Serious problems often aren't discovered until it's been prescribed hundreds of thousands of times.

That's why the cholesterol drug *cerivastatin* (Baycol)…the diabetes medication *troglitazone* (Rezulin)…and the heartburn drug *cisapride* (Propulsid) are no longer available. Serious—sometimes deadly—side effects were discovered after the medications had been on the market for a while. Such side effects are unlikely with drugs that have been around for several years.

Cheaper drugs are sometimes more effective, too. Several large studies have shown that diuretics ("water pills")—among the oldest and cheapest drugs for high blood pressure—reduce heart failure and stroke more effectively than newer compounds.

If you have high blood pressure and your doctor isn't prescribing a diuretic, ask why. If you need two or more drugs (about 70% of the time, that's necessary), a diuretic usually should be one of them.

REPORT #243
Medical Emergency? Calling 911 May Not Be Wise

Charles B. Inlander, consumer advocate and health-care consultant based in Fogelsville, Pennsylvania. He was the founding president of the nonprofit People's Medical Society, a consumer advocacy organization credited with key improvements in the quality of US health care in the 1980s and 1990s, and is author of 20 books, including *Take This Book to the Hospital with You: A Consumer Guide to Surviving Your Hospital Stay* (St. Martin's).

When faced with a medical emergency, our first instinct is to dial 911. But calling 911 may not be your only—or even your best—choice. The 911 emergency response program began in the US about 40 years ago. Most people assume that if they call 911 in response to a medical emergency, an ambulance and medical personnel will arrive in a matter of minutes. That's not necessarily true. Operators at 911 call centers are trained to assess the situation by asking the caller about the person in need, his/her symptoms, whether he is conscious, the nature of the injury and any other pertinent information that is necessary to provide the appropriate response. In some cases, such as a bad sprain or a nonlife-threatening broken bone, the 911 operator may suggest that the caller take the person to a hospital emergency room. In other instances, such as a possible heart attack, a stroke, a severe in-jury from a fall or a sudden severe fever in a child (above 104° F), the operator will almost always dispatch an ambulance.

Most emergency medical services units consist of an ambulance with two or more emergency medical technicians (EMTs) and, in some cases, a paramedic. EMTs receive 150 to 250 hours of training from programs typically conducted at community colleges. Paramedics get 1,000 to 1,300 hours of training, usually culminating in a two-year college degree. Paramedics are allowed to start intravenous lines, give shots and insert airway devices to assist breathing. EMTs are usually restricted to using oxygen masks and performing other noninvasive procedures, such as applying bandages or compresses.

As you can see, it's preferable to have a paramedic on the team, so check with local emergency medical services to see if the emergency response units in your area are staffed by both EMTs and paramedics. Emergency response units are required to take the patient to the nearest or most appropriate emergency facility. The patient and family have no say in this. Each unit is in constant contact with the local hospital emergency room, notifying nurses and physicians of the patient's status.

In some cases, medical care might start sooner if you take the patient to an emergency room on your own, particularly if the patient is able to move and/or you live more than 30 minutes from an ambulance service. Important: Arriving at a hospital in an ambulance does not necessarily mean you will get quicker care. Most emergency rooms make an immediate assessment of each patient and quickly move the most severe into care units, no matter how they arrived.

In many areas of the country, "urgicare" and "emergicare" centers—freestanding facilities that usually are not affiliated with any hospital—are available for minor medical emergencies, such as ankle sprains, minor rashes and sore throats. These facilities, which are typically staffed by doctors and nurse practitioners, are often less crowded than hospital emergency rooms. The centers accept most types of insurance and are usually open 12 to 24 hours a day.

REPORT #244
Is Safety a Problem at Teaching Hospitals?

Charles B. Inlander consumer advocate and health-care consultant based in Fogelsville, Pennsylvania. He was the founding president of the nonprofit People's Medical Society, a consumer advocacy organization credited with key improvements in the quality of US health care in the 1980s and 1990s, and is author of 20 books, including *Take This Book to the Hospital with You: A Consumer Guide to Surviving Your Hospital Stay* (St. Martin's).

Are teaching hospitals safer and better than community hospitals...or less so? A friend was recently diagnosed with an unusual form of leukemia. His prognosis is pretty good and the cancer center at our local hospital has an excellent reputation—but he's decided to get treatment at a well-known academic medical center, even though he'll have to travel more than 100 miles each way. He wants to be sure he's doing "everything possible" to beat his cancer—and sometimes that means going outside the community to get access to new or cutting-edge treatment options. There are many factors to consider when deciding what hospital is best suited to your medical care needs, from the facility's quality rating and cost to your own condition, needs and personal comfort. Teaching hospitals aren't always tops in all those areas. We discussed the pros and cons of teaching hospitals with noted medical consumer advocate Charles B. Inlander, author of *Take This Book to the Hospital with You: A Consumer Guide to Surviving Your Hospital Stay*.

TEACHING HOSPITALS GET AN "A" FOR...

Also called academic medical centers, teaching hospitals often provide routine care, but are better known for innovative, sophisticated services, technologically advanced equipment and research laboratories that investigate cutting-edge, experimental treatments. Each teaching hospital is affiliated with a university medical school and staffed with residents from the school doing their clinical training, as well as the licensed attending physicians who supervise them. There are also "fellows," which is what they call physicians pursuing advanced training beyond residency to learn a particular specialty. This range of personnel means that teaching hospitals, by their very nature, have more layers. The ratio of full-fledged doctors to residents varies from one teaching hospital to another, but generally speaking the benefit of academic medical centers is that patients have access to expertise plus the newest thinking and treatments.

In Inlander's opinion, teaching hospitals offer a particular advantage for people with rare, complex or multiple medical conditions. Specialists are theoretically up to date on the latest research and treatment advances. A specialist's extensive experience translates to more refined skills and a wider breadth of knowledge that is valuable in making obscure diagnoses and performing difficult or uncommon procedures—more so than at community hospitals where unusual cases truly are unusual. Since they have more patients with unique needs, both the specialists and the hospital staffs generally have much more experience in caring for people who are seriously ill. And certain teaching hospitals specialize at a very high level in the diagnosis and treatment of particular conditions, such as heart disease or cancer.

WHEN COMMUNITY HOSPITALS ARE A BETTER CHOICE

Community hospitals may be easier to navigate, friendlier and more comfortable, while also providing high-quality care. In addition, Inlander is quick to note that there are some situations where community hospitals may be a better choice than teaching hospitals, especially for people visiting a hospital for more routine care (such as chemotherapy for common cancers or cardiovascular screening) or straightforward procedures—such as childbirth or a lumpectomy or stenting.

Factors that may weigh against teaching hospitals include...

• **Higher cost.** Since the cost of educating and supervising residents is high, the bill for a procedure may be larger at a teaching hospital than at a community one—and then you may need to add in travel costs as well. With consumers currently paying a higher percentage of medical costs out of pocket, this can be a serious consideration.

• **Higher infection risk.** Simply being in a hospital can be hazardous to your health nowadays, given that hospital-acquired infections now kill more than 90,000 patients annually. Teaching hospitals have a greater number of severely ill patients who are therefore more vulnerable to hospital acquired infections... increasing risk to those around them as well. "A higher number of sicker people with more severely compromised immune systems can mean higher rates of infections," Inlander warns.

• **There may be an "agenda."** The fact that teaching hospitals receive research funding from sponsoring drug companies or equipment manufacturers may translate directly into care recommendations.

• **Doctors who work longer hours make more errors.** Though there has been systematic reform of the long hours required of medical residents, many routinely work longer days than is recommended. Ask your resident how long he/she has been on duty. A Harvard study reported that two-thirds of residents work 30-hour shifts, while other studies show that residents who work more than 20 consecutive hours are more prone to fatigue, lapses in concentration and medical errors. You always have the right to ask for a different doctor if you are concerned.

SAFETY CONSIDERATIONS IN THE HOSPITAL

Compare how your local community hospital stacks up against the nearest teaching hospital. You can research this kind of information about hospitals (such as standards of care, rates of medical errors and outcomes) at Web sites such as The Joint Commission at *www.qualitycheck.org*...the US Department of Health and Human Services at *www.hospital compare.hhs.gov*...and The Leapfrog Group at *www.leapfroggroup.org*.

Whatever hospital you go to, make sure to ask questions. Always know who is treating you. Be on guard at all times to make sure medical care is carried out safely (eg, that practitioners wash hands, that medications and dosages are correct, etc.). Patients in teaching hospitals should insist that an experienced physician—not just a resident in training—supervises care... and remember, you can opt not to have residents treat you, even at a teaching hospital. On the other hand, it's not necessarily a bad thing to develop a relationship with the residents in addition to your doctor, since they are usually more accessible.

REPORT #245
It's Good to Second-Guess Your Doctor

Michael S. Sabel, MD, associate professor of surgery at University of Michigan Health System. Dr. Sabel is coauthor of the new University of Michigan Comprehensive Cancer Center's study "Changes in Surgical Management Resulting from Case Review at a Breast Cancer Multidisciplinary Tumor Board," which was published in *Cancer*.

Mehmet C. Oz, MD, professor of surgery at Columbia University College of Physicians and Surgeons and attending surgeon at New York-Presbyterian Hospital. He is medical director, Integrative Medicine Program and attending surgeon at New York Presbyterian. He is coauthor, with Michael F. Roizen, MD, of *You: The Smart Patient: An Insider's Handbook for Getting the Best Treatment* (Free Press).

My friend was recently diagnosed with breast cancer, and told by her doctor that she should have a mastectomy. Yet rather than rush to have surgery, she is seeking a second opinion...a very good idea. A new study has found that a second opinion from a team of specialists after an initial diagnosis of breast cancer resulted in a significant change in treatment protocol in more than half of the cases...and six of the women were found not to have breast cancer at all! This study underscores what many medical experts have been telling us for years—getting a second opinion for a major medical problem is one of the most important things you can do to protect your health and life.

SOMETIMES THERE WAS NO CANCER

In the study, 149 patients diagnosed with breast cancer were referred to a breast cancer clinic at the University of Michigan Comprehensive Cancer Center, where a multidisciplinary review board consisting of oncologists, surgeons, radiologists, pathologists, radiation oncologists and nurses reviewed and discussed the patients' medical information including mammograms, biopsy slides and their referring surgeons' treatment recommendations. This second evaluation of these patients led to changes in the recommendations for surgical treatment in 77 patients studied (52%). The specialists had differing opinions regarding everything from the interpretation of the patients' mammograms to the necessity for the mastectomy.

"We certainly expected that there would be some impact on these cases from the multidisciplinary review board, but we were surprised that more than half of the patients had some kind of change in their management," said Michael S. Sabel, MD, study coauthor and a surgical oncologist at University of Michigan Comprehensive Cancer Center.

The study supports the growing body of evidence that second opinions can provide patients with critical information when making difficult treatment decisions. "I encourage patients to get a second opinion," said Dr. Sabel. "Patients need to know what their choices are. There may be new treatment approaches to consider, or they may find that the diagnosis is entirely wrong, as was the case for some patients in this study."

FINDING THE BEST TREATMENT

The study's findings come as no surprise to Mehmet C. Oz, MD, who is a professor of surgery at Columbia University Medical Center in New York. He emphasizes the importance of getting a second opinion in his bestselling book, *You: The Smart Patient: An Insider's Handbook for Getting the Best Treatment* (Free Press). He told me that overall, not just with breast cancer, "research has shown that getting a second opinion results in new diagnoses in as many as 30% of all cases."

However, in spite of the apparent value of second opinions, few people get them. "Only 20% of people who seek medical care every year get a second opinion," said Dr. Oz. "Many people are embarrassed about it or they don't want to offend their doctors."

Always seek a second opinion if...

• **Your doctor says you need surgery.**

• **Your doctor is stumped by your condition and can't diagnose it.**

• **Your doctor isn't a specialist in the disease you have.**

• **Your treatment isn't working.**

* **Your doctor doesn't seem to be taking your symptoms seriously.**

• **You want to try other treatment options.**

• **A serious diagnosis has been made (to confirm its accuracy).**

You should also get a second opinion if you are taking several medications simultaneously, Dr. Oz told me, noting that "a recent study showed if you're on six or more medications, the chance of having a drug interaction is 94%. This means if you're on more than six drugs, you'd better get a second opinion about them."

HERE'S HOW TO DO IT

Not only will most insurance companies cover second opinions, since it makes financial sense, many insurers actually require one before they'll pay for certain major procedures. Medicare typically covers most or all of the cost for second opinions for important treatments such as surgery. (*Note:* Some Medicare managed care plans require a referral from your primary doctor prior to the visit.) HMOs usually will pay for second opinions from doctors who are in the plan's network. And, more and more often, cancer centers automatically review cases with a multidisciplinary tumor board, making second opinions routine for their patients.

Once you've decided to get a second opinion, learn as much as you can about your medical problem. According to Dr. Oz, patients who do their homework use their appointment time more productively and are better able to make decisions regarding their treatment. Internet Web sites, such as *www.nlm.nih.gov/ medlineplus, www.cancer.gov*—can provide a wealth of useful health information, research and resources. Also, says Dr. Oz, "the Internet is a great way to find top experts in a medical field. Many people don't know that they can research academic papers that are written by health experts in their field, and find out where the authors of these papers are from. Even if they don't live nearby, these experts can always refer you to someone who does live near you." Another good source for referrals is Castle Connolly Medical Ltd., a health information resource company that researches and makes available lists (*www.castleconnolly. com*) of the country's most highly regarded physicians in every specialty.

Once you find a doctor for a second opinion, ask what you should bring to your appointment, which may include all relevant X-rays, test results and reports. It is also a good idea to make a list of questions ahead of time, and to bring a friend or relative along for moral support and to listen to what the doctor is recommending, which may be a great help afterward.

VIRTUAL SECOND OPINIONS MAY BE AN OPTION

If you'd rather consult with a doctor without leaving the comfort of your home or if the best doctor to meet with is very far away, several Internet Web sites (sponsored by private organizations, medical universities and hospitals) offer second opinions for a small fee, such as Cleveland Clinic, *http://eclevelandclinic.org/ myconsult*. You submit your X-rays or test results to specialists who review them and send an opinion back to you via e-mail. Although this approach can provide you with additional information, Dr. Oz believes it does not compare with a face-to-face meeting with a doctor. "It's hard to believe that someone who is sitting across from you and knows the nuances of your case wouldn't be a much better choice," he said, adding "but it is better than doing nothing."

Of course, in the event that there is a real difference of opinions, you may need a third opinion, says Dr. Oz. Some insurance plans will pay for it—but if not, this may be an occasion when it makes sense to dig as deeply as you need to for the real, right answer.

REPORT #246
Individual Radiation Exposure Up Six-Fold

E. Stephen Amis, Jr., MD, professor and chair, department of radiology at the Albert Einstein College of Medicine and chairman of radiology at Montefiore Medical Center, Bronx, New York.

First of all, let me say this: I don't think anyone will argue with the idea that improved imaging tests—MRIs, CT scans and the like—have revolutionized medicine. Take CT scans, for example. This imaging technique creates highly detailed cross-sectional images of your body. These precisely detailed "slices" not only show bones, but also organs, blood vessels and other tissue, giving doctors information they need to diagnose muscle and bone disorders, pinpoint the location of a tumor, identify and monitor diseases such as cancer or heart disease, and detect internal injuries and internal bleeding, among other problems. In fact, the effectiveness of these imaging tests has profoundly changed the way medicine is practiced and they've helped doctors make decisions that have saved countless lives. But this progress comes at some cost—excessive exposure to radiation.

FOLLOWING THE NUMBERS

According to research revealed by the National Council on Radiation Protection's 39th National Conference on Radiation Control, over the last two decades the per-capita dose of ionizing radiation from clinical imaging exams has grown six-fold. This is a huge increase but not a surprising one, given dramatic technological innovations in imaging tests that utilize radiation. Some startling numbers were also revealed in the "American College of Radiology White Paper on Radiation Dose in Medicine" published in the *Journal of the American College of Radiology*. The number of CT scans performed each year grew from three million in 1980 to more than 60 million in 2005. The seven million nuclear medicine exams ordered in 1980 increased to 20 million in 2005.

So why is this a problem? According to the American College of Radiology report, "Ionizing radiation, especially at high doses, has long been known to increase the risk for developing cancer." The paper also notes that the International Commission on Radiological Protection has reported that collective CT scan doses a patient receives can approach or exceed radiation levels that have been shown to increase risk for cancer. The obvious questions are: Does taking a test to prevent cancer actually give me cancer? What's being done about this? Should we be worried? And what can a person do to protect him or herself?

THE INSIDE STORY

To get to the important information and find out what we really need to know about this issue, we contacted E. Stephen Amis, Jr., MD, chair of radiology at both the Albert Einstein College of Medicine and Montefiore Medical Center in Bronx, New York, and lead author of the ACR's white paper. He advises people to take an active role in their care, keeping track of imaging tests that involve radiation. This report was intended to raise awareness of the issue of cumulative radiation exposure, Dr. Amis says, not to scare anyone away from imaging exams they need. The goal is for both patients and health-care providers to be alert to the risks of cumulative radiation from imaging tests and take reasonable steps to reduce unnecessary exposure. The emphasis is on "unnecessary."

Dr. Amis believes that, in general, the benefits of imaging tests far outweigh the risk of having them done. In fact, another article on the same subject, published in *In Practice,* a publication of the American Roentgen Ray Society (the oldest radiology society in the US), noted that "...of 62 million CT scans delivered in a year, nearly 14 million of those patients would die of cancer without the benefit of the scan."

REPEATED EXPOSURE IS WHAT'S RISKY

Dr. Amis stresses that the concern isn't with the safety of the tests themselves—it is repeated exposure to radiation through imaging tests that the ACR is warning us about. "For example," says Dr. Amis, "we're worried about the 30-year-old with chronic kidney stones who comes to the emergency department every six months. He gets a CT scan every time he walks through the ER door—so after six years he's had 12 scans." In response to my question about the radiation exposure of, say, annual mammograms, Dr. Amis reassured me that traditional x-rays, like mammograms and chest x-rays, use significantly lower radiation doses and it would take many such exams to result in a cumulative exposure that might be worrisome. It's the bigger exams—CT, full body imaging—that add up quickly.

This is where being an educated consumer comes into play. In order to minimize your risk but still receive the best medical care for your condition, you can ask your doctor questions—and keep records for yourself. *Here's what you need to remember...*

• **Know the dose.** Not all imaging exams use radiation—for example, ultrasound and MRI are radiation-free. And some (such as CT scans) provide a much higher dose than others (bone density tests and standard X-rays, for example, require very little radiation). To educate yourself about dose levels from various procedures, click on the "Patient Safety" link at *RadiologyInfo.org*.

• **Keep track.** If you have had numerous CT scans or other tests involving radiation (like Dr. Amis' example of the patient with kidney stones) start keeping notes of the procedures you undergo, what they were for and when they were done. Then if a doctor recommends another such exam, you can refer to your previous history, voice your concerns and ask if a radiation-free alternative might be just as effective. For the kidney stone patient described above, an ultrasound or simple X-ray would likely have given sufficient information to help with a diagnosis, without adding to his radiation exposure.

• **Push back.** In a serious medical situation, a CT scan or other higher-radiation-dose test could deliver the diagnosis that saves your life —and if that's the case, you need to have it done. But if you feel that the procedure is unnecessary (either because you've been through it before or you suspect your doctor is being overly aggressive) and you don't believe your concerns are being taken seriously, be vocal— get a second opinion or ask the radiologist or imaging specialist about alternatives. Or, if the situation is not acute and dangerous, consider waiting and seeking advice on less invasive options.

MONEY TALKS

Remember, too, that money and convenience often play a role. Not only are these tests very profitable for hospitals, they also require an enormous capital investment in equipment—which is recouped by doing lots and lots of procedures. Also, the tests are fast, easy and painless for the patient, many of whom may feel especially well cared for when lots of tests are done.

"Everything in moderation" seems to once again be true. Being an informed consumer —and requesting radiation-free imaging tests whenever possible—will reduce your lifetime radiation exposure. By doing so, you can limit your doses to the times when no radiation-free alternative is available.

REPORT #247
Medical Interventions...
A Leading Cause of Death

David J. Sherer, MD, board-certified anesthesiologist in clinical practice in the Washington D.C. area. He is coauthor of Dr. David Sherer's Hospital Survival Guide: 100+ Ways to Make Your Hospital Stay Safe and Comfortable *(Claren).*

Not long ago we read a report that made the astonishing claim that the leading cause of death in the US is the American medical system. Medicare's recent announcement that it will no longer reimburse hospitals for the cost of treating certain "serious preventable events," such as an object left in a patient's body after an operation or giving a patient the wrong kind of blood, and particular infections amounts to a frightening acknowledgement of how bad things have gotten in mainstream health care.

Authors of the report on causes of death, published in *Life Extension* magazine, attributed nearly 800,000 deaths each year to medical interventions, in contrast to approximately

650,000 deaths from heart disease and 550,000 from cancer. The methodology they used to calculate that number didn't stand up to our analysis, so I don't think the numbers are quite so high. However, it did get my attention since the figures came from credible sources including peer-reviewed medical journals, citing for instance, 106,000 deaths annually from adverse drug reactions, 98,000 from medical errors and 88,000 from infections. This compares with 160,000 deaths from lung cancer each year. Death can't be held off forever, of course—but preventable deaths from hospital-acquired infections, especially if due to poor hygiene such as those transmitted by not washing hands, are particularly egregious.

For greater insight into the risks we face, we spoke with David J. Sherer, MD, a board-certified anesthesiologist in Falls Church, Virginia, and the coauthor of Dr. David Sherer's *Hospital Survival Guide: 100+ Ways to Make Your Hospital Stay Safe and Comfortable* (Claren). He said that although this report is controversial and somewhat alarmist, it has elements of truth. Numbers can always be crunched and interpreted in different ways, but the indisputable point here is that medical errors and complications or adverse effects from medical interventions have reached a crisis point in this country—one that needs to be addressed. That's beginning to happen.

Dr. Sherer and I discussed what's behind this alarming trend and how we can protect ourselves.

BEHIND THE RISE IN
MEDICAL-RELATED DEATHS

First of all, the problem is not that medical practitioners have suddenly and inexplicably become sloppy and careless. That's far too simplistic an explanation. *Instead, Dr. Sherer chalks up the alarming statistics to a number of different factors...*

• **The American public is getting older and sicker.** Growing numbers of graying baby boomers are developing the diseases of aging —heart disease, diabetes, orthopedic problems, etc. In the meantime, in people of all ages, ballooning rates of obesity contribute to these same health challenges. More sick people mean more medical interventions...and in hard numbers, that adds up to more mistakes or complications.

• **In a kind of medical "perfect storm,"** just as more Americans are developing serious health problems, we're struggling with a shortage of medical support personnel including nurses, which decreases the attention paid to patient needs and details of treatment. Also, managed care has meant doctors have less time to devote to patients during office visits and, as a result, are less likely to know the particulars of their history. Dr. Sherer warns that this sets up a system ripe for errors.

• **Americans today take more medications than anyone else in the world**—and drug companies are working hard to get us to take even more. Spending on direct-to-consumer drug advertising has increased over 300% in nearly a decade, to $4.2 billion in 2005 from $1.1 billion in 1997. With that much money aimed at advertising drugs not just to save lives, but to enhance mood or correct erectile dysfunction or alleviate restless legs syndrome, Dr. Sherer points out that drugs are often being taken by people who don't need them. More drugs mean more drug reactions and interactions to juggle than ever before... again, many more opportunities for errors.

• **We're paying closer attention to medical errors and preventable complications and**—paradoxically, the harder we look for them, the more we find. This makes the numbers look terrible in the short run, but in the long run this increased vigilance and accountability should result in improved care.

HOW TO PROTECT YOURSELF

Forewarned is forearmed: There are many proactive steps you can take to shield yourself and your loved ones from this epidemic of deaths related to medical interventions. *At the doctor's office or in the hospital, Dr. Sherer recommends...*

• **Bring an up-to-date list of all medications you take.** Make sure that you list not only prescription drugs, but also over-the-counter medications, herbal remedies, vitamins and other dietary supplements. These can all react with one another. Also list the condition for which you take each drug.

• **Include correct name, spelling, usage and dosage.** Dr. Sherer cautions that many drugs—for example, Xanax (for anxiety) and Zantac (to treat ulcers)—sound similar. A comprehensive and accurate list that includes the condition for which a drug or supplement has been prescribed will help ward off confusion and errors. This is especially important when dealing with health-care professionals who don't speak English as their first language.

• **Tell practitioners about any drug allergies or sensitivities and all pre-existing conditions.** For example, perhaps you are allergic to penicillin. While this information should appear on your chart, don't take for granted that it does. Reminding health-care providers of your medical history, including drug allergies, is a simple and effective way to avoid potentially life-threatening medical errors.

• **Do your homework.** If you are scheduled to take a new drug or undergo a test or procedure, first research it at reliable government, hospital or university-based Web sites such as *www.medlineplus.gov* or *www.mayoclinic.com* or *www.jhu.edu* (Johns Hopkins). Peer-reviewed journals such as the *Journal of the American Medical Association* (*jama.ama-assn.org*) and the *New England Journal of Medicine* (*www.nejm.org*) can also be excellent sources of information. An objective non-biased drug assessment database is available through both print and online subscription (*www.factsandcomparisons.com*)—ask your health-care provider and/or pharmacist whether they use it.

• **Speak up.** Ask your doctor the right questions. Why do I need this drug/test/procedure? What are the risks versus benefits? Is this the best drug/test/procedure for my condition? What about side effects? In the case of tests, are the results typically straightforward or subject to interpretation? How often is this test/procedure performed at your facility? How often does the surgeon or other medical practitioner perform it? In both cases, the more often, the better. Will there be pain or discomfort? If your physician can't or won't take the time to answer your questions, it's time to get a new physician.

• **Designate a friend or family member to be your advocate.** When you're ill, it's all too easy to become nervous and forget the questions you want to ask, or fail to recall your physician's advice. It's not only comforting to have a trusted advocate by your side at such moments, it also contributes to a better understanding of the situation on your part, and more accountability on the part of your caregivers. If you're in the hospital, try to have someone with you or visiting frequently so that they can get help/nurse's attention if need be.

• **Take personal responsibility.** In the long run, you remain in charge of your own health. Responsibility includes not just your interactions with medical practitioners, but also making lifestyle changes that reduce your risk of illness.

No doubt we will continue to hear more about this vitally important health topic. Given that hospitals will now have to absorb the costs of their mistakes due to Medicare's refusal to provide coverage for "serious preventable events," with a stipulation that prevents billing patients for them, too, it's clear that they will focus intently on reducing these events, which can only be good news. And meanwhile, Medicare's new hospital inpatient provisions will result not only in an estimated savings for the government of more than $20 million annually—but, we can only hope, the saving of many lives as well.

REPORT #248
Survival Odds 70% Better at Top Hospitals

Rick May, MD, vice president of Clinical Excellence Research and Consulting, HealthGrades in Golden, Colorado.

The death rate at the highest-ranked US hospitals is 70% lower than at the lowest-ranked ones, according to a recent report from HealthGrades, the leading independent healthcare ranking organization. If all hospitals performed at the level of the top-rated hospitals, researchers found that 237,420 deaths might have been prevented over the three years of the study.

SIGNIFICANT REGIONAL VARIATION

We spoke with Rick May, MD, a senior physician consultant at HealthGrades, to learn more about how consumers can use this information to their benefit. Hospitals in the US are required to report a variety of quality data including information on infection rates, how sick their patients are, what percentage of patients have complications and how many die. Some states require even more information, including hospital charges, lengths of stay and whether patients were discharged to home or a nursing facility. This type of public reporting is intended to make hospitals more accountable for their performance and HealthGrades uses advanced statistical analysis to help consumers make sense of this mass of data so they can take control over their medical care. As it turns out, doing your research and making an informed decision about which hospital to go to may make the difference between life and death.

ABOUT THE STUDY

The HealthGrades study (which is available at *www.healthgrades.com/business*) involved more than 41 million Medicare hospitalizations from 2005 to 2007, at more than 5,000 hospitals nationwide. Investigators looked at deaths for patients being treated for 17 procedures and conditions, including heart and lung problems, stroke, gastrointestinal disorders and diabetes. According to Dr. May, the analysis included death for any reason—not just those attributable to errors. Though the analysis included death from all causes (for instance, patients who came in having a heart attack and subsequently died from it were counted), Dr. May told me that "we found that there are very few patients who would have died no matter where they went. Even for serious conditions like heart attacks, many of the deaths were preventable."

Based on risk-adjusted death and complication rates, hospitals were awarded a rating of one, three or five stars. One-star hospitals had poor performance. Three-star hospitals were performing about as expected (average), and five-star hospitals had great outcomes.

Patients in the five-star hospitals were 70% less likely to die while in the hospital for treatment of one of the listed conditions compared with a one-star hospital. As Dr. May explained, "If 100 patients with heart attacks went to a one-star hospital, maybe 10 of them would have died...whereas, if those same 100 patients went to a five-star hospital, only three would have died and the other seven would have lived. There's an incredible difference."

More than half of all deaths were associated with four diagnoses…

- **Heart failure**
- **Respiratory failure**
- **Pneumonia**
- **Sepsis (a whole-body infection)**

Not surprisingly, Dr. May's team found significant regional differences in hospital performance. For example, death rates were lowest in the part of the country classified as the East North Central region (Illinois, Indiana, Michigan, Ohio and Wisconsin), while the East South Central region (Alabama, Kentucky, Mississippi and Tennessee) was highest. It's surely no coincidence that the East North Central region also had the highest percentage (26%) of best-performing hospitals.

COMPARE ONE HOSPITAL TO ANOTHER

Dr. May advises carefully researching and comparing local hospitals against one another in terms of patient outcomes and volume for your particular procedure or condition. As a rule, the more often a procedure is performed at a hospital, the better the outcome. There are enormous variations among hospitals across regions and within the same region in terms of overall mortality and individual procedure outcomes, so be a smart consumer and do your research.

REPORT #249
Protect Yourself Against Medication Mistakes

Jack M. Rosenberg, PharmD, PhD, a professor of pharmacy practice and pharmacology and director of the International Drug Information Center at Long Island University in Brooklyn, New York.

If you're taking prescription medication, there's a 50/50 chance that you're doing something wrong, the FDA reports. The possible consequences range from delayed recovery from illness to potentially life-threatening problems.

Worrisome: Medication errors injure about 1.5 million Americans per year. *Common mistakes and how to avoid them…*

MIXING MEDICATIONS

In a recent survey, 68% of older adults using prescription medication also were taking over-the-counter (OTC) drugs, dietary supplements or both.

Concern: This increases the risk for dangerous drug interactions. *Examples…*

- **Combining a nonsteroidal anti-inflammatory drug (NSAID),** such as aspirin or ibuprofen, with the blood thinner *warfarin* (Coumadin) can cause hemorrhaging.

- **Some antacids, allergy drugs, cold drugs** and other medications alter the effectiveness of, or interact dangerously with, the heart medication *digoxin* (Lanoxin).

- **Using potassium supplements** along with a blood pressure–lowering ACE inhibitor, such as *lisinopril* (Prinivil), may disrupt heart rhythm.

- **St. John's wort,** a mood-lifting herb, alters the effectiveness of, or interacts dangerously with, many drugs, including digoxin and antidepressants.

- **The herb ginkgo biloba** may cause bleeding problems when taken with NSAIDs or blood thinners.

Self-defense: In your purse, carry a list of every drug and supplement that you take. When told to begin a new drug, show the list to your doctor and pharmacist, and ask about possible interactions. Use the same pharmacy for all your prescriptions so the pharmacist can cross-check each medication. Read warning labels before taking anything new.

NOT FOLLOWING DIRECTIONS

When patients decide on their own to modify dosage instructions, consequences can be serious. *Errors include…*

•**Taking too much—often due to a false belief that "if some is good, more is better."**

Reality: A higher dosage increases the risk for adverse side effects. With sleeping pills and narcotic painkillers, an overdose can be deadly.

•**Taking too little—usually due to worries about a drug's safety or expense.**

Study finding: Diabetes patients who were most concerned about the safety of blood pressure drugs and/or blood sugar drugs tended to take less than the prescribed amount. But, in fact, underdosing increases the risk for diabetes complications, such as stroke and kidney failure.

•**Stopping too soon or too abruptly—which often occurs when people start feeling better and think that the drug is no longer necessary.**

Problems: Prematurely halting antibiotics, for instance, allows the hardiest bacteria to survive and reinfect you…suddenly discontinuing antidepressants increases relapse risk. In other cases, people stop taking medication because they do not feel better, so they think the drug doesn't work. But many drugs—such as those that lower blood pressure or cholesterol—do not make you feel any better day-to-day, yet still do their job of reducing health risks.

Recommended: Follow directions on the label. If you think a drug is not effective, have concerns about safety, experience side effects or cannot pay for the medication, tell your doctor without delay. The doctor should be able to explain why the drug is appropriate for you…or suggest alternatives.

BEING FORGETFUL

It can be difficult to keep track of medications. *The more drugs you take, the more likely you are to have problems with…*

•**Not remembering to take your medication**—and therefore not getting enough to be fully effective.

•**Double-dosing**—because if you don't recall that you already took a scheduled dose, you take it again.

•**Forgetting to check expiration dates.** Over time, drugs lose potency or break down into harmful substances. Some medications, such as eyedrops, may become contaminated with microorganisms as they age.

Helpful: To keep track of when to take—and whether you already have taken—each of your medications, use a pillbox marked with the hours of the day and days of the week. At the start of each week or month (depending on how many days' worth of medication your pillbox holds), place your medication in the appropriate spots so that you can easily see if and when you're due for a dose.

High-tech: Try a programmable electronic pillbox, which beeps to alert you when it is time for each dose (available at drugstores for about $8 to $20).

All OTC drugs are labeled with expiration dates. If a prescription label does not include an expiration date, ask your pharmacist to add it.

Good habit: Remember to check the date before taking a drug.

STORING IMPROPERLY

Drugs exposed to moisture or temperature extremes may break down. *Safe storage…*

•**Remove cotton from pill bottles**—once the bottle is opened, cotton may collect moisture.

•**Most medications should be kept in a cool, dry place.** Never store drugs in a car, above the stove, near a sunny window or on a sink or countertop that's likely to get wet.

•**Refrigerate medications if directed on the label.**

•**Keep medications in their original bottles** so that you know what they are and how to take them. Transfer to your day-by-day pillbox only as many pills as the box is designed to hold.

ASSUMING THE DOCTOR IS RIGHT

Patients must protect themselves from inadvertent medication errors committed by health-care professionals.

Reason: Every year in the US, an estimated 51 million dispensing errors are made at outpatient pharmacies...and 400,000 preventable drug-related injuries occur in hospitals. Even the new bar-code labeling technology that is supposed to reduce errors has glitches.

Self-defense: When your doctor gives you a prescription, clarify the name and purpose of the drug, its strength (for instance, milligrams per tablet) and dosage. At the pharmacy, check the label to be sure you are given what was prescribed.

If hospitalized, ask for a list of names and dosages of all drugs that you are supposed to receive and find out what each one looks like. Before you accept a dose, make sure the nurse checks your ID bracelet—so you aren't given a drug meant for another patient.

REPORT #250
Beware of the Other Killer 'Superbug'

Carolyn Gould, MD, a medical epidemiologist and infectious-disease specialist in the Division of Healthcare Quality Promotion at the Centers for Disease Control and Prevention and a clinical assistant professor of medicine at Emory University, both in Atlanta. Her research interests include the prevention of antibiotic resistance and health-care-associated infections, including those from Clostridium difficile.

With all the recent media attention, most people now have heard of *methicillin-resistant Staphylococcus aureus* (MRSA), a bacterial strain that has emerged as one of the nation's top threats to public health. Less well-known—but of similar concern to infectious-disease experts—is *Clostridium difficile* (C. difficile), a potentially deadly organism that's spreading fast.

In the US, the number of hospital discharges in which C. difficile was listed as a diagnosis doubled between 2000 and 2003, with a disproportionate increase in cases involving elderly patients—perhaps due to their generally weakened immunity. Over a recent five-year period, it is estimated that C. difficile was responsible for about 20,000 deaths.

FUELED BY ANTIBIOTICS

C. difficile bacteria can be found in stool (animal and human) and on many surfaces. Up to 3% of healthy Americans are colonized with C. difficile—that is, they have the bacterium in their intestinal tract, but don't get sick from it. By comparison, 20% to 40% of patients in hospitals may be colonized with C. difficile.

Main risk: The use of antibiotics. The vast majority of patients infected with C. difficile are either taking—or have recently taken—antibiotics, and most acquire the infection in the hospital. One problem with antibiotics is that they not only kill disease-causing germs but also the beneficial organisms in the intestine, which normally prevent C. difficile from proliferating.

Once C. difficile multiplies, it produces highly virulent toxins that cause inflammation and damage cells in the lining of the large intestine. The newer "superstrains" of the bacterium are thought to produce up to 20 times more of these toxins than the usual strains.

Result: Watery, often violent diarrhea...severe intestinal cramps...blood or pus in the stools...and sometimes life-threatening colitis (inflammation of the colon).

Important: If you get diarrhea that is prolonged (more than two to three days) and/or severe, do not ignore it. See a doctor immediately. You should assume that it might be caused by C. difficile if you've taken antibiotics in the last few months, have recently been discharged from the hospital or have cared for someone with C. difficile.

Caution: The most widely used test for C. difficile, a stool test, is about 70% to 90% sensitive—some patients who test negative for the organism are later found to be infected.

A colonoscopy (examination of the colon using a long tube with a camera attached) may be performed to check for pseudo-membranes, patches of inflammatory cells that are characteristic of C. difficile infection.

DIFFICULT TO ERADICATE

Unlike many disease-causing bacteria, C. difficile produces spores. These hardy, heat-resistant forms allow the bacterium to survive in a dormant form for months or even years in the intestinal tract...and on surfaces, such as floors and doorknobs, for weeks.

People acquire C. difficile by ingesting the spores, which resist the acidity of the stomach and germinate in the small intestine. Disruption of the normal flora (bacteria) of the colon—typically through exposure to antibiotics—allows C. difficile to flourish.

Those who are exposed to the spores could get infected—and, even if they do not have symptoms, can pass the infection on to others. This is a serious problem in nursing homes and hospitals, where people tend to have weakened immune systems and often take antibiotics. In these settings, C. difficile typically is spread via the hands of contaminated health-care workers or through exposure to contaminated surfaces.

Treatment: Two antibiotics, *metronidazole* (Flagyl) and *vancomycin* (Vancocin), appear to be equally effective in treating mild-to-moderate infections caused by C. difficile.

Doctors usually start treatment with metronidazole—it's much cheaper than vancomycin and may be less likely to lead to antibiotic-resistant organisms in the colon. For severe infections, however, vancomycin is thought to be the better choice.

BEST PREVENTION STRATEGIES

There's some evidence that people who take antacids, including proton-pump inhibitors, such as *esomeprazole* (Nexium), and H2 blockers, such as *ranitidine* (Zantac), have a higher risk for C. difficile—possibly because antacids decrease stomach acid, thereby making it easier for the bacterium to survive and germinate in the intestine. However, antacid use alone is unlikely to increase C. difficile risk significantly unless the patient is taking antibiotics and/or is hospitalized. *Effective ways to guard against C. difficile infection...*

•**Avoid unnecessary antibiotics.** Since active C. difficile infection is almost always associated with antibiotic use, patients can reduce their risk by taking antibiotics only when they're truly necessary. Do not ask your doctor for antibiotics when you have a viral illness, such as a cold or flu.

Important: Doctors are just as likely to prescribe antibiotics unnecessarily as patients are to ask for them. If your doctor recommends that you start taking an antibiotic, ask what it's for...if he/she is sure that you have a bacterial (rather than a viral) illness...and if it's possible that the condition will improve on its own without antibiotics.

•**Ask for a culture.** If you need an antibiotic, ask your doctor to perform a culture (whenever possible) to target the drug to the infection. Virtually all antibiotics have been implicated in C. difficile infection, but the infection is more common in patients who take broad-spectrum antibiotics, such as *fluoroquinolone* and *cephalosporin* antibiotics, that have a greater tendency to disrupt the colon's normal flora.

•**Wash your hands frequently**—particularly when you're in the hospital—or if you're caring for someone infected with C. difficile. Use warm water and regular soap, and wash for at least 15 seconds to remove spores.

•**Decontaminate.** If you've been infected with C. difficile—or you are caring for someone who has had it—disinfect surfaces daily. Hospital rooms, especially bathrooms and frequently touched surfaces, are also commonly contaminated with C. difficile.

REPORT #251
In the Hospital? Know Your Rights

Charles B. Inlander, consumer advocate and health-care consultant based in Fogelsville, Pennsylvania. He was the founding president of the nonprofit People's Medical Society, a consumer advocacy organization credited with key improvements in the quality of US health care in the 1980s and 1990s, and is author of 20 books, including *Take This Book to the Hospital with You: A Consumer Guide to Surviving Your Hospital Stay* (St. Martin's).

If you're one of the roughly 35 million Americans who is admitted to a hospital this year due to a chronic illness, an emergency or a need for surgery, you may feel like you're in custody. Hospitals are so intimidating to most people that they don't realize that, thanks to federal and state laws, they have many rights as patients.

For example, when you're hospitalized, you can…

• **Say "No"!** You not only have the right to refuse any procedure or test you do not want, but also can say no to having a specific doctor, nurse or resident-physician treat you. (Of course, you may not have a choice if your case is an emergency.)

Bonus: My research has found that saying no is the best way to get hospital personnel to fully explain something you don't understand so that you can then make more-informed medical decisions.

• **Have a loved one with you.** Hospital visiting hours are not laws, but hospital-imposed restrictions. No matter what visiting hours the hospital lists, you have the right to have a personal advocate, such as a family member or friend, with you. However, visitation may be limited or barred in such areas as recovery rooms, trauma centers and quarantined areas.

Smart idea: In choosing someone to stay with you or nearby at all times, consider asking the person you've designated as your representative in a living will or medical durable power of attorney to make medical decisions for you if you are unable to do so.

• **See your medical records.** State and federal laws allow you to see and obtain copies of your medical records (except psychotherapy notes). But you—and, in general, your designated representative—also have the right to look at your medical chart (a detailed record of your medical care and status) while you are in the hospital. Just ask your nurse or doctor.

• **Check your bill.** State and federal consumer-protection laws give you the right to an itemized bill that includes every service, product, medication and procedure for which you are charged during your hospitalization.

Helpful: Since hospitals usually keep a running tab as charges occur, ask the billing office for a copy of your bill each day you are in the hospital. Hospital personnel may balk, but you have that right.

• **Insist on knowing who is treating you.** Doctors and nurses should have nametags that include their medical degrees. You should know if your nurse is a registered nurse (RN) or licensed practical nurse (LPN). (RNs have more training.) You also have the right to ask anyone his/her job title and qualifications. Don't let uniforms fool you. A white coat and stethoscope hanging around the person's neck means nothing in terms of their training or their qualifications.

• **Check out.** By law, you can check yourself out of a hospital at anytime, even if your doctors don't recommend it. You must sign an "Against Medical Advice" form, but you can leave whenever you like—for example, if you disagree with the proposed treatment.

REPORT #252
Protect Yourself from Pharmacy Drug Errors

David Wood, freelance consumer advocate and writer on senior scams and fraud, Washington, DC.

At least 1.5 million patients annually in the US are harmed or killed by prescription drug errors.

Major causes: Doctors' poor handwriting that is misread by pharmacists…distractions that cause doctors and pharmacists, as well as nurses and other caregivers—including those working in hospitals—to make mistakes.

Self-defense: Know your prescription and its purpose…

• **Ask your doctor the exact name of the drug and its dosage.** Check the name and dosage on the label when you receive it.

• **Ask your doctor to write the purpose of the drug on the prescription form**—the pharmacist will be alerted if the purpose doesn't fit the name of the drug.

• **If your doctor sends a prescription to a pharmacy electronically, get a copy for yourself.**

• **If a drug bottle arrives in a box or other packaging,** check to be sure the label on the bottle matches that on the packaging.

• **Take your prescription to the pharmacist during his/her off-peak hours.** Then talk to the pharmacist about it to verify it and ask any questions you have.

Key: During off-peak hours, the pharmacist is more free to talk—and less likely to be rushed in a way that could cause a mistake.

• **Learn about drugs that are prescribed to you from online sources.**

Good sites: Drugs.com (*www.drugs.com*)… RxList (*www.rxlist.com*).

For other online sources of information about a particular drug, enter its name in the Web search engine of your choice.

REPORT #253
Medical Tests—No News Is Not Good

Trisha Torrey, patient advocate, newspaper columnist, radio talk show host and national speaker based in upstate New York. Torrey is author of *You Bet Your Life: The 10 Mistakes Every Patient Makes* (Langdon Street). Visit her blog at *EveryPatientsAdvocate.com/blog*.

W hat a relief it is when a few days… or a week…or even several weeks go by after you've had an important medical test and no one has called you with results. No news is good news—right?

Not necessarily. Disconcertingly, new research has revealed that one in 14 patients who had routine blood tests or screenings were not informed of clinically significant findings. That's right—patients were never told that their test results were abnormal.

COMMUNICATIONS BREAKDOWN

At Weill Cornell Medical College in New York City, researchers examined the medical records of 5,434 individuals aged 50 to 69 at 23 primary-care practices around the country. They focused on patients who had had abnormal findings on at least one of 14 standard medical tests in the preceding year, searching specifically for evidence that results had not been communicated. They also asked doctors to describe their office policies for communicating test results.

Researchers discovered that the rate of failure to communicate abnormal test results exceeded 7%. *Specifically, they found…*

• **In 117 out of 1,889 significant clinical findings,** doctors did not inform patients, while for an additional 18 patients, the doctors said that they had communicated results but had not documented that they had done so.

• **Very few of the practices reported having a specific process and rules for communicating test results to patients,** and in eight practices, the policy was to tell patients that if they heard nothing, they could assume all was well.

These findings were reported in the *Archives of Internal Medicine*.

DANGEROUS OMISSION

This is a very big deal—not learning your test results may mean that you don't get medical care you need. It's not an exaggeration to say, in fact, that it can put your health at serious risk by leading to delays in potentially lifesaving treatment. After reading about this research, we spoke with patient advocate Trisha Torrey, author of *You Bet Your Life: The 10 Mistakes Every Patient Makes*. She said it is important to take charge to be sure this doesn't ever happen to you. Here is her advice for all patients getting medical tests, including blood work, imaging tests, cultures, genetic tests and anything and everything your doctor might order for you…

• **Ask to be notified of test results no matter what the findings are.**

• **Ask when you will be notified of results.** Some tests can be read immediately while others take a week or even several weeks (for instance, to grow a culture or analyze genes). If you don't get your results by the time you are told to expect them, don't wait—call the office. If your results are not yet available, ask for clarification on when they will be. Reiterate that you expect to learn your results no matter what they are.

• **Ask how you will be notified.** If it is by telephone, be specific about whether you prefer to be called at home, at your office or on your cell phone.

• **Ask to receive a copy of the results in the mail.** This serves as your official record in case of future difficulties or future misunderstandings.

In today's overburdened health-care system, we all need to be more proactive than ever about our care. Don't assume that you're fine because you don't hear back after a test—call and ask.

REPORT #254
Surviving Your Hospital Stay

Charles B. Inlander, consumer advocate and health-care consultant based in Fogelsville, Pennsylvania. He was the founding president of the nonprofit People's Medical Society, a consumer advocacy organization credited with key improvements in the quality of US health care in the 1980s and 1990s, and is author of 20 books, including Take This Book to the Hospital with You: A Consumer Guide to Surviving Your Hospital Stay *(St. Martin's).*

I recently had to put all my years of experience as a medical-consumer advocate to the test when I found myself in the hospital recuperating from surgery for an enlarged prostate gland. My surgery was a success—in part because I chose a surgeon who had done the procedure, a *transurethral resection of the prostate* (TURP), more than 1,000 times. But my hospital stay went without major incident also because I knew what to do to avoid problems. *Here's what you—or a loved one—can do to have an equally successful hospital stay…*

• **Bring a list of your medications.** I always advise people to bring a list of all their medications—and the dosages—when they go to the

doctor, but the same applies if you're headed to the hospital. Coming prepared with your medication list is one of the best steps you can take to protect yourself against medication errors. I brought my medication list and kept it on the adjustable table by my bedside. One nurse thanked me and used it to be sure that her records were correct.

• **Hang signs.** The 84-year-old man in the bed next to mine was nearly deaf and couldn't understand the questions that the doctors and nurses asked him. He would just nod and say "yes" to everything. When I realized this was happening, I made a sign with bold print that read, "You have to speak directly into my ear!" and hung it on the wall above his head. It worked. Once my roommate was able to hear the staff, they got real answers. You can make a sign for a variety of messages, such as "Contact my son/daughter (and give phone number) for any medical permissions."

• **Use the phone.** One night, I needed the nurse but was getting no response when I pushed the call button. I waited 20 minutes and finally picked up the phone, dialed "0" and asked for the nurses' station on my unit. A nurse answered on the first ring. I asked her to come to my room, and she showed up about 10 seconds later. I never had a problem again when I pushed the call button.

• **Bring earplugs.** Hospitals are noisy places. Knowing this, I brought earplugs with me and slept peacefully. A portable music player with earphones or noise-canceling headphones can provide the same escape.

• **Call home.** Twice during my three-day hospitalization, my doctor visited when no one from my family was around. So when my doctor entered the room, I got on the phone, called my wife and had the doctor talk to her at the same time he was talking to me. This is the best way to keep your family informed, and it is especially helpful if you are not feeling well or need someone to ask questions for you.

• **Check the bill.** I received a bill from the hospital that said I owed $2,600. I knew this was wrong. By going over the itemized bill (which I had requested at my discharge), I discovered that I had been inadvertently charged for services received by another patient.

Bcause I was diligent and made a lot of calls, the insurer found the error. Since an estimated 85% of all hospital bills have errors in them, it's buyer beware!

REPORT #255
Surgery Danger For Women

Patients often receive *unfractionated heparin* to prevent postsurgical blood clots. Sometimes this leads to *heparin-induced thrombocytopenia* (HIT), a decrease in platelet count that paradoxically increases clotting risk.

New finding: HIT is more common in women than in men.

Self-defense: Studies show that HIT risk is lower with low-molecular-weight heparin or the anticoagulant *fondaparinux* (Arixtra)—ask your doctor before surgery.

Theodore E. Warkentin, MD, professor of pathology and molecular medicine, McMaster University, Hamilton, Ontario, and leader of a study of 290 people, published in *Blood*.

REPORT #256
Surviving the Intensive Care Unit

Richard P. Shannon, MD, chair of the department of medicine at Allegheny General Hospital in Pittsburgh, where he pioneered a highly effective model program for reducing catheter-associated bacterial infections. Dr. Shannon also is chair of the department of medicine at the University of Pennsylvania School of Medicine and the Hospital of the University of Pennsylvania, both in Philadelphia. His efforts to improve patient safety were highlighted in the PBS television series *Remaking American Medicine*.

Having a loved one in the intensive care unit (ICU) is unavoidably stressful. Patients placed in this part of the hospital are seriously injured or ill enough to require the most sophisticated around-the-clock medical care.

Frightening: About 12% of the estimated 5 million Americans admitted annually to ICUs die before leaving intensive care. While the seriousness and uncertainty of your loved one's condition may leave you feeling powerless, there are ways you can help.

AVOIDING INFECTIONS

Approximately 2 million infections are acquired in hospitals each year—about 260,000 of them fatal. ICU patients are most vulnerable—their immune systems are already greatly challenged because of their illnesses or injuries, and they frequently require invasive procedures that can inadvertently introduce bacteria into the body.

What you can do...

Be aware of the two steps for hand hygiene. Although you may not always be able to stay in the patient's room, when you are present, remind health-care staff and visitors to wash their hands with soap and water and use an alcohol hand-sanitizing gel upon entering the room.

Alcohol hand-sanitizing gel is highly effective against bacteria, while soap and water is necessary to eliminate hardy, infection-causing spores, such as those formed by the bacterium *Clostridium difficile*, a primary cause of severe diarrhea in hospitalized patients taking antibiotics.

BREATHING TUBES

Here is what to do to help protect a patient who has trouble breathing...

If a breathing tube is recommended for your loved one, ask the doctor if it is absolutely necessary. Patients who are unable to breathe on their own due to heart failure or severe pneumonia are often "intubated" (a plastic tube is passed through the nose or mouth into the trachea to force air from a mechanical ventilator into the lungs). Because intubation is an invasive procedure that greatly increases the risk for infection, it is often safer to first try a *noninvasive bilevel positive airway pressure* (BiPAP) mask. The BiPAP mask, which fits snugly over the nose and mouth to open the airways, delivers oxygen to the lungs and assists exhalation. This device is an appropriate first step in cases of mild respiratory failure.

Ask the doctor daily, "Is this breathing tube still necessary?" The longer a patient remains on mechanical ventilation, the greater the threat for an often-fatal complication known as *ventilator-associated pneumonia* (VAP). Patients on mechanical ventilators are routinely sedated to reduce anxiety and discomfort. But some studies suggest that lightening the sedation for a brief and carefully monitored period daily, to assess the patient's readiness to breathe independently, may reduce time on the ventilator by an average of two-and-a-half days.

Make sure the head of the patient's bed is always elevated at least 30 degrees if mechanical ventilation is necessary. Studies suggest that elevating the head significantly reduces the risk for VAP, probably by preventing mucus from pooling in the back of the throat and becoming a reservoir of bacteria that can be inhaled into the airways. A semi-upright position also may minimize reflux (backup of stomach acid), reducing the chances that gastrointestinal bacteria will be inhaled into the lungs. If the bed doesn't have an elevation indicator, the desired elevation can be measured and marked on the wall.

Confirm that your loved one's mouth is being thoroughly cleaned and swabbed twice daily with *chlorhexidine*, an antiseptic that prevents the growth of oral bacteria. A recent study at the University at Buffalo School of Dental Medicine found that patients' own dental plaque is often the source of VAP-causing bacteria.

CARING FOR CATHETERS

Central venous catheters—which often are inserted through the patient's jugular (neck) vein to allow for the delivery of medication and ready access for blood withdrawal—give bacteria direct access to the bloodstream, greatly increasing a patient's risk for a *bloodstream infection* (BSI). Such infections cause more than 26,000 deaths in US hospitals each year.

A new lifesaving approach: At Allegheny General Hospital in Pittsburgh, we developed a program to prevent BSIs after one of our heart-transplant candidates died as a result of a catheter-associated infection. The program (consisting of basic measures, such as always cleansing the insertion site with a topical antiseptic) reduced catheter-associated BSIs by 87%.

Unfortunately, not all hospitals are equally vigilant, which means you must be. *What you can do...*

•**Ask daily, "How many catheters are being used?"** Many ICU patients require several catheters to deliver medications and nutrients and eliminate wastes. Make a daily note of the number and location of the patient's catheters. Ask each day whether any of the catheters can be removed.

•**Watch to ensure that the catheters are being properly maintained.** Nurses should check the condition of all catheters and dressings each time they see the patient.

•**Ask daily, "Are any of the catheters at risk of causing an infection?"** Speak up if you notice red skin and/or oozing of a watery substance around an insertion site.

OTHER WAYS TO HELP

Researchers have recently identified other ways that family members or friends can help protect an ICU patient. *My advice...*

•**Inquire about early physical therapy.** A recent two-year study found that patients on mechanical ventilation who received early physical therapy (PT)—within 48 hours of intubation—cut their ICU stays by more than a day and their overall hospital stays by about three days, on average, compared with completely immobilized patients. A nursing assistant or physical therapist, for example, can flex a mechanically ventilated patient's arm and leg joints three times daily, until he/she recovers sufficiently to participate in more active therapy.

•**Request a weekday transfer before 7 pm.** The ICU is fully operational 24 hours daily, but the same is typically not true of less intensive hospital units, where ICU patients are transferred before going home. That's why I am generally reluctant to transfer patients out of the ICU after 7 pm. A recent Canadian study involving about 79,000 ICU patients at 31 hospitals found that those transferred at night had about a 22% higher risk for death following the transfer, compared with those transferred during the day. While you won't always be able to choose when your loved one leaves the ICU—it will depend largely on the demand for ICU beds—it's worth lobbying for a weekday, daytime transfer.

• **Communicate with the ICU team.** Within two hours of your loved one's admission to the ICU, try to arrange an initial meeting between family members and the ICU physicians and nurses to discuss your loved one's status and treatment plan. Find out who will be leading the care (in the ICU, this is typically a specialist called an *intensivist*) and ask when he makes daily rounds.

Arriving at the hospital and asking, "Is the doctor here?" is an inefficient and often frustrating way to try to stay updated on your loved one's progress.

Better: Call ahead to the ICU nurses' station and ask, "When will the doctor be there?"—and time your hospital visits accordingly. Jot down any questions ahead of time—that way, you'll remember to ask them when seeing the physician. Communicating regularly with the doctor may ease your own anxiety while helping to ensure that your loved one receives optimal care.

REPORT #257
Is the Doctor Who Is Treating You a Novice?

Charles B. Inlander, consumer advocate and health-care consultant based in Fogelsville, Pennsylvania. He was the founding president of the nonprofit People's Medical Society, a consumer advocacy organization credited with key improvements in the quality of US health care in the 1980s and 1990s, and is author of 20 books, including *Take This Book to the Hospital with You: A Consumer Guide to Surviving Your Hospital Stay* (St. Martin's).

You may have heard that July is not the best time to be admitted to a hospital because that's the month that new interns (doctors who have just graduated from medical school) join the staff. Over the years, medical experts have pooh-poohed that admonition, insisting that the quality of medical care does not suffer when new interns arrive at hospitals. But that's not the finding of a recent multi-institution study. This research found that not only are first-year interns more prone to mistakes than more experienced physicians, but so are all residents (the general term for doctors, including interns, who have been assigned to a hospital for advanced training in a medical specialty following four years of medical school).

The errors that these doctors in specialty training programs make, including misdiagnoses, not ordering necessary medical tests, etc., stem not only from their lack of judgment and technical competence, but also from inadequate supervision by senior physicians, who should review the doctors' diagnoses, test orders and treatment recommendations.

How to protect yourself or a loved one from such mistakes…

• **Know who is treating you.** After one year of training at a hospital, an intern is generally referred to as a "resident" or "resident physician." Residencies can last from two to five or more years, depending on the specialty in which the doctor is training. For example, internal medicine residencies average three years, while surgical residencies can last five or more years.

Self-defense: Always ask the doctor who is treating you in the hospital or emergency room whether he/she is a resident. If so, ask to see a senior physician (who always should be present or on call) to confirm the diagnosis or suggested treatment.

• **Don't be afraid to ask for a specialist's opinion.** Several months ago, I accompanied a female family member who was experiencing unexpected vaginal bleeding to an emergency room. A resident was the first to see her and, after examining her, he said he thought the problem was a minor irritation. He was about to discharge her with a recommendation to see her gynecologist later in the week when we asked to see the gynecologist on call. This doctor arrived about a half hour later. He immediately ordered a biopsy and imaging scans and within four hours determined that she had a growth in her uterus. Within a day, it was determined to be cancerous and surgery was quickly scheduled.

Self-defense: Don't be afraid to ask for a board-certified specialist to deal with your suspected or known problem.

•**Be on the lookout for fatigue.** Residents are often on call for 24 hours or more at a time, and many are dead tired from overwork and lack of sleep.

Self-defense: Whether you're in the emergency room or an inpatient at a hospital, don't hesitate to ask how long any resident who is treating you has been on call or on duty. If it is more than 12 hours, ask for a second opinion on any medical advice this doctor gives you.

REPORT #258
The Pros and Cons of "Off-Shore" Medicine

Charles B. Inlander, consumer advocate and healthcare consultant located in Fogelsville, Pennsylvania. He was the founding president of People's Medical Society, a consumer health advocacy group active in the 1980s and 1990s, and is the author of more than 20 books, including *Take This Book to the Hospital with You: A Consumer Guide to Surviving Your Hospital Stay* (St. Martin's).

I n years past, "medical tourism" referred mainly to the practice of bringing people from foreign countries to the US for high-quality medical care. In recent years, the term has assumed a new definition, as US citizens leave the country for more affordable surgery and other treatments. Hundreds of thousands of Americans are seeking foreign medical care each year, and this trend is expected to grow as US insurance companies consider covering "off-shore" medicine. *But before you jump on a plane, here are some important points to consider…*

•**Is it safe?** Americans have long assumed that foreign medical care is more dangerous than that offered here at home. But high-quality medical care can be found in many places throughout the world. The Joint Commission on the Accreditation of Healthcare Organizations, the private group that accredits hospitals in the US, has an international branch (*www.jointcommissioninternational.org*) that accredits foreign hospitals. If you are thinking about going abroad for medical care, make sure that the facility you are considering has been accredited by the joint commission. Also, check on the training of the doctors who would be caring for you. Look for physicians who were educated at US medical schools and completed a residency in their area of specialty at a US hospital. This is not a guarantee that you will receive high-quality care, but it does give you some reassurance because it is easier to check the reputation of medical schools and residency programs in the US.

•**Will I really save money?** MedSolution (*www.medsolution.com*), a Canadian medical-tourism firm, recently released these cost comparisons…

•**Hip replacement**—$40,000 in North America, $15,000 in France and $5,800 in India…

•**Coronary angioplasty**—$35,000 in North America, $18,400 in France and it is $3,700 in India.

Many people going abroad for face-lifts and other cosmetic procedures are paying 30% to 50% of US prices.

•**Do I have all the facts?** It's usually best to use a medical-tourism firm. To find one, search the term "medical tourism" on the Internet and/or consult the informational Web site *www.medicaltourismguide.org*. The firm you select will ask for your medical records to review, and you will then be matched with a doctor and hospital. These firms handle all the details, including travel and hotel arrangements. But make sure you get references for the firm (check for complaints with the Better Business Bureau or the attorney general's office in the firm's home state) as well as the hospital and doctors they recommend to you (ask the firm for contact information for patients treated at these medical facilities).

Buyer beware: If something goes wrong with your overseas medical care, emergency treatment will be provided (your insurance probably won't cover the cost, though). Also, you have no legal recourse in the US against the overseas provider. Each country has its own malpractice laws. Most are not as protective as those in the US. Very few foreign hospitals or doctors will be of much help to you once you return to the US. Make sure that you have a doctor here who is ready to provide follow-up care.

Volume 24
New Medical Ripoffs and Scams

REPORT #259
Are You Being Overcharged for Medical Care? How to Fight Back

Three-quarters of hospital bills have overcharges, and the average overcharge is about $1,000, according to People's Medical Society, a nonprofit medical consumer rights organization. Doctors, too, are handing inflated bills to patients.

Good news: It's simple to fight back.

If your health insurance completely covers hospital and doctor visits, these steps might not be necessary, though making the extra effort to eliminate overcharges can help bring down medical costs for everyone. Also, be aware that your insurance coverage might not be as comprehensive as you think—call your insurance carrier or review the exclusions section of your policy.

DOCTORS' BILLS

To avoid paying more than you should...

•**Negotiate.** If you have no health insurance, ask your doctor for a discount. Only 13% of patients ever make this request, but when they do, the majority secure a lower price, according to a survey of 2,118 adults conducted by Harris Interactive.

Ask the doctor in person. Requests made by phone or to an office assistant rarely work.

Keep in mind that insurance companies typically pay doctors one-half to two-thirds of the billed amount. If you will be paying out-of-pocket, you can offer to pay somewhere in that range when negotiating a price.

•**Get blood tests done at a lab.** When your doctor does a blood test, he/she charges you for the office visit...plus an added fee for

Sid Kirchheimer, investigative reporter and author of the "Scam Alert" column in AARP Bulletin. He is author of *Scam Proof Your Life: 377 Smart Ways to Protect You and Your Family from Ripoffs, Bogus Deals & Other Consumer Headaches* (Sterling).

drawing your blood…plus the amount a lab charges to run the test.

Ask the doctor to waive his fees, or go directly to a lab to have the test done and pay only for the test (ask the doctor to supply any necessary paperwork).

Look in your local *Yellow Pages* under "Laboratories—Clinical, Medical, Diagnostic" or "Laboratories—Testing" for labs in your area.

•**Don't pay for the follow-up visit.** When you see a doctor about a health problem, you often have to see him again a few weeks later to confirm that the treatment was successful. Chances are, your doctor will look you over for a few seconds during this follow-up, pronounce you well—then bill you another $50 to $100 for the second appointment.

During your initial appointment, tell the doctor that you're paying out-of-pocket and ask if he'll waive or reduce the charge for the follow-up visit, assuming that it takes only a moment. Many doctors will agree to this, particularly for regular patients.

•**Confirm that tests are necessary.** Doctors often order unnecessary medical tests out of fear that not conducting these tests might open the door for negligence lawsuits later. Unless your health insurance is picking up the entire bill, question whether recommended tests—including MRIs, CAT scans and X-rays—really are necessary. Ask what these tests will determine.

HOSPITAL OVERCHARGES

Here's how to spot overbilling on hospital bills…

•**Ask for a daily itemized bill.** When you check into the hospital, tell the staff member who takes down your insurance information that you want an itemized bill brought to your bed every day. Hospitals are required to provide this upon request.

When you receive these daily bills, review each listing (or ask a family member to do so for you). Were you billed for two doctor visits yesterday even though you saw a doctor only once? Were you billed for tests that you don't recall getting? Are there vague entries, such as "miscellaneous costs" or "lab fees?" Are there listings you can't understand? Tell the nurse you would like to speak with the hospital's

patient advocate, then ask the advocate to explain any charge that isn't clear. You might be appalled by what you're told.

Examples: Some hospitals have been known to call a box of tissues a $12 "mucus recovery system" and a bag of ice cubes a $30 "thermal therapy kit."

Save the daily bills so you can reconcile them later with the final bill.

If the patient advocate won't help remove the mistakes and reduce egregious overcharges from your bill, hire an independent medical billing advocate. He/she will examine your bill and fight to remove any overcharges, usually in exchange for a percentage—typically 35%—of the amount he saves you.

To find a medical billing advocate: Contact Medical Billing Advocates of America (540-387-5870, *www.billadvocates.com*)… American Medical Bill Review (530-221-4759, *www.ambr.com*).

•**Bypass the hospital pharmacy.** Hospitals dramatically overcharge for drugs. A patient might be billed $5 to $10 for a pill that retails for 10 cents elsewhere.

If you are taking medications on an ongoing basis and are not fully covered by insurance, bring your drugs with you to the hospital.

When you consult with your doctor prior to entering the hospital, find out which drugs you're likely to be given during your stay. Ask the doctor to write you prescriptions so that you can buy these drugs at your local pharmacy in advance and avoid the hospital mark-up. Even if your doctor won't do this, you can bring any nonprescription pills you're told you'll need, such as vitamins.

If you must get drugs through the hospital pharmacy and your insurance isn't footing the bill, ask your doctor to specify generics whenever possible. When you get your itemized daily bill, double-check that you weren't charged for brand-name drugs instead.

•**Watch for double billing.** Hospitals often bill patients twice for certain things. If your bill lists sheets and pillows, ask the hospital's patient advocate if these items are included in your daily room rate. If you're billed for the scrubs, masks and gloves worn by surgical staff, find out if these were included in your bill for operating room time.

Also double-check the times on your operating room bill. Hospitals charge from $20 to $90 for every minute you're in the operating room, so if the time you spent in surgery is padded even a little, it will add a lot to your bill. Your anesthesia records will say how long your operation really lasted.

•**Don't pay for your last day.** Hospital patients are charged the full day's room rate for the day they check in—even if they arrive at 11:59 pm. In exchange, patients are not supposed to be charged for their last day, but hospitals often try to bill for the final day anyway. Sometimes these last-day room bills are simply removed when you complain, but there are hospitals that insist the last-day charge is legitimate for patients who aren't discharged by a certain hour, often noon.

During your hospitalization, ask the hospital's patient advocate whether you'll be billed for your room on the final day of your stay. If the answer is, "Yes, if you're not out by a certain hour," ask your doctor on the next-to-last day of your stay to give you your final checkup and discharge the following morning, rather than waiting until the afternoon. If the doctor says this doesn't fit his schedule, tell the patient advocate that you shouldn't have to pay because the delay is the doctor's fault.

REPORT #260
Medical Scams, Cons and Rip-Offs

Chuck Whitlock, journalist whose work exposing scams has been featured on many television programs, including *Inside Edition* and *Extra*. He is author of several books about scams, including *MediScams: Dangerous Medical Practices* and *Health Care Frauds* (St. Martin's Griffin). *www.chuckwhitlock.com*

Bogus "miracle cures" and quack physicians probably have been around as long as the health-care profession. Con artists prey upon the unhealthy because sick people may be so desperate to find a cure that they will try any possible treatment, however expensive and farfetched.

These snake oil salesmen have been on the rise in recent years, as our aging population has more medical problems...millions of underinsured and uninsured Americans search for health-care options that they can afford... and the surging popularity of "alternative medicine" makes unscientific treatments seem more mainstream.

Sometimes it's obvious when a claim is fraudulent—but certain scams and unethical practices are difficult to spot...

UNETHICAL PRACTICES

•**Bonuses from HMOs and PPOs to doctors who skip useful tests.** HMOs and preferred provider organizations (PPOs) often give cash bonuses to doctors who don't perform pricey tests—even when those tests are in the patient's best interest. They are essentially bribing doctors to scam their patients.

Example: Your HMO or PPO doctor tells you that he/she is going to spare you the invasive thallium stress test (where radioactive dye is injected into your bloodstream) and perform a routine treadmill test without thallium, though the thallium test is warranted.

What to do: When your HMO or PPO doctor tells you that you have a particular health condition, research that condition on a reliable Internet Web site, such as WebMD.com or MayoClinic.com. If the site mentions a test that your doctor has not performed, ask him why it was skipped. If the doctor's response seems evasive, consider getting a second opinion.

•**Unqualified plastic surgeon.** Many doctors have switched to plastic surgery in recent years, drawn by the lucrative nature of the specialty and its lower reliance on insurance payments. (Most plastic surgery procedures are elective and not covered by insurance.) No law or regulation prevents doctors from changing their specialty to plastic surgery—even if they have no background or training in this field. Patients likely have no idea that they are trusting their lives and appearances to what are essentially unqualified, untrained novices.

What to do: If you're considering plastic surgery, ask the surgeon...

281

- •**Are you board-certified in plastic surgery?** He/she should be.

- •**At what hospital do you have physician's privileges?** A general hospital is fine, but a university hospital is even better—university hospitals tend to have very high standards.

- •**Who will be handling my anesthesia?** Don't trust a plastic surgeon who says he'll handle it himself. He may be trying to cut corners and putting your health at risk in the process.

REPORT #261
Latest Medicare Scam: Old Bills

Nora Johnson, certified compliance professional with Medical Billing Advocates of America, a nationwide network of independent medical billing advocates, Caldwell, West Virginia. *www.billadvocates.com.*

Recently, bill-collection agencies have been contacting some seniors saying that Medicare claims from years past have been denied, and these individuals must pay up. Some agencies have legitimately purchased lists of unpaid debts from hospitals—but others might be scams. Under no circumstances should you immediately pay any such bill.

Better: Send a certified letter to the collection agency stating that you're disputing the bill and that you want to see a copy of the Medicare denial. By law, you are entitled to receive this.

Many collection agencies will give up at this point, but if you are sent a copy of the Medicare form, try to determine the reason for the denial. Medicare claims often are denied because of coding mistakes or missed deadlines—these things are the fault of the hospital or health-care provider. If that's the case, contact the billing department at the hospital or the health-care provider, explain that the fault was theirs and ask to be sent a new bill showing a balance of zero.

Helpful: Medicare forms are difficult to interpret. If you can't figure out the reason for the denial, contact Medicare at 800-633-4227.

Even if the Medicare claim denial wasn't the hospital's fault, you can be billed only if the hospital can prove you signed an "Advanced Beneficiary Notice" form when you received treatment, establishing that you knew the procedure might not be covered.

Also, you might not have to pay the bill if the statute of limitations on debt collections has expired.

That could be from three to eight years, depending on your state. Check with the office of your state's attorney general.

Don't make even a small partial payment to the collection agency without confirming the charge is legitimate—doing so can reset the statute-of-limitations clock on the rest of the bill.

REPORT #262
Health Insurance Trap

Even though a hospital is in your insurer's network, some procedures may incur out-of-network charges.

Reason: Certain individual practices, such as anesthesiology and pathology, may not be in-network.

Self-defense: Before scheduling a procedure, ask your provider, the hospital and the insurer if all services are in-network.

Emergency room treatment: If the hospital is in-network, ER services will be reimbursed at the in-network rate.

Charles B. Inlander, consumer advocate and healthcare consultant located in Fogelsville, Pennsylvania. He was the founding president of People's Medical Society, a consumer health advocacy group active in the 1980s and 1990s, and is the author of more than 20 books, including *Take This Book to the Hospital with You: A Consumer Guide to Surviving Your Hospital Stay* (St. Martin's).

REPORT #263
Medical Scams—How Greedy Doctors and Hospitals Threaten Your Well-Being

Evan S. Levine, MD, assistant clinical professor of medicine at Albert Einstein College of Medicine and a practicing internist and cardiologist at Montefiore Medical Center, both in Yonkers, NY. He is the author of *What Your Doctor Won't* (Or Can't) Tell You (Penguin Group).

Even though the overwhelming majority of physicians are honest and hard-working and make medical recommendations based only on their patients' well-being, some doctors and hospitals allow their desire to turn a profit to interfere with good medical practices.

To learn more, we spoke with Evan S. Levine, MD, an internist and cardiologist at Montefiore Medical Center in New York City. *Based on his 18 years' experience as a physician and his extensive research in the area of unscrupulous medical practices, Dr. Levine advises medical consumers to beware of...*

Scam: Using bait-and-switch tactics to get new patients. Sometimes a store will advertise a "hot" product for a rock-bottom price, but when you go to buy it, you're told that it's "sold out." This type of bait-and-switch tactic—advertising a great-sounding product that is available only in limited numbers—is used by some hospitals.

Example: You see an ad for an impressive new doctor who trained at the most prestigious institutions, but when you call to make an appointment, he/she is too busy to see you for six months. You get an appointment with his junior partner instead, and the big-name doctor has successfully attracted another patient to the hospital.

My advice: Do your research when looking for a new physician. Don't rely on advertising to find one. Get referrals from a doctor you've seen for a long time (if you have one) and/or family members and friends whose judgment you trust. Schedule a "get acquainted" meeting with the doctor to make sure that you like his demeanor and overall treatment philosophy. (Your insurance provider may cover such a visit.)

Also helpful: If you are diagnosed with a serious illness, such as cancer or Parkinson's disease, promptly see two physicians for an initial consultation—one who specializes in research on the condition and one involved in patient care.

This will greatly increase your odds of getting information on state-of-the-art treatments and the personal care you need. You can find a doctor who conducts research on a particular condition via an Internet search or by calling a local university-affiliated hospital and asking for such specialists.

Scam: Giving costly medical tests that patients don't really need. More and more internists and specialists, such as cardiologists, are performing costly medical tests in their offices to increase profits.

Example: *Computed tomography angiograms* (CTAs), which examine blood flow in the arteries. This noninvasive test can be useful in determining the extent and severity of suspected or existing coronary artery disease.

But some doctors tell patients who don't have heart disease symptoms, such as chest pain or shortness of breath, to get the test—even though the American College of Cardiology (ACC) does not recommend it in these cases.

The machine used to perform a CTA costs at least $1 million, so there's a financial incentive for these doctors to recommend the test even when it's not needed. Aside from the unnecessary expense for the patient, the radiation from this test is equivalent to having more than 100 chest X-rays.

My advice: Only a cardiologist should determine if you need a CTA, and it should be performed at an outpatient hospital center—not in his office.

To read the ACC's guidelines for this test: Go to *www.cardiosource.org/acc* and click on "Science & Quality" then "Practice Guidelines & Quality Standards."

Another red flag: Sonography machines in an internist's office. Sonograms should be performed under the supervision of a cardiologist or radiologist. Internists don't have the appropriate training.

Scam: Pushing patients out of the hospital prematurely to boost profits. Some hospitals strive to get patients checked out as quickly as possible to make room for more patients. That's because insurance companies typically pay set fees based on a patient's diagnosis rather than the length of hospital stays. Shorter stays mean more turnover—and more money.

Some hospital administrators pressure doctors to check out patients quickly, and some doctors may even get bonuses if their patients have short lengths of stay.

Where the danger is greatest: Beds in the intensive care unit (ICU) are far more costly than regular beds, so to make room, patients are sometimes sent out of the ICU too soon. If a loved one is moved from an ICU to an area with fewer monitors and nurses, it can be dangerous—or even deadly.

My advice: Speak up. If you think a loved one is too sick to leave the ICU or hospital, complain to the head nurse on the floor or to the hospital administrator or patient advocate. (Get the administrator's or patient advocate's phone number from the hospital's operator.)

Scam: Prescribing expensive or unnecessary drugs. Some doctors are swayed by perks (such as free meals) from drug companies and prescribe costly brand-name medications that are no better than generic alternatives.

Oncologists are one of the few types of physicians who can sell medication in their offices in addition to prescribing it. To increase his bottom line, an oncologist could recommend pricey chemotherapy that won't necessarily make you feel better or prolong your life.

My advice: If your doctor recommends a drug that he sells, ask if there are studies showing that the medication is more effective in treating your condition than other drugs.

If it's chemotherapy, ask if research has shown that the treatment prolongs life. And seek a second opinion from another oncologist—preferably one based at an academic center.

Scam: Referring patients to friends, spouses or business partners. Unfortunately, some doctors refer their patients to their friends or spouses or doctors who rent office space from them. In these cases, your doctor's judgment may be affected by his personal relationship with the physician to whom he is referring you.

My advice: For reliable doctor referrals, look for an internist you trust. When you find such an internist, stick with him. If your health insurance changes, it's usually better to switch plans to stay with a good doctor—even if there's a higher co-pay.

REPORT #264
Health Rip-Off Tip-Offs

Eduard F. Goodman, JD, LLM, CIPP, chief privacy officer, Identity Theft 911, LLC, Scottsdale, Arizona. Goodman is an expert in privacy and personal data protection, wireless networking liabilities and cyberterrorism. He served as the 2008-2009 Section chair of the State Bar of Arizona's Internet, E-Commerce & Technology Law Practice Section.

In our computerized world, crime gets ever more conceptual...as with medical identity theft. This is a type of fraud that occurs when someone "steals" the identity of a person with health insurance and then uses his/her name—and, in the latest twist, insurance coverage—to get treatment that can include doctor visits, drugs and even hospital stays.

While insurance companies bear the financial brunt, this is by no means "not your problem." If your medical identity is stolen, you and your family may pay a very high price. Your insurance coverage can get used up...unpaid bills can ravage your credit rating...and dangerous incorrect information can enter your medical files, making it difficult for healthcare workers to accurately diagnose and treat you in the future—especially in emergencies when you might not have a chance to speak with them first.

There's another kind of health insurance fraud that you have to be alert to as well—in which, appallingly, the criminal is your doctor. With this type of fraud, physicians may fabricate diagnoses…engage in a practice called "upcoding" (falsely billing for a higher-priced treatment than was provided)…or "unbundling" (billing each stage of treatment as if it were a separate procedure). These aren't victimless crimes either—such fraud boosts the cost of health care, translating into higher premiums and out-of-pocket payments and reduced benefits or coverage.

UNDER THE RADAR

Health insurance fraud is a fast-growing and highly underreported type of white-collar crime, warns Eduard F. Goodman, JD, LLM, an expert in privacy and personal data protection law and chief privacy officer at Identity Theft 911, LLC in Scottsdale, Arizona. The most recent estimate from the National Health Care Anti-Fraud Association is that about 3% of annual health-care spending in the US goes down the drain in the form of fraud, resulting in costs of about $70 billion. Goodman told me that seniors, in particular, are frequent targets of health insurance fraud, especially Medicare schemes. Yet if this happens to you, you likely won't even know—until perhaps much later when something weird occurs, like you get a collection notice in the mail for treatment you didn't have or you are turned down for a loan because your credit rating plummeted due to unpaid medical debts incurred in your name by an imposter. Messes like these can take years to unravel.

HOW TO AVOID GETTING RIPPED OFF

Goodman and I discussed what might be some red flags that someone has stolen, or is trying to steal, your medical identity…

• **You are offered a "free" medical screening or equipment (such as a wheelchair,** walker or diabetic supplies)—all you have to do is provide your Social Security number, Medicare information and/or health insurance policy number. Sometimes free medical offers are legitimate—for example, your community hospital may offer periodic free or discounted health screenings, such as mammograms or blood pressure tests. Be suspicious, however, of such offers at or near commercial settings such as shopping malls or health clubs—they

may be "rolling lab" schemes in which scammers skip from mall to mall or gym to gym, administer tests (which may themselves be bogus), then bill them to your insurance or Medicare. And, as for that free wheelchair, why would a company simply give you medical equipment? Once an unscrupulous company has your signature, it can try to bill Medicare for equipment or services you do not need or do not receive.

• **You (and/or your insurance company) are charged for services that were not provided.** Crooked physicians involve themselves in schemes to obtain "reimbursement" for medical visits you never made or tests you never had. They assume that you won't look closely at your statements and that if you do, you won't know one treatment from another. You can protect yourself by keeping careful records of all medical appointments and procedures and comparing them with statements from your doctor and insurer. If you detect a discrepancy, immediately contact your insurance company to challenge it. Many companies offer ways to report suspected fraud on their Web sites.

VICTIM-PROOF YOURSELF

Goodman gave advice on how to minimize the likelihood that you will become a victim of health insurance fraud…

• **Request copies of your current medical files from all medical providers.** You have a legal right to these documents under HIPAA (the Health Insurance Portability and Accountability Act of 1996). Carefully review them and correct any false or incorrect information.

• **Be careful with your Social Security, Medicare and insurance policy information—these are the tools thieves use to steal medical identities.** Though you can do little to keep them from gaining access by hacking into a company's database or breaking into a doctor's office, you should protect this information in every way you can. Shred all documents with these numbers so that they can't get them from your trash.

A common trick: Calling and requesting a policy number or other private information because it is necessary "in order to process a payment or claim." If someone wants your Social Security number or other such information, always ask why. Sometimes there are legitimate reasons—for instance, perhaps a hospital requires this information to be paid for treating you. In that event, verify that it is a legitimate request by asking for the caller's name—then you can call the hospital and ask to speak to that person. If you discover that there's no such person, promptly report the incident to your insurance company (as you should with any suspected fraud).

• **Never sign a blank insurance form.** Fill out, sign and date only one claim form at a time. Giving blanket authorization to providers to bill for services can lead to overcharges and other abuses. Keep copies of all such forms.

• **Don't agree to let your health-care provider keep your credit card number on file.** When you conduct medical transactions online—such as refilling prescriptions or purchasing contact lenses—Goodman advises minimizing data exposure by typing in your information each time you order. When you trust your credit/debit card data to these institutions, you are also trusting that they are safeguarding it adequately, and all too often that is not the case.

• **Use care when disposing of confidential information since any private information can be used to get more.** Shred ATM and credit card receipts and take security measures with stored paper documents, computers, iPods, PDAs, smart phones, computer printers and other electronic devices that can store personal data.

• **Do not assume that all is well because you don't owe money.** Once every few months, make a point of sitting down to compare your medical bills with the Explanation of Benefits (EOB) statements from your insurer. Follow up on any discrepancies, such as services you did not get, office visits you did not make or medical equipment you did not use.

• **Always scrutinize your monthly credit card statements, including health-care charges.** Promptly report any unauthorized transactions to the issuer and any instance of suspected fraud to your insurer.

• **Monitor your credit report.** Request a free copy from each of the three nationwide consumer credit-reporting agencies at least once a year and review it for suspicious entries. If you detect any, challenge them. If necessary, file a police report. To get your report, go to *www.annualcreditreport.com* or call 877-322-8228.

REPORT #265
Painkillers Can Kill

Amanda Risser, MD, MPH, assistant professor of family medicine at Oregon Health and Science University (OHSU), Portland, who has investigated the potential risks from NSAID use. Her article on NSAID-related precautions appeared in *American Family Physician*. She practices family medicine at OHSU Family Medicine at Richmond, a community health center in Portland.

Millions of Americans regularly take one or more nonsteroidal anti-inflammatory drugs, known as *NSAIDs*. Drugs in this class include over-the-counter analgesics (painkillers), such as aspirin and ibuprofen, as well as prescription medications, such as *celecoxib* (Celebrex), *indomethacin* (Indocin) and *diclofenac* (Cataflam).

NSAIDs are not as safe as people think. In 2004, an NSAID known as *rofecoxib* (Vioxx) was withdrawn from the market after it was found to increase the risk for heart attack and stroke. Other NSAIDs, including aspirin, have a high risk for side effects, including internal bleeding.

The occasional use of NSAIDs is unlikely to cause serious problems. The risks start to rise when people use these drugs too often or if people have certain risk factors. *Main dangers…*

CARDIOVASCULAR RISKS
Low-dose aspirin therapy (100 mg or less daily) has been shown to decrease the risk for heart attack and stroke in high-risk patients. Other NSAIDs, however, don't fare so well.

People who regularly take NSAIDs other than aspirin have an average increase in blood pressure of about five points. These drugs also can worsen congestive heart failure and increase risk for heart attack. The Cox-2 inhibitor Celebrex is believed to increase these risks more than other NSAIDs.

Self-defense: Avoid Celebrex if you have cardiovascular risk factors, such as hypertension or high cholesterol, or if you've previously had a heart attack. With other NSAIDs, we advise patients to check their blood pressure within a week or two after starting the drug. If blood pressure is going to rise, it usually does so during that time.

Also important: Don't exceed the dose recommended on the label. People who take high doses of ibuprofen or diclofenac, for example, are more likely to have cardiovascular "events" than those who take the amounts recommended on the label.

While it would be easy to assume that people who regularly take a non-aspirin NSAID may reduce cardiovascular risk by taking low-dose aspirin as well, studies have shown that this isn't the case and that this combination of medications is risky, especially for gastrointestinal (GI) complications.

ASTHMA

About 21% of adults with asthma experience a worsening of symptoms when they take aspirin. In rare cases, aspirin can cause respiratory problems, such as difficulty breathing, in people without a history of asthma.

Warning: People who experience respiratory problems when they take aspirin usually have a high cross-reactivity to similar drugs—they'll experience similar symptoms when they take ibuprofen, *indomethacin* or other NSAIDs. The risk for aspirin-exacerbated asthma is highest in patients who also have nasal polyps and/or recurrent bouts of sinusitis.

Self-defense: In general, asthma patients should avoid aspirin and other NSAIDs, particularly if they also have polyps or sinusitis. These patients can safely substitute acetaminophen. Asthma patients who need additional pain relief should ask their doctors about such prescription non–NSAID drugs as *gabapentin* (Neurontin) and *nortriptyline* (Aventyl, Pamelor).

KIDNEY COMPLICATIONS

Up to 2% of patients who regularly take NSAIDs will have to stop taking them because of kidney problems.

Self-defense: Patients undergoing dialysis or those with kidney disease should not take NSAIDs—acetaminophen is a better choice.

I advise patients with diabetes or other risk factors for kidney disease to have a baseline *creatinine* test when they start NSAID therapy and then subsequent monitoring. Creatinine is a metabolic by-product that indicates how well the kidneys are working. Patients can keep using NSAIDs if their creatinine remains stable.

Important: Patients who have developed kidney disease as a consequence of liver disease should never take NSAIDs. They have a high risk for complications, including total kidney failure.

LIVER DISEASE

Some studies have shown that patients who take the painkillers *sulindac* (Clinoril) or diclofenac have an increase in liver enzymes circulating in the bloodstream. This increase is less likely to occur with other NSAIDs.

Self-defense: Stop taking NSAIDs if your doctor determines there's an increase in liver enzymes. The complications usually reverse when the drugs are discontinued.

Important: NSAID-related liver damage is rare. It usually occurs in patients who already have a liver disease, such as hepatitis C or cirrhosis. (Liver problems are rare with acetaminophen as well, but be sure not to take too much—follow directions on the label.)

CENTRAL NERVOUS SYSTEM

Older adults who take NSAIDs will sometimes develop central nervous system problems. Aspirin, for example, can cause or worsen tinnitus (ringing or other sounds in the ears). Indomethacin has been linked to cognitive changes, including psychosis in rare cases.

Self-defense: Follow the dosing instructions on the label. These disorders mainly occur when people take NSAIDs in excessive doses—and will resolve when the drugs are discontinued or are taken in a lower dose.

GI COMPLICATIONS

It's estimated that at least 10% to 20% of people who regularly take one or more NSAIDs experience GI irritation. Many eventually will develop ulcers in the stomach, duodenum (the part of the small intestine nearest the stomach) and/or esophagus.

What happens: The NSAIDs reduce levels of prostaglandins, substances that help maintain the protective linings of the digestive tract. These drugs also are acidic—they can irritate tissues and potentially cause internal bleeding.

An analysis of data from the 1990s showed that NSAID-related bleeding was responsible for 32,000 hospitalizations and 3,200 deaths annually. The risk for bleeding is especially high among people 75 years old or older.

Self-defense: Older adults, particularly those with ulcers, should avoid NSAIDs—so should anyone who also is taking an anticoagulant, such as *warfarin*. The risk for bleeding in those who take both types of drugs is five to six times higher than for those who are taking only an anticoagulant.

Patients with a high risk for NSAID-related bleeding can take acetaminophen. It rarely causes GI irritation. People with arthritis also might try the supplements glucosamine and chondroitin or capsaicin cream.

REPORT #266
"Slow" Medicine—Take The Time to Choose the Care You Need

Dennis McCullough, MD, family physician and geriatrician, and associate professor in the department of community and family medicine at Dartmouth Medical School in Hanover, New Hampshire. He is the author of *My Mother, Your Mother: Embracing "Slow Medicine," The Compassionate Approach to Caring for Your Aging Loved Ones* (Harper).

The 86-year-old mother of a friend of mine recently underwent surgery for a problem that was not life-threatening.

She developed an infection when she was in the hospital, and because of her frail state, she also developed heart and kidney failure. She ultimately died as a result of the treatment.

Doctors in the US save perhaps millions of lives every year with a disease-focused approach that includes diagnosing and treating problems such as high blood pressure and elevated cholesterol. But in some people age 80 and older, this approach can lead to "death by intensive care" if the physical and mental frailties that come frequently with age aren't considered. And some people in their 70s are already frail. Preliminary research from *The Dartmouth Atlas of Health Care* points out that carefully considered (i.e., less) care may lead to equal or better outcomes.

Recent development: Some older adults are now opting for an approach known as *slow medicine*, which allows families and health professionals to put more careful thought into recommended testing and treatment.

THE BIGGER PICTURE

The tests and treatments used most often in our medical system are primarily based on studies of adults age 60 and younger.

The same data are *not* available for older adults, yet doctors usually treat both age groups the same. Imagine an 85-year-old with no symptoms or history of heart disease. Most doctors would advise him to have an occasional cholesterol test, followed by therapy with a statin drug if the numbers weren't ideal.

However, age alone is the biggest risk factor for heart disease, and patients and families are rarely told how little is changed by recommended treatments. There's no solid evidence that a statin will change the life course in an older adult with no history of heart problems.

Always ask: Why do this test or start this treatment? What if I don't do it? A certain percentage of people taking a statin will develop muscle pain or other side effects.

TAKE IT SLOW

In my opinion, a "slow medicine review" should replace the standard medical exam for many older adults. It includes some of the same components as any other checkup (including having another person present to help process information from the doctor), but with important differences. *For example…*

•**No rush.** Most of the decisions made during office visits, such as writing prescriptions and ordering tests, are not urgent. The doctor can give his/her advice, then let the patient decide what to do later.

Example: Suppose you have sleep problems. A doctor might recommend over-the-counter Tylenol PM. This medication is generally safe, but the doctor should explain that it contains *diphenhydramine*, an antihistamine that can impair cognition and increase the risk for falls in older adults. You might take a few days to weigh the risks and benefits of the drug—then decide whether to take it or whether to ask for an alternative.

•**Check and double-check.** Since there's a greater risk for adverse effects from drugs and treatments prescribed for older adults than for younger adults, both doctors and patients should be cautious about making changes.

Example: An 80-year-old with a history of high blood pressure might have an elevated blood pressure reading during an office visit. The standard advice would be to change the drug or dosage, but higher doses and new drugs increase the risk for side effects.

In a slow-medicine review, the doctor would tell the patient to check his pressure at home or at a senior center or pharmacy for a few weeks to make sure that the high readings accurately reflect what's happening. Only then would he recommend making changes.

My advice: You rarely need to make *any* changes based on the findings of one visit. Few problems are life-threatening.

UNNECESSARY SCREENINGS

Many tests are unnecessary in older adults.

It's estimated that 90% or more of men in their 80s will have some degree of prostate cancer. In the majority of cases, the cancer will never cause problems. Why put patients through *prostate-specific antigen* (PSA) testing—and the risk for subsequent biopsies—for a condition that will never need treatment?

It does make sense for all men to have a digital rectal exam during an office visit. If a tumor is large enough to feel, it's large enough

to treat. However, health outcomes are rarely improved by routine PSA screening for men over age 80.

Similarly, mammograms in women over age 80 are rarely necessary.

REPORT #267
How to Get Out of the Hospital Alive

Peter J. Pronovost, MD, PhD, professor in the departments of anesthesiology, critical care medicine and surgery at Johns Hopkins University School of Medicine in Baltimore. He is the medical director for the Center for Innovation in Quality Patient Care, which promotes patient safety at Johns Hopkins Hospital. He is coauthor, with Eric Vohr, of *Safe Patients, Smart Hospitals* (Hudson Street).

Hospital-acquired infections are among the most common *preventable* causes of death due to medical errors, but hospitals still aren't doing enough to prevent these and other mistakes.

New research: A recent survey of hospitals found that 87% don't always follow infection-prevention guidelines—including basic hand-washing protocols.

Result: As many as one in 10 patients will acquire a potentially deadly hospital infection.

Most doctors know what they need to do to prevent unnecessary mistakes. The challenge is to consistently implement proven safety measures. Until this occurs, there are steps you can take to help protect yourself if you are hospitalized.

To learn more about hospital risks—and what patients can do to stay safe—we spoke with Peter J. Pronovost, MD, PhD, a patient-safety researcher at Johns Hopkins University School of Medicine.

•**You refer to the "toxic" culture in hospitals. What does this mean?** Most patients assume that medical care is guided by scientific principles—that doctors do things in ways that are safe as well as effective.

But its not that simple. Doctors are human. They often are overconfident and have strong personalities and big egos that cause them to do things that conflict with the patient's best interests.

Recent example: At our hospital, an otherwise healthy patient suffered serious complications after kidney surgery. It was clear that the patient needed to return to the operating room, but the surgeon refused because a CT scan indicated that there was nothing wrong.

We all know that test results can be misleading. Even though the patient had serious complications, the surgeon wouldn't admit the possibility of error. And surgeons often have complete authority in such cases.

As the intensive care physician on call, I explained the situation to another surgeon and he agreed to operate. It turned out that the first surgeon had accidentally cut the pancreas and intestine during the procedure—an error that could be lethal.

Surgery is not a perfect science—even the best surgeons make mistakes. Had systems been in place to keep personality issues (such as a surgeon's insistence that he couldn't make a mistake) out of the equation, much of this patient's suffering could have been prevented.

• **What kinds of systems can help?** Teamwork is a big one. Johns Hopkins researchers did a study that looked at errors and liability claims at a number of hospitals. We found that in nearly 90% of cases, at least one of the team members knew that something was wrong but was either afraid to speak up or was ignored by the person in charge.

At Johns Hopkins, we created a system in which nurses *must* attend rounds with the attending physician and head resident. This helps prevent subsequent errors in communication and has caused medication errors to drop to almost zero. It also cut the time that patients spent in *intensive care units* (ICUs) by about half.

Patients also should be active team members. Speak up and ask questions if you do not understand something. Always ask all health-care practitioners who enter your room to please wash their hands.

• **You've pioneered the use of checklists.** How do they help? A checklist virtually eliminates the hierarchal mind-set that I discussed above. A doctor or surgeon cant get away with merely saying, "Because I said so." He/she is required to follow step-by-step procedures that have been shown to improve safety.

Example: About 31,000 Americans a year die from infections caused by central lines (catheters placed in a vein in the neck, groin or chest). We examined data from the CDC in order to summarize the most important points in developing the checklist. Our checklist included things like hand-washing…cleaning the patient's skin with the disinfectant *chlorhexidine*…draping the patient…and the use of a surgical mask, hat, gown and gloves.

In Michigan, where the checklist was first adopted, the incidence of central-line infections dropped by 66% within 18 months after the protocols were implemented—a reduction that has now been sustained for more than three years.

If you're planning a surgery: Ask what the hospital's rate is for catheter-related bloodstream infections—and be concerned if it is much above one out of every 1,000 catheter days. If you or a family member has a catheter, ask every day whether it is still needed.

• **Should patients ask about checklists before choosing a hospital?** Absolutely. Virtually every procedure can be done more safely when the medical staff follows clear and consistent guidelines.

Checklists don't have to be long and complicated. Take hand washing. It's among the most effective ways to prevent hospital infections. Yet even doctors and other health-care workers in hospitals working on infection prevention do *not* do it about 30% of the times that they should. It's perfectly reasonable for a patient who is scheduled to undergo surgery to ask his surgeon whether he follows an infection-prevention checklist.

Another example: Wrong-site surgery. Nearly 3,000 times a year in the US, surgeons operate where they shouldn't. There are cases in which the surgeon has operated on the wrong side of the body (such as amputating the left leg instead of the right) or even on the wrong patient.

The Joint Commission (a nonprofit group that regulates hospital standards and safety) now mandates that operating room teams perform a "time-out" before surgery. During this time, the surgeon marks the surgical site. The case is then reviewed both by surgeons and nurses to confirm the patient's name and the nature of the surgery.

If you're planning a surgery: Prior to the operation, ask your surgeon if he uses the time-out period. If so, ask him to perform the step *before* you're sedated so that you can participate. That way, you can confirm your name and other details. For example, the surgeon might touch your right knee and say something like, "This is where we're operating, right?" When you're awake, the risk for error is further reduced.

• **Hospital-acquired pneumonia is a big risk for patients.** What can patients do to prevent it? If you spend time in an ICU, there's a good chance that you'll be put on mechanical ventilation to help you breathe. We've found that elevating the head of the bed so that it's raised at least 30° will help mucus from the mouth and nose drain into the stomach instead of the lungs. Yet the beds in ICUs are often kept in a horizontal position. Inhaling mucus is one of the main causes of *ventilator-associated pneumonia*.

Also important: A family member should ask each day whether mechanical ventilation is still needed for the patient.

• **How can patients who are allergic to latex—widely used in many hospitals—protect themselves?** We went latex-free at Johns Hopkins three years ago. Some hospitals, however, continue to use latex gloves during surgery even though about 1% of Americans are allergic and could experience a life-threatening anaphylactic reaction.

The allergy tends to occur in people who have had frequent exposure to latex in the past. This includes health-care workers (who often wear the gloves) or patients who have undergone multiple surgical procedures in which latex gloves were used.

My advice: Before having a procedure, tell your surgeon that you don't want to be exposed to latex. Latex-free gloves are readily available—hospitals should use them.

REPORT #268
Do You Really Need Surgery?

Dennis Gottfried, MD, associate professor of medicine at the University of Connecticut School of Medicine, Farmington, and a general internist with a private practice in Torrington, Connecticut. He is the author of *Too Much Medicine* (Paragon House). *www.DrDennisGottfried.com.*

Up to 30% of surgical procedures in the US are unnecessary. This shocking statistic was recently released by the respected nonprofit, nonpartisan policy analysis group The Rand Corporation.

The analysis confirms why it's so crucial to request a second opinion from a physician who is not associated with your doctor before agreeing to any elective surgery.

Procedures that may not be necessary—and alternatives to consider…

STENTS

Each year, more than one million heart patients are treated with angioplasty and stents, which restore normal circulation to the heart and reduce angina (chest pain).

With angioplasty, a deflated balloon is threaded into the coronary artery. It's then inflated to flatten plaque (fatty deposits), and a metal stent is placed inside the artery to prevent arterial deposits from reblocking the opening.

Problem: Angioplasty and stents are overused. A study of more than 2,300 patients presented at a recent meeting of the American College of Cardiology found that patients with stable angina, in which discomfort occurs in a consistent pattern (such as during exertion), who were treated with medications (such as *nitroglycerine* to dilate the blood vessels) had the same outcomes as those treated with stents—without the dangers of an invasive procedure.

Who is helped by stents: Patients with a recent worsening of chest pain (unstable angina). For people with a significant blockage in the left main coronary artery or with three coronary arteries blocked and a weakened heart muscle, bypass surgery (which involves grafting a vein from another part of the body to bypass the blockage) improves the patient's life expectancy.

Who isn't helped by stents: People with stable angina. These patients usually should be treated with medications to control the pain and to reduce blood pressure and cholesterol. Medications are just as effective at preventing future heart attacks and preventing death as stenting in these patients—without the risks of a surgical procedure. Stenting and bypass surgery should be used only in patients for whom medication fails to adequately control chest pain.

CAROTID ENDARTERECTOMY

About 20% of all strokes are related to blockages in the carotid arteries in the neck. With a procedure known as *carotid endarterectomy*, the blockages are surgically peeled away to improve circulation to the brain and potentially prevent a stroke.

Problem: Severe carotid blockages (generally blockage of 80% or more) occasionally can lead to "ministrokes"—*transient ischemic attacks* (TIAs), which often precede a full-blown stroke. But if a person has a severe obstruction and no TIA symptoms, the likelihood of having a major stroke is very small. Performing a carotid endarterectomy in those people decreases the chance of having a stroke by only 0.7%.

Who is helped by carotid endarterectomy: People with severe carotid blockage and TIAs have a 13% risk of having a disabling stroke over the next two years. When a carotid endarterectomy is performed, the risk drops to 2.5%.

Who isn't helped by carotid endarterectomy: People with a blockage of less than 60% even if they have a history of ministrokes. In this group, the risk for stroke is higher *after* surgery—perhaps because the risk of stroke-producing plaque being dislodged during the operation may exceed the patient's initial stroke risk.

In groups of people with severe obstruction and no TIA symptoms, more than 140 endarterectomies must be performed to prevent one stroke. For obstructions of 60% to 79%, there is no convincing scientific evidence for surgery. Nonsurgical treatment, including the use of aspirin and cholesterol-lowering drugs, is preferable in all of these cases.

PROSTATECTOMY

About 180,000 American men are diagnosed with prostate cancer each year and about 30,000 die from the disease. Surgical removal of the prostate (*prostatectomy*) often is recommended, but risks include infection, impotence and incontinence.

Problem: The majority of prostate cancers grow slowly. Most men with the disease would eventually die from an unrelated condition even if the prostate cancer weren't treated.

In a recent study that was published in *The New England Journal of Medicine*, older men with early prostate cancer who were treated with prostatectomy died at about the same rate as older men with similar cancers who had no surgery.

Who is helped by prostatectomy: Men who are in their 50s and younger with biopsy findings that show an aggressive form of prostate cancer are generally candidates for prostatectomy.

Who isn't helped by prostatectomy: Men whose life expectancy is less than 10 years at the time of diagnosis. They're less likely than younger men to die of their cancer and face a high risk for surgical complications. Older men with prostate cancer often do better with hormone therapy and/or radiation.

BACK SURGERY

Surgery for a herniated (ruptured) disk is among the most commonly performed orthopedic procedures in the US.

Problem: A herniated disk that presses on a nerve can be excruciatingly painful. But in 80% to 90% of cases, enzymes secreted by the body break down disk material and the nerve pain disappears in time. This can take many months, so surgery promises faster relief.

Disk surgery, however, has serious potential risks, including nerve injuries, buildups of scar tissue, infection and chronic back pain. A recent study in the *Journal of the American Medical Association* compared the long-term outcomes of back patients who had surgery with those who didn't. The likelihood of recovery was virtually the same.

Who is helped by back surgery: People with severe, intractable back pain that radiates into a leg (sciatica) or those with a progressive neurological deficit, such as foot weakness, or a loss of bowel or bladder control, which indicates compression of a spinal nerve, require prompt surgical treatment.

Who isn't helped by back surgery: People whose only symptom is low back pain. Studies have shown that individuals with local symptoms do better with nonsurgical treatment, including anti-inflammatory drugs, acupuncture, massage therapy and physical therapy. For most people with mild sciatica, the pain usually disappears within a few months as the disk breaks down.

KNEE REPAIR

You shouldn't assume that you need surgery if you suddenly develop pain, inflammation and swelling in one or both knees. Sometimes the pain is from a medical problem such as gout or Lyme disease.

Problem: Even with knee injuries, many surgeons want to repair or remove damaged tissue without waiting enough time to see if normal healing will take place.

Who is helped by knee surgery: People in whom a ligament or tendon is completely severed. For these patients, the knee will rarely heal well enough on its own to restore adequate function and reduce pain. For people who engage in intensive sports, arthroscopic surgery (using a keyhole incision) for lesser injuries often is recommended since they may not be willing to wait for healing to occur.

Who isn't helped by knee surgery: For most people with knee injuries, surgery—even arthroscopic—is the last resort. First, rest the leg, use anti-inflammatory drugs and try physical therapy and braces. Follow this approach for at least one to two months before considering knee surgery.

REPORT #269
The Great American Heart Hoax

Michael D. Ozner, MD, cardiologist and medical director of Cardiovascular Prevention Institute of South Florida in Miami. He is the symposium director for "Cardiovascular Disease Prevention," an annual international meeting highlighting advances in cardiology. He is author of *The Great American Heart Hoax: Lifesaving Advice Your Doctor Should Tell You About Heart Disease Prevention (But Probably Never Will)* (BenBella). *www.DrOzner.com.*

Americans get more than 1.5 million cardiac bypass surgeries and angioplasty procedures a year, which makes heart surgery among the most commonly performed surgical procedures in the US.

Fact: These procedures have not been proved to extend lives or to prevent future heart attacks except in a minority of patients. Between 70% and 90% of angioplasties and bypass surgeries are unnecessary in stable patients with coronary artery disease.

While American patients are seven times more likely to undergo coronary angioplasty procedures and bypass surgery than patients in Canada and Sweden, the number of Canadians and Swedes who die from cardiovascular disease is nearly identical (per capita) to the number of people who die from heart disease in this country.

These are not harmless procedures. About 30% of angioplasties fail, requiring patients to repeat the procedure—and eventually, many of these angioplasty patients will undergo bypass surgery. People who have bypass surgery are nearly four times more likely to suffer a stroke at the time of surgery and are vulnerable to postsurgical infections. Between 3% and 5% of patients die from bypass surgery—that's 15,000 to 25,000 lives lost a year.

So why do we keep doing these procedures?

A FLAWED MODEL

Cardiologists used to compare the coronary arteries to simple pipes under a sink. The thinking went that these arteries sometimes accumulated sludge, called *plaque* (cholesterol deposits within an artery wall), that impeded the flow of blood to the heart. Treating this sludge with angioplasty or shunting blood around it with bypass surgery seemed obvious.

That approach, however, is flawed. We now know that the arteries are highly dynamic structures. What happens within the artery wall is more significant than blockages that obstruct the *lumen* (arterial openings).

The majority of heart attacks can be linked to small, yet highly inflamed, plaques. These small plaques have no effect on circulation, because they take up little space within the lumen. Yet they may rupture and cause a sudden heart attack due to a clot that forms at the site of the rupture.

What happens: Cholesterol-carrying particles that enter an artery wall undergo oxidation and modification that trigger an immune response. White blood cells flood the area and engulf the oxidized cholesterol particles and cause plaque to form. Then the white blood cells secrete substances, such as *proteinases*, that break down the fibrous cap that covers the plaque. When the fibrous cap ruptures, blood enters the plaque and a blood clot forms that can block the artery.

Sudden clots that form following plaque rupture are the cause of most heart attacks. Angioplasties and bypass surgery do nothing to prevent plaque rupture or clot formation.

HEART-SAVING STEPS

The following steps may save lives. Of course, always ask your doctor about the best heart-health strategies for you.

• **Test for high sensitivity (hs)-C-reactive protein (CRP).** It's a "marker" that indicates simmering inflammation in blood vessel walls and can be measured with a simple blood test. Inflammation within arterial plaques contributes to plaque rupture and clot formation and subsequent heart attacks.

The landmark JUPITER study looked at more than 17,000 participants with elevated hs-CRP (above 2 mg/dL) and normal cholesterol. Those who were treated with medication to lower hs-CRP were significantly less likely to have a heart attack or stroke or to die than those in the control group. CRP can be lowered with lifestyle changes (diet, exercise, weight loss, smoking cessation) and medical therapy (including statin drugs).

• **Test for apolipoprotein B (apoB).** This is a better indicator of heart disease than standard cholesterol levels (including HDL, LDL and triglycerides). Even if your LDL "bad" cholesterol level is normal, you still could have elevated particle numbers, which means that your LDL cholesterol is distributed across a lot of very small, dense particles. These small, dense particles are the most dangerous kind—they are more likely to squeeze through the lining of the artery and more likely to become oxidized once they're there, leading to *atherosclerosis* (hardening of the arteries). You can check your "bad" particle number by testing for apoB. Blood tests for apoB are performed routinely in Europe and Canada but not in the US. Ask for this test when you have your usual cholesterol screening.

The optimal level of apoB is less than 90 mg/dL (or even lower for high-risk patients). To lower apoB, follow the recommendations for lowering CRP.

• **Choose an anti-inflammatory diet.** People who follow a Mediterranean-style diet—high in plant foods and cold-water fish (such as salmon) and low in red meat and processed foods—can reduce inflammation.

The Lyon Diet Heart Study compared a Mediterranean diet to a diet resembling the American Heart Association's cholesterol-lowering Step 1 Diet. Participants on the Mediterranean plan were 70% less likely to die from all causes and 73% less likely to have a recurrent cardiac event than those on the standard "healthy" diet.

The Mediterranean diet is effective partly because it limits saturated fat and does not contain trans fat. The fat present in the Mediterranean diet, mainly from olive oil and fish, has anti-inflammatory effects. Also, the antioxidants in fruits and vegetables reduce the oxidation of cholesterol-containing particles within artery walls.

Avoid high-fructose corn syrup, which goes straight to the liver, where it causes an increase in triglycerides, a major risk factor for heart disease.

• **Laugh, pray, get a pet.** Anything that reduces stress can significantly reduce your risk for heart disease. Research at the University of Maryland Medical Center, for example, found that laughing is almost as effective as exercise at improving arterial health.

Laughter relaxes blood vessels and improves circulation to the heart. And like other stress-control strategies, including prayer, loving relationships (with pets as well as people) and yoga, it lowers *cortisol*, a stress-related hormone.

• **Get moving.** There is a dose-response relationship between exercise and the heart—more exercise gives a greater benefit. Aim for 30 to 45 minutes of exercise most days of the week.

Good news: Walking for as little as 30 minutes five to seven days a week can significantly decrease the risk of dying from heart disease.

REPORT #270
Who Needs Surgery?

Americans often undergo needless heart surgery, but stents or bypass surgery can be lifesavers for a select group of patients, including those with...

• **Unstable angina with increasing frequency** and intensity of chest pain, often occurring at rest.

• **Disabling chest pain that does not respond to lifestyle intervention** or optimal medical therapy.

• **Significant obstructions in the left, right and middle coronary arteries** and a weak heart muscle.

• **Significant blockage in the main trunk of the left coronary artery.**

Michael D. Ozner, MD, cardiologist and medical director of Cardiovascular Prevention Institute of South Florida in Miami. He is the symposium director for "Cardiovascular Disease Prevention," an annual international meeting highlighting advances in cardiology. He is author of The Great American Heart Hoax: Lifesaving Advice Your Doctor Should Tell You About Heart Disease Prevention (But Probably Never Will) (BenBella). www.DrOzner.com.

REPORT #271
New Warnings About Long-Term-Care Insurance—Watch Out For These Traps

Bonnie Burns, training and policy specialist with California Health Advocates, a nonprofit organization in Sacramento, California. Burns is consumer representative for the National Association of Insurance Commissioners. She coauthored the report "Comparing Long-Term-Care Insurance Policies: Bewildering Choices for Consumers" for the AARP Public Policy Institute in 2006. www.CAHealthAdvocates.org.

Long-term-care insurance is supposed to help protect us from the ever-increasing costs of nursing home and in-home care. But the policies are complex and typically are purchased decades before their benefits are needed. That makes it difficult for consumers to know what they will need and what will and won't be covered.

Adding to the confusion is a new federal program to be funded by individuals' automatic payroll deductions at businesses that choose to participate—part of the government's health-care system overhaul. The program—whose premiums and many other details have yet to be decided—is meant to help consumers pay for some features of long-term care.

Here, potential pitfalls surrounding long-term-care coverage...

TRAP: THE NEW UNCERTAINTIES

Until the Department of Health and Human Services sets the premiums and rules for the new federal program, possibly as late as October 2012, there's no way to know whether it's a good deal.

The program, officially called the *Community Living Assistance Services and Supports Act* (CLASS), will be required to accept participants regardless of their age or health. Add up the potential costs, and it's possible, though not certain, that healthy people might be able to obtain better deals on long-term-care coverage from private insurers. On the other hand, people living below the poverty line will have to pay a premium of only $5 per month.

Even if the program does offer attractive terms…

• **It won't be available for enrollment to those who are already retired or about to retire**—the program will be tied to employment, much like Social Security. If your employer offers the program, you will be enrolled automatically unless you opt out. Also, you must pay premiums for five years before you can collect benefits.

• **It won't pay any benefits before 2018, and its benefits might be insufficient to fully cover nursing home costs.** The Congressional Budget Office estimates that benefits might average around $75 per day—enough to help pay for a home health aide but well below nursing home costs, which currently average $200 per day and are climbing fast.

The program might turn out to be best used in conjunction with a private long-term-care policy…or with some future insurance product designed specifically to supplement the federal program.

What to do: If it makes sense for you to obtain private insurance now to protect your assets, do so. Otherwise you might find yourself in need of long-term care before the government program is up and running.

TRAP: SOARING PRIVATE INSURER PREMIUMS

Don't purchase a private long-term-care insurance policy unless your retirement budget has enough flexibility to cover a 50% premium increase.

That's because premiums—which are not locked in when you obtain a policy—have been soaring. Policyholders who can't or don't want to pay the higher rates often abandon their policies.

What to do: If you want to buy a policy, do so through an independent insurance agent who sells policies issued by more than one company. Such an agent is more likely to provide frank opinions about which insurers strive to limit rate increases. Many of these agents can be found through the Web site of the Independent Insurance Agents & Brokers of America, a trade organization (*www.iiaba.net*), or the National Association of Professional Insurance Agents (*www.pianet.com*). Your

agent should have at least 10 years of experience selling long-term-care insurance in the community. As a rule of thumb, choose a policy from one of the top six to eight companies selling long-term-care insurance. They are less likely to increase rates dramatically than those that do little long-term-care business. Contact your state insurance department to find one of these companies.

TRAP: ENDLESS PREMIUMS

Some policies now continue to charge premiums even as they are paying benefits. Traditionally, long-term-care policies stop charging premiums when they begin paying benefits. That's an important feature—long-term-care policies rarely pay 100% of long-term-care costs, and many retirees cannot afford to pay both out-of-pocket care expenses and insurance premiums.

What to do: Make sure that the policy includes a "waiver of premium" clause, either as a basic feature or as a rider, before signing a contract.

TRAP: NO INFLATION PROTECTION

Insurance agents sometimes encourage customers to skip inflation riders, which increase benefits to keep pace with the cost of care, in favor of less expensive policies that include "future purchase options." These options give policyholders the right to buy additional coverage later, regardless of their age or health—but they don't guarantee that the added coverage you can buy in the future will be affordable.

What to do: Insist that your policy include a rider that covers annual inflation of at least 5%, compounded, especially if you are younger than 60. It could be decades before younger people require long-term care, which means it is likely to be more expensive than it is today.

TRAP: NO NURSING HOME COVERAGE

A policy covering only in-home care is not a good one even if in-home care is what you want. As much as seniors want to remain in their homes, failing health sometimes means they cannot.

What to do: Do not buy a policy unless it provides coverage for in-home care, nursing home care and assisted- living facilities—all at levels sufficient to pay most or all of the bills charged for these care options in your area.

TRAP: LANGUAGE TRICKS

Key words and phrases often are not noticed or are misinterpreted.

Examples: One policy defined an "assisted-living facility" as having at least 10 beds. A policyholder received no benefits when he entered a facility with only six beds.

If you hire a family member rather than a professional caregiver to care for you, it is unlikely to count toward your "exclusion period"—the period before you can start getting benefits for a preexisting condition.

What to do: Read the "definition of terms" section of your policy carefully. If you are uncertain how to interpret something in your policy, contact your agent or your state's agency on aging or insurance department to ask for help. Seek an exclusion period of no more than three months.

REPORT #272
7 Things Doctors Don't Tell You About Anesthesia (But Should)

David Sherer, MD, anesthesiologist in the suburbs of Washington, DC, and former physician-director of risk management for a major HMO. His interests include medical malpractice reforms and testimony, the use of anesthesia in starting intravenous lines and the importance of patient advocacy. He is author of *Dr. David Sherer's Hospital Survival Guide* (Claren).

All forms of anesthesia can cause side effects or complications, yet doctors don't always take the time to address these issues with patients. *Here are seven things you must know...*

• **Your supplements can increase your risk.** Some herbs and nutritional supplements can be lethal when they're combined with anesthesia. Ginkgo, for example, can elevate blood pressure. Because some anesthetic drugs have the same effect, patients taking both can experience sharp rises in blood pressure. This increases the risk for stroke and heart attack.

Risks from supplements are greatest with general anesthesia, but even with regional anesthesia (such as spinal or epidural), there are dangers.

Example: Garlic supplements will thin the blood, which can cause additional bleeding with regional anesthesia.

During the presurgery interview with your anesthesiologist, mention everything that you're taking. Also, talk with the doctor or naturopath who prescribed the supplements about any possible interactions.

• **Nausea can be controlled.** Many forms of anesthesia stimulate the *chemoreceptor trigger zone*, a part of the brain involved in nausea. Older anesthetic drugs, such as *nitrous oxide* (laughing gas), are far more likely to cause nausea than newer agents. But postoperative nausea and vomiting still are among the most common side effects of anesthesia.

Better control: A relatively new class of drugs, known as *5-HT3 antagonists* (such as *Kytril* and *Zofran*), may reduce postsurgical nausea more effectively than their predecessors. *Scopolamine patches*, which are commonly used to prevent motion sickness, also can be helpful.

Important: If you've had surgery and experienced nausea in the past, tell the anesthesiologist during the presurgery interview. He/she will make sure that you get the appropriate kinds and doses of medication.

• **Constipation and urinary retention are likely.** Analgesic narcotics, such as codeine, Demerol and Percodan, have a tendency to make it difficult for patients to urinate or have a bowel movement—problems that can persist for days or even weeks after the surgical procedure.

Helpful: Ask the anesthesiologist if your procedure can be done with an ultrasound-guided nerve block instead of general anesthesia. Patients given this type of anesthesia typically require lower doses of narcotics, which can reduce the side effects.

• **Snoring is a danger sign.** Patients who snore or make snoring sounds during sleep may suffer from *sleep apnea*, a condition in which breathing may stop and start, leading to the lowering of oxygen levels.

The danger: Patients with sleep apnea tend to have more complications during *intubation*, the insertion of an endotracheal tube into the patient's windpipe (trachea) that delivers oxygen and many inhaled anesthetics. Problems with intubation can be the riskiest part of anesthesia—diminished airflow can cause brain damage or death.

•**Dantrolene should be on hand.** It's the only drug that can reverse *malignant hyperthermia*, an anesthesia-related complication that can lead to increases in body temperature and a breakdown of multiple organ systems. This occurs in perhaps one in every 65,000 patients. Without treatment, it is fatal in more than 80% of cases. When *dantrolene* (Dantrium) is administered, the death rate is less than 10%.

Hospitals are required to stock dantrolene, but some outpatient facilities might not have it. Don't undergo any procedure involving general anesthesia unless this lifesaving drug is available and can be administered if necessary.

•**A "local" prior to an IV reduces pain.** Most procedures start with the insertion of a large-bore intravenous (IV) needle into a vein. The IV is used to deliver some forms of anesthesia and/or other drugs during surgery.

Because these needles are so large, they can cause a lot of pain. An injection of *lidocaine* works to numb the skin before an IV is inserted. Many hospitals don't do this, so be sure to ask for it.

•**The anesthesiologist should be board-certified.** Anesthesia can legally be administered by a medical doctor (anesthesiologist), an anesthesia assistant or a certified registered nurse-anesthetist. Except for the simplest procedures, it's always best to have a board-certified anesthesiologist administer the anesthetic. He/she has the most experience and training. He can administer the anesthesia alone or in conjunction with other professionals. You can find out if the doctor is board-certified by contacting your state board of medicine or the American Board of Anesthesiology (*www.theaba.org*).